KU-875-772

WITHDRAWN FROM
THE LIBRARY

UNIVERSITY OF
WINCHESTER

KA 0303727 4

NEW PERSPECTIVES ON

Charles Willson Peale

Charles Willson Peale, *Self-Portrait in the Character of a Painter,* 1824. Oil on canvas, 26 x 22". *Courtesy of the Pennsylvania Academy of the Fine Arts, Philadelphia. Gift of the artist.*

NEW PERSPECTIVES ON

Charles Willson Peale

A 250TH ANNIVERSARY CELEBRATION

————◆◈◆————

Lillian B. Miller and David C. Ward
Editors

Published for the Smithsonian Institution
by the University of Pittsburgh Press

Published by
the University of Pittsburgh Press, Pittsburgh, Pa., 15260

Copyright © 1991, University of Pittsburgh Press

All rights reserved

Baker & Taylor International, London

Manufactured in the United States of America

LIBRARY OF CONGRESS CATALOGING-IN-PUBLICATION DATA
New perspectives on Charles Willson Peale : a 250th anniversary
celebration / Lillian B. Miller and David C. Ward.
        p.   cm.
    ISBN 0-8229-3660-7
    1. Peale, Charles Willson, 1741–1821 — Criticism and interpretation.
I. Peale, Charles Willson, 1741–1821.   II. Miller, Lillian B.
III. Ward, David C.
ND237.P27N48   1990
759.13 — dc20   90-39185
                                                   CIP

UNIVERSITY OF WINCHESTER

03037274

CONTENTS

———◆———

v

FIGURES

———◆———

Frontispiece:

Charles Willson Peale,
Self-Portrait in the Character of a Painter, 1824

1. Unknown, *Daniel of St. Thomas Jenifer.* Attr. to John Hesselius, ca. 1760–1770

2. Sir Joshua Reynolds, *Charles Carroll of Carrollton, 1763*

3. Charles Willson Peale, *Margaret Tilghman (Mrs. Charles) Carroll,* ca. 1770

4. Charles Willson Peale, *Charles Carroll, Barrister,* ca. 1770

5. Charles Willson Peale, *John Beale Bordley,* 1770

6. Herman van der Myn, *Charles Calvert, Fifth Lord Baltimore,* ca. 1730

7. Charles Willson Peale, *William Pitt,* 1768

8. Charles Willson Peale, *Thomas Ringgold,* miniature, ca. 1770

9. Charles Willson Peale, *Thomas Ringgold,* ca. 1773

10. John Hesselius, *Charles Carroll, Barrister,* ca. 1760

11. John Singleton Copley, *Mrs. Theodore Atkinson,* 1765

12. Charles Willson Peale, *Judge James Arbuckle of Accommac,* 1766

13. Charles Willson Peale, *Mrs. James Arbuckle and Son,* 1766

14. Matthew Pratt, *The American School,* 1765

15. Benjamin West, *Charles Willson Peale,* 1767–69

16. Benjamin West, *Pylades and Orestes,* 1766

17. Charles Willson Peale, *Elisha Restoring to Life the Shunammite's Son,* after West, 1767

ix

SYMBOLS AND ABBREVIATIONS

A(TS):   Horace Wells Sellers's Transcript of Charles
                  Willson Peale, Autobiography, P-S, F:IIC.

CWP   Charles Coleman Sellers, *Charles Willson Peale*
                  (Philadelphia, 1969).

DAB   *Dictionary of American Biography.*

Daybook 1   Charles Willson Peale, 1806–22 Daybook, P-S,
                  F:IIE/4-6.

Daybook 2   Charles Willson Peale, 1810–22 Daybook, P-S,
                  F:IIE/4-6.

F: Microfiche edition. Lillian B. Miller, ed., *The
                  Collected Papers of Charles Willson Peale and His
                  Family* (Millwood, N.Y., 1980).

P&M   Charles Coleman Sellers, *Portraits and Minia-
                  tures by Charles Willson Peale,* American Philo-
                  sophical Society, *Transactions,* n.s., vol. 42,
                  pt. 1 (Philadelphia).

P&M Suppl.   Charles Coleman Sellers, *Charles Willson Peale
                  with Patron and Populace: A Supplement to Portraits
                  and Miniatures by Charles Willson Peale with a Sur-
                  vey of His Work in Other Genres,* American Philo-
                  sophical Society, n.s., vol. 59, pt. 3 (Philadelphia,
                  1969).

P-S   Peale-Sellers Papers, American Philosophical
                  Society, Philadelphia.

Selected Papers 1   Lillian B. Miller, Sidney Hart, Toby A. Appel,
                  eds., *The Selected Papers of Charles Willson Peale
                  and His Family,* vol. 1: *Charles Willson Peale: The
                  Artist in Revolutionary America, 1735–1791* (New
                  Haven, Conn., 1983).

Selected Papers 2   Lillian B. Miller, Sidney Hart, David C. Ward, eds., *The Selected Papers of Charles Willson Peale and His Family,* vol. 2: *The Artist as Museum Keeper, 1791–1810* (New Haven, Conn., 1988).

Sellers, *Mr. Peale's Museum*   Charles Coleman Sellers, *Mr. Peale's Museum: Charles Willson Peale and the First Popular Museum of Natural History and Art* (New York, 1980).

PREFACE

———◈———

THE original purpose of this volume was to bring together recent articles about Charles Willson Peale that introduced a new approach to his life and work. We limited our choice of articles to those published after 1969, the date of Charles Coleman Sellers's definitive biography, *Charles Willson Peale*. In examining the collection of articles as a whole, however, we became aware that some scholars were engaged in researching aspects of Peale's life and work that we believed opened up fruitful avenues for further exploration. Therefore, we invited these individuals to submit essays indicating their findings up to date. Undoubtedly, we have missed research still in progress, but since this volume is not the last word on Peale and his family, we believe and hope that as scholars become more aware of the richness of Peale material, they will be encouraged to make further contributions.

We have edited the published articles included here so that they conform to a uniform mode of presentation. Our editing has extended primarily to quotations and citations; that is, we have checked the quotations against the original documents, corrected some errors in transcribing, and presented Peale in his original orthography, grammar, and punctuation. We have brought the footnotes up to date by citing Peale documents according to their appearance in either *Selected Papers of Charles Willson Peale and His Family* or *The Collected Papers of Charles Willson Peale and His Family,* the microfiche edition. Documents that have been reproduced in microfiche are indicated by "F:" and followed by alphanumerical coding: series, card, row, and frame. For example, a document that appears in the series assigned to Charles Willson Peale and that bears the citation "IIA/24F5–6" may be found in Series IIA, card 24, line F, frames 5 and 6. Preceding the fiche reference appears the abbreviation of the institution that houses the document. (See the list of symbols and abbreviations, above.)

We are grateful to the various journals that have graciously given us permission to republish articles and to the institutions that have allowed us to quote from their documents and to reproduce their paintings. At the National Portrait Gallery, we would like to thank Alan Fern, Director; Cecelia Chin and the staff of the Library; Rolland G. White, Photographer; Rose S. Emerick, Editorial Assistant on the Peale Family Papers staff; and Abigail Goldberg, Smith College Intern at the Peale Family Papers, 1990, for her assistance in compiling the index. We also wish to express our appreciation to Catherine Marshall, Managing Editor of the University of Pittsburgh Press, and to Jane Flanders, Editor, for their enthusiastic support and encouragement of this project.

NEW PERSPECTIVES ON
Charles Willson Peale

Introduction

————◆————

THIS volume celebrates the 250th birthday of one of America's eminent old masters. Charles Willson Peale's contribution to the cultural development of the nation extended beyond his more than a thousand portraits of prominent — and not so prominent — Americans to embrace natural history, institutional development, technological innovation, and social and political thought and practice. Maligned and admired in both his own time and thereafter, he and his art have frequently been dismissed with faint praise for his artistic achievement and an amused glance at his varied career and numerous progeny. His reputation began to improve after 1939, and particularly after 1969, guided by the affectionate pen of a descendant, Charles Coleman Sellers, whose graceful biography followed a thorough and meticulous catalogue raisonne of his entire oeuvre (1952, 1969).[1] The catalogue brought to scholarly attention the scope, variety, and aesthetic charm of Peale's artistic achievement, but even so, it has taken a number of years for scholars of American art and culture to give serious attention to the details of Peale's accomplishments, and it has taken almost as long for his art to receive similar recognition in the marketplace.

Some of the new interest in Peale has developed out of the expansion of concerns and methodologies marking American Studies during the post-Vietnam years; some is due to the enormous surge of interest among art collectors and institutions to acquire American paintings, an interest that has sent the price of almost all American art works soaring; and some has arisen from the recognition by scholars that Peale's life and work provide a window into the American past, clarifying and illuminating the sources, influences, and complexities of American history, art, and culture.

This is a good time, then, to stop and assess the Peale terrain, to see

3

where we came from, what we have done, and from this, to realize what still remains to be done by future scholars of the American scene. There are a number of lessons to be learned from this kind of examination. The history of Peale criticism in itself provides an understanding of the course of American intellectual history during the past one hundred years. Why Peale was neglected, disdained, or admired reveals much about how Americans perceived themselves and their culture during this period. Peale was so intrinsically American in his experiences, attitudes, methods of working, and value system that his countrymen's response to him at different times has inevitably paralleled their response to their culture in general.

Peale's Americanism derived from the Maryland soil that nurtured him from his birth to young manhood and from the Philadelphia environment that later molded and influenced his adult mind and activities. However, Peale also was influenced by the London world he lived and studied in briefly while a student of Benjamin West from 1767 to 1769, and by the literary world of England and France, which provided an intellectual structure into which he fitted his American experiences. The integration of these various worlds in Peale's life and art is worth examining, for if Peale is to be considered uniquely American, then these European elements must receive close attention as contributing to his national character. In his cosmopolitanism as well as his nationalism, Peale was very much a man of his own day. Although his world may be a "lost" world, as Daniel Boorstin has termed it, the value system he espoused and the general ideology that formed that value system have remained essential ingredients of an American tradition, one that historians have termed Jeffersonian. As friend and correspondent of Jefferson, Peale participated in the creation of that tradition, which, as Boorstin writes, "has played and should continue to play a vital and valuable role in American history." Boorstin's justification for his study of that tradition is as pertinent for us forty years later as it was in 1948: "If we can improve our definition of the original Jeffersonian world of ideas," he wrote, "we will have gone a long way toward . . . strengthening the philosophical foundations of a moral society in our day."[2] These new perspectives on Charles Willson Peale 250 years after his birth are presented with that hope.

Charles Willson Peale was born near Chestertown, Maryland, in 1741, the eldest child of a Maryland schoolteacher. His father had been exiled to the colonies for his participation in a forgery scam that occurred while he was a clerk in the London Post Office. Unhappy in the Maryland wilderness, Charles Peale constantly looked back to England seeking help and the possibility of a return. His was a short life in Maryland, however; he died when his eldest child was nine years old. The family, consisting of his widow and five young children, was forced to move to Annapolis where the mother supported her brood with her sewing. Young Charles was apprenticed to a saddler at age thirteen and began his career in the crafts — a training that figured largely in his activities for the rest of his life and that has consistently been noted by biographers as an important characteristic of his work. During his apprenticeship, Charles learned how to work in metal, how to upholster furniture and repair watches, and particularly, how to handle tools. While still a craftsman, he learned how to paint portraits by observing how they were painted, by buying a book and the requisite supplies, and then, by doing. His early portraits were rough, but still conveyed a recognizable image. Study with Benjamin West in London polished the roughness and turned him into a more sophisticated artist capable of composing complicated portraits in good London style.

The coming of the American Revolution and radical political activities diverted Peale for a time from his work as a portrait artist in America, but he carried his miniature painting kit into battle and into army camps, thus providing us with some of our only images of revolutionary heroes. By this time, Peale had settled in Philadelphia and identified his life with the city's progress. He abandoned his political activities; taking advantage of the city's cultural interests, wealth, and intellectual ferment as the new nation's capital, he furthered his career as a portraitist and participated in the development of a more interesting civic life through the founding and development of cultural institutions devoted to art and education — the Philadelphia Museum (1791) and the Pennsylvania Academy of the Fine Arts (1805).

The museum became an intimate part of Peale's domestic life. His family and collection of animals, plants, and minerals shared lodgings at Philosophical Hall, home of the American Philosophical Society. He spent his second honeymoon on a bird-hunting expedition; his daughter was married in Philosophical Hall, the children were initiated into the art of taxidermy and museum management there, and sons were born and named in the hall — Charles Linnaeus and Benjamin Franklin. The museum became his personal world as well as "a world in miniature" for the rest of the citizenry. Work in the museum helped to crystallize his thought, especially about the role of museums in public education. By 1810, the time of his first retirement from the museum's management, Peale had developed a fully reasoned conception of the proper organization of museums and their role in national, social, and moral development.

In 1801, Peale exhumed the bones of the mastodon in the marshes of Newburgh, New York, and reconstructed them into two skeletons, thereby providing paleontologists with evidence from which they could develop new definitions of the origins and nature of animal life. Peale's curiosity about the natural world was paralleled by his interest in invention, in the development of stoves, bridges, and machines that would "encrease the Comforts of Life." And when in 1810, Peale decided to buy a farm in Germantown and retire as a gentleman farmer, he created Belfield, meaning a land devoted to beauty, and began to transform the farm into another kind of museum — an outdoor institution that combined nature, art, and invention in "a world in miniature." Throughout his adult life, he continued to paint portraits, improving in his art as he worked and creating works that were highly respected as portraits and, in many instances, aesthetically pleasing.

Peale's accomplishments, then, were varied and extensive. Ironically, it has been the variety of his undertakings that diminished his reputation as artist and dissuaded historians from taking him seriously. Beginning soon after his death in 1827, the sense that Peale had dissipated his energies in too many directions influenced biographers to hedge their evaluations of him as an artist. His was an "overloaded stock," wrote William Dunlap, the first American art historian, in 1834. "It was a sturdy stem; but no stem can bring to maturity the best fruit of so many different kinds if, as is the case with man, its life is too short to bring any one to perfection." Dunlap dismissed Rembrandt Peale's apology for his father — that Peale, possessing a "*more lively genius*" than Benjamin West, might have achieved more in artistic excellence than West if "his attention" had not been so diverted. Nonsense, expostulated the offended Dunlap, one of Benjamin West's many devoted students. "Mr. Peale's *genius* was devoted to making money." West's work "will go down to posterity; those of Charles Willson Peale will soon be forgotten."[3]

In 1867, Henry T. Tuckerman viewed Peale more sympathetically. The Civil War had produced in the North "sudden prosperity" for "an imperfectly educated class, who, with little discrimination, and as a matter of fashion, devote a portion of their newly acquired riches to the purchase of pictures." The relationship that formerly had existed between art and the American public had changed, in Tuckerman's view. The "vocation" of artist was "no longer precarious," but ironically, art in America was "deficient": like American life, American art was "too subject to vicissitude and cosmopolitan influences, too dependent on the market." Tuckerman's purpose, then, at the onset of the so-called Gilded Age, was to hold up as models for contemporary artists who were flocking to European centers for training and absorbing European styles, "the early and isolated struggles, and the actual appreciation and success, of the genuine artist in America." To advance a national art that would equal the greatest achievement of European past and present art, to change the direction of American life from "the fever and hurry bred by commerce, political strife, and social ambition," and so to improve the national character and taste—these were Tuckerman's grand aims that were reflected in his assessment of Charles Willson Peale.[4]

Tuckerman emphasized Peale's "genial enterprise and . . . national sympathies," his "liberal . . . and public spirit." Although "there was more versatility and aptitude than positive genius in Peale," Tuckerman did not disparage the artist's mechanical skills, nor his varied interests. Peale's greatest achievement, however, was his collection of historical portraits, which "however deficient in the more brilliant qualities of artistic genius have the charm of fidelity, and often are the sole authentic likenesses of the eminent men delineated."[5]

A decade later, Samuel G. W. Benjamin, anxious to improve American art in the face of what he considered the greater accomplishments of Europe, agreed with both Dunlap's and Tuckerman's assessment. Peale was not a "specialist": "Like so many born in America, [he was] gifted with a general versatility that enabled him to succeed moderately well in whatever he undertook without achieving the highest excellence in any department." Peale owed his fame, according to Benjamin, to having painted "several excellent portraits of Washington" which lacked "many of the qualities of good art," but were "yet faithful likenesses of the father of his Country, and as such are of great interest and value."[6]

The twentieth century saw no great change in the critical appraisal of Peale and his art. During the thirties, again a period of national self-consciousness, Peale was appreciated for his historical portraits, but dismissed as an artist. "If he had confined his amazing energy to his art," wrote Suzanne LaFollette in 1929, "he could no doubt have been a much better [painter]."[7] Sadakichi Hartmann also found him "a portraitist of some merit," but in his one sentence evaluation, emphasized his gallery of historical portraits.[8] Eugene Neuhaus was intrigued by the "romantic and interesting details" of Peale's life, his whimsical naming of his children after artists, and his "fairly good portraits." Peale's "greatest claim to recognition," however, was his portrait of Washington (which one of the seven that Peale painted Neuhaus does not designate); however, Peale, as a painter of externals, showed Washington as "a stolid personage in the prime of life without any spiritual qualities."[9]

Neuhaus, like other critics in the thirties, was writing during a period when American folk art was being discovered and enjoyed for its naive charm and expression as the spirit of the genuine American; but the rest of American art generally — except for the work of Copley and Stuart — suffered. Despite increasing nationalism, most American art critics agreed with John McAndrew, who, in explaining American architecture in 1938 to a French audience of an exhibition of American art sponsored by New York's Museum of Modern Art, wrote: "For the last 300 years American architecture, like our culture in general, has had its principal sources in Europe." As examples of American painting, along with the requisite Copleys, Stuarts, and a Trumbull, that exhibition featured American folk and popular art — cigar store Indians, weathervanes, watercolor paintings on china and velvet, and the *Peaceable Kingdom* of Edward Hicks. Raphaelle Peale's *After the Bath* (now called *Venus Rising from the Sea — A Deception* [1822? Nelson-Atkins Museum of Art, Kansas City]) was included as an example of "the new and naive taste for realism" that marked the rise of democracy during the administrations of Andrew Jackson. Later — almost as an afterthought — the elder Peale's "large portrait of Washington" was added to the exhibition, probably because it was owned by the museum in Versailles.[10]

The tide of opinion began to change after World War II, as American art began to be examined more seriously and the work of early American artists other than Copley and Stuart were researched by young scholars. Still, Peale suffered in comparison. Virgil Barker, for example, corrected Dunlap's accusation of Peale's moneygrubbing, but conceded that Peale "was not a great painter, and much of his work has only the narrowly historical importance of bridging two periods." However, Barker did single out the *Self-Portrait in His Museum*, *The Family Group*, *The Exhumation of the Mastodon*, and *The Staircase Group* as artistically important, garnishing his praise with adjectives such as "genial," "pleasing," and "blandly extrovert."[11] Having available the two-volume life and letters prepared by Charles Coleman Sellers (1939, 1947), Oliver Larkin (1949), E. P. Richardson (1956), and James Thomas Flexner (1954) viewed Peale's long life from a more intimate vantage point, finding in the artist charm and some artistic skill. Larkin enjoyed Peale's "rich personality deeply concerned with the life around him, biased toward what was alive and forward-moving in his world and therefore capable of taking from others what he needed for full expression, and no more."[12] Richardson believed that Peale "was not only an admirable portrait painter but a man of generous enthusiasms and fertile intellectual curiosity." He was also "ardent, hopeful, enthusiastic, affectionate."[13] And Flexner, also, was impressed by "the friendliness of [Peale's] temperament."[14] Even in their praise, however, they continued to present an image of Peale as a jack-of-all-trades, an amusing personality, father of many talented children, a largely self-taught American who became the visual historian of the American past.

These critics also tended to stress the American character of Peale's work. Peale "discarded everything he had learned in England that was more than a refinement of the style he had practiced before he had left home," wrote Flexner; "he adhered to the method of seeing that had long been typical of the Colonial South."[15] Richardson wondered how Peale "arrived so early and unaided, cut off from artistic contacts, at so interesting a parallel to the neoclassic portrait style worked out in France by David," and produced paintings "never wholly free from naivete and provincial awkwardness, but cogent, amiable and, at their best, of penetrating candor."[16] Peale's democratic bias — his belief that art was for everybody — was also a matter of remark, usually coupled with mention of his ingenuity and public spirit — all of which made him intrinsically American.

In the 1970s and 1980s, scholars began to place Peale and his work in a more specific social, intellectual, and aesthetic context. The publication of his and his family's papers in microfiche and print by the Peale Family Papers project at the National Portrait Gallery[17] has made available thousands of documents illuminating the life of the family and the times in which they lived. Social historians interested in analyzing American family structure and relationships, class structure, and problems relating to gender and race have found in these documents important evidence for their special concerns. New interests in the history of American technology, in republicanism, in institutional development and organization, in transatlantic influences on art and culture have invited attention to the Peale family and their achievements. The essays included in this volume have just begun to graze the surface of what promises to be fertile ground for these new historical explorations. This volume, therefore, is designed not only to celebrate the birth and life of Charles Willson Peale, but also to invite new considerations of the period, events, and accomplishments associated with this highly important cultural figure.

NOTES

1. *CWP; P&M; P&M Suppl.*

2. Daniel Boorstin, *The Lost World of Thomas Jefferson* (Boston, 1948), pp. xi–xii.

3. William Dunlap, *History of the Rise and Progress of the Arts of Design in the United States* (New York, 1834), 1:138.

4. Henry T. Tuckerman, *Book of the Artists. American Artist Life* (New York and London, 1867), pp. 7–39; at pp. 22, 27.

5. Tuckerman, *American Artist Life,* pp. 50, 53.

6. S.G.W. Benjamin, *Art in America. A Critical and Historical Sketch* (New York, 1880), p. 21.

7. LaFollette did add, however, that Peale's later portraits were "drawn with greater facility" than those executed in his colonial period, which show "a certain archaic stiffness of pose" (Suzanne LaFollette, *Art in America* [New York, 1929], p. 18).

8. Sadakichi Hartmann, *A History of American Art* (Boston, 1932), p. 26.

9. Eugen Neuhaus, *The History & Ideals of American Art* (Palo Alto, Calif., 1931), p. 26.

10. *Trois siècles d'art aux États-Unis* (Paris, 1938), p. 21. The Peale *Washington* at the Musée Nationale at Versailles is a replica of the full-length portrait of 1779 (*Washington at the Battle of Trenton*). Sellers believes that the painting is not by Charles Willson Peale but a copy after the portrait now at the Pennsylvania Academy of the Fine Arts (*P&M,* p. 228).

11. Virgil Barker, *American Painting* (New York, 1950), pp. 315–20.

12. Oliver W. Larkin, *Art and Life in America* (New York, 1949), p. 67.

13. E. P. Richardson, *Painting in America* (New York, 1956), pp. 98, 99.

14. James Thomas Flexner, *The Light of Distant Skies. American Painting 1760–1835* (1954; rpt. New York, 1969), p. 23.

15. Ibid.

16. Richardson, *American Painting,* p. 100.

17. See F:; *Selected Papers* 1 and 2.

I

Generous Marylanders

Paying for Peale's Study in England

———◆———

ROBERT J. H. JANSON-LA PALME

AMONG the many histories of American colonial painting, very little attention has been paid to the extraordinary show of support Charles Willson Peale received enabling him to study in England in 1767.[1] Eleven fellow Marylanders of differing degrees of wealth and prominence contributed a sum sufficient to support the aspiring painter for an entire year in London. And, contrary to William Dunlap's assertion of 1834, their donations were made freely, without any expectation of repayment.[2] No other budding student of art in colonial America received the same broad-based, generous patronage prior to 1790.[3]

Some historians — Samuel Isham and Royal Cortissoz (1936), Carl Bridenbaugh (1950), James Thomas Flexner (1954), Wayne Craven (1966) — following Dunlap have credited Peale's support rather loosely to a group of "gentlemen" or even, somewhat misleadingly — Edgar P. Richardson (1956) — to "his friends."[4] Others — Alan Burroughs (1936) and Flexner (1939/80) — aware perhaps of the presence in the subscription list of Proprietary Governor Horatio Sharpe, attributed the financing of Peale's study trip to the Governor's Council.[5] Still other writers, such as Virgil Barker (1950), remained essentially silent on the subject, or like John Wilmerding believed it sufficient to say that Peale left for London carrying letters of introduction.[6] One of those letters, of course, was addressed to Benjamin West, whose own maiden trip abroad had not been underwritten, as is so often thought, out of pure altruism.[7]

Who were the eleven interested supporters of the still infant art of painting in the small colony along the upper Chesapeake? The full story began to emerge in 1939 with the publication of the first volume of Charles Coleman Sellers's biography of Peale.[8] Sellers and his father, Horace Wells Sellers, had obtained a large quantity of unpublished Peale documents, including the detailed autobiography, written in the 1820s, which had hitherto gone practically unnoticed.[9] From this material Sellers not only listed each subscriber by name and amount, but also attributed the leading role to John Beale Bordley, Peale's friend and patron. Bordley initiated the idea of English study and also submitted a full proposal to Charles Carroll, Barrister, who became the principal contributor. Despite the fact that this account of the events was taken almost verbatim from Peale's recollection, it was to be many years before the story would be fully incorporated into the literature on the artist. Aside from Sellers's further writings, Edgar P. Richardson was really the first to highlight most of the narrative in his 1983 essay on Peale.[10] The complete text from Peale's autobiography is as follows:

> A painting of his was carried to Miss Eliz'th Bordleys and the Hon'ble J. B. Bordley being then at Annapolis to attend the Governors counsel of which he was a member, this piece was left for Mr. Bordley to see it, when he rose in the morning he went into a cold room where the picture was put, before he had gartered up his stockings, and staid there Viewing it near 2 hours, and when he came out, he said to his sister, something must and shall be done for Charles, and he immediately sent for him, and after some conversation he asked him if he was willing to go to England to get improvement, if the means could be provided. this was readily agreed to, and Mr. Bordley drew up a paper, intended to obtain the assistance of the wealthy to bear his Expences, and desired him to show it to Barrister Carroll, who having approved the measure Mr. Bordley gave 10 Guineas, Mr. (Barrister) Carroll 26 Gui., Gov'r Sharpe £8 Ster'g., Daniel Dulany 10 Gui's., Robert Lloyd Esqr. 5 guis., Benj'n Tasker Esqr. 3 gui's., Tho's Ringold Esq'r 3 Gui's., Benj'n Calvert Esq'r. 5 Gui's., Thomas Sprigg 5 Gui's., Daniel of St. Thomas Genefer 3 Gui's., Cha's Carroll Esq. 5 Gui's., amounting to £83 – 12 – 0. Sterling.
>
> The next step was to get letters of recommendation, Mr. Bordley wrote to Edmond Jenings Esq. Dan'l Dulany Esq'r. wrote to the Rev'd Mr. Douglas, an intimate acquaintance of Mr. Ramsey the Kings painter. He also obtained a letter from Wm. Allen Esq. of Phild'a to Benjn. West who was then in high estimation for his great Merit in painting. Mr. Allen had been Mr. Wests patron on his going abroad for his Improvement.[11]

Many, indeed most, of the eleven subscriber names are quite familiar to the growing number of students of Chesapeake and Maryland
culture. Nearly all of the subscribers were active politically, their positions shifting from time to time according to their perceived self-interest;
and several were connected with the colony's largest fortunes. Their
wealth, which put virtually all of them within the top 4 percent of
Marylanders (unlike the bulk of John Singleton Copley's patrons), tended
to be associated first and foremost with holding and cultivating large
tracts of land.[12] As there was somewhat more diversity within the group
than these brief generalizations suggest, it may be well to review as con-
cisely as possible the separate circumstances of each subscriber and to
suggest reasons for their interest in Peale and/or the potential benefits
his developed talent might bring to the colony.

To begin with the instigator: John Beale Bordley (1726/27–1804) was
a descendant of Anglican clergy, a lawyer and subsequently a planter,
an agronomist, and a learned member of the American Philosophical
Society. He was particularly close to the Peale family from the 1740s
on. During the days of Charles Willson's boyhood in Chestertown, Maryland, Bordley had studied in the Kent County School under Charles
Peale, the future artist's father. Known for his benevolence, in 1750 Bordley had helped Peale's unexpectedly widowed mother and her five young
children move to Annapolis, where their prospects for gaining a liveli-
hood would be greater.[13] It was predictable that, on seeing a picture
of Peale's after his return from a Massachusetts sojourn (which included
a visit to Copley's studio), Bordley, as a kind of family protector, would
offer the maximum encouragement and foster a plan to mobilize some
powerful backers for Peale's further advancement.

Beale Bordley was well known in Annapolis social and legal circles
in the sixties, but there was a further reason why he would have sent
his young protégé to Charles Carroll, Barrister (1723–83).[14] Not only
was the Barrister a man of artistic discernment with strong London connections, he also seemed a likely patron because of his wife's family ties
with Maryland's Eastern Shore, and specifically with the town of Chestertown.[15] Mrs. Carroll (fig. 3) was a member of the numerous and
influential Tilghman clan, and her uncle was Peale's godfather.[16] A second uncle, Robert Lloyd, who gave five guineas toward Peale's study
abroad, was a highly active member of the richest family on the Eastern Shore.[17] Moreover, Mrs. Carroll was a first cousin of Anna Maria
Tilghman Earle, wife of Thomas Ringgold, well-to-do Chestertown mer-

chant and planter, and supporter of the same Kent County School where Peale's father had spent his final years.[18] Ringgold too subscribed to the proposed London trip. Such family networking was carried still further as Ringgold's partner on the Western Shore, Samuel Galloway of Tulip Hill, was linked through marriage to another subscriber, Thomas Sprigg.[19]

Recent studies confirm how important kinship was in Chesapeake culture. The Bordley scheme to help Peale through family sympathies was effective in attracting at least half of the donors, including Daniel Dulany, Jr., to whom Bordley was closely related through his wife's family.[20] Dulany, English-educated, was a shrewd and often outspoken lawyer whose pamphlet *Considerations on the Propriety of Imposing Taxes in the British Colonies, for the Purpose of Raising a Revenue, By Act of Parliament* (1765), was freely used by William Pitt and Lord Camden as they argued for the repeal of the Stamp Act in 1766. Dulany's gift of ten guineas equaled Bordley's donation and may have been partly motivated by Dulany's hope of enlisting Bordley's support for his brother Walter's nomination to the Governor's Council. Governor Sharpe was understandably reluctant to see another Dulany on his council.[21] Bordley was a clear favorite in the governor's sphere in the 1760s, being appointed to several judgeships and recently to the Governor's Council.[22] Thus it was doubtless he who directly sought the patronage of Governor Sharpe, a man who had arrived in the colony in 1753 and who was without local family connections.[23]

Sharpe, often thought of as a military man primarily interested in horse racing, was in fact an effective political leader. He tried to establish a college in the colony during his tenure, and, at the time of the solicitation for Peale, was building one of the colony's most sophisticated residences, called Whitehall. The name Whitehall had been applied to the land after it was purchased by Deputy Governor Nicholas Greenberry in 1695; that Sharpe used the same name with all its implications of the English establishment and monarchical officialdom for his new elegant dwelling, begun in 1764, no doubt reflects his outlook. It is easy, therefore, to understand how such a man could have been persuaded to send a promising youth to London in order to improve the cultural atmosphere of his capital city. Sharpe's support may, in turn, have strongly influenced such perennial insiders of the proprietary government as Benjamin Tasker and Benedict Calvert to contribute.[24] Tasker, born about 1690 and the oldest of the subscribers, was on familiar terms with both Governor Sharpe and his predecessor Governor Ogle. Tying him to the subscription group also was the fact that his daughter was the wife of Daniel Dulany, Jr. As for the planter Calvert, his family connection with the proprietor, Lord Baltimore, was in itself sufficient to secure him a seat in the upper house of the Assembly when he was in his twenties. He served continuously in the post from the mid-1740s until well after Peale's return from London. During this time, Benjamin Tasker also served without interruption as the president of the upper house until his death in 1768; so these two men were in frequent contact with each other as well as with Governor Sharpe from the time of the latter's arrival in the province.

An unusually generous contributor to Peale's journey was Daniel of St. Thomas Jenifer, an unmarried planter-merchant, who was also in favorable standing with the government of Horatio Sharpe. His generosity was demonstrated in his remarkable will, which thoughtfully provided for no fewer than thirty-one individuals from every station in life. In cultural matters, his library contained books in both English and French; and, judging from the good quality of a portrait taken of him at about the time of the Peale subscription, he seems to have had an instinct for competency in art (fig. 1).[25]

Still more knowledgeable about portrait painting was the final personage on the list of contributors, Charles Carroll of Carrollton. Because he came from a strong Roman Catholic background, he could not have been closely related to any of the foregoing subscribers, although he was a distant cousin of the Anglican Charles Carroll, Barrister; and because of legal prohibitions, he could not have held colonial or provincial office, as all of the others did at one time or another. As scion of the richest family of the Western Shore of Maryland, however, he had just returned in 1765 from London and the Continent where he had studied and conducted business for several years. While abroad, he had had his portrait painted by Joshua Reynolds, "the best hand in London" (fig. 2). This beautiful work with its soft, painterly detailing, Rembrandtesque lighting, and simple but sophisticated placement of the figure is utterly unlike anything painted in the Maryland area before or during the 1760s. And so it was that even though he was just twenty-eight years old, Carroll, perhaps more than any other Annapolitan of his day, found himself in a position to judge the caliber of portrait painters available to his social peers. When the subscription for Peale was taken up, Carroll had not yet inherited his fortune and was still dominated by his sixty-five-year-old father. He thus contributed a mere five guineas to the would-be painter whom he scarcely knew.[26]

Other subscribers had in the fifties and sixties commissioned portraits locally with greater or lesser success from such itinerant practitioners as the English-trained John Wollaston and John Hesselius, who had studied art with his Swedish-born father, Gustavus, in Philadelphia.[27] Indeed, in 1763 Hesselius became a resident of Annapolis, and his stiff, predictable productions doubtless represented the most effective pictures that Chesapeake patrons could hope to obtain during this period — short of voyaging to England. The best-known piece by Hesselius, done in 1761 for Benedict Calvert, one of the subscribers, portrays his young son Charles in the company of a slave-boy companion (Baltimore Museum of Art).[28] Although this well-recognized painting exemplifies to many today the style and quality of John Hesselius's work, students of this artist detect a higher level of quality in his paintings of the seventies — interestingly enough, after Peale's return from London.

An improvement in Peale's abilities is almost certainly what most of the subscription group hoped their generosity would help bring about. Instructive in this regard is Peale's portrait of Charles Carroll, Barrister, of 1770–71 (fig. 4). This sitter was not only the most generous of the subscribers, he was the most impressively educated — the English School, Lisbon, Portugal; Eton College; Clare College, Cambridge; and Middle Temple, London — and the most wedded to the visual arts. What kind of image of this patron was the freshly trained artist able to contrive as a result of his studies? The picture may be compared with one painted a decade earlier, almost certainly by Hesselius (fig. 10).

Peale shows the Barrister seated at ease by the window of his country mansion, Mount Clare. Visible is the newly built entrance portico and beyond it in perspective the forecourt and entrance gates to the house.[29] This elaboration of personalized setting was not entirely new to American portrait painting, and specific views as seen through windows in portrait backgrounds may be found in European painting from the late fifteenth century onward. By and large, however, except in the case of some successful military officers or high officials, mid–eighteenth-century portraitists in America and England tended to prefer vague, often imaginary, garden backdrops for their figures if the out-of-doors were to be shown at all.[30] The Hesselius view of Carroll shows him standing impassively against a blank background, with much of the visual interest centering on the elegant trim of his costume. The broader proportions of the head differ from Peale's likeness where the head appears as an elongated ovoid. A recorded Peale miniature of Carroll (1770–71, private collection) that came to light in 1958 appears to confirm that Hesselius was portraying this sitter in much the same way he did all his males and that the acute vision of Peale had made a necessary correction.[31] The Peale canvas, then, brought a new degree of verisimilitude to Maryland painting, a new casualness of pose and a new specific recognition of the sitter's circumstances. These qualities were to appear again and again in Peale's more ambitious portraits of the seventies and eighties.

The young artist went to still greater lengths in the seven-foot canvas honoring his chief ally, John Beale Bordley (fig. 5). Created at the behest of Edmund Jenings, Bordley's London step-brother who had been of service to Peale during his two-year stay there, this monumental work is an outgrowth of Peale's studies under West. Bordley appears as a full-standing figure surrounded by a profuse amount of rather unrelated detail assembled to proclaim his concern for American liberty.[32] This well-meant tribute fits into the tradition of baroque allegories, such as Herman van der Myn's portrait, *Charles Calvert, Fifth Lord Baltimore,* which hung in the Annapolis city chambers and for which Peale had a lifelong admiration (fig. 6).[33] Its more immediate predecessor, however, was Peale's own *William Pitt* (1768; fig. 7), also ordered by Jenings. In this well-known early attempt at a large-scale picture, Peale had shown the English statesman against an architectural background of the Whitehall Banqueting House, prefiguring his frequent use of associated architectural motifs, such as he had done in Barrister Carroll's portrait.[34] The Bordley figure shows improvement over the clumsily robed Pitt, and doubtless reflects Peale's intense study of West's eight-foot allegorical portrait *The Drummond Brothers* (1767, Addison Gallery of American Art, Andover, Mass.). Symbolic statuary appears at the right in both pictures, and Peale is attempting to endow his sturdy American friend with a little of West's more fluid ease. A gratuitous tree trunk seems to flow and merge with Bordley's body, but Peale errs in the proportioning of the arms, in the awkwardness of the leg placement and in the tipping of the perspective. The painting paves the way, however, for such full-lengths of the seventies as the *William Paca* (1772, Maryland Historical Society) and *Conrad Alexandre Gérard* (fig. 74). Perhaps the finest portion of the Bordley painting is found in the wonderfully gentle, introspective facial expression that Peale captured with heartfelt warmth.

A third supporter of Peale's trip to London benefited from the artist's improved skills. A miniature of *Thomas Ringgold,* brought to light in 1985, shows the Chestertown merchant-planter's head rendered with a convincing grasp of solid form and also with a delightfully keen expression (fig. 8).[35] One is reminded of the considerable experience Peale had with miniature painting in London and of his submitting examples of them to exhibitions there, and also of Barrister Carroll's caution against his concentrating on such painting.[36] Peale also did a half-length of Ringgold that has a certain frozen, lackluster rigidity about it (fig. 9).[37] It is probable that the subject's widow commissioned the canvas shortly after his death in 1772 along with a companion piece showing herself in mourning. But Peale could not quite recapture the spirit of his living model in transferring the miniature's head to the larger format. We know that Peale was not entirely satisfied with the Ringgold canvases from remarks in his autobiography for the year 1790. "The shadows," he wrote, were "too cold almost black. . . . Had I used Vermillion or light Red how much better these paintings would have been."[38]

The above classes of portraiture — the interior sitter with a significant outside view juxtaposed, the complex full-length, the exquisite miniature, and the straightforward standard half-length — all became part of Peale's repertory thanks to his London trip. A fifth class, the conversation piece, which Peale was to develop so attractively during the seventies and eighties, was considered but not executed for a fourth subscriber, Charles Carroll of Carrollton. Sellers believes that sometime before September 1770 Peale began a large design of the picture, which would have shown father, mother and recently born daughter.[39] Had such a composition been carried out, the picture might have become Peale's most winning effort — certainly if it resembled *The John Cadwalader Family* of 1772, as Sellers supposes (fig. 27).[40] Thus, while only a small number of the original subscribers reaped immediate results from their generosity, the pictures Peale created for them displayed his talent in virtually every category of portraiture that was later to make him famous. But these beneficiaries were not in the majority. Many of the subscribers had already been portrayed more or less competently and perhaps did not want to make further expenditures for works of art. Even the retired Governor Horatio Sharpe seems to have been content to continue living with an older type three-quarter-length portrait in his newly decorated, magnificent quarters at Whitehall.[41] New portraits did not appear to them necessary.

It seems certain that all the subscribers were motivated by a concern to make of Annapolis a southern town that would outdo Williamsburg in the quality of its cultural amenities and would begin to approximate the level of refinement that was so evident in Philadelphia by mid-century.[42] In Annapolis there was a significant rise in the purchase of luxury goods, and Thomas Jefferson in 1766 was ready to admit that "the houses are in general better than those in Williamsburgh."[43] Jefferson's statement was made well before the erection of structures designed or embellished by the very accomplished William Buckland, who was active in Annapolis and the nearby areas between 1771 and 1774.[44] Recent studies have shown a conscious aping, on a reduced scale, of English architectural "pattern" books in the city during the 1760s and 1770s.[45] Surely Horatio Sharpe in building his remarkable templelike retreat Whitehall in the fall of 1764 (with its subsequent lateral wings when he decided to make it his retirement home) was in the vanguard of sophisticated Annapolitans who were busy adapting English taste to their own needs and pleasure. Sharpe's decoration of the twenty-foot-high central saloon with exuberant allegorical carvings as well as his enthusiasm for gardening imply that this supporter of Peale was attempting to elevate on as broad a basis as possible the artistic climate of his colonial capital.[46]

T. J. Wertenbaker, in his still interesting synthesis *The Golden Age of Colonial Culture,* recognized the strong English proclivities of the merchant-planter class living in and around Annapolis.[47] He described the Annapolitan as suave and refined but at the same time more relaxed and less serious than the Philadelphian. The combination of light as well as serious reading, clubs, and theater, together with an admiration of large-scale—even lavish—urban architecture, could clearly be enhanced by the establishment of a local school of painters to be led by an ambitious, optimistic, and charming young man who showed definite promise. Annapolitans, indeed the gentry of the Chesapeake, would no longer have to rely on itinerants for their portraits and decorations. They would not have to depend on Philadelphia or even England, now that the Stamp Act crisis had ushered in some strain with the mother country.[48]

It may be that not all subscribers had altruistic motives or that they were as interested in things artistic as their support of Peale seems to suggest. Perhaps Beale Bordley, Barrister Carroll, and Governor Sharpe had to exert some pressure to encourage the generosity of the others.

But the confidence that Bordley, the Carrolls, and Sharpe placed in Charles Willson Peale proved to be more than justified. A conscientious person, Peale worked hard in London and did all that he could to please his benefactors on his return. Very much a man of the Chesapeake, he took the values of enterprise and independence, combined with a strong sense of kinship and English cultural attitudes, along with him to Philadelphia in 1776, on the very eve of the Revolution. And despite all its wealth derived from its well-located trade and port facilities, its already established cultural institutions, and its large class of skilled and talented craftsmen, that most populous of American cities had no strong local tradition of portrait painting before Peale's arrival on the scene.[49]

Peale's career from then on was unlike that of most painters born during the colonial period. Whereas other major artists in America suffered from frustration or a decline in technical powers, or they grew out of touch with the public—as might be said of Trumbull, Vanderlyn, or possibly Allston—Peale could still claim competency and even verve as a painter in his eighties during the third decade of the nineteenth century.[50] He not only showed his own worth: he passed on to his very considerable kin a love—in some instances, a mastery—of the visual arts. In supporting and encouraging his tightly knit family, he repaid what he had received as a youth and proved himself a true son of the Chesapeake.[51]

NOTES

1. Charles Coleman Sellers, *The Artist of the Revolution, The Early Life of Charles Willson Peale* (Hebron, Conn., 1939), p. 67. Peale also obtained free passage to England.

2. "[Peale] decided upon a voyage to England as soon as practicable. His wishes were seconded by several gentlemen of that city, and a subscription made to forward that enterprise, he engaging to repay the loan with pictures on his return." William Dunlap, *A History of the Rise and Progress of the Arts of Design in the United States,* ed. F. W. Bayley and C. E. Goodspeed, (Boston, 1918), 1:157. In one of the few other cases of group sponsorship of an American artist for study under West, Dorinda Evans notes that Thomas Sully in 1809 agreed to copy one "excellent picture in London" for each of the seven subscribers to his trip (Dorinda Evans, *Benjamin West and His American Students* [Washington, D.C., 1980], p. 151).

3. For the encouragement of the fine arts after 1790, see Lillian B. Miller, *Patrons and Patriotism. The Encouragement of the Fine Arts in the United States, 1790–1860* (Chicago, 1966).

4. Samuel Isham, *The History of American Painting,* ed. Royal Cortissoz (New York,

1936), p. 68; Carl Bridenbaugh, *The Colonial Craftsman* (New York, 1950), p. 102; James T. Flexner, *History of American Painting 1760-1835: The Light of Distant Skies* (New York, 1954), p. 20; Wayne Craven, *Colonial American Portraiture* (New York, 1986), p. 384; Edgar P. Richardson, *Painting in America* (New York, 1956), p. 99.

5. Alan Burroughs, *Limners and Likenesses, Three Centuries of American Painting* (Cambridge, Mass., 1936), p. 77; James T. Flexner, *America's Old Masters* (1939; rev. ed. New York, 1980), p. 184. Flexner is entirely in error in stating that "ten members of the council" subscribed.

6. Virgil Barker, *American Painting, History and Interpretation* (New York, 1950); John Wilmerding, *American Art* (New York, 1976), p. 55.

7. Following the accounts of John Galt, West's first biographer, and William Dunlap, most writers have assumed that Justice Allen and Governor Hamilton financed West's trip to Italy in 1760. However, Allen Staley, using extensive research material on the artist, states that "accounts of the trip do not suggest that [West] expected to receive any financial support" from them (Helmut von Erffa and Allen Staley, *The Paintings of Benjamin West* [New Haven, Conn., 1986], p. 20). It is well known that Allen and Hamilton purchased pictures painted by West and that his passage was arranged by Provost William Smith.

8. Sellers's 1939 publication apparently did not receive wide circulation, for he was able to make available the unissued sheets to the American Philosophical Society for publication, with an extra sheet, in 1947 as *Charles Willson Peale,* vol. 1, *Early Life (1741-1790).* This biography is, unfortunately, not fully footnoted.

9. Horace Wells Sellers rendered the manuscript autobiography, [*The Selected Papers of Charles Willson Peale and His Family,* vol. 5 (New Haven, Conn., forthcoming] into 487 typed pages (F:IIC). He drew upon this source for his article "Charles Willson Peale, Artist Soldier," *Pennsylvania Magazine of History and Biography* 38 (1914): 257-86, which was noted by Burroughs and Flexner, among others.

10. E. P. Richardson, Brooke Hindle, and Lillian B. Miller, *Charles Willson Peale and His World* (New York, 1983), p. 28.

11. P-S, A(TS): 29-30. The listing of the subscribers for this account was taken from Peale's diary for 1767 (*Selected Papers* 1:57-58). The most notable discrepancy between the diary and the autobiography is that Peale raised Barrister Carroll's contribution from 25 to 26 guineas and placed Sharpe's name above Dulany's in his later version.

12. Edward C. Papenfuse et al., eds., *A Biographical Dictionary of the Maryland Legislature, 1635-1789* (Baltimore, 1979-85) presents well-researched data pertaining to the occupations and verifiable wealth of all of Peale's patrons. Many held local rather than provincial office, and only half served in the Proprietary Assemblies from 1758 to 1766 (*Selected Papers* 1:59-62). Copley's patrons were studied and analyzed by Jules D. Prown, in *John Singleton Copley, In America 1738-1774* (Cambridge, Mass., 1966), 1:129-30. In his summary analysis, Prown indicates that Copley's sitters consisted of a preponderance from "big business," the landed gentry, and the professional class. For the stratification of wealth in Maryland, see Aubrey C. Land, "Economic Base and Social Structure: The Northern Chesapeake in the Eighteenth Century," *Journal of Economic History* 35 (1965): 639-54, esp. p. 653. Subscribers' wealth has been taken from Papenfuse et al., *A Biographical Dictionary.*

13. See *CWP,* pp. 15-16. See also entry in Papenfuse et al., *A Biographical Dic-*

tionary 1:145–46 for details about this highly praiseworthy gentleman who had condemned slavery; also see *Selected Papers* 1:48.

14. During the 1750s, while Charles Carroll, Barrister, was serving several consecutive terms in the lower house of the Assembly, John Beale Bordley was an active member of a jovial group known as the Tuesday Club. See Elaine G. Breslaw, ed., *Records of the Tuesday Club of Annapolis 1745–56* (Urbana, Ill., 1988), *passim.* Carroll maintained two residences, one in Annapolis and the other a splendid estate near Baltimore called Mount Clare.

15. The Barrister's standing as a critic of portrait painting is given credibility by a letter sent by his distant cousin Charles Carroll of Carrollton to Edmund Jenings in London, April 8, 1771. The letter refers to husband and wife portraits recently completed for the writer by Peale: "I have sent you by this opportunity Mrs Carroll's and my portraits. I question whether you will discover any great likeness of your old acquaintance in my picture. Mr and Mrs Carroll will give you their opinion on both" (Charles Carroll of Carrollton Letterbook, 1771, Ms. 203.2, Maryland Historical Society). Jenings, Bordley's half-brother, had looked out for Peale during his London stay, 1767–69, and the Barrister was visiting London at the time of Carroll's letter. Charles Carroll of Carrollton was known to be sly in seeking out compliments. (I owe this insight to Sally D. Mason of the Carroll Papers.)

16. William Tilghman (1711–82) was the son of an early trustee of the Queen Anne's County Free School, where Charles Peale first found employment as a schoolmaster. His lineage was intimately linked with that of the Lloyd family, by far the largest landowners on the Eastern Shore. See E. H. Brown, "The First Free School in Queen Anne's County," *Maryland Historical Magazine* 6 (1911): 14.

17. Robert Lloyd (ca. 1712–70), who owned residences in both Talbot and Queen Anne's counties, was highly active in the lower house of the Assembly in mid-century. Edward Lloyd was his first cousin.

18. Thomas Ringgold (1715–72) maintained a large plantation in Kent County and bought a well-situated residence in Chestertown in 1767, which he began enlarging before his death. He left a legacy to the school and to one male heir, Thomas, Jr., who like himself was both an astute businessman and active politician.

19. Thomas Sprigg (1715–81) of Anne Arundel County had been president of the Jockey Club and was married to Elizabeth Galloway, Samuel's first cousin. See J. Reany Kelly, *Quakers in the Founding of Anne Arundel County, Maryland* (Baltimore, 1963), p. 55. The Galloway-Ringgold relationship grew even closer when Samuel's daughter married Thomas Ringgold, Jr. There is a portrait of Sprigg attributed to Hesselius (ca. 1770) at the North Carolina Museum of Art, Raleigh.

20. At the time of the Peale subscription, Dulany's step-sister, Margaret Chew, was married to John Beale Bordley. Although there is a large literature on the subject, Allan Kulikoff's *Tobacco and Slaves: The Development of Southern Cultures in the Chesapeake, 1680–1800* (Chapel Hill, N.C., 1986) is especially enlightening on the importance of kinship; see chap. 7, "The Rise of the Chesapeake Gentry."

21. See Aubrey C. Land, *The Dulanys of Maryland* (Baltimore, 1955), pp. 236–67, 279–80.

22. Bordley was appointed to four different judgeships in the 1760s as well as to the commission that would decide the Maryland-Delaware boundary line.

23. Horatio Sharpe (1718–90), English-born proprietary governor of Maryland from 1753 to 1769, was a close contemporary of all but a couple of the subscribers. From a military background, he developed a breadth of interests and left a large body of correspondence. Edward C. Papenfuse, *In Pursuit of Profit: The Annapolis Merchants in the Era of the American Revolution 1763–1805* (Baltimore, 1975), p. 31, speaks highly of Sharpe's "well-run administration." His initiative in 1754 in founding a college is pointed out in Tench Tilghman, "The Founding of St. John's College 1784–1789," *Maryland Historical Magazine* 44 (1949): 76–77. In the same journal, vol. 46 (1951): 8–26, Charles Scarlett, Jr., presents much new and important information about Whitehall in his "Governor Horatio Sharpe's Whitehall" (see esp. pp. 9–10).

24. The "Benj'n Calvert, Esq'r" listed by Peale in both his diary and autobiography is surely Benedict Calvert, Esquire (ca. 1724–88) of Mount Airy, illegitimate son of Lord Baltimore, who came to America in 1747 and served on the governor's council for a quarter century and throughout Sharpe's tenure. No suitable Benjamin Calvert, Esq., appears in contemporary records. A certain Benjamin Calvert, living on the Patuxent River, is mentioned as owing back rent in 1763 (Maryland Hall of Records: Provincial and General Court Records, Liber DD 2, f. 317); but such a person would not be called "Esquire," nor would he be likely to contribute five guineas to an art student. Mistaken first names do occur elsewhere in Peale's papers. See John Thomas Scharf, *History of Maryland* (1879; rpt. Hatboro, Pa., 1967), 1:436; *Selected Papers* 1:57.

25. Daniel of St. Thomas Jenifer (1723–90) served in the Proprietary Assembly shortly after Sharpe's arrival and, more significantly, after he left office. He had received several judicial appointments by the time of the Peale subscription. In his will he revealed unusual generosity in forgiving debts, helping the needy, and freeing slaves (Maryland Hall of Records: Anne Arundel County, Wills, November 16, 1790, JG 1/194).

This rather solemn portrait has been attributed to John Hesselius, but it is not included in Richard K. Doud, "John Hesselius, Maryland Limner," *Winterthur Portfolio* 5 (1969): 128–53. The work has been dated ca. 1760, but from the subject's apparent age it could have been taken ca. 1770, or even later, when Hesselius was in his last and best phase. See Richard J. Cox, "From Feudalism to Freedom: Maryland in the American Revolution," in *Maryland Heritage, Five Baltimore Institutions Celebrate the American Bicentennial,* ed. John B. Boles (Baltimore, 1976), p. 177.

26. Charles Carroll of Carrollton (1737–1832), youngest of the subscribers and a signer of the Declaration of Independence, was the wealthiest, longest-lived, and best known of the group. His father, Charles Carroll of Annapolis, writing in April 1762, desired that his son's picture be drawn by the "best hand in London." The son reported in November 1763 that his picture was done three-quarter length by Reynolds. There is definite evidence that the famous English painter did paint the portrait. See Ann C. Van Devanter, *"Anywhere So Long As There Be Freedom": Charles Carroll of Carrollton, His Family & His Maryland* (Baltimore, 1975), pp. 17–19, 142–43; Thomas Hanley, *Charles Carroll of Carrollton* (Washington, D.C., 1970), pp. 141–44; Richard H. Saunders and Ellen G. Miles, *American Colonial Portraits, 1700–1776* (Washington, D.C., 1987), pp. 256–57. The soft subtlety of this work must have greatly impressed other Marylanders who saw it.

27. The itinerant English painter John Wollaston arrived in New York in 1749 and gradually moved south to Virginia, painting about three hundred portraits in just a few years. He was in Annapolis during 1753–54, just as Horatio Sharpe assumed the governorship. John Hesselius (1728–77), on the other hand, was a native-born American painter, who not only was in Annapolis during much of Sharpe's tenure but also became his immediate neighbor seven miles outside the capital city. There are records of Hesselius selling part of the land inherited through his wife's family to Sharpe as the latter enlarged his farm and gardens. For a good study of Hesselius in Maryland, see Doud, "John Hesselius."

28. See Craven, *Colonial American Portraiture,* p. 370; Saunders and Miles, *American Colonial Portraits,* pp. 251–52.

29. The Peale picture has suffered damage, especially noticeable about the window area where the new classical portico that Carroll had installed in 1768 is visible. See Michael F. Trostel, *Mount Clare, Being an Account of the Seat Built by Charles Carroll, Barrister, Upon his Lands at Patapsco* (Baltimore, 1981), pp. 42–43, 53.

30. A well-known early prototype of the foreground figure seated beside a window that looks out on a specific view is Ghirlandaio's portrait *Old Man with a Child* (ca. 1480, Louvre). Similarly, an early American example of what might be called a "window of significance" is seen in the upper right of Thomas Smith's *Self-Portrait* (ca. 1690, Worcester Art Museum). Though less distinctly framed by a window, the portrait of *Rev. James Blair* (ca. 1740, College of William and Mary) shows the "Wren" building of William and Mary alongside the sitter in a picture by the English-born Charles Bridges. Sir Joshua Reynold's *Dr. Thomas Newton, Bishop of Bristol* (exhibited 1774, Lambeth Palace, London) illustrates St. Paul's Cathedral through a window opening; and in an even more exact parallel with Peale's *William Buckland* (1774–87, Yale University Art Gallery), Reynolds revealed his sitter's profession as architect in *Sir William Chambers, R.A.* (1780, Royal Academy, London) by placing a portion of his classically designed Somerset House in a window view. West employed this idea from time to time, and it is interesting to note that Peale first began to place a specific building (St. Paul's Cathedral) beside his sitters in the miniature of *Mathias and Thomas Bordley* (fig. 19) that he painted for their father John Beale Bordley when he first arrived at West's studio.

31. See *P&M Suppl.,* p. 56. The miniature is illustrated in Richardson, Hindle, and Miller, *Charles Willson Peale and His World,* p. 29. The Hesselius portrait of Carroll was not accepted by Doud, although he lists as probable a picture of Dr. Charles Carroll, the Barrister's father, a work Doud only knew of through written sources. It is possible that the painting Doud thought to be of the father was really of the son, as both the written source and the painting described here can be traced back to the same private collection. See Doud, "John Hesselius," p. 149.

32. The painting was never sent to London as intended. Hidden from view for about a century, the picture was variously attributed until a cleaning in the 1960s revealed Peale's signature. Almost as soon as Peale's name became visible on the foreground rock, Charles Sellers (in *P&M Suppl.,* pp. 55–56, and "Charles Willson Peale and John Beale Bordley," *Pharos* 7 [1969]: 20–25) was prepared to explain the heavy-handed apparatus of Peale's encomium down to its last detail. In Sellers's reading of the piece, both the artist and Bordley were united against the perils of

British tyranny. Bordley, the Maryland country gentleman, was in effect instructing the very people he had earlier sent Peale to learn from; one wonders how Governor Sharpe would have reacted to this contrivance (see chap. 4).

33. (Ca. 1730, Baltimore City Life Museums; the Peale Museum, Baltimore).
In 1823, Peale contracted with the city corporation of Annapolis to paint portraits
of six Maryland governors in exchange for this work, which he wanted for his Philadelphia Museum. The status of Peale's ownership was unclear at the time of his
death in 1827, but the work was ultimately purchased for the Baltimore institution.
See Wilbur H. Hunter, *The Story of America's Oldest Museum Building* (Baltimore, 1964),
pp. 22-23; Saunders and Miles, *American Colonial Portraits,* pp. 148-50.

34. The device of a large and pointedly significant building being used to focus
attention on the central figure was a feature of Benjamin West's *Spencer Compton,
Eighth Earl of Northampton, with His Wife and Children* (ca. 1764-65, Castle Ashby,
Northampton). In this eight-foot canvas, West joins a perspective view of Castle
Ashby with the head and shoulders of the earl. Probably West passed this compositional idea along to Peale, who declared in a fragmentary 1790 preliminary draft
of his autobiography that he received from Mr. West "all the satisfaction he could
desire" (unpaginated manuscript, P-S, F:IIC/1).

35. The provenance of this previously unpublished work is striking in that it
appears to have been included in the will of Mary Galloway Ringgold, daughter-in-
law of the sitter, dated October 10, 1803. Many of the specified items, such as marked
silver, were sold at Christie's in New York, May 31, 1985. The will lists "her grand-
father and grandmothers pictures" as bequeathed to "my daughter Maria Tilghman." The itemization, which would refer to portraits almost certainly, doubtless
comprises the pair of portraits now in the Baltimore Museum of Art as well as the
miniature, since all three works passed through the same hands. It is highly unlikely that the miniature could have come into the possession of the descendants
at a later date, for this particular line moved to California in 1848.

36. For the Bordley miniature that Peale submitted to the Society of Artists' exhibition in 1768, see Saunders and Miles, *American Colonial Portraits,* pp. 282-83; for
the best rendering and annotation of the well-known letter to Peale of October 29,
1767, from Barrister Carroll, see *Selected Papers* 1:70-71.

37. This 30 by 20 inch canvas was acquired by the Baltimore Museum of Art
in 1985 and is one of the paintings left by Mary Galloway Ringgold to her daughter
Anna Maria Ringgold Tilghman, mentioned above (note 35). (I am much indebted
to William V. Elder III for confirming this information.) The painting has been
cleaned since it was first published by Sellers in *P&M Suppl.,* p. 77. The simple
isosceles triangle of the composition is a reminder of the fact that Peale named his
first son to be born (February 1774) after his return from England in honor of Raphael. (West had named his eldest son Raphael in 1766.) The small pile of papers
that anchors the composition at bottom right includes some partly legible writing
which Sellers took to mean that the sitter was Thomas Ringgold, Jr.: ". . . rds of
the Gen . . . Assembly . . . Annapolis 177 . . ." In point of fact, Thomas, Senior,
appears in all of the Assembly lists of the sixties and was elected but did not serve
in 1771. On the other hand, Thomas Ringgold, Jr. (1774-76), though active politically, was never elected to the Assembly. Moreover, the facial features indicate a

man who has reached more than thirty-two years. It is interesting that the family of this highly successful merchant-planter seems to have preferred having him remembered as legislator (his gravestone likewise praised his public service).

38. For a fuller quotation, see *P&M Suppl.*, p. 78.

39. In *P&M,* p. 49, Sellers gives a description of this design based on sources available to him. It should be noted that Carroll also was portrayed in miniature as well as in half-length at this time. These works are unlocated. A half-length of Mrs. Charles Carroll of Carrollton, signed and dated 1771, has been found (*P&M,* pp. 20–21).

40. Also unlocated are half-length portraits of the son and daughter of Daniel Dulaney, Jr., which, according to a list kept by Peale from 1770 to 1775, the father commissioned (*P&M,* pp. 20–21).

41. The Sharpe portrait was returned to Whitehall from the Johns Hopkins University after Charles Scarlett, Jr., began restoring the building. The painting was cleaned and some older restorations removed. Cox, "From Feudalism to Freedom," attributes the portrait to John Hesselius, ca. 1760. If the work is by Hesselius, it could have been painted at an earlier date, for the anatomical understanding and the drapery folds are inferior to Hesselius's later work.

42. For some visitors' observations, favorable and unfavorable, about Williamsburg prior to the Revolution, see John Reps, *Tidewater Towns, City Planning in Colonial Virginia and Maryland* (Williamsburg, Va., 1972), pp. 183–85. A good summary of the status of Philadelphia just after the mid-eighteenth century may be found in Theodore Thayer, "Town into City, 1746–1765," in *Philadelphia, A 300-Year History,* ed. Russell F. Weigley (New York, 1982), pp. 68–108.

43. Jefferson's observation is quoted in *The Founding Fathers: Thomas Jefferson, A Biography in His Own Words,* ed. J. L. Gardner (New York, 1974), p. 33. For an explanation of the increase in lavish spending, see Papenfuse, *In Pursuit of Profit,* pp. 16–31. The market in fine furniture is discussed in Gregory R. Weidman, *Furniture in Maryland 1740–1940* (Baltimore, 1984), pp. 44–45. Fabrics, silver, and wine figured in the luxury import trade, and several Annapolitans were notable for their book collecting — among them at least two of the Peale subscribers, Charles Carroll, Barrister, and John Beale Bordley. See Robert Brugger, *Maryland, A Middle Temperament* (Baltimore, 1988), pp. 76–83, on the subject of libraries and other signs of an elevation of culture and taste.

44. See Barbara A. Brand, "William Buckland, Architect in Annapolis," in *Building by the Book 2,* ed. Mario di Valmarana (Charlottesville, Va., 1986), pp. 65–100.

45. See *Building by the Book 2,* esp. the articles by Michael F. Trostel, Marcus Binney, and John Harris, as well as that by Barbara Brand.

46. Although Whitehall was known and mentioned extensively by such architectural historians as Fiske Kimball seventy years ago, a proper understanding of its very special character began to emerge only after Charles E. Scarlett, Jr., purchased it. His important article, "Governor Sharpe's Whitehall," cited above, made available basic new information that brought about his restoration of the structure in conformity with Sharpe's original concept. Hugh Morrison reported and saw the significance of Scarlett's researches in *Early American Architecture from the First Colonial Settlements to the National Period* (New York, 1952), pp. 386–90, but many architectural

historians since have overlooked it. The introduction of the true temple form into house building in the 1760s is comparable in its uniqueness to eleven men banding together to send a painting student to London during that same decade. For color illustrations of Whitehall, see George B. Tatum, "Great Houses from the Golden Age of Annapolis," *Antiques,* January 1977, pp. 181–82. Some of the building components were imported from England, according to Scarlett.

47. T. J. Wertenbaker, *The Golden Age of Colonial Culture* (New York, 1949), pp. 85–104; Richard Beale Davis's *Intellectual Life in the Colonial South 1585–1763* (Knoxville, Tenn., 1978) presents in volumes 2 and 3 a vast amount of detail concerning the arts, literature, and libraries in Maryland and Virginia, but does not contrast such centers as Annapolis and Williamsburg as Wertenbaker does. Moreover, Philadelphia is not within the scope of his study.

48. See Ronald K. Hoffman, *A Spirit of Dissension: Economics, Politics, and the Revolution in Maryland* (Baltimore, 1973), pp. 47–50, for the involvement with England of some of the Peale contributors in the early sixties. In Land's *Colonial Maryland,* Governor Sharpe's disagreements with some of the contributors — as well as other aspects of his administration — are discussed on p. 239ff. This masterful book points out that in Annapolis during the decade prior to the Revolution the cost "of only the thirteen largest houses put almost £60,000 currency in circulation" (p. 185). It is interesting to see how the higher artistic and cultural aspirations of the Peale subscription group transcended politics.

49. Among the cultural institutions of Philadelphia in the 1760s, so well established that they still exist today, one might cite the Library Company of Philadelphia. For concurring opinions on the pivotal role of Peale in the history of Philadelphia portrait painting, see Craven, *American Colonial Portraiture,* p. 382; and Saunders and Miles, *American Colonial Portraits,* p. 34. Philadelphia's enormous population advantage ought to be noted: 40,000 persons versus 3,700 for Annapolis (1775), according to Carl Bridenbaugh, *Cities in Revolt: Urban Life in America, 1743–1776* (New York, 1964), pp. 216–17.

50. For Trumbull, see Irma B. Jaffe, *John Trumbull, Patriot-Artist of the American Revolution* (Boston, 1975), pp. 269, 285. Of John Vanderlyn's decline, there seems little doubt; but in the more complex case of Allston, see William H. Gerdts and Theodore E. Stebbins, Jr., *"A Man of Genius," The Art of Washington Allston* (Boston, 1979), pp. 161–62.

51. See Charles H. Elam, ed., *The Peale Family, Three Generations of American Artists* (Detroit, 1967); Maryland Historical Society, *Four Generations of Commissions: The Peale Collection of the Maryland Historical Society* (Baltimore, 1975).

2

Charles Willson Peale
in London

———◆———

JULES DAVID PROWN

I F one had to choose a single word to characterize Charles Willson
Peale, that word would undoubtedly be "versatile." Saddler, metal
and silversmith, clock and watchmaker, artist, soldier, naturalist,
taxidermist, museum entrepreneur, inventor, landscape architect, and
more — Peale was indisputably versatile. And, if we look closely at just
one aspect of Peale's activity — his art — the same versatility prevails. He
produced portraits, landscapes, still lifes, figure pieces, miniatures, drawings, watercolors, signs, banners, transparencies, mezzotints, line engravings, an etching, and sculpture. Considering the range and quality
of Peale's art, as well as the unlikely circumstances of his beginnings
in colonial Maryland, the question inevitably arises, how did he get to
be what he became? What shaped him as an artist?

Although it is somewhat reductive, it is possible to isolate three early
events most likely to have affected the trajectory of Peale's long career
as an artist — the Hesselius episode, the Copley episode, and the London visit. We know little about the first two events, but the influence
of John Hesselius and John Singleton Copley as reflected in Peale's earliest surviving portraits does not seem to have been profound or lasting.
The London experience, however, transformed Peale as an artist. The
primary purpose of this essay is to shed light upon what happened to
Charles Willson Peale in London, especially the artistic influences to
which he was exposed. Beyond offering a few suggestions concerning
Peale's continuing awareness of John Singleton Copley which affected
the character of his art, I suggest certain specific links with Benjamin

West and Francis Cotes. This, however, merely introduces the subject of English influence on Peale's early work, and a more thorough stylistic study needs to be undertaken.

Unlike his slightly older contemporaries, Copley and Benjamin West, who began their full-time artistic careers at the age of fifteen and seventeen, respectively, Peale got a late start. The dawn of his professional interest in painting apparently occurred when he was about twenty-one, a married and settled man.[1] After completing his apprenticeship as a saddler, he had gone into business for himself in Annapolis. With his clever hands and agile, curious mind, Peale branched out from saddling into metalwork, then the crafting of simple silver items, and then into watch and clock repairs. While on a trip to Norfolk, Virginia, probably in 1762, Peale saw some landscape paintings and a portrait by an artist identified only as "a brother of Mr. Joshua Fraizers." He thought they were wretched, and, confident that he could do better, painted a landscape, a portrait of himself working on a clock, and some family portraits (all unlocated). In December 1762 he went to Philadelphia for the express purpose of improving himself as a painter: he met an unknown artist he identified only as Mr. Steel (Steele?), he visited the studio of the able artist James Claypoole who unfortunately was out of town, and he purchased Robert Dossie's two-volume *The Handmaid to the Arts* (1758) at Rivington's Book Store.[2]

On his return to Annapolis, Peale arranged to get instruction from John Hesselius, a successful local artist. Hesselius's impressive double portrait of *Charles Calvert and his Black Slave* (1761, Baltimore Museum of Art), painted approximately a year earlier, suggests his contemporary style. In exchange for a saddle, Peale watched Hesselius paint two portraits and, in a practical exercise, Hesselius painted half a face and Peale completed it under the older artist's direction. Although this training was surely valuable to Peale, it is not possible for us to gauge Hesselius's influence with any precision, in part because no comprehensive study of Hesselius has yet been published and, more to the point, because no painting by Peale from this period survives. The earliest Peale portraits in which we can look for Hesselius's influence are the portraits of the children of Nathaniel Carter—Joshua and Thomas—(private collection) painted about two and a half years later. They suggest that the influence was more technical than stylistic.

In Annapolis, Peale was unable to work his way out from under the burden of debt he had assumed when he left his apprenticeship to go on his own, and in 1765 he was forced to abandon temporarily his young wife and infant son and flee as a debtor. He went first to Virginia and then sailed for Boston, arriving there on July 14, 1765. Still pursuing his interest in art, he visited John Moffatt's color shop on Queen Street. Moffatt had inherited the shop from his uncle, the artist John Smibert. Peale bought some prints and subsequently was led up the rear stairs into a well-lighted room. There, on walls covered with green baize, hung Smibert's copies of old master paintings that throughout the eighteenth century served young American artists from Copley to Allston as sources of inspiration and instruction — copies of Van Dyck's *Cardinal Bentivoglio* (Harvard University),[3] Poussin's *Continence of Scipio,* and Raphael's *Madonna della Sedia* — as well as some of Smibert's own paintings, including *Dean George Berkeley and His Entourage* (Yale University Art Gallery).

From Boston, Peale traveled north to Newburyport. As an advertisement he painted a *Self-Portrait* (unlocated) which led to a few, but only a few, portrait commissions, notably the Carter children paintings, which provide scanty evidence of the influence of any of the artists whose works Peale had undoubtedly seen — Justus Englehardt Kühn, Gustavus and John Hesselius, or John Wollaston, all of whom worked in Maryland and Virginia between 1753 and 1757 during the early years of Peale's apprenticeship.[4]

In the fall of 1765, Peale returned to Boston where he visited John Singleton Copley, the leading local artist. Copley lent him "a head painted by candlelight" to copy, probably a portrait of the artist's half-brother, Henry Pelham.[5] Although only two and a half years older than Peale, Copley had been painting professionally for a dozen years. Copley may have been especially sympathetic to young Peale's concern about his artistic future, because at the time of Peale's visit he was thinking about his own career. For all his success in Boston, the ambitious Copley wondered how his paintings compared with the work of contemporary English artists, which he had rarely seen except in the form of black-and-white engravings. He had just sent (probably in early September, 1765) his *Boy with a Squirrel* (Museum of Fine Arts, Boston), a better-known portrait of Henry Pelham, to London to be exhibited at the Society of Artists, and was awaiting some word as to how it had been received. In Boston Peale could hardly have looked upon Copley's impressive paintings of 1765, such as *Mrs. Theodore Atkinson* (fig. 11), without a sense of his own inadequacy. This might have depressed him, but it might also have motivated him to think of going abroad to study, if only to be able to compete eventually with an artist like Copley.

Peale did not linger in Boston to study with Copley. Before the year was out, he returned to Virginia, still a fugitive from creditors in Maryland, and spent six months with Mr. and Mrs. James Arbuckle at Accomac. His portraits of them painted late in 1765 or early 1766 (figs. 12 and 13) show little Copley influence, except perhaps compositionally, although in his many paired portraits, Copley as a rule did not place the husband and wife in the same chair. The portrait of Mrs. Arbuckle and her son Edward is the earliest of Peale's mother/child groupings, a favored theme after his return from England. While staying with the Arbuckles, Peale made a copy in oil of an unidentified print after Joshua Reynolds, perhaps one of the prints he had purchased from Moffatt in Boston.[6]

Peale, although a debtor, was held in high personal regard by a number of prominent Marylanders, including John Beale Bordley, a former pupil of Peale's schoolteacher father. Bordley had kept a friendly watch on the family since the elder Peale's death. Peale showed his recent work to Bordley, and also sent his copy of the Reynolds print as a gift to Charles Carroll in Annapolis.[7] Favorably impressed, these influential friends decided that Peale should be sent to London to further his art. They not only hoped that he could thus secure skills enabling him to work his way out of debt but also, with the same motivation that had prompted leading Pennsylvanians to send Benjamin West abroad a few years earlier, they hoped that he would return as a well-trained artist to make a contribution to the cultural life of the colony.

Bordley, Carroll, Gov. Horatio Sharpe, and others contributed funds to send Peale to England. William Allen of Philadelphia gave him a letter of introduction to Benjamin West, and Bordley gave him one to his half-brother in London, Edmund Jenings. Peale sailed in December 1766 and arrived in London on February 13, 1767. He was promptly taken in as a pupil by Benjamin West. Like Copley only two and a half years older than Peale, West was also an experienced and successful artist. He had arrived in London in the fall of 1763 after three years in Italy. Combining talent, a pleasing person and personality, and a gift for getting ahead, West rose rapidly in the London art world. His legendary generosity to aspiring young American artists is celebrated in Matthew Pratt's *American School* (fig. 14), a view of West's studio in 1765. West stands on the left criticizing a drawing; one of the foreground figures must be Pratt himself, and another student may be Abraham Delanoy, a young

New York artist then studying with West.[8] Peale located a convenient place near West on Silver Street, Golden Square, for one guinea a month rent. A neighbor, with a studio in Golden Square, was the artist Angelica Kauffmann (fig. 101), whom Peale later visited, admired, and after whom in 1775 he named a daughter.[9]

Peale went on a shopping spree in London as soon as he got settled. He bought a light blue suit, seven ruffled shirts, black stockings, silk stockings, worsted hose, a beaver hat, gloves, a surtout (overcoat) and a cork wig. As for art supplies, he purchased a palette, a palette knife, twenty-five yards of linen, "pencils" (brushes) and other tools, and colors including a bladder of flake white. For drawing he bought a porte-crayon, which appears in his right hand in the portrait West painted of him in London (fig. 15), and a drawing book; he acquired a set of "crayons" (pastels); for miniature painting he bought a miniature paint box and palette, a miniature stand, tin divisions for paint, cases for miniatures, and colors including one dram each of lake, ultramarine, Prussian blue, and peach black. He recorded that he bought some prints and books, including Boyer's French-English dictionary, Leonardo Da Vinci's *Treatise of Painting,* "Webs Encaustic Painting," and "Kirby's Perspective."[10]

Peale fitted easily into West's studio routine. When he arrived in February, West was at work on a full-length portrait of Gov. James Hamilton of Pennsylvania (Independence National Historical Park Collection, Philadelphia). West immediately pressed Peale into service posing for the hand resting on a table. Peale reported to his patrons in Maryland, "I am at my Studies under Mr. West who promises me all the Instruction I can desire and from his Behaviour to me in the Short Time I have been with him is a Person Extreemely affible and Good natured — His Paintings are Elegant." He added, "Mr. West is Pleased to give me Encouragement to persue the Paint.g Business so that I have great Hopes of Returning Home a tolerable proficient and give Some Satisfaction to my Benefactors."[11]

Peale, being generally handy, partially repaid West's kindness by making himself useful around the house; he repaired locks and bells, helped as a studio assistant with such tasks as painting drapery, so well mended a broken palette that West was about to throw out that West used it for the rest of his life, and probably helped out when the Wests moved from Castle Street to new premises on Panton Square the following year.

When Peale arrived, West was preparing his pictures for the annual exhibition of the Society of Artists, to open in the Great Room at Spring Gardens, Charing Cross, on April 22. Peale wrote home that West had "two Pieces ready for the Exhibision," identifying them as "Venus and Adonis," and "Jupitor Coming to Celemna in thunder."[12] The former was West's *Venus Relating to Adonis the Story of Hippomones and Atalanta* (private collection), a large picture with life-size figures in which West was aspiring to achieve the rich coloristic effects of the Venetians. The other, a pendant to *Venus and Adonis,* was *Jupiter and Semele,* a picture subsequently lost at sea and known today only through a 1771 engraving by Thomas Cook.[13] Peale also noted that in West's studio *Pylades and Orestes* (fig. 16), which had been one of West's major entries in the previous year's exhibition, was set on one easel; *Jupiter and Europa,* a painting exhibited at the Society of Artists two years earlier, but now unlocated, rested on another. Although he did not mention them, Peale also undoubtedly saw the other pictures West submitted to the Society of Artists' 1767 exhibition. One of these, *Pyrrhus When a Child brought to Glaucias King of Illyria for Protection,* painted for Dr. Robert Hay Drummond, Archbishop of York, is known today only through the 1769 engraving by J. Hall. Another entry, perhaps a companion picture to *Pyrrhus Before Glaucias,* with a child as the central character, was the *Fright of Astyanax,* commissioned by another important clergyman, Thomas Newton, Bishop of Bristol. This painting, now also lost, can be partially seen in the background of West's portrait of *Bishop Newton* (Trinity College, Cambridge, England), engraved by Richard Earlom in 1767. *Elisha Restores to Life the Shunammite's Son,* another emotion-laden scene that West sent to the exhibition, was the picture Peale got to know best. As one of his first lessons from West, Peale was instructed to make a watercolor copy of this painting (fig. 17).[14]

Both West and Peale were aware of one special problem in their teacher/student relationship; Peale wanted to be a portrait painter, and West conceived of himself as a history painter, even though he regularly painted portraits. And indeed, although Peale specifically studied painting in London with West, the portraits he produced upon his return to America, with their muted, cool, pale, sometimes powdery color, and emphasis on clarity of form, do not resemble West's portraits as much as they do the 1760s portraits of other English artists, notably Joshua Reynolds, Reynolds's pupil Hugh Barron, Francis Cotes, and, to a lesser extent, Allan Ramsay. In an early letter to John Beale Bordley, Peale reported that he had visited the studios of Reynolds and Cotes, who were, he said, considered to be the best portrait painters in London.[15] He opined, however, that West was better, but that judgment may have been colored by personal and nationalistic considerations; his later portraits speak louder than words of the greater influence of Reynolds and Cotes. Peale does not mention visiting Ramsay, the king's portrait painter, although he had a letter of introduction to a friend of the artist;[16] nevertheless, he surely saw Ramsay's work.

The general portrait style that seems most to have influenced Peale in London is characterized by solid forms defined by a steady flow of light, simple balanced compositions, strong outlines, and plain color. It is an anti-rococo style that traced its roots back to the 1740s and English portraitists such as Thomas Hudson and George Knapton rather than French artists in England or French-influenced artists — Phillippe Mercier, Jean Baptiste Van Loo, Francis Hayman, and eventually Thomas Gainsborough. The plain style, continued in the 1750s by Hudson, became fully developed and popularized by Ramsay in the late 1750s and early 1760s after his return from Italy; it was emulated by Ramsay's chief rival, Reynolds, also recently returned from Italy and working under a similar classicizing as opposed to French rococo influence; and was subsequently picked up by Cotes.[17] Some of West's early portraits, such as his *Peale* (fig. 15), have similar qualities of clear outlines, simplicity of form, and emphasis on the plasticity of individual figures, but his intense reds, as in the drapery background of the *Peale* portrait, often darkened with black, differ from the cool restraint that characterized the palette of these other artists in the 1760s.

Early on in London, Peale decided that within the broad category of portrait painting, he wanted to specialize in miniatures. He wrote to Bordley that although West did not paint miniatures himself, he was "intimate with the Best miniature Painter," and intended to borrow some miniatures for him to copy.[18] The question is, who was that "best" miniaturist? The most likely candidate is Jeremiah Meyer (1735–89), a prolific and successful miniaturist with a studio in Covent Garden who had studied under Reynolds. As the only miniaturist selected to be a founder-member of the Royal Academy in the following year, 1768, Meyer might well have been the miniaturist most highly regarded by and closest to West, who played a pivotal role in the establishment of the Royal Academy.[19]

In April 1767, Peale undoubtedly visited the Society of Artists exhibition. West was a major exhibitor and a director of the society. A principal attraction was David Martin's portrait of a prominent American, *Benjamin Franklin* (White House, Washington, D.C.), whom Peale had visited shortly after his arrival in London.[20] Peale also went to the competing exhibition of the Free Society of Artists at Pall Mall, and recorded that he spent a shilling to buy a pamphlet of criticism on the exhibition.[21]

One picture in the 1767 Society of Artists exhibition that held special interest for Peale was Copley's *Young Lady with a Bird and Dog* (fig. 18). In the previous year's exhibition, Copley's *Boy with a Squirrel* had been shown. Peale of course did not see that exhibition, although while in Boston he had presumably heard from Copley about that painting having been sent to London. West had been much impressed with it, and the picture was taken to West's studio after the 1766 exhibition closed. West sent a long and helpful critique to Copley in Boston, and urged him to send him another picture to enter in the 1767 exhibition. Peale in West's studio would have been one of the first to see Copley's new picture and compare it, presumably adversely as did West and Reynolds, with the *Boy with a Squirrel*.[22]

As noted earlier, Peale began his studies with a watercolor copy of West's *Elisha Restoring to Life the Shunammite's Son* (fig. 17). Of the other documented pictures he painted during his stay in London, some may well have been study works executed under West's direction, but most have disappeared and few can be dated more precisely than 1767–69. He painted a pastoral scene of cows;[23] copied three seascapes after Francis Swaine: *Moonlight at Sea, Ship on Fire,* and *Storm at Sea;*[24] and also may have painted an Italianate landscape, *Mercury and Argus.*[25]

In 1767 John Beale Bordley sent his two children, Matthias, ten, and Thomas, twelve, from Annapolis to London in care of his half-brother, Edmund Jenings, for their education. Jenings first got the boys a clergyman tutor, and then sent them to Eton. At the request of Jenings, Peale painted a miniature double portrait of the boys after their arrival (fig. 19). It shows the dome of St. Paul's in the background and a bust of Minerva, goddess of wisdom, on the table, symbols that reflect the purpose of the boys' trip, the furtherance of their religious and secular education.[26] Jenings also commissioned from Peale a large miniature double portrait of *Mrs. James Russell and her Granddaughter* (unlocated).

By the fall of 1767, Peale, quite lonely, was planning to return to America. But his friends in America, especially Charles Carroll, Barrister, urged him to remain. Since it was unlikely that such an opportunity to study would arise again, Carroll felt that Peale should take full advantage of it. Carroll raised more money in Annapolis for Peale, West offered to give him free board if he stayed, and Jenings commissioned a few portraits. Peale agreed to stay, and as a result was in the studio at a time when West was at the center of dramatic changes in the English art world, leading to the establishment of the Royal Academy in December 1768.

The archbishop of York, Robert Drummond, who commissioned West's *Agrippina returning to Brundisium with the Ashes of Germanicus* (Yale University Art Gallery; see fig. 67), was so pleased with his picture that he arranged to have West show it to George III. Peale was in the studio when West set off in court dress, wearing a sword, to see the king; he subsequently shared the excitement of West's account of his visit, during the course of which he had received a commission from the king to paint *The Departure of Regulus.* Later Peale posed for the figure of Regulus. It was in conversations with West while this painting was in progress that the king expressed interest in lending support to his own Royal Academy. Through the efforts of West and others, this led to the establishment of the academy, which received its royal charter in December 1768.

Meanwhile, the 1768 exhibition of the Society of Artists opened on April 28. West exhibited *Agrippina,* the picture which had led to the king's commission of *Regulus;*[27] *Venus and Europa;*[28] a whole-length *Portrait of Two Gentlemen,* probably the double portrait of the sons of Archbishop Drummond (*Robert & Thomas Drummond,* Addison Gallery, Phillips Academy, Andover, Mass.); and *Jacob Blesseth Joseph's Two Sons* (Dudley Peter Allen Memorial Art Museum, Oberlin, Ohio), a pendant to *Elisha Restoring to Life the Shunammite's Son,* the picture Peale had copied earlier. Peale, having been elected a fellow of the society, also exhibited four pictures—three miniatures and a three-quarter-length *Portrait of a Young Gentleman.* The only one of these that can be identified with some certainty is the miniature of *Two Young Gentlemen,* presumably *Thomas and Matthias Bordley.* The other miniatures were identified simply as *A Lady* and *Two Ladies.* Peale was listed in the catalogue as a "Miniature Painter."

A special exhibition was held by the Society of Artists in the autumn of 1768 in honor of the visit of Christian VII, king of Denmark. Peale exhibited *A Portrait of a Girl,* which Charles Coleman Sellers has suggested, I believe correctly, was the portrait of a *Little Girl with a Toy*

Horse (fig. 20), signed and dated 1768.[29] While Peale's picture seems modest in comparison with West's entries such as *Cleombrotus Ordered Into Banishment by Leonidas II, King of Sparta* (Tate Gallery, London), and certainly different in subject, it seems specifically to have been intended to rival, indeed outshine, Copley's *Young Lady with a Bird and Dog* (fig. 18) exhibited the previous year. It is significant that Peale responded competitively not to his English contemporaries but to the major American artist, perhaps in preparation for a future contest with Copley for domination of the American market, or at least for the reputation as the best painter in America.

During 1768, with a year of study under his belt, Peale not only began to exhibit his newly acquired skills, but was able to supplement his financial resources by painting miniature portraits of provincial customers for two guineas apiece on commission for a jeweler on Ludgate Hill. Later he raised his price to three pounds and then to four pounds, whereupon the flow of commissions slowed to a trickle and finally stopped. As he expanded his artistic activities, the curious Peale also became interested in experimenting with various media. He took lessons from a sculptor named Capizoldi in modeling and casting, and then made bust portraits of himself, West, and Jenings.[30] He also spent some time in the studio of the leading contemporary British sculptor, Joseph Wilton, in connection with a major unexpected commission.

In the wake of the repeal of the Stamp Act, a group of gentlemen in Westmoreland County, Virginia, raised a sum of money to secure a portrait of the earl of Camden to hang in the county courthouse to commemorate his efforts in opposition to the act. On their behalf, Richard Henry Lee wrote to Edmund Jenings in London in the summer of 1767, saying that the subscribers wanted the commission to go to Reynolds, but that for his part, "I think Mr. West being an American ought to be preferred in this matter, if his skill should approach near to that of the best limners, as I am told that it does." Agreeing with this, Jenings arranged for West to paint Camden, but Camden kept finding excuses not to sit.[31] After a year of frustration, it occurred to Jenings, who had previously commissioned portraits from Peale and was solicitous of his well-being, to ask Peale to paint a full-length portrait of that other great opponent of the Stamp Act and friend of the colonies, William Pitt the Elder, earl of Chatham.

Peale's portrait of *Pitt* (1768, Statehouse, Annapolis, Maryland), his first major work, reflects two theoretical factors as well as the practical results of his London training. One theoretical influence was his own political background. As a member of the Sons of Liberty, he had been actively involved in Maryland politics in the 1764 campaign against the "court party" in Annapolis and, in specific reference to the Stamp Act, had painted a political banner when he was in Newburyport at the time of the Stamp Act crisis. He was therefore politically sympathetic with the intent of Jenings's commission to paint Pitt. Second, Peale had absorbed from West an awareness of the intellectual potential of a work of art, but rather than paint a history picture, he painted a portrait in historical guise, somewhat in the manner of Reynolds's contemporary "mythological" portraits.

Peale was at work on the Pitt portrait by the summer of 1768. He did not secure a life sitting, but based the likeness on a portrait bust by Wilton, another founding member of the Royal Academy close to Benjamin West who had already produced several full-length statues of Pitt on commission for Ireland and America. That is how Peale came to be in Wilton's studio in the summer of 1768 when he was specifically interested in sculpture.

After completing the large picture, Peale became aware of certain compositional shortcomings, perhaps in the wake of a critique from West. At any rate, he set about painting an improved replica (fig. 7) in which, among other changes, he altered the perspective to make the cornice of the Banqueting House at Whitehall loom more prominently above the head of Liberty. Consistent with his interest in different media, Peale also engraved a large, remarkably good, mezzotint plate. On November 1, 1768, Jenings forwarded the second version of the large painting to Lee as a gift to the gentlemen of Westmoreland if they found it acceptable, noting that it had been painted by a young artist of "merit and modesty," Charles Willson Peale, and adding that he hoped "he may meet with every encouragement on his return to America."[32]

Peale's full-length *Pitt* was an ambitious undertaking, especially for an artist who fancied himself a miniature painter. Like Wilton's full-length statues, it presents the figure in classical dress, in this case a Roman "consular habit," holding the Magna Carta. Defending the claims of the American colonies on the basis of the British constitution, Pitt points to a statue of British Liberty trampling underfoot a petition of the Congress at New York, a petition that had been rejected by the House of Commons. On the plinth of the statue, a relief depicts an Indian with bow in hand and dog at his side, symbolizing American faithfulness

(the dog) and firmness (the bow). West may well have made an icono-
graphical contribution here, having noted a few years earlier in connection with a published depiction of an American Indian that when an
Indian goes to war, as opposed to going hunting, he leaves his dog behind.[33] Thus America is armed, but not yet ready to undertake hostili-
ties. On an altar a flame indicates that the cause of liberty is sacred,
a duty to God. In relief on the altar are heads of Sidney and Hampden,
who gave their lives in defense of liberty in the seventeenth century,
a message echoed in the background by the menacing presence of Whitehall, where Charles I, who tried to restrict the rights of liberty, had been
executed.

It is doubtful that George III would have appreciated Peale's picture, especially with the veiled threat suggested by Whitehall. Indeed,
it seems unlikely that West, working closely at the time with George
III on the *Regulus* commission and the planning for the Royal Academy, would have allowed himself to be closely identified with Peale's
Pitt project, and Peale presumably did not execute it in West's studio.[34]

With the completion of the mezzotint, the Pitt project was finished
and so was Peale's period of study and work in London. Although he
must have been tempted to remain for the opening exhibition of the
new Royal Academy on April 26, 1769, he had to leave on March 8 to
take advantage of the offer of free passage back to Maryland from James
Russell, a merchant handling Maryland and Virginia business, whose
wife and granddaughter Peale had painted in miniature earlier. Before
he sailed, Peale may have helped West paint a large transparent painting which was to decorate the left side of the facade of the Royal Academy at its opening. If so, the experience was useful preparation for the
many transparencies Peale later was to produce in America in celebration of victory at the end of the War of Independence.

Before he left, Peale probably saw a large work by Henry Benbridge,
an American artist he had not yet met — a full-length portrait of the
Corsican hero *General Paoli* (Fine Arts Museums of San Francisco). Commissioned by James Boswell in 1768, the painting presumably arrived
in London from Italy early in 1769, since a mezzotint engraving of it
was published by Carrington Bowles on May 1. Because of the personal
interest in Benbridge of two prominent Philadelphians in London, Franklin and West, Peale almost certainly would have had access to the picture if it had arrived before his departure.

As a farewell gift, West gave Peale a "throne chair" he had used himself for portrait painting, a large armchair on a revolving platform which could be adjusted as to height and turned to position the sitter in relation to the light source.[35]

After a crossing of twelve weeks, Peale arrived in Patuxent, Maryland, on June 8, 1769. His first major painting after his return to America was an ambitious American counterpart to *Pitt,* a full-length portrait of his friend and patron *John Beale Bordley* (fig. 5), also commissioned by Jenings. Standing in an American landscape, Bordley points to a statue of a female figure holding the scales of justice in her right hand and a liberty pole in her left hand with a cornucopia at her feet. On the pedestal is inscribed *"Lex / Angliae."* On a rock is placed a book, its open pages headed *"Nolumus Leges / Angliae Mutari"* ("We do not want the laws of England to be changed").[36] A torn piece of paper on the ground in the left foreground reads "Imperial Civil / Law — Summary / proceeding." In the landscape a peach tree is in fruit, a building is under construction, and sheep graze in the meadow, while a horse laden with a wool pack (local produce of the sheep) heads for market, all suggesting the self-sufficiency of America.

The resonances between *Pitt* and *Bordley* are many and pointed. The statue of British Liberty in *Pitt* crushes beneath its feet a document protesting the infraction of liberty; in *Bordley* a cornucopia rests at the feet of a statue whose justice (the scales) insures liberty (the pole). In the portrait of the lawyer Bordley, the law — English law as inscribed on the pedestal — is the protector of liberty in America, whereas in England there has been a betrayal of her own laws and constitution. The building in *Pitt,* Whitehall, is a threatening reminder from the past; the building in *Bordley* is a promise of the future.

When Peale returned from England in mid-1769, the best artist in America was still John Singleton Copley. Peale, after two years of study and practice in London, had reason to believe that now he was ready to compete with Copley, who had not yet been to Europe. That Peale seems to have been especially aware of Copley as his major American rival is not surprising, inasmuch as it may have been his initial encounter with Copley and Copley's paintings in Boston four years earlier that had fixed his sights on Europe in the first place. And his depiction of the *Little Girl with a Toy Horse* (fig. 20) in evident response to Copley's *Young Lady with a Bird and Dog* (fig. 18) also suggests that competition with Copley was one of his intentions.

Copley was at the zenith of his American career when Peale came

back to Maryland. By means of his art, he had risen from modest origins — his father had been a tobacconist on the Boston docks — to achieve
prosperity and social acceptance. In the year of Peale's return, Copley
had begun to acquire a twenty-acre estate atop Beacon Hill next door
to John Hancock, and in November he married Susanna Clarke, daughter of the Boston agent of the British East India Company. Copley was
thus for Peale both a formidable rival in art and an example of what
a successful artist could hope to achieve in America.

Peale was able to rival Copley more effectively in certain categories
of art than others. For example, his full-length *John Beale Bordley* seems
awkward in contrast with Copley's more elegant and assured *Jeremiah
Lee* of the same year (Wadsworth Athenaeum, Hartford, Conn.). On
the other hand, Peale had specialized in miniature portraits in London,
and his miniature of his wife, *Rachel* (fig. 21), also painted shortly after
his return, compares favorably with Copley's *Mrs. Samuel Cary* of the
same period (fig. 22). And it can be argued that in three-quarter-length
portraits, the handsome pair of *Charles Carroll, Barrister* and *Margaret
Tilghman Carroll* (figs. 3 and 4) can, unlike the pre-London *Arbuckle* portraits (figs. 12 and 13), hold their own reasonably well with Copley's contemporary work.

The evidence that Peale had Copley on his mind and wanted to impress him is quite clear. Disguising rivalry with politeness, Peale sent
Copley an impression of his *Pitt* mezzotint along with a flattering letter
in November 1770. Copley promptly thanked him for the kind words
and the print, and said that he wished he could see the painting from
which it had been taken. While he remained in Boston, Copley was too
far away to be a damaging rival for Peale; but as the political situation
in America worsened, portrait commissions became increasingly hard
to secure, and even such a successful artist as Copley found it necessary
to travel in pursuit of work.[37] When he spent six months in New York
in 1771 skimming off the cream of the available patronage there, he became more of a threat. Taking note of Copley's New York trip, Peale
wrote to Bordley from Philadelphia in November 1772 of "a Number
of New Yorkers haveing been here, who have given me the character
of being the best painter of America — that I paint more certain and
handsomer likenesses than Copley. What more could I wish?"[38]

If imitation is the highest form of flattery, then Copley paid Peale
an even greater compliment in his portrait of *Sam Adams* (fig. 23), which
seems to owe something in spirit and iconography if not composition

to Peale's *Pitt.* Copley seems to have been clearly aware of real competition from Peale as an artist who had had the advantage of several years of study in London under the guidance of Benjamin West. Just as years earlier he had taken advantage of the arrival of a more fashionable English artist, Joseph Blackburn, as an opportunity to learn,[39] so now too he seems to have been interested in picking up what he could from Peale of contemporary English practice. Although any substantial influence was limited by distance — and we do not know what paintings by Peale Copley actually viewed — he surely saw some works during the second half of 1771 in New York and, especially, in Philadelphia during his brief visit there in November.

Although the effect of Peale's London study on the work produced during the years following his return to America may be clearly seen in his miniatures, it is reflected more importantly in a series of family groups and double portraits. In these we can detect the convergence of two distinct influences from the London years, that of the portrait painter Francis Cotes, whose studio he visited, and, more subtly, that of his mentor, Benjamin West.

Cotes had been primarily a pastellist during his early career, but in the 1760s he had developed an oil style based on that of Reynolds, although simplified, and emphasizing the depiction of men or women in outdoor settings and military portraits, two portrait categories on which Peale was to concentrate later.[40] Considering that Cotes was one of the foremost English pastellists, that Peale was a compulsive experimenter in various media and had purchased a set of pastels when he first arrived in London, and that Copley was a superb pastellist (Peale would have seen Copley's pastel of a *Young Lady* exhibited at the Society of Artists in 1768), one wonders why Peale did not also challenge Copley in this medium in America. His failure to do so may reflect the fact that West viewed the medium with disdain;[41] and even more, that during the very years that Peale was in London, 1767–69, Cotes began to turn his attention away from pastels and toward the creation of a series of novel double portraits, such as *Mr. and Mrs. Thomas Crathorne* (fig. 24). These works were marked by unusual subjectivity, a warm and overtly affectionate interchange between the figures — often reinforced by the direction of the glances — that was quite different from the cool and dispassionate formality of conventional double portraits such as Reynolds's *Mr. and Mrs. Godfrey Wentworth* (fig. 25).[42] Peale seems to have been especially influenced by Cotes's paintings. Similar warmth, affection, and intimacy characterize *The Johnsons of "Rose Hill"* (fig. 26), *The John Cadwalader Family* (fig. 27), and *The Peale Family Group* (fig. 28), all of 1772 (although the *Peale Family* was not completed until much later).

With original portrait groups such as these, Peale became a force to be reckoned with in American art, and Copley was not unaware of the challenge. Although it is questionable whether any of these specific works was far enough advanced or accessible for Copley to have seen them on his 1771 trip, he undoubtedly saw something and, subsequently, heard more. When a pair of prominent Philadelphians, Mr. and Mrs. Thomas Mifflin, came to Boston in 1773 and commissioned portraits, Copley, who since early in his career had painted only single-figure portraits, was prompted to tackle the more complicated compositional problems of a double portrait (Historical Society of Pennsylvania). He may, in fact, have tried his hand at the double format earlier in *William Vassal and His Son Leonard* (ca. 1770–73, Fine Arts Museums of San Francisco). He came closest to Peale in one of the last paintings he produced before leaving for England in 1774, *Mr. and Mrs. Isaac Winslow* (Museum of Fine Arts, Boston). Copley seems to have been stung by the challenge of the impressive double and family group portraits that Peale was producing in the Middle Colonies.

These works by Peale also reflect West's influence. Indeed, it would be remarkable if Peale had remained unaffected by his exposure to West, and (in West's studio) to ancient history, classical mythology, Renaissance literature, and the Bible, West's major sources of artistic inspiration. Several years after Peale's return to America, a poem appeared in a local newspaper praising his portrait of his wife (unlocated). Sellers believed the poem to have been written by Peale himself, but felt that the "classic allusion to Arria, the heroic and devoted wife, is unexpected."[43] However, Peale surely knew West's *Non Dolet, the Story of Paetus and Arria* (Yale Center for British Art, New Haven, Conn.), done in 1766, which helps to confirm the attribution of the poem to Peale and to document West's influence. The first two paintings by West that Peale reported seeing in West's studio were *Venus and Adonis* and *Jupiter and Semele,* a pair of amatory works that moralizingly advocated gentle love in preference to destructive passion.[44] Peale, like West, was romantic and uxorious, and the affection celebrated in West's early depictions of lovers is manifest in Peale's love-infused portraits painted in America (figs. 26 and 27), a type of representation that eventually culminated in the almost erotically explicit double portrait of Benjamin and Eleanor Ridgely Laming (fig. 29).

Peale's multifigure compositions also suggest that he picked up from West certain devices for linking figures through the use of outline, the connection of arm to arm, of shoulder to shoulder, and of flanking curves that bracket the composition as in *Cleombrotus*. And a comparison of Peale's *Little Girl with a Toy Horse* with *Cleombrotus,* pictures exhibited simultaneously at the Society of Artists in 1768, shows that Peale learned from West a sense of the use of background geometry as an ordering or structuring device.

Peale seems to have absorbed West's instinct for large issues, his lack of concern for niggling details. In his paintings West concentrates on the central figures and those elements that link them — the significant exchange of glances, of gestures, and of facial expressions, as in *Pyrrhus before Glaucias*. When the king of Epirus was overthrown, his infant son, Pyrrhus, was taken to his uncle, who adopted him and eventually by force of arms restored his kingdom. West depicts the moment when the king and his councillors weigh the consequences of giving refuge, while the queen and her attendants are touched with pity for the child. The picture was highly praised when exhibited for its truth of expression, that is, the range of appropriate responses in gesture and facial expression to the event, and the artist's ability to display and reconcile a wide range of emotions — pity and terror, hope and fear.

Recognition of the importance of expression was a lesson Peale must have learned. Although there was little opportunity for such a dramatic range of expression in the portrait commissions he received after his return to America, Peale in his multifigure portraits made effective use of the significant exchange of glances, of gestures, and of facial expressions to link the figures. And when the opportunity presented itself, as in the 1772 portrait of his wife Rachel weeping over the body of their deceased infant daughter, Margaret (fig. 30), Peale invested the image with a considerable sentimental and emotional charge. The painting by West that Peale actually copied, *Elisha Restoring to Life the Shunammite's Son* (fig. 17), also related to *Rachel Weeping,* at least thematically, but in Peale's tragic real-life portrait there is no hope offered of a miraculous resurrection.

Peale's two years of study and work in London had been well spent. Whereas the few surviving works of his early years are crude and awkward, the miniatures and full-size portraits produced after his return rival in quality the work of Copley. In London he had enjoyed an opportunity to work in West's studio when that American artist was emerging as a major history painter, with the first of a series of commissions from the king, and was playing a prominent political role in the establishment of the Royal Academy. Through West, Peale had access to the leading artists, major works, and central ideas of the contemporary English art world. He gained experience in many media, both on a small and large scale. He absorbed technical and stylistic influences from a number of sources, but, unlike West and later Copley, he never aspired to an English career. He seems always to have had the American market firmly in mind. In particular, he seems to have been driven to compete with Copley, and in the early 1770s he did so effectively. But Copley left America in 1774, never to return, and Peale's own life and work were profoundly redirected by the events of the American Revolution. Peale's English years had prepared him for a rivalry that never came to full fruition, but it also provided the base for a long and distinguished artistic career in America.

NOTES

This chapter was originally presented as a paper by invitation at the conference "Charles Willson Peale: An Interdisciplinary Study of His Work," held at the National Portrait Gallery October 23, 1981, in cooperation with the Winterthur Museum and Gardens.

1. For a brief account of the earliest glimmerings of Peale's boyhood and adolescent interest in art, see *P&M Suppl.*, p. 11.

2. Unless otherwise noted, biographical information is taken from *CWP;* information about portraits is taken from *P&M;* and information about Peale's other works of art comes from *P&M Suppl.* For Steele, see Richard H. Saunders and Ellen G. Miles, *American Colonial Portraits* (Washington, D.C., 1987), pp. 31–34.

3. Formerly assigned to John Trumbull, but now correctly reattributed to Smibert. See Irma B. Jaffe, "Found: John Smibert's Portrait of Cardinal Guido Bentivoglio," *Art Journal* 35 (Spring 1976): 210–15.

4. Sellers also suggests that Peale admired a portrait of *Charles Calvert, Fifth Lord Baltimore,* attributed to Herman Van der Myn and painted in about 1730, that hung in the Maryland Statehouse (*CWP*, p. 33; fig. 6).

5. Jules David Prown, *John Singleton Copley* (Cambridge, Mass., 1966), vol. 1, fig. 95. It is possible but much less likely that the picture Peale copied was Copley's *Nun with Candle,* presumably itself a copy from a European print (ibid., 1:34n, 1:61).

6. This might reflect his awareness of Copley's occasional reliance upon English prints. See Waldron Phoenix Belknap, Jr., *American Colonial Painting: Materials for a History* (Cambridge, Mass., 1959).

7. This was Charles Carroll, Barrister, a distant cousin of the better-known Charles Carroll of Carrollton, signer of the Declaration of Independence.

8. Pratt had left London by the time Peale arrived in the city, and Delanoy was also believed to have sailed. Peale reported that Delanoy seemed embarrassed to be discovered in his flat when West and Peale went apartment hunting shortly after Peale's arrival. See Charles Willson Peale to Rembrandt Peale, October 28, 1812, P-S, F:IIA/51F13-G6.

9. In November 1767, the year Peale arrived, Angelica Kauffmann married a bogus count (de Horn), and had to spend £500 to shed him within a few months. West presumably had a personal interest in this affair, because he and Angelica Kauffmann had been close friends in Rome where they exchanged portrait drawings in the early 1760s. See Arthur S. Marks, "Angelica Kauffman and Some Americans on the Grand Tour," *American Art Journal* 12 (Spring 1980): 7–9.

Peale may have initially absorbed the idea of naming children after artists from West, whose son Raphael was born April 8, 1766, less than a year before Peale's arrival. Besides Angelica Kauffman (1775) Peale gave artists' names to Raphaelle (1774), Rembrandt (1778), Titian [I] (1780), Rubens (1784), Sophonisba Angusciola (1786), Rosalba Carriera (1788–90), Vandyke (1792–d. in infancy), and Titian [II] (1799).

In 1770, after Peale returned to America from England, Edmund Jenings sent him a copy of Matthew Pilkington's *Gentleman's and Connoisseur's Dictionary of Painters* (1770), on the flyleaf of which Peale recorded family dates as in a Bible (perhaps because of frequent use of the book as a reference work to supply artists' names for Peale children?).

10. Charles Willson Peale, "Diaries, 1765–67," P-S, in *Selected Papers* 1:59, 61, 64. Some, but not all, of the books Peale purchased can be identified readily. Abel Boyer, *The Compleat French Master for Ladies and Gentlemen* was first published in London in 1694, and regularly thereafter. Peale probably bought the twentieth (London, 1764) or twenty-first (Edinburgh, 1767) edition. Leonardo Da Vinci, *Traitté de la peinture,* was first published in Paris in 1651, and again in 1716. An English edition, *A Treatise of Painting,* done from the French edition, was published in London in 1729. *Selected Papers* 1:61n21 identifies A Webley as the bookseller/printer of John Henry Muntz, *Encaustic; or, Count Caylus's Method of Painting in the Manner of the Ancients to Which is Added a Sure and Easy Method for Fixing Crayons* (London 1760). Webley's name appears on the title page "Printed for the Author; and A. Webley, at the Bible and Crown near Chancery Lane, Holborn" (*Selected Papers* 1:61, 119). Peale owned the Müntz work (*Selected Papers* 1:118–19) but he may in this instance have confused Webley and Webb; Daniel Webb's *An Inquiry into the Beauties of Painting* (London, 1760) was an influential book that Peale would have been likely to buy. The last book Peale mentions was John Joshua Kirby, *Dr. Brook Taylor's Method of Perspective made easy both in theory and practice* (Ipswich, 1754).

11. Charles Willson Peale to [Mr. Lancelot Jaques], 1767, P-S, F:IIA/2B13.

12. *Selected Papers* 1:47–48; *CWP,* p. 57.

13. John Galt, *The Life, Studies, and Works of Benjamin West* (London, 1820), 2:225.

14. *P&M Suppl.,* p. 12.

15. *Selected Papers* 1:47–48; *CWP,* p. 57. Peale's visit to Reynolds's studio may have been prompted by Charles Carroll of Carrollton, another patron who had subscribed funds for his trip to London. The year before Peale departed for England,

Carroll had returned to Maryland from London, where Reynolds had painted his portrait (ca. 1763, fig. 2).

When Peale visited Reynolds's studio on Leicester Square and Cotes's elegant house on Cavendish Square, Cotes's prices were a little more than half those of Reynolds (Edward Mead Johnson, *Francis Cotes* [London, 1976], p. 15).

16. From Daniel Dulany to Rev. Mr. Vaughan, quoted in Charles Coleman Sellers, *Charles Willson Peale* (Philadelphia, 1947), 1:67–68.

17. There was a political dimension to this stylistic difference. The French rococo style was favored by the heir apparent, Frederick, Prince of Wales, George II's son and father of George III, as well as by his Tory courtiers. Following the death of Frederick and the ascension of George III, the simple Anglo-Italianate classical style of Ramsay and Reynolds flourished.

18. *Selected Papers* 1:47–48; *CWP*, p. 57. Peale's patrons in America were not convinced of the wisdom of his decision to specialize in miniature painting. Charles Carroll, Barrister, advised him that in America there would be more demand for portraiture on a larger scale, although he acknowledged that it would be better to be a first-rate miniaturist than a second-rate painter of regular portraits (Charles Carroll to Charles Willson Peale, October 29, 1767, P-S, in *Selected Papers* 1:70–72).

19. Among other possible candidates, John Smart, Richard Cosway, and Ozias Humphry were still on the rise and probably not yet identifiable as "best." G. M. Moser was closely allied with West in art politics, but he painted enamel miniatures and Peale did not. Francis Cotes's brother Samuel was a miniaturist, but not the "best."

20. And surreptitiously sketched in a naughty tête-à-tête (*CWP*, p. 59).

21. *Selected Papers* 1:66. I have not been able to locate any surviving critical pamphlet on the Free Society exhibition. There were, however, two pamphlets on the Society of Artists exhibition, *A Critical Examination of the Pictures, Sculpture, etc., Exhibited in the Great Room at Spring Gardens,* and *Le Pour et la Contre.* William T. Whitley, *Artists and Their Friends in England, 1700–1799* (1928; rpt. New York and London, 1968), 1:221. Perhaps it was one of these that Peale bought.

22. For the correspondence, especially between Copley and West, concerning Copley's *Boy with a Squirrel* and *Young Lady with a Bird,* see Guernsey Jones, ed., *Letters and Papers of John Singleton Copley and Henry Pelham, 1739–1776,* vol. 71, *Massachusetts Historical Society Collections* (Boston, 1914), pp. 35–36, 41–45, 49–66.

23. At the time of his death, West owned "a group of cows, in romantic woody scenery" by George Barratt and Sawrey Gilpin. This may have been the picture that Peale copied (*P&M Suppl.,* p. 12).

24. *P&M Suppl.,* pp. 12–13. These titles correlate closely with three pictures Swaine had exhibited at the Society of Artists in 1765.

25. *P&M Suppl.,* p. 13.

26. While there is no necessary connection, it might be noted that West had close links with clergymen educators, notably William Markham, headmaster of Westminster School until 1765, whose portrait he painted. In the year Peale painted this miniature, West painted *William Young* (Eton College), the first of his four Eton "leaving portraits," portraits of boys from prominent families presented to the headmaster of Eton upon their graduation.

27. West exhibited *Regulus* the following year at the first exhibition of the Royal Academy.

28. West painted two versions of this subject. The one exhibited in 1768 was probably the version now in the North Carolina Museum of Art, despite the fact that the picture is signed and dated 1770 (Helmut von Erffa, "Benjamin West's Venus and Europa," *North Carolina Museum of Art Bulletin* 8 [June 1969]: 22–26; Helmut von Erffa and Allen Staley, *The Paintings of Benjamin West* [New Haven, Conn., and London 1986], p. 238).

29. *P&M Suppl.*, pp. 83–84; *CWP*, pp. 71–72.

30. He also may have made a clay bust of Cicero, perhaps a cast or a copy of a classical bust; it appears on the left in the full-length portrait of *William Paca* (1772, Maryland Historical Society, Baltimore) (*P&M Suppl.*, p. 57).

31. Charles Coleman Sellers, "Virginia's Great Allegory of William Pitt," *William and Mary Quarterly* 9 (1952): 59–60; see also Charles Henry Hart, "Peale's Allegory of William Pitt, Earl of Chatham," *Massachusetts Historical Society Proceedings* 48 (Boston, 1915): 291–303.

32. *CWP*, p. 71; mezzotint and broadsides are reproduced on pp. 68 and 69.

33. William Burke, *Storia degli Stabilimenti Europei in America* (Venice, 1763): 1:vii.

34. Sellers, "Pitt," p. 59.

35. *CWP*, p. 74.

36. The correct reading of the word *"Nolumus"* occurred after this paper was initially given. See chap. 4.

37. In another example of this situation, Henry Benbridge, who returned to Philadelphia from London with a good reputation at the end of 1769, by 1772 had moved to Charleston, South Carolina where there was less competition.

38. *CWP*, p. 104.

39. Prown, *Copley* 1:22–26.

40. Johnson, *Cotes*, p. 17.

41. West wrote to Copley on August 4, 1766, that his next picture for the Society of Artists should "be Painted in oil, and make it a rule to Paint in that way as much as Posible, for Oil Painting has the superiority over all other Painting." Replying on November 12, 1766, Copley asked West to "be more explicit on the article of Crayons, and why you dis[ap]prove the use of them" (*Copley-Pelham Letters*, pp. 45, 51).

42. See also Johnson, *Cotes*, figs. 92, 94, and 102. Peale undoubtedly saw many double portraits in London, including Reynolds's *James Paine and His Son* (Ashmolean Museum, Oxford University) and West's *Robert and Thomas Drummond* (Addison Gallery, Phillips Academy, Andover, Mass.), both exhibited at the Society of Artists while he was in London.

43. *CWP*, p. 93; see also *Selected Papers* 1:94.

44. According to Ovid's *Metamorphoses*, after Semele was impregnated by Jupiter, jealous Juno, betrayed and enraged, urged Semele to persuade Jupiter to make love to her in his full divine glory. She did, reluctantly he did, and his lightning burnt the mortal Semele to a crisp.

West had begun the series of mythological pictures on the theme of romantic love during his impressionable years as a young man in Rome, where, like a number of other young artists, he may have enjoyed a brief emotional attachment with

Angelica Kauffmann. The first of these pictures, begun in Italy and perhaps reflecting his feelings toward Angelica, was *Angelica and Medoro* (State University of New York, Binghamton) from Ariosto's poem *Orlando Furioso* (1532) in which the lovers sit hand in hand by a tree on which the name "Angelica" has been inscribed. This painting was followed, perhaps with a touch of romantic disillusionment, by *Rinaldo and Armida* (Rutgers University Art Gallery), a scene from Tasso's *Gerusalemme Liberata* in which Rinaldo falls in love with but eventually abandons the virgin witch Armida.

3

"Encouragement Exceeding Expectation"

The Lloyd-Cadwalader Patronage of Charles Willson Peale

———◄◆►———

KAROL A. SCHMIEGEL

LATE in the spring of 1769, Charles Willson Peale returned to Annapolis. After two years spent in Benjamin West's London studio the twenty-eight-year-old artist arrived home with the knowledge that one patron in England already desired a number of paintings. Who else would want his pictures? Would the eleven men who had financed his trip abroad request their portraits? Would they recommend him to their influential friends and relatives? Would he succeed in this, his second career? The aim of this chapter is to discuss the patronage of Charles Willson Peale during the first crucial years after his return to Annapolis from England. From a perusal of most histories of colonial American painting, it might be concluded that an artist was selected either because his work was obviously superior to whatever else was available or because he had no competitors. Presumably the subject of a portrait sat — and paid the bill — but did no more. The role of the eighteenth-century patron in America largely has been ignored, primarily because so few of those commissioning works of art functioned as patrons. The usual American customer, in John Singleton Copley's estimation, regarded portrait painting as no more than any other useful trade.[1] Only a few colonists recognized art as distinct from a craft, ordered a number of paintings that included subjects other than portraits, and thereby promoted the career of the professional artist. The activities of these colonial patrons were not on the scale of the Catholic church, contemporary European mercantile families, or nobility, but were the first American manifestations of an interest in art for its own sake that blossomed into the commissions and collections of the nineteenth century.

Shortly after his return from England, Peale established artist-patron relationships with three men — John Cadwalader (1742–86) of Philadelphia and his two brothers-in-law, Edward Lloyd (1744–96) and Richard Bennett Lloyd (1750–87), both of Talbot County, Maryland. The three commissioned at least sixteen paintings from Peale. A study of these, the reasons why they were ordered, the attitudes of the recipients, and their relationships with the painter and with his other patrons provide insight into the beginnings of Peale's successful career and into the attitudes of affluent Americans toward art and artists.

Peale's was not the only important arrival in Annapolis in the late spring of 1769. Robert Eden, the new royal governor, brought with him to the capital city of the colony clothes and furnishings in the latest English fashion. His additions to and redecoration of his house encouraged Marylanders to build their own new and lavish townhouses, many designed by the English-trained architect William Buckland. Eden thought of himself as an art collector, for he owned a portrait of his family's benefactor, Charles I, one of his own patron (and brother-in-law) Frederick Calvert, Lord Baltimore the sixth, some landscapes by Francis Smith, and numerous city views. Eden's "Picture Parlor" may have inspired the wealthy and prominent of Maryland to acquire paintings for their own homes. The governor gained and retained his personal popularity even with those who were growing antagonistic to the royal rule he represented. During his six years in Annapolis, Eden enjoyed much hospitality and soon became a leader among the fashionable party-going, horseracing set. His assistant, William Eddis, recorded that "assemblies and theatrical representations were the amusements of the evening, at which the company exhibited a fashionable and brilliant appearance." Annapolis was likened to Bath, where the latest styles of London were instantly adopted.[2]

The man who had been primarily responsible for Peale's trip to England was John Beale Bordley (1727–1804), a lawyer and agriculturist who had attended the Chestertown, Maryland, school where Peale's father had taught. In 1767, after studying a painting left for his perusal by the aspiring artist, Bordley decided to help Peale gain some proper training and convinced ten other men, all on the Governor's Council, to join him in providing a purse to finance Peale's studies in London. He also encouraged his half-brother, Edmund Jenings, a London lawyer with an independent fortune and a former Maryland resident, to look out for Peale as well as for Bordley's own two sons, Thomas and Mathias, who were to attend school in England.[3] During Peale's sojourn Jenings commissioned the portrait of William Pitt, earl of Chatham, as a gift for the gentlemen of Westmoreland County, Virginia (fig. 7). The painting, whose two versions were completed in 1768 in London, served as the basis for the mezzotint Peale made to sell after he returned to America. It was Jenings who sent Peale home to Annapolis in 1769 with orders for several paintings — portraits of his friends Bordley, John Dickinson, and the Charles Carrolls of Carrollton — and specified that the pictures include views with flora that would proclaim their American origin.

First to be completed but last to be shipped was the 1770 three-quarter-length portrait of Dickinson with the falls of the Schuylkill River in the background (fig. 41). Bordley's portrait (fig. 5), sent to Jenings in April 1771, showed his house and representations of his agrarian interests in the background. In the foreground, nearer the sitter, were a statue of Justice, legal documents, and the poisonous jimsonweed. The painting of Charles and Mary Carroll and their daughter, although begun, was not completed. Instead Peale substituted a half-length portrait of Mr. Carroll (fig. 4) and another of Mrs. Carroll (fig. 3), each of which included dogwood blossoms. In the summer of 1771 Jenings received these two, as well as an unsolicited painting of Peale's wife and child (unlocated) and the Bordley portrait.[4]

An enduring patron and friend, Bordley remained Peale's strongest supporter. The two men painted landscapes together, and the professional kept the amateur's paints in order. Bordley had requested two pictures while Peale was in London: a copy of an English portrait and a miniature of his sons, both of which were done in 1767 (fig. 19). In 1770 Bordley's unmarried sister Elizabeth sat for a portrait that included her Annapolis house in the background (private collection). Peale executed a picture of Sarah Turner, her companion, as a pendant (the Chase Home, Annapolis). In 1771 Peale produced an idealized double portrait of Bordley's sons dressed as archers in a romantic landscape (private collection). Mathias was still at Eton; earlier that year, Thomas had died. This painting remained as an exhibition piece in Peale's Annapolis studio until the artist moved to Philadelphia in 1776. Peale also executed a portrait of Bordley's daughter Henrietta Maria (fig. 34), miniatures of the lawyer's stepchildren John and Sarah Mifflin (1776, unlocated), possibly a miniature of Bordley (1775 or 1776, private collection), a portrait of his second wife, Sarah (1789, private collection), and a bust of Bordley (1790, private collection). Peale later made two replicas of the bust and in 1808 completed a portrait of Bordley's daughter Elizabeth, begun earlier that year by Peale's son Rembrandt (unlocated).[5]

Of the other ten subscribers to Peale's study trip, five, whose portraits had been executed by John Hesselius earlier, did not commission paintings from Peale. Horatio Sharpe was no longer governor and was living in reduced financial circumstances by the time Peale returned to Maryland. Robert Lloyd, Daniel of St. Thomas Jenifer, and Thomas Sprigg did not patronize Peale. Benjamin Tasker had died in 1768, and Thomas Ringgold died in 1772. The widow and son of the latter did have their portraits executed by Peale, probably in 1773 (both in private collections). In 1770 and 1771 Charles Carroll, Barrister, required a miniature of himself (private collection), possibly one of his wife, Margaret Tilghman Carroll (unlocated), and full-size portraits of each of them, which included views of their home, Mount Clare, near Baltimore (figs. 3, 4). In 1788 for their nephew and heir, Nicholas Carroll, Peale made copies of these two large paintings (private collection). He executed at least two landscapes for the barrister in 1775. During the winter of 1770–71, Daniel Dulany commissioned Peale to make portraits of his daughter Ann and son Benjamin (both unlocated) and may have recommended Peale to his half-brother Lloyd Dulany, whose picture Peale also executed that same winter (unlocated). Benedict Calvert wanted portraits of his children; about 1770 Peale painted Eleanor in her riding costume (private collection), and Charles's portrait was taken about 1773, probably just before his departure for school in England (Maryland Historical Society). Charles Carroll of Carrollton ordered a miniature of himself in 1770 (unlocated) and probably a double portrait of his daughters, Elizabeth and Mary in 1775 (unlocated).[6] Thus only sixteen commissions, other than the eleven from Bordley, came from the group of men whom Peale had regarded as potential patrons. He had to look elsewhere for additional commissions.

John Cadwalader was not among the group who had funded Peale's study with Benjamin West, but he was a close friend of Bordley and the favorite cousin of John Dickinson. Cadwalader seems to have become acquainted with Peale's work during the summer of 1770 and immediately became interested in the artist. Cadwalader first commissioned a miniature of his wife, Elizabeth (unlocated), and some landscapes. Subsequently he ordered portraits of his mother, father, sister, brother, a miniature of himself, a group portrait of himself with his wife and his eldest daughter, Anne, and a copy of a portrait of his mother-in-law.[7] With these nine commissions, all occurring within a space of three years, Cadwalader seems to have provided Peale with more orders than any other individual except John Beale Bordley.

John Cadwalader was a man of fashionable tastes and the elder son of a prestigious family. His father, Thomas, was a physician, a founder of the Pennsylvania Hospital, an active member of the American Philosophical Society, and a trustee of the College of Philadelphia.[8] John and his brother Lambert attended the college and furthered their education by a trip abroad. In 1763, shortly after their return, the two established a successful business as importers of dry goods. John Cadwalader's marriage in September 1768 to twenty-six-year-old Elizabeth Lloyd (daughter of Edward Lloyd of Wye, Talbot County, Maryland) added considerably to the merchant's financial resources, for Miss Lloyd had already received property valued at £10,000 including a sizable farm that she managed herself. The couple acquired a house on Second Street in the Society Hill section of Philadelphia and undertook a major redecoration program that made their home one of the most lavish townhouses in the city. Abiding by the nonimportation agreements, the Cadwaladers commissioned woodwork and a large quantity of furniture from local craftsmen who excelled in the elaborately carved Chippendale style. Robert Kennedy, a local merchant, supplied them with prints displaying a variety of subjects from the Bible, classical mythology, the English theater, and romantic peasant scenes.[9] In addition to the engravings Cadwalader wanted paintings — fashionable, to be sure, but of an American family and of American scenes. He saw a potential protégé in Charles Willson Peale: a new and aspiring artist whom Cadwalader could sponsor in Philadelphia. He knew that Peale had acquired the necessary technical competence and knowledge of current fashions in the London studio of the American-born master Benjamin West and now sought patrons whose commissions would support him and his family. Another bond between the prospective patron and artist was their agreement on the necessity of the colonies' attaining relief from the taxes imposed by England. Cadwalader had signed the nonimportation agreement in

1765, and Peale had joined the Sons of Liberty in Maryland in 1764.

In Annapolis and Philadelphia, Peale was not without competitors. By 1769 John Hesselius (ca. 1728–77), who in 1762 had given Peale a few lessons in painting, lived near the Maryland capital and still accepted a limited number of commissions. Matthew Pratt (1734–1805), a pupil of West, after returning to Pennsylvania in 1768, executed a number of portraits for leading Philadelphians, such as William Hamilton, Samuel Powel, Thomas Willing, and John Dickinson. Although Pratt took a brief trip abroad in the spring of 1770, went to New York City in 1772, and to Virginia in 1773, his residence remained Philadelphia, and he continued to paint portraits. Henry Benbridge (1743–1812), after studying first in Italy and later in West's studio, returned from London in October 1770. His stay in Philadelphia was brief, and by 1772 he had moved to Charleston, South Carolina, with his wife, the miniature painter Esther (Hetty) Sage. William Williams, Jr. (1727–91), was painting in Philadelphia from 1767 until 1775, but his weak pictures were based on engravings and did not compare with Peale's elegant likenesses. Pierre Eugène Du Simitière, absent from Philadelphia only between 1772 and 1774, remained active until his death in 1784; however, his interest in natural history and the American Philosophical Society may have left him short of time to compete with Peale for portrait commissions. He did execute some miniature drawings and pastel pictures during this period.[10] Thus Peale was not without competitors, two of whom had received their training from the same master as himself.

Despite the availability of other established artists in Philadelphia, John Cadwalader turned to Peale during the summer of 1770. By early September, Peale had completed the miniature of Elizabeth Cadwalader; however, the artist informed Cadwalader that his landscapes were not begun: "Mr Bordly has expected me over to the Island [Wye] some time, and I intend to paint your Landscapes there, if I can find Views that will look well in painting, I can there amuse Mr. Bordly with a part of the art which he is exceedingly fond of." The commission of the miniature was not at all extraordinary, but landscapes were not the usual product of American artists in the eighteenth century. Most commonly used for overmantels, landscapes were often ordered from England to fit the space available, or purchased from European artists such as Alexander Stewart of Edinburgh, who worked in Philadelphia during 1769. The landscape commission may have presented difficulties to Peale. Seven months later, in 1771, he explained: "I hope you will pardon my neglect of the Landscapes for realy too much difidence prevented my attempt after nature had lost her green mantle. The peices you get from Eng[l]and I hope will be very clever I could not promise myself to make any thing of that way in the l[east wo]rthy of the Place you intend."[11]

Cadwalader's waste book for 1770 shows £110 credited to Peale. This generous payment, made before the commissioned paintings were completed, portended a successful career for Peale in Philadelphia and must have been a major impetus in his early decision to move there as soon as he had fulfilled his obligations in Annapolis.[12]

John Cadwalader intended the portraits of the members of his family to hang in his front parlor. Martha Cadwalader (1740–91), later Mrs. John Dagworthy (Philadelphia Museum of Art), is shown standing with her right hand holding her drapery and her left arm resting on a carved plinth supporting fruit. Lambert Cadwalader (1743–1823) (private collection) is depicted standing also, with his elbow resting on the elaborately carved crest rail of a side chair owned by his brother, below an oval landscape painting and with an outdoor scene in the right background. Each of the elder Cadwaladers is represented seated, the doctor holding a book and his wife Hannah sitting at a tea table in front of a window (both at Philadelphia Museum of Art). Three of these paintings were probably delivered before March 15, 1771, when Cadwalader purchased frames from James Reynolds, but which three is uncertain. Peale finished the group portrait (fig. 27) and exhibited it in his studio during the summer of 1772.[13]

Although Cadwalader recommended Peale's works to his cousin John Dickinson, it cannot be said that the Philadelphian was solely responsible for the requests of his two Lloyd brothers-in-law for portraits. During the previous summer and fall of 1770, Cadwalader and the Lloyds were involved with the settlement of the estate of the senior Edward Lloyd, who had died January 27, 1770, and during the following winter Richard Bennett Lloyd stayed in Philadelphia as a house guest of his sister and brother-in-law, Elizabeth and John Cadwalader. There was ample opportunity for John Cadwalader to urge his wife's brothers to engage Peale. However, the nudge that actually effected a commission was apparently provided by John Bordley. In March 1771 Peale suggested to Bordley that Mrs. Lloyd might want a miniature painted during the artist's impending visit in the neighborhood. Elizabeth Tayloe Lloyd apparently agreed, and, as had been the case with the Cadwaladers, Peale's first work for the Lloyds was a miniature of the wife (private collection), which likewise resulted in orders for additional pictures. The relative success in obtaining new commissions surprised even Peale:

> Since my return to America the encouragement and patronage I have met with exceed my most sanguine expectation, not only in Annap:s Maryld. which is my native place but also in Philadelphia I have had considerable business for wh[ich] I was very genisley rewarded, and my vanity much flatte[red] by the general approbation which my performance hath hitherto met with — The people here have a growing taste for the arts, and are becoming more and more fond, of encouraging their progress amongst them, I fondly flatter myself they will here find patronage, and an Assylum, when oppression and tyranny shall perhaps banish them from seats where they now flourish — [14]

Edward Lloyd (1744–96) and Richard Bennett Lloyd (1750–87) were members of a family already prominent in Maryland for a hundred years. The first Edward Lloyd (died 1696) arrived from Wales by way of Virginia before 1650. His grandson served from 1709 to 1714 as governor of the colony. Thus began a two-hundred-year-long tradition by which the eldest son in every generation (invariably named Edward) held political office in Maryland. The Lloyd landholdings were extensive and the family's wealth considerable by the time Edward Lloyd (1711–70) died. His will of 1750 described its writer's intentions for his family. The children — Elizabeth (born 1741), Edward (born 1744), and the baby Richard (born 1750) — under the supervision of a tutor were to learn "such Languages as they are capable of Receiving and that he is Master of." At age twelve the sons were to be sent "home to England to such school as may be most fitting to perfect them in their education." They were to remain abroad to attend the university and then to study law at the Inns of Court. The father intended to support both sons in England until they received degrees or reached the age of twenty-five. Elizabeth was to be sent to the best school in Annapolis or Philadelphia for a few years.[15] It is uncertain whether Edward received part of his education in England, though it is known that Richard clearly did. Neither son chose a legal career. Information about Elizabeth's education is minimal; possibly she did go to a boarding school.

By 1771, Edward Lloyd had married Elizabeth Tayloe, daughter of John Tayloe, of Mount Airy, Richmond County, Virginia, and had become the father of a two-year-old daughter, Anne. He had finally settled his father's estate and agreed on an equal division with his brother,

Richard, and his sister's husband, John Cadwalader. Edward Lloyd retained the family home at Wye. Within the year, he would be elected to the state legislature, purchase Samuel Chase's scarcely begun Annapolis house, engage the architect William Buckland to complete it, and watch his imported mare win the September Jockey Club purse of 100 guineas. Lloyd's second child, Rebecca, was expected in late October, and this impending event probably prompted the commissioning of his wife's miniature, which in turn led to the painting of one of the most successful and most "English" group portraits by Charles Willson Peale.[16]

Like the John Cadwaladers, the Edward Lloyds insisted upon being up to date. Their tastes may have been influenced by Governor Robert Eden, but they relied on Mathias Gale, a trusted London agent, to keep them apprised of the latest fancy. Even the selection of English-trained William Buckland to complete the building and the elaborate decoration of the Annapolis house indicated Edward Lloyd's intention to be fashionable. The results of Buckland's labors were elaborately carved mantels, interior shutters, volutes, overdoors, and friezes, all as stylish as the architect's talent and collection of English design books could make them. The second-floor hall boasted niches for sculpture. The relatively plain exterior with its central pedimented projection was easily visible, for Lloyd's was the only three-story house in Annapolis.[17] Quite possibly Edward Lloyd saw it not only as the finest house in the capital but also as the rival of his brother-in-law's Philadelphia townhouse.

From such a concern for fashion, the Lloyds made the logical choice of Charles Willson Peale to be their artist. English-trained, like Buckland he had come from London recently enough to know the current style of painting. His pictures had been exhibited there, but in America he was as yet recognized by only a few connoisseurs. Thus, by engaging Peale, the Lloyds would obtain portraits by an artist worthy of their notice. Who else was there? Lloyds of an earlier generation had patronized John Hesselius, whose portrait of James Hollyday was at Wye and who had executed portraits of Colonel and Mrs. Robert Lloyd, Queen Anne County cousins (ca. 1761).[18] Hesselius's formula recalled the work of Robert Feke in the 1740s and of John Wollaston in the 1750s. To engage another English-trained artist, the Lloyds would have had to look to Pratt or Benbridge in Philadelphia. Peale was close at hand and beginning to enjoy the attention of prominent Marylanders, friends such as Bordley and both of the Carroll families.

The group portrait of the Edward Lloyd family (fig. 31) was Peale's second attempted and first successful conversation piece. This charac-teristically English composition required that the group be depicted in-formally in familiar surroundings, such as their library, their park, or with their property in the background; that only the family, with the possible inclusion of a few intimate friends, be portrayed; and that each figure be engaged in a customary pursuit. After a twenty-year hiatus, the informal family group portrait was revived in England around 1766, at which time the royal family commissioned one by John Zoffany. Peale had studied conversation pieces at the Free Society of Artists' 1768 ex-hibition in London and would have noted the popular features used to express the overall theme of domestic harmony. The Lloyds probably chose a group portrait because it was the current English fashion. Some years earlier, however, John Wollaston had painted Mrs. Lloyd's mother with a younger sister. The Lloyds saw this painting at the Tayloe home, Mount Airy, when they visited in the spring of 1771, and it, too, may have prompted them shortly after their return to Wye to commission a portrait that would emphasize the family group.[19]

Not surprisingly, Peale's first attempt at a conversation piece — the portrait for Edmund Jenings of Mr. and Mrs. Charles Carroll of Car-rollton and their daughter — was not successful and was abandoned. American artists rarely produced a composition containing more than one, or at the most, two figures. Before his work on *The Lloyd Family,* Peale had completed only three pictures that included two figures: *Mrs. James Arbuckle and Son* (1766, fig. 13), *Mrs. James Russell and Granddaughter* (1768, unlocated), and *Matthias and Thomas Bordley* (1768, fig. 19). The last two were miniatures executed while Peale was in England. The art-ist produced a second double portrait of the Bordley brothers in a land-scape, very English in feeling and in composition, painted during the same spring that he completed the Lloyd group (private collection).[20]

Peale's group portrait of Edward, Elizabeth, and Anne Lloyd is one of the artist's best paintings of several figures. The composition con-forms to the requirements of the type. Edward Lloyd, his body curving into Hogarth's line of beauty, is the most prominent figure. He is depicted as a country gentleman with his home in the left background. The im-age of the mansion apparently was taken from a plate in Isaac Ware's *A Complete Body of Architecture* (London, 1756).[21] Anne Lloyd stands on a sofa between her parents. Her father's arm encircles her and his large hand holds her small one. Her mother is seated to Anne's left holding a cittern. Their closely placed heads are the focal point in the center of the painting.

Elizabeth Lloyd's musical instrument serves two artistic purposes: it implies domestic harmony by alluding to the theme of "Virtuous Love" from James Thomson's *The Seasons,* an influential poem in the second half of the eighteenth century; and, employing one of the imagery devices of English painting, it proclaims Mrs. Lloyd an accomplished woman. In all probability, Mrs. Lloyd had been trained in music and owned the cittern. Since the instrument differs from those shown in Peale's portraits of Mrs. Benjamin Rush (1776, Winterthur Museum, Delaware) and Mrs. Robert Innis (1775, Kennedy Galleries, New York), it was not a studio prop. The Lloyds' elegant clothes, including Edward's recently imported English-made suit, and jewelry reinforced their self-image as a family of wealth and position in need of a painting that was in itself fashionable.[22] Peale's result pleased the Lloyds, who ordered a miniature of Edward Lloyd (private collection). A close study of the sitter indicates that Peale may have made it by copying Lloyd's head from the conversation piece, for the position of the head and the costume are identical in both.

Peale began the conversation piece during the late spring or early summer of 1771, June was the likely month for much of the painting's execution. On July 18 Peale wrote to Edmund Jenings: "[I] was prevail'd on to do some pieces for Mr. Loyd who intends leaving the Country very soon, one of them you will see when he arrives in England, vizt. a family Piece of three figures."[23]

This tantalizing letter allows several possible interpretations. One is that Peale, knowing Richard Lloyd was returning to London, painted the conversation piece with the hope of sending it for exhibition either at the Society of Artists or in West's studio. A second possibility is that Richard Lloyd was taking the group painting as a memento of his brother's family. In either case, exposure to an English audience would enhance Peale's reputation at home and might encourage Englishmen or expatriate Americans to commission portraits of their friends in the colonies. The references in Peale's list of paintings of 1770–75 to "Mr. Lloyd a co[n]versation" and "Mr. R. Lloydd ½ Length" suggest that the "Mr. Lloyd" of the letter was Edward, not Richard.[24] Thus one might infer that the elder brother was planning to accompany the younger on the trip abroad and was obliging Peale by taking the painting to show to Edmund Jenings. Despite any intent to the contrary, both Lloyd portraits apparently remained in Maryland.

The commission for the portrait of Richard Bennett Lloyd (fig. 32) came to Peale the same summer and was completed as the sitter celebrated his twenty-first birthday on August 27, 1771, and preparing to return to England. Peale depicted his subject standing with one arm resting on a pedestal bearing a neoclassical swag, a prevalent motif of the Adamesque style enjoying popularity in England but not well known in America until after the Revolution. Lloyd's pose is the relaxed stance of an Englishman interpreted à la the Vatican Antinous and the Apollo Belvedere. Peale thought "this attitude does admit of good gracefull lines if well drawn." Behind Richard Lloyd a stream flows over a rocky cliff into a river, and in the distance a spire rises above the landscape. Because Peale's contemporary portraits illustrate specific sites and because the artist believed in painting landscapes from nature, the view seen in the background of Lloyd's portrait is assuredly significant. Presumably, it represents Richard Lloyd's landholdings and connotes the sitter's status as a wealthy country gentleman. Fashionably and richly attired, young Lloyd looks out of the composition with an air of detachment. Lloyd sailed from Maryland a few days after August 29, 1771, and temporarily left the management of his estate to his overseer.[25]

The portraits of the Edward Lloyd family and of Richard Lloyd give a definite English impression; however, with the exception of the portraits of Martha and Lambert Cadwalader, those Peale executed for John Cadwalader are decidedly American in feeling. The difference is most clearly shown in the group pictures. The group picture (fig. 27) depicting John, Elizabeth, and Anne Cadwalader was completed during the summer of 1772. Peale exhibited it in Philadelphia where it was "greatly admir'd."[26] Intended to be displayed in the parlor with the other four portraits Peale had executed for Cadwalader, it conformed to them in size and in its vertically rectangular format. Cadwalader stands at the right of the composition and offers a peach to his daughter, who sits on an elaborately carved Chippendale card table. Elizabeth Cadwalader, also seated, supports Anne in her arms and looks at her husband. The tenderness of facial expressions, the proximity of hands near the fruit, and the unity achieved by the directions of the sitters' looks proclaim the theme of domestic harmony with simpler means and as much effectiveness as the symbolism and complex composition of the Lloyd family portrait. The latter, with its landscape setting utilizing an indoor sofa outside, was typical of the English conversation piece. The Cadwalader family picture with its plain background was comparable to the American works of John Singleton Copley. In the Philadelphia picture, Peale captured an unmomentous event in his subjects' lives;

in the Maryland painting, he depicted three individuals posing for their portraits.

Although Cadwalader had urged Peale to settle in Philadelphia as early as 1770, the latter retained his residence in Annapolis and visited Philadelphia when he felt it expedient. This arrangement worked relatively well and led to another commission from Edward Lloyd. In 1774 Lloyd paid Peale £35 for "a picture of Venus rising from the Sea."[27] This painting, now lost, places Lloyd and Peale among the American cognoscenti. Few colonists understood classical literature, and still fewer appreciated its illustration. Similarly, few American artists could render nudes successfully. By 1774 Peale had seen those of John Smibert, Gustavus Hesselius, and Henry Benbridge. The *Venus* executed for Lloyd is one of two known commissions for mythological subjects that Peale received. Earlier, during 1772, he had painted and retained for exhibition a copy of Benjamin West's *Venus of Urbino* (after Titian, 1538), which was then owned by Chief Justice William Allen of Philadelphia. From this model, or from an engraving by R. Strange, Peale painted a version of Titian's *Venus* for Col. William Hamilton in 1776.[28]

Over the years, Peale made a number of drawings of European works of art which he kept in his studio.[29] Prospective clients could view these drawings and his copy of West's *Venus,* which demonstrated Peale's ability to render idealized subjects, and could select from them a composition to be translated into an oil painting. Peale's two-year sojourn in London had introduced the aspiring artist to the works by, and collections of, contemporary Englishmen and especially to the paintings of Benjamin West, his teacher, in whose studio Peale observed the painting of mythological subjects. Several antique statues — the Laocoön, Apollo Belvedere, and Venus di Medici — served as models for figures, and Titian's palette was the inspiration for tones of flesh colors. George Ogle's *Antiquities Explained* (1737) contained engraved plates that suggested compositions to the artists in West's studio. Many of West's mythological paintings were begun during the 1760s, worked over and retouched during the next thirty years, and exhibited after the artist's reputation was firmly established. In 1800 he exhibited at the Royal Academy *Venus Rising from the Sea.*[30] Quite possibly this painting with its full-length standing figure was in the studio during the two years that Peale was in London. If so, it may have served as the model for Peale's 1774 commission. Another possible composition to which Peale had access is a standing Venus, attended by Cupid rising from the sea in a chariot drawn by four horses. This also appeared in Ogle's book, from which Peale could easily have made a drawing while in London and brought it home to Maryland. This particular representation may have appealed to Lloyd, who owned and raced horses.

How long the owner enjoyed his picture is not recorded. A relative's account of the pirates' looting of Wye House in 1781 did not refer to its loss. Peale's *Venus* was most likely among the twenty-one paintings not identified by subject or artist in the 1796 inventory of Edward Lloyd's estate and left, like most of the property, to his eldest son. Listed with the books in the library were "1 piece of painting on canvas," a series of Hogarth's prints, and the West portrait of Richard Bennett Lloyd."[31] Quite possibly Lloyd had chosen the more private gentleman's library rather than the drawing room for contemplation of *Venus Rising from the Sea.*

In 1776, when the Revolution was imminent, Peale moved his family to Philadelphia. He served as a lieutenant in the Philadelphia militia, and his great benefactor, John Cadwalader, was a general. The artist recorded wartime meetings of the two in his autobiography, but Peale knew that his political activities as president of the Whig Society and chairman of the Constitutional Society in 1777 had alienated his former patrons, "those whom before he had considered his best friends." These conservative men of wealth and education were merchants who opposed Peale's published liberal views on a unicameral legislature, election procedures, and market manipulation. Many ceased to request his paintings, among them Cadwalader. The last commission Peale had received from him was late in 1772 for a copy of an earlier painting of his late mother-in-law, Elizabeth Rousby Lloyd (died 1769).[32]

With the loss of orders for portraits of politically conservative sitters after 1777, Charles Willson Peale turned his attention to recording for his gallery of portraits the faces of those active in the War for Independence. The Revolution had given America its own heroes and history, and he began painting and selling a new type of painting that pictured these men and events. Peale's full-length portrait *George Washington at the Battle of Princeton* (fig. 33), commissioned by the Supreme Executive Council of Pennsylvania in 1779, became a state picture to be copied for the courts of Europe and for private gentlemen. Richard Bennett Lloyd was one of the latter group, and in 1782 he obtained one of Peale's numerous replicas. Most of the individuals who purchased these paintings had a personal association with the sitter and the ending of the Revolution: Henry Laurens, Joseph Wilson, Hugh Shiell, Thomas

Nelson, Elias Boudinot, James Tilghman, and Robert Goldsborough.[33] Lloyd, too, knew Washington — at least well enough to ask for his assistance on behalf of a relative — and possibly played a minor role in the diplomacy with France, where he had spent two years in the circle of Benjamin Franklin. Lloyd's collection of prints indicated where his political sympathies lay, for it included portraits of America's heroes such as Franklin, Gouverneur Morris, Baron von Steuben, and John Wilkes.[34]

Yet Richard Bennett Lloyd has been branded a Tory by historians because he served for a time as an English soldier, married an Englishwoman, and did not fight in the Continental army. Lloyd had served in the second, or Coldstream, Regiment of Foot Guards between early 1773 and the fall of 1775. He had written to his brother-in-law of his intention to settle in America, but confessed to "a sad raging passion for the military life."[35] The army was an acceptable career for younger sons of peers and gentlemen; commissions and even promotions were purchased, not awarded on the basis of merit. The Coldstream Regiment was the same prestigious one in which Lloyd's friend and Maryland's royal governor, Robert Eden, had served. Lloyd's marriage to Joanna Leigh, daughter of an English merchant, in July 1775, as well as the growing enmity between England and America, prompted his resignation. After the birth of their second son in the fall of 1777, the Lloyds moved to France, where they enjoyed the company of Benjamin Franklin. They returned to England for at least several months before embarking for New York in the fall of 1780. Joanna Lloyd's beauty was widely acclaimed in America. She was fêted with Martha Washington in Philadelphia and aroused her husband's jealousy by flirting with the French officers stationed in Maryland. The Lloyds had their portraits painted in London — his by Benjamin West (1773), hers by Sir Joshua Reynolds (1775), and their miniatures executed by Richard Crosse (1775, 1780), who, like the other two artists, enjoyed royal patronage. The Lloyds required no portraits of themselves while in America but wanted one of Washington.[36]

The letters from Peale to Richard Lloyd regarding the portrait of Washington dealt with the business at hand and contained no evidence of personal friendship:

> I fully intended to have wrote you before this time, but a hurry of Business prevented me. I have recd the Thirteen Guineas, some of them were light. The Charge which Mr. Reynolds makes for the Frame is 7£ 10 and the packing Case will be 1-2-6. The Picture I will pack up myself and send it as you direct.

And:

> I have sent your whole length Portrait of Genl Washington by the stage
> before last, directed for you at Annapolis and to be left with Mr. Grant
> in Baltimore town, for the Carriage of which I have paid 10/shillings. I
> return you thanks for the money received by Mr. Chew.[37]

There was no indication that artist and customer recalled their meeting of eleven years earlier when Peale had painted Lloyd's portrait.[38]

The artist and the elder Lloyd brother remained on good terms. After
1774 Edward Lloyd commissioned no pictures but was host for several
visits. Peale wrote in his autobiography:

> He [Peale] expected business here and at Major Kerr in Easttown but
> is disappointed and goes to Col. Lloyd where he had painted several por-
> traits and always recd a hearty welcome. . . . The Col'l is possessed of
> immense property, he had 400 acres of land in a park to keep deer, round
> which was a fence of 20 rails high. Maise were planted within for the
> sustenance of his deer. He also had on his farm an immense number of
> wild turkies, the writer has seen 20 of them in a flock. His seat being
> on the Wye river he had a seine of immense length and breadth, requir-
> ing at least 20 men to haul it, of course the quantity of Fish which at
> times has been taken is wonderfull, at one time, and in winter he fed
> sheepshead so that at all times of the summer season he could have them
> fresh for his table.[39]

During this 1790 visit to Talbot County, Peale, recently widowed,
courted but failed to win the hand of Mary Tilghman of Gross Coate,
whose family thought her too far above him socially.[40] A year later he
married Elizabeth DePeyster of New York and returned to the Eastern
Shore with his bride. The new Mrs. Peale apparently was not acceptable to the Lloyds, who failed to extend their usual hospitality. The 1791
trip was the last Peale made for a number of years. Rebuffs from his
friends and patrons and the competition of Jean Pierre Henri Elouis
encouraged Peale to give up portrait painting in Maryland and turn
full-time to his natural history museum and gallery of heroes in
Philadelphia.[41]

Until the 1830s America had no major art patrons in the usual sense
of the word. A few men owned small groups of paintings, sometimes
including copies of old masters; but the seemingly few paintings inherited or ordered by the Lloyd brothers and their Cadwalader brother-
in-law placed them among the minority of colonial Americans who

collected works of art and hired professional artists. Fewer still were benefactors such as John Beale Bordley and John Cadwalader. The latter's prepayment of £110 for undelivered portraits and landscapes, his recommendations of Peale, and his early encouragement of the artist to relocate in Philadelphia exemplified his role as a patron — one who gave the painter financial support and a chance to demonstrate his ability where it would be observed by others who would offer commissions. John Cadwalader's efforts on Peale's behalf proved that talented artists were indeed welcomed and encouraged on the western side of the Atlantic. Both Edward and Richard Bennett Lloyd utilized Peale's services because he was an artist who could provide the paintings they required. Their desire for fashionable portraits was the same as that of other colonial American sitters; but because the Lloyds were closely attuned to English fashions and employed an artist "lately from London," they obtained what they sought instead of a limner's product. Unlike the usual colonist, who required only portraits of himself and his family, Edward and Richard Bennett Lloyd commissioned paintings of other subjects. The former's *Venus Rising from the Sea* demonstrated the existence of a connoisseur with a classical education and cosmopolitan taste. The latter's purchase of a full-length portrait of George Washington represented the growing interest in American history, which would support the artist's gallery of heroes' portraits. The pictures Peale executed for the Lloyds and Cadwaladers preserved their images, adorned their homes, commemorated events, and demonstrated their taste and knowledge. The same paintings illustrated the role different types of patronage played in establishing the successful career of Charles Willson Peale.

NOTES

This chapter was originally published in the *Winterthur Portfolio* 12 (1977): 87–102.

1. Copley to [Benjamin West or Capt. R. J. Bruce], n.d. [1762?], in *Letters and Papers of John Singleton Copley and Henry Pelham, 1739–1776*, Massachusetts Historical Society, *Proceedings* 71 (1914): 65–66.

2. Rosamund Randall Beirne, "Portrait of a Colonial Governor: Robert Eden," *Maryland Historical Magazine* 45 (September 1950): 153–66; William Eddis, *Letters from America* (Cambridge, Mass., 1969), pp. 54–58.

3. *P&M*, pp. 36–37; Charles Coleman Sellers, *Charles Willson Peale* (Philadelphia, 1947), 1:66–67.

4. *P&M*, pp. 172–73, 37, 49, 68; *P&M Suppl.*, pp. 55–56.

5. *P&M*, pp. 36–38, 87, 141, 213. See also notes 11 and 14, below. For *Henrietta Maria Bordley,* see chap. 5. Also see *P&M Suppl.,* p. 55.

6. Beirne, "Portrait of a Colonial Governor," p. 159; *P&M Suppl.,* pp. 56, 76–77; *P&M,* pp. 47–50, 60, 71–72; Peale to Charles Carroll, Barrister, April 11, 1775, P-S, in *Selected Papers* 1:140: "I have been at work on your other Landscape and I hope to have it ready for the figures by next week, when I shall send them to Annapolis with Mrs. Peale."

7. *P&M,* pp. 44–56, 61–62. Sellers does not list the copy of Cadwalader's mother-in-law's portrait. Peale mentions it in a letter of November 1772 to John Beale Bordley: "Mr. Cadwalader is a good deal disappointed in your not coming up, he would be glad to See you here. . . . I must copy a piece of Mrs. Cadwa[la]der's Mother" (P-S, in *Selected Papers* 1:126–27).

8. *DAB.*

9. Nicholas B. Wainwright, *Colonial Grandeur in Philadelphia: The House and Furniture of General John Cadwalader* (Philadelphia, 1964), pp. 2–3, 37, 49–50. A list of the titles of these engravings shows the range of the Cadwaladers' taste in pictures.

10. Richard K. Doud, "John Hesselius, Maryland 'Limner,'" in *Winterthur Portfolio 5,* ed. Richard K. Doud (Charlottesville, Va., 1969), pp. 130–42; George C. Groce and David H. Wallace, *The New-York Historical Society's Dictionary of Artists in America* (New Haven, Conn., 1957), p. 515; Robert G. Stewart, *Henry Benbridge (1743–1812)* (Washington, D.C., 1971), p. 18; Edgar P. Richardson, "William Williams: A Dissenting Opinion," *American Art Journal* 4 (Spring 1972): 18–21; Edgar P. Richardson, "James Claypoole, Junior, Re-Discovered," *Art Quarterly* 33 (Summer 1970): 159–74; Paul G. Sifton, "Pierre Eugène Du Simitière: Collector in Revolutionary America" (Ph.D. diss., University of Pennsylvania, 1960), pp. 457–61, 582–84.

11. Charles Willson Peale to Cadwalader, September 7, 1770, P-S, in *Selected Papers* 1:82–84; the Stewart advertisement appeared in the *Pennsylvania Journal* (Philadelphia), July 13, 1769; Peale to Cadwalader, March 22, 1771, P-S, in *Selected Papers* 1:89–92.

12. Wainwright, *Colonial Grandeur,* p. 47. Sellers (*Charles Willson Peale,* 1:95; *P&M,* pp. 20–21) illustrates Peale's record of his paintings and their prices. This list reports the price of Dr. Cadwalader's portrait as £12.12.0, his wife Hannah's and their son Lambert's half-lengths together as £25.4.0, and the miniatures of John and his wife together as £21.0.0, for a total of £58.16.0. Assuming Martha Cadwalader's picture (signed and dated 1771) also cost £12.12.0, the sum remaining of the £110 was probably meant as payment for the landscapes. If these were not delivered, possibly the portrait of John, Elizabeth, and Anne Cadwalader was executed instead.

Sellers interprets the entry for Lambert's and Hannah's pictures as being of the John Cadwalader family. His assumption seems incorrect for two reasons: for similar paintings containing more than one figure, Peale noted the number of subjects in the margin (that is, "3" next to the Lloyd group); and the entry, "Son & wife ½ lengths," is indented under Thomas Cadwalader's entry and implies that these individuals are the wife and son of the doctor, especially since the next entry, "Mr. J. Do. & wife Mins," is at the margin line and suggests a different person and his wife.

13. Wainwright, *Colonial Grandeur,* p. 47; *P&M,* pp. 45–46, 61–62. The two au-

thors disagree on the dating of the portraits of Dr. and Mrs. Thomas Cadwalader and of their son Lambert. Sellers suggests ca. 1772. Since the portrait of Martha Cadwalader is dated 1771, Reynolds's account is for three frames, and none of these paintings shows the interior of the Cadwalader house, it would seem that the portraits of Martha and her parents were completed by early 1771. Because the paintings of the John Cadawalader family and of Lambert include new furnishings in the house, it is logical that they were executed at approximately the same time, i.e., before July 29, 1772, when the group portrait was exhibited in Peale's studio.

14. Charles Willson Peale to Benjamin Franklin, April 21, 1771, P-S, in *Selected Papers* 1:98–99; see also Peale to Cadwalader, March 22, 1771.

15. Lloyd Papers, Maryland Historical Society.

16. Lloyd Papers; Rosamund Randall Beirne, "The Chase House in Annapolis," *Maryland Historical Magazine* 49 (1954): 180–82.

17. Rosamund Randall Beirne and John Henry Scharff, *William Buckland: Architect of Virginia and Maryland* (Baltimore, 1958), pp. 82–89.

18. James Bordley, Jr., *The Hollyday and Related Families of the Eastern Shore of Maryland* (Baltimore, 1962), p. 101; Doud, "John Hesselius," p. 149.

19. Sacheverell Sitwell, *Conversation Pieces: A Study of English Domestic Portraits and Their Painters* (London, 1936), p. 9; Alice Winchester, "English Conversation Pieces from the Mellon Collection," *Antiques* 83 (April 1963): 444; Ellis Waterhouse, *Painting in Britain 1530–1790* (Baltimore, 1969), p. 219. Other examples of the conversation piece that may have influenced Peale may be seen in Mary Webster, *Francis Wheatley* (London, 1970), figs. 28–30; Wheatley used a studio prop musical instrument. The portrait by Wollaston is still at Mount Airy and is owned by Col. and Mrs. H. Gwynn Tayloe, Jr.

20. *P&M,* pp. 24–25, 38, 49, 188. Among the few colonial American conversation pieces painted are John Smibert's *Bermuda Group* (1729, 1739), John Singleton Copley's *Gore Children* (ca. 1753), Robert Feke's *Isaac Royall Family* (1741), Joseph Blackburn's *Winslow Family* (1757), and Henry Benbridge's *Gordon Family* (ca. 1762).

21. Issac Ware, *A Complete Body of Architecture* (London, 1756), plate 39. Whether the building in the painting was Wye House as it existed in 1771 is doubtful. Possibly the painting showed a house Lloyd was considering building in Annapolis later in 1771, for construction did not begin at Wye until after the Revolution.

22. For a discussion of Mrs. Lloyd's probable musical training, see Philip Vickers Fithian, *Journal and Letters* (Princeton, N.J., 1900), p. 124 (Fithian was the tutor at Nomini Hall, the Carter family seat, not far from the Tayloe home); also see John Winter (tailor to Edward Lloyd), March 9, 1771, Lloyd Papers.

23. Charles Willson Peale to Edmund Jenings, July 18, 1771, P-S, in *Selected Papers* 1:100–02.

24. P-S, in *Selected Papers* 1:632.

25. Charles Willson Peale to John Beale Bordley, n.d., 1770, P-S, in *Selected Papers* 1:86–87 (In this letter, Peale is referring to the pose in his portrait of Lloyd Dulany); Lloyd to John Cadwalader, August 26, 1771, Cadwalader Papers, Historical Society of Pennsylvania.

26. Charles Willson Peale to John Beale Bordley, July 29, 1772, P-S, in *Selected Papers* 1:123–24.

27. Lloyd Papers.

28. Sellers, *Charles Willson Peale* 1:61, 52; Roland E. Fleischer, "Gustavus Hesselius: A Study of His Style," in Ian M. G. Quimby, ed., *American Painting to 1776: A Reappraisal* (Charlottesville, Va., 1971), pp. 139–43; Stewart, *Henry Benbridge*, pp. 15–16. Strange's *Venus* was engraved in 1768 after a drawing made at the Medici collection in Florence in 1764; the print Peale is thought to have owned is now in the collections of the American Philosophical Society, Philadelphia (*P&M Suppl.*, p. 13).

29. *P&M Suppl.*, p. 13; John Adams reported: "Yesterday Morning I took a Walk, into Arch Street, to see Mr. Peele's Painters Room. . . . Peel shewed me some Books upon the art of Painting, among the rest one by Sir Joshua Reynolds. . . . Also a Variety of rough Drawings, made by great Masters in Italy, which he keeps as Modells" (John Adams to Abigail Adams, August 21, 1776, in *The Book of Abigail and John*, ed. L. H. Butterfield [Cambridge, Mass., 1975], p. 157).

30. Charles Willson Peale to John Beale Bordley, n.d., 1767, P-S, in *Selected Papers* 1:47–51; Daniel Webb, *An Inquiry into the Beauties of Painting and into the Merits of the Most Celebrated Painters Ancient and Modern* (London, 1760), p. 43; Franzika Forster-Hahn, "The Sources of True Taste: Benjamin West's Instructions to a Young Painter for his Studies in Italy," *Journal of the Warburg and Courtauld Institutes* 30 (1967): 378; Grose Evans, *Benjamin West and the Taste of His Times* (Carbondale, Ill., 1959), plate 16; *The Gallery of Pictures Painted by Benjamin West Esqr., Historical Painter to His Majesty, and President of the Royal Academy, Engraved in Outline by Henry Moses* (London, n.d.), plate facing p. 18. West used the plates in Ogle's *Antiquities Explained* (London, 1737) and similar books as sources for some of his mythological paintings.

31. Lloyd Papers.

32. Sellers, *Charles Willson Peale* 1:156–69, 193–95. See also note 7, above. Elizabeth Cadwalader died on February 16, 1776, and her husband John on February 10, 1786.

33. Sellers, *Charles Willson Peale* 1:213, 192–93, *P&M*, pp. 226–33.

34. An application to Washington through Lloyd is mentioned in Henry Hollyday to James Hollyday, February 20, 1785, Hollyday Papers, Massachusetts Historical Society; Richard Bennett Lloyd to Benjamin Franklin, July 13, 1778, Franklin Collection, Historical Society of Pennsylvania; inventory of R. B. Lloyd's estate, Lloyd Papers.

35. Lloyd to John Cadwalader, November 8, 1772, Cadwalader Papers.

36. Lloyd to John Cadwalader, January 17, 1775, Cadwalader Papers, mentions Eden's friendship with the two men; see also Beirne "Portrait of a Colonial Governor," p. 155. In America, Joanna Lloyd "was soon celebrated as Very Handsome, Very Accomplished, and, in short, it was the general enquiry, 'Have you seen Mrs. Lloyd?'" (Mrs. Shoemaker to [her daughter] Rebecca Rawle, Jan. 18, 1781, Shoemaker Papers, Historical Society of Pennsylvania). The following year, John F. Mifflin wrote to his mother Mrs. John B. Bordley, "I have been to wait on Mrs. Captain Lloyd. I think she looks more beautiful than ever I saw her. . . . Mrs. A[llen] made a *small* party for Mrs. Washington and Mrs. Lloyd the other Evening. The Company consisted only of 31 Ladies and Gentlemen" (February 6, 1782, Bordley-Calvert Papers, Maryland Historical Society); Karol A. Schmiegel, "The Patronage of the Lloyd Family of Maryland" (M.A. thesis, University of Delaware, 1975), pp. 32–40.

37. Charles Willson Peale to R. B. Lloyd, October 15, 1782, P-S, F:IIA/11E1; Charles Willson Peale to Richard Lloyd, December 24, 1782, P-S, in *Selected Papers* 1:378.

38. *P&M,* pp. 129-30, reports that Peale's autobiography calls Richard Lloyd "Poor Dickey Wye." A careful reading of the original text, however, shows that the nickname belonged to Richard Bennet (died 1749), the relative for whom Lloyd was named. Peale may have confused the two men. See A(TS): 146.

39. A(TS): 144-45.

40. Sellers, *Charles Willson Peale* 2:20-21.

41. Sellers, *Charles Willson Peale* 2:34-35. The artist described the events of the 1791 visit in his autobiography: "Peale goes to Col. Lloyds to thank him for the use he made of his vessel in his passage here, and then makes a perspective drawing of his house, which is a handsome building with wings, one wing for the kitchen and other purposes, the other served as an office for his clerk"; and later; "Col. Lloyd and his family were gone to dine with Col. Hineman, which Peale was glad of, for he did not wish to carry Mrs. Peale to his house, because neither himself or lady had given an invitation since his coming to Wye, which from his long acquaintance with the family he thought he had a Right to expect, wherefore he did not, Peale will not undertake to say, they might have resons for their conduct and if just they had acted Right, if otherwise, they act foolish and wrong themselves, which being no fault of Peale's ought not to trouble him. If we endeavor to do well and do not gain respect by doing so, the Guilt is not with us" (Peale, A[TS]: 171, 175).

4

A Graphic Case of
Transatlantic Republicanism

———◆———

SIDNEY HART

ALTHOUGH primarily remembered as a portrait painter, Charles
Willson Peale was also a fervent republican who in his art and
his actions supported the colonial cause from an early date in
the revolutionary crisis. Peale's political identification with the country, or antiproprietary party, in Maryland can be traced to the 1760s
when he was an artisan residing in Annapolis. Peale had struggled to
support his family as a saddle-maker, upholsterer, silversmith, and watch
repairer, and by the 1760s was just beginning to try his hand at portrait
painting to supplement his income.[1] In the bitterly contested election
of 1764 for the Maryland Assembly, Peale supported the antiproprietary Samuel Chase against the court candidate George Steuart.

Despite "threats of persecution" from the creditors who were court
men, Peale joined the opposition Sons of Freedom. Peale later analyzed
the court-country conflict of 1764 as a harbinger of the revolutionary
crisis, describing the election as a "remarkable period in the annals of
Annapolis . . . which greatly agitated the minds of every class of inhabitants of that city." He described the court party as enjoying an "ascen-
dancy over the minds of the inhabitants, as to have any of their friends
elected into any & every public office," and as possessing the "influence
of office" and "the power of wealth [which] carried like a rapid stream
all that fell within its Vortex."[2]

After the election, Peale's creditors made good their threats. In
1765, in order to avoid imprisonment for debt, Peale fled to New England. There he read a pamphlet by James Otis and assisted "in making

73

emblematical Ensigns used at Newbury Port . . . in July 1765" for a Stamp Act demonstration. He also met John Singleton Copley and strength- ened his skills and his determination to become a portrait painter.[3] In 1776, the political factionalism of the previous two years having subsided, Peale returned to Annapolis. By then Peale's talents as an artist had grown considerably, and both court and country parties joined together for the honor of Maryland to assist the struggling artist. Peale was sent to England to study under the American artist Benjamin West. But while West cautiously stood aloof from politics and enjoyed the patron- age of George III, his student refused to "pull off his hat as the King passed by" because of the passage of the Townshend Acts.[4]

Peale's most significant political act while in England was embodied in his portrait of William Pitt, earl of Chatham. The Pitt portrait (fig. 7) was commissioned by a group of Virginia planters, led by Richard Henry Lee, who sought an American artist to portray a British states- man who had been active in defending American rights. The painting would be placed in the lower house of the Virginia legislature. An artist was to be selected by Edmund Jenings, an English gentleman friendly to colonial interests and the half brother of Peale's friend and patron, John Beale Bordley. Jenings first selected Benjamin West to paint a por- trait of Charles Pratt, Baron Camden, who had opposed the Stamp Act. When West was unable to paint Camden, Jenings then suggested that Peale, "a Young Man of Merit & Industry," do a portrait of William Pitt. Peale used the opportunity to make a strong political and artistic statement.[5]

Peale was not able to persuade Pitt to sit for the portrait; he used, instead, a recent bust by Joseph Wilton as a model. His first artistic and political decision was selecting Pitt's costume. Pitt had recently ac- cepted a peerage, an appointment that not only weakened his leader- ship among English Whigs but also damaged his popularity in the colo- nies. Peale decided to present his subject in classical dress, perhaps to associate Pitt with Roman republican heroes, but more likely to avoid painting him in the robes of an earl, a costume not likely to appeal to the Virginia planters. The artist utilized conventional symbols from the eighteenth-century Anglo-American political vocabulary: Magna Carta, a statue of British Liberty, busts of Hampden and Sydney, and an alert native American representing America. Two features, explicitly repub- lican in tone, are imposed on this standard symbolism. Occupying the background of the painting is the Banqueting House of Whitehall from

which Charles I had been led to his execution — a reminder of the regi-
cide and revolution that had occurred when British law was violated
by the monarch. There was also a "Statue of BRITISH Liberty trampling under Foot the Petition of the CONGRESS at NEW YORK."
Peale explained this apparently improper action, "so contrary" to the
spirit of liberty, in a broadside that accompanied an engraving of the
portrait. Quoting Montesquieu, he wrote, "The Painter principally intended to allude to the Observation . . . that the *States which enjoy the
highest Degree of Liberty are apt to be oppressive of those who are subordinate to
them.*"[6] The twin themes of violence and the fragility of liberty mark
the portrait as a republican document.

After Peale returned to Maryland, he completed four more portrait
commissions from Jenings: Charles Carroll of Carrollton (unlocated)
and his wife Mary Darnall Carroll (private collection); John Dickinson
(fig. 41); and John Beale Bordley (fig. 5). Jenings had requested that
Peale include American flora and scenery in the backgrounds. Jenings's
own political actions during the Revolution — placing John Adams's and
his own pro-American writings in British newspapers — suggest that he
asked Peale to make Bordley's portrait a political statement like the Pitt
painting, and that he was involved with Peale's devising the political
symbolism in that painting. The portrait was to be sent to Jenings, perhaps to be shown to British statesmen friendly to the colonial cause.[7]

John Beale Bordley (1726/27–1804), lawyer and agriculturist, had been
close to the Peale family since he had been a student of Peale's father
in Chestertown, Maryland. Bordley held several important judicial and
political posts in colonial Maryland, including judge of the Maryland
Provincial Court in 1766, judge of the Admiralty in 1767, and member
of the Governor's Council during the administrations of Sharpe and Eden.
Bordley's sympathies were firmly with the country party, as evidenced
by his election to the Maryland Committee of Public Safety. Bordley,
however, refused to serve. A deep, ingrained shyness and a strong dis-
taste for the rough-and-tumble popular participation of Maryland's politics caused him to make his home on the 1,600-acre farm he had acquired on Wye Island in the Wye River on the Eastern Shore. There
he could put into practice his agricultural theories and turn his land
into a model plantation.[8]

Peale began his portrait of Bordley in 1770 and continued to work
on the painting during the following year. On March 18, 1771, Peale wrote
to Bordley, indicating that he would visit shortly; "[I will] do any thing

you may think necessary to your Portrait," he wrote. The last record of the painting occurs on April 20, 1771, when Peale wrote to Jenings to say that he had, as much as possible, followed Jenings's instructions. The Carroll portraits included "Blossoms of the Dog Wood"; Dickinson's, the falls of the Schuylkill River. The Bordley portrait, Peale wrote, "needs no description." Peale then went on to explain his addition of a white plant, a flowering jimsonweed found in Virginia, which if eaten brought on madness and "violent" death. Perhaps Peale expected to make engravings of the portrait and, as with the *Pitt* piece, include a broadside explanation of the symbolism. For some reason, however, while Jenings acknowledged the other three portraits, the Bordley portrait was not mentioned. Instead, Jenings thanked Peale for a painting of "Mr. Bordley & His son." Perhaps Peale did not send the political portrait in deference to the planter's diffidence and retirement from politics. The Bordley portrait remained unlocated for almost two hundred years and was then discovered in an exhibition at the Ringling Museum of Art in Sarasota, Florida.[9]

The Bordley portrait may be said to represent what Peale, Bordley, Jenings, and perhaps other important colonial leaders thought to be the most important concepts underlying the colonists' opposition to Great Britain. Moreover, this portrait provides an unusual kind of republican expression. In defining and explicating the term *republicanism,* historians have amply documented the transmission of ideas between England and the American colonies in books and pamphlets.[10] The Bordley portrait, however, provides a graphic depiction of Anglo-American republican ideas. Furthermore, the portrait may be used to illustrate how historians may interpret works of art as political and social documents.

The Bordley portrait should be viewed as Peale's American version of the *Pitt* portrait. It contains two strong themes of colonial opposition to British imperial policies, themes of particular concern to Bordley: agricultural plenty and self-sufficiency that would insulate the colonies from British economic restrictions and create a strong and independent people, and a deep-seated reverence for English law. There is also the potential threat of colonial resistance symbolized by the jimsonweed. Bordley is portrayed as the gentleman farmer on his Maryland plantation. In contrast to the classical and British context of the *Pitt* work, the *Bordley* setting is rural and American. The formal altar of the *Pitt* portrait is replaced by a natural rock pedestal; the vertical lines in the background in the *Pitt* portrait, supplied by Whitehall and a massive

Roman column, are replaced by a large tree drawn in the form of Hogarth's line of beauty. Only the statue of British Liberty, symbolizing colonial reverence for British law, is retained in the American portrait.

Peale divided the portrait into two distinct and contrasting parts, each representing a theme of colonial opposition. The background is given over to the rural setting of the Eastern Shore, and it represents Bordley's agrarian republican ideal of staple agriculture and economic self-sufficiency: a pack horse loaded with agricultural produce, a peach tree, sheep in the fields, and a building under construction. Although by 1770 Bordley had retired from both law and politics and was to remain reticent about those subjects even during the Revolution, he was quite active in promoting agricultural reforms that in his mind related to the political crisis between Great Britain and her American colonies. In 1769 Bordley wrote a pamphlet entitled *Necessaries: Best Product of Land: Best Staple of Commerce,* supporting an agricultural economy based on staples rather than cash crops (such as tobacco) or luxury items (such as silk or wine). The pamphlet, in addition to its agricultural content, is a clear statement of the agrarian republican ideal. In it, Bordley observed that Maryland farmers who grew wheat instead of tobacco "became more happy and independent of the British store keepers who had kept them in debt and dependent." He compared the "silk and wine" countries of southern Europe to the "bread and beer" countries of the north and found the former "miserably dependent on foreign countries for a supply from them." Bordley drew a direct connection between an agrarian staple-producing nation in which the inhabitants were "well employed" and an independent and virtuous people.[11]

Peale used the foreground of his portrait for the second theme: the colonists' legal arguments against the British empire. The tone of this part of the painting is in stark contrast to the almost pastoral scene of the background. Bordley, trained as a lawyer, appears stern as he points to a statue of British Liberty, a reminder to the intended English audience that the American colonists are living under and are protected by British law. As in the Pitt portrait, Peale resorts to a torn sheet of paper to symbolize a British legal violation. The paper, ripped in half by Bordley and lying at his feet, bears the inscription, "Imperial Civil / Proceeding," and was probably intended to symbolize the arbitrary proceedings by which the new customs duties after 1763 were being collected.

Occupying a central location in the foreground of the portrait, integral to its meaning, is an open book upon which Bordley's arm rests. The book's legible Latin inscription has been transcribed as *"Notamus Leges Angliae mutari"* ("We observe the laws of England to be changed"). Such a transcription indicates colonial opposition to a change in the British law that had already occurred. But the opposition would not be meaningful in a republican context. The republican opposition of the early 1770s sought to prevent any changes in the British law or constitution that would upset the balance in government and thus endanger liberty. For Peale and Bordley to have acknowledged that change had occurred would, in a republican context, lead them logically from opposition to revolution — from protest within the British empire to the next step, open rebellion and independence from a nation that had become corrupt and had lost its liberty.

The transcription errs in the verb *"Notamus."* The phrase instead should read *"Nolumus"* — a change in verb that renders the phrase to "We are unwilling that the laws of England be changed."[12] British Liberty, the symbolic statue to which Bordley defiantly points, remains tenuously intact; in 1770–71 its preservation is still the central tenet of republican thought. With the correct transcription of the *"Nolumus"* phrase, the Bordley portrait may be viewed not only as a simple statement of colonial opposition, but as a republican document designed to communicate a very specific message to an English audience presumed to understand its contents.[13]

As a legal phrase, *"Nolumus Leges Angliae mutari"* dates back to the statute of Merton of 1235. It was used in the barons' reply to the bishops who wished to alter the law regarding the illegitimacy of children born before marriage. There is no indication, however, that the phrase had become a common Latin tag used by lawyers.[14] The phrase became significant in 1642 when Parliament issued the *Nineteen Propositions* demanding an increased role in the government. Charles I's *Answer to the Nineteen Propositions* argued that such an increased role for Parliament would lead to the total subversion of the English constitution and concluded with the *"Nolumus"* phrase. The *Answer* startled both royalists and parliamentarians. Having rejected Parliament's demands, Charles enunciated a theory of mixed monarchy or mixed government. While claiming the monarch to be supreme, Charles acknowledged that the power to govern was shared with the two Houses of Parliament. Theories concerning the mixed nature of the English constitution had previously been proposed by lawyers and scholars, but it was only after the king's public approval that such theories rapidly became accepted by both Whigs and Tories as the basis of the English constitution. The *Answer* was reprinted frequently in the seventeenth century. In the 1680s both the *Nineteen Propositions* and the *Answer* were used extensively in parliamentary debates regarding the nature and theory of mixed government. After 1689, Charles I's theory of mixed government may be said to have triumphed, for numerous pamphlets on the Bill of Rights referred to the *Answer* as the authoritative source.[15]

Theories of mixed government have been known to appear during periods of turbulence and social instability. Charles I's interpretation resulted from the constitutional crisis preceding the English Civil War. Both Aristotle and Machiavelli, in propounding similar theories, praised mixed governments because such governments seemed the most resistant to rapid change and to decay. Thus, the constitutional consensus supporting the idea of mixed government in the seventeenth and eighteenth centuries contained within it a fear of change or decline. This same fear motivated the political forces opposed to the established government in both England and America. The *Answer*—with its code phrase *"Nolumus"*—came to be used by the republican opposition to refer to the dangers involved in any alteration to the mixed English constitution.[16]

The *Answer* was reprinted in the eighteenth century in such popular works as Rapin's *History of England* (1724–35). Writers such as Montesquieu, Blackstone, Paley, and Burke elaborated on the theory of mixed government as it had been expressed in the *Answer*.[17] John Dickinson, whose portrait Peale had taken also in 1770, used the phrase in his *Essay on the Constitutional Power of Great Britain Over the Colonies* (1774). Dickinson argued in this pamphlet against the "unbounded power" of Parliament. The colonies, he wrote, were accused of being "criminal" by refusing to acknowledge such power, but just the opposite was true. If the colonies were to submit to parliamentary supremacy, they would be guilty of the greatest crime against themselves and their posterity. It would mean submission to a change in the existing laws of England, laws that protected and provided justice for British subjects throughout the empire: "NOLUMUS."[18] Although the pamphlet is heavily annotated, no source for the *"Nolumus"* phrase is provided. Dickinson evidently assumed that readers familiar with English constitutional law would be conversant with it and its historical context.

Historians of republicanism have recognized the importance of the *Answer* and have assumed that the colonists were familiar with the document as a literary source.[19] There were, however, no American reprints of the *Answer* in the eighteenth century. Nor has much evidence been uncovered to show that the document was cited in the pamphlets of the revolutionary era. The Bordley portrait—a graphic rather than a printed source—indicates that some educated colonists knew the phrase and its political meaning, and had chosen to present it to an English audience as a prominent symbol of colonial opposition. Historians should sometimes turn to paintings as well as to traditional written sources to demonstrate the currency of ideas.

NOTES

This chapter was originally published in the *Pennsylvania Magazine of History and Biography* 109 (1985): 203–13. For their assistance, the author would like to thank Bernard Bailyn, Lance Banning, George A. Billias, Milton M. Klein, Ellen Miles, Lillian B. Miller, Jim Oldham, Edward C. Papenfuse, Gregory A. Stiverson, and David C. Ward.

1. *CWP,* pp. 17–37; for Peale's later involvement in the Revolution, see *Selected Papers* 1:138–327.

2. A(TS): 18–19; see also Charles Albro Barker, *The Background of the Revolution in Maryland* (1940; rpt. New Haven, Conn., 1967), p. 333; Ronald Hoffman, *A Spirit of Dissension: Economics, Politics, and the Reconstruction of Maryland* (Baltimore, 1973), pp. 47–49.

3. A(TS): 19–25, 40.

4. Ibid., pp. 27–36.

5. Edmund Jenings to Richard Henry Lee, November 7, 1768, June 28, 1769, Virginia State Library, Richmond, Personal Papers Collection; Charles Coleman Sellers, "Virginia's Great Allegory of William Pitt," *William and Mary Quarterly,* 3d ser. 9 (1952), 58–66; Lyman H. Butterfield, Leonard C. Faber, Wendell D. Garrett, eds., *Diary and Autobiography of John Adams* (Cambridge, Mass., 1961) 2:355–56n.

6. *CWP,* pp. 65–71; *P&M,* pp. 88–91; see also chap. 11.

7. Butterfield, Faber, and Garrett, eds., *Diary and Autobiography of John Adams* 2:355–56n.

8. *DAB;* Edward C. Papenfuse, Alan F. Day, David W. Jordan, and Gregory A. Stiverson, eds., *A Biographical Dictionary of the Maryland Legislature* (Baltimore, 1979), 1:145–46; Elizabeth Bordley Gibson, *Biographical Sketches of the Bordley Family of Maryland* (Philadelphia, 1865), pp. 65–159; David Hackett Fischer, "John Beale Bordley, Daniel Boorstin, and the American Enlightenment," *Journal of Southern History* 28 (1962): 327–42; *Selected Papers* 1:48–49n.

9. *Selected Papers* 1:86–104, 123; *P&M Suppl.,* p. 55; *CWP,* pp. 83–85.

10. Bernard Bailyn, *The Ideological Origins of the American Revolution* (Cambridge, Mass., 1967); Gordon Wood, *The Creation of the American Republic, 1776–1787* (Chapel Hill, N.C., 1969).

11. In 1776 Peale made a fair copy of this pamphlet for the printer, and it was published that year in Philadelphia. Bordley republished the pamphlet in 1799 and in a preface indicated that he had first written the piece in 1769 (*Selected Papers* 1:167–68; John Beale Bordley, *Essays and Notes on Husbandry and Rural Affairs* [Philadelphia, 1799], pp. 299–315).

12. For previous transcriptions, see *P&M Suppl.*, p. 55; Edgar P. Richardson, Brooke Hindle, Lillian B. Miller, *Charles Willson Peale and His World* (New York, 1982), pp. 38, 40. A letter dated December 8, 1982, from John Landsdale of Harwood, Maryland, to John A. Mellin, a reporter for the *Capital*, an Annapolis newspaper, first called attention to this Latin phrase. Lansdale read Mellin's column on Peale and had visited the Peale exhibition at the National Portrait Gallery (1982–83). In his letter, he noted that previous transcriptions of this phrase had all incorrectly rendered it as *"Notamus."* Mellin brought the letter to the office of the Peale Family Papers at the National Portrait Gallery. A careful examination of the painting confirmed Lansdale's reading.

13. Lance Banning, *The Jeffersonian Persuasion. Evolution of a Party Ideology* (Ithaca, N.Y., 1978), pp. 40–45; Bailyn, *Ideological Origins of the American Revolution*, pp. 70–71n; Bailyn, letter to author, February 1, 1983.

14. A. S. Oppé, *Wharton's Law Lexicon*, 14th ed. (London, 1938). A search of some of the most popular legal handbooks and dictionaries used in England and the colonies in the eighteenth century failed to turn up this phrase. See, for example, Giles Jacob, *A New-Law Dictionary* (London, 1729); Giles Jacob, *Every Man His Own Lawyer* (London, 1765); Thomas Blount, *Nomo-Lexicon: A Law-Dictionary* (London, 1670).

15. Corine Comstock Weston, *English Constitutional Theory and the House of Lords, 1556–1832* (New York, 1965), pp. 5, 23–24, 26–34, 37–38, 92, 92n, 113, 115.

16. Banning, *The Jeffersonian Persuasion*, pp. 40–45.

17. Weston, *English Constitution Theory and the House of Lords*, pp. 7, 123; for the likelihood that Bordley owned a copy of Rapin's *History of England*, see Joseph Towne Wheeler, "Reading Interests of the Professional Classes in Colonial Maryland, 1700–1776," *Maryland Historical Magazine* 36 (1941): 291, 294, 297.

18. John Dickinson, *Essay on the Constitutional Power of Great Britain Over the Colonies* (Philadelphia, 1774), pp. 48–50.

19. Banning, *The Jeffersonian Persuasion*, pp. 40–45; Bailyn, *Ideological Origins of the American Revolution*, pp. 70–71, 71n.

5

The Portrait of a Little Lady

Charles Willson Peale's *Henrietta Maria Bordley*

——◆——

CHARLES COLEMAN SELLERS

HE emergence of children as individuals with minds and rights and voices of their own, a friendly world within our world, came to America as one of the liberating influences of the eighteenth-century Enlightenment. Families adhering to Puritan orthodoxy still regarded the young as vials of original sin, awaiting such redemption as parent and pastor could enforce. Stern views of that sort, prevalent in New England, had far less currency to the south, and very little among the easygoing planter aristocracy of the Maryland and Virginia lowlands. In that country scriptural dogma was in large measure replaced by an ideal of nature. Here was not only an Age of Reason but of freely released emotions, laughter, tenderness, and tears. Annapolis and Williamsburg were capitals of this world of bay and river, wide and fertile fields. After mid-century, Philadelphia became the intellectual and financial center.

Annapolis and the Enlightenment were formative influences in the life of Charles Willson Peale (1741–1827), in whose oeuvre as a portrait artist the themes of domesticity and childhood recur year after year to the end. His own childhood had been a troubled one, and so, becoming himself the father of a large family, he saw to it that his boys and girls grew up within a pattern of painting and poetry — fancy-free. It was a philosophy that encouraged undisciplined enthusiasms, but, whatever the end result, he never doubted that he had been basically right.

Peale's earliest surviving portraits are those of the little sons of Nathaniel Carter of Newburyport, Massachusetts, 1765,[1] and his full-lengths of Judge James Arbuckle (fig. 12) and his wife (fig. 13), painted soon afterward on his return to Virginia, Mrs. Arbuckle posing with little Edward at her knee in a composition borrowed from a British mezzo-tint.[2] For a young artist of unestablished reputation to paint children was usual enough, but the children and the parent and child groups continued to appear in Peale's work over and over — a theme approached with pleasure and an almost missionary zeal. Portraits of young fathers and mothers did not seem to him to be complete without the children; in some instances, when Peale was only able to persuade the parent at the last moment to include the child, coherence of the group pose is markedly lacking, unlike the group portraits in which the painter had had his own way from the start.

In 1768 in London as a student of Benjamin West, Peale had an opportunity to show a painting in the special exhibition of the Society of Artists honoring the visit of the king of Denmark to the capital. His entry, no. 84 in the catalogue, "A portrait of a girl," is a young painter's very purposeful effort to shine, and perhaps to outshine Copley's *Mary Warner* (fig. 18) shown at the society's annual exhibition of the year before.[3] Peale, delighting in poetry and a poetaster himself, had taken much to heart the contemporary view of poetry and painting as sister arts. It is set forth in the opening lines of Charles Alphonse Du Fresnoy's *De Arte Graphica:*

> As Painting, Poesy, so similar
> To Poesy be Painting; emulous
> Alike, each to her sister doth refer,
> Alternate change the office and the name;
> Mute verse is this, that speaking picture call'd.[4]

This from the translation by James Wills, inferior to Dryden's and yet the one recommended to Peale as "the best precept for a painter."[5] Thus, for the Society of Artists and the king of Denmark, Peale composed a representation of childhood built up upon a repetition of rectangular lines apparently intended to give it the simple, alliterative character of a nursery rhyme. The painting itself is even repeated in its background as a picture on the wall. This is the *Little Girl with a Toy Horse* (fig. 20), signed and dated 1768, which was found in London in 1954 and is now in the Bayou Bend Collection, The Museum of Fine Arts, Houston.[6] It is, of course, the same painting mentioned above as "A portrait of a girl."

Returning to Maryland in 1769, Peale brought with him an impulse to be monumental and strenuously poetic; yet his last portrait in that vein was painted in 1770. This was his huge full-length of the American patriot John Beale Bordley,[7] shown on his Wye Island plantation as a champion of American rights in the ancient tradition of British liberty (fig. 5). Bordley was the painter's closest friend. He had taken the lead in sending Peale to London, and now the two spent many happy days together at Wye, with Bordley as a student and amateur of art. The great portrait, full of symbolism and with inscriptions in English and Latin to reinforce its allegory, had been intended for exhibition in London, where Peale meant that it should teach the British something of American determination and spirit. That never came about, probably because Bordley was as diffident and sensitive a soul as his friend and dreaded the idea of his portrait becoming a target of the London critics.

In Maryland Peale was in his own milieu, among his own people, enjoying their admiration and a prosperity he had never known before. Here, as that poetic feeling matured, it was more lightly and spontaneously felt and expressed. When he set out to compose a masterwork for an exhibition in his Annapolis studio, the symbolism was far more natural, more truly poetic. The theme of the *Peale Family* (fig. 28) is domestic harmony, developed around the action of a drawing lesson, one brother guiding another while all the family — mother, brothers, sisters, babies and even Peggy Durgan their old nurse — have gathered beside them in the studio.[8] There is an easel behind them and at first, to clarify his concept, Peale had inscribed *"Concordia Animae"* upon it — only one explanatory label, whereas his *Bordley* and its earlier counterpart, *William Pitt,* (fig. 7),[9] had had many. Later, however, he painted out even this, replacing the words with a more effective statement, a lightly sketched design of three figures, arms intertwined.

In 1776, soon after Peale's removal to Philadelphia, John Adams saw this picture and was moved by it. He wrote home of it to Abigail: "Peale is from Maryland, a tender, soft, affectionate creature. He showed me a large picture containing a group of figures, which, upon inquiry, I found were his family. . . . There was a pleasant cheerfulness in their countenance, and a familiarity in their air towards each other."[10]

The *Peale Family* was begun about 1773, according to Peale's recollection of thirty-five years later, at the time of its final completion. If so, it was conceived in the same year as his *Henrietta Maria Bordley* (fig. 34),[11] the work of a day or two, painted purely for love and pleasure but holding within it all the warmth and tenderness of the larger piece. This was no attempt at an artistic tour de force, as was the *Little Girl with a Toy Horse* of 1768; as a result, its poetic feeling is more direct and genuine. *Henrietta* was in the nature of a message about the child in the city to her parents who were at the plantation away to the south on the great bay. It was lightly done, a gift of love and friendship, a floral offering on the altar of *concordia animae*.

This child, in Philadelphia to begin her education as a lady of fashion, bore a queen's name, with an authentic touch of royal splendor behind it. Her ancestor, Captain James Neale, had been a favorite of King Charles I, and his wife, a lady-in-waiting at the court of Henrietta Maria, daughter of Henry of Navarre. The princess of France and queen of England had stood sponsor at the baptism of her little namesake, Henrietta Maria Neale, our Henrietta's great-grandmother. The Neales, Catholics, came to Maryland after the execution of Charles, bringing with them the jewels given them at the king's command before he died. The queen's name and the king's jewels would remain as heirlooms in their line.[12]

In her *Biographical Sketches of the Bordley Family,* written in 1826, Elizabeth Bordley Gibson recalls that her much older half sister Henrietta had been sent "in the spring of 1773" to "the best school in Philadelphia . . . on the earnest recommendation" of John Cadwalader, whose wife was a relative of the Bordleys.[13] Actually, she had gone in the autumn before, since we have Peale's letter of November 1772 assuring her father, "Henrietta looks charmingly well, and I hope may be as well educated here as at any other place."[14]

It is probable that "best school" consisted of private instruction in the three R's and in music, and, above all, in sharing the life of the Cadwalader home where she could acquire the manners and poise of a lady. Nicholas B. Wainwright's *Colonial Grandeur in Philadelphia* describes in full detail the magnificence of the newly completed Cadwalader mansion on Second Street near Spruce. George Washington's diary notes that he dined there on May 20, 1773, before going with the family "to the Ball." A year later Silas Deane dined "with Mr. Cadwalader, whose furniture and house exceeds anything I have seen in this city or elsewhere," and John Adams wrote of it at the same time in the same terms.[15]

It is, therefore, as a little lady that the artist has posed and portrayed Henrietta. Unlike the young sitters in his other child portraits, she has no doll or toy in hand, and the mood goes beyond the winsomeness of childhood which he so loved to depict — as we see it for instance, in his delightful little piece of *Ann Proctor* (fig. 35), now at the Hammond-

Harwood House in Annapolis.[16] Henrietta is a little lady of the world. The books on the table beside her are appropriate to the schoolgirl, but also an attribute of the lady of accomplished tastes. The lilacs in her hands might possibly be taken as dating the picture in April of that year, but, more certainly, are there to carry a suggestion of early springtime in harmony with the painter's theme. In adult portraiture that black cord about a young woman's throat, drawing the eye along a graceful line toward where the miniature of her lover lay concealed in a locket at her breast, was many a picture's major element of attraction and romance. So here Henrietta has the same — perhaps with a miniature of her mother hidden there in the minuscule bosom.

Henrietta's mother is present in this painting as still another poignancy. Margaret Chew Bordley had been slowly failing in health. Her illness and its expected end may have been one reason for sending the child away. One purpose of the portrait surely had been to console and reassure. Margaret was able to visit Philadelphia late in the year, but died in Maryland on her return journey before quite reaching home, November II, 1773.[17] Peale himself had been fond of this wife of his best friend and had named his own daughter, born January II, 1772, for her. Little Margaret Bordley Peale also died sometime in this year 1773.

Eight years later in 1781, Henrietta Maria was married to Major David Ross, an officer in one of the regiments of the Maryland Line raised to make good the Continental army's terrible losses of 1776. Her father had been supplying the army from the Wye Island plantation through those campaigns, and she herself would tell of seeing the cattle driven away. Peale, too, had been in the field, a captain under General John Cadwalader. In 1800 the Rosses moved from Maryland to Chambersburg, Pennsylvania, and there Henrietta, mother of a family of nine, died in 1823.

Her portrait has a history of continuous family ownership until 1972, moving with her descendants from Pennsylvania to California, unexhibited and unrecorded. Its acquisition by the Honolulu Academy of Arts brings to us for the first time this small pictorial lyric of friendship and young life, of love and the breaking of love's circle by death — the half-smiling tenderness of two hundred years ago.

NOTES

This chapter was originally published in the *Honolulu Academy of Arts Journal* I (1974): 9–15.

1. *P&M,* pp. 51-52.

2. *P&M,* pp. 24, 277.

3. Jules David Prown, *John Singleton Copley* (Cambridge, Mass., 1966), vol. 1, fig. 164.

4. Charles Alphonse Du Fresnoy, *De Arte Graphica; or, the Art of Painting. Translated from the Original Latin by Mr. Wills, with Notes miscellaneous and explanatory* (London, 1754), p. 3.

5. The Wills version is commended by Peale in a marginal note on p. 514 of his copy of Matthew Pilkington, *Gentleman's and Connoisseur's Dictionary of Painters* (London, 1770), American Philosophical Society.

6. *P&M Suppl.,* p. 113.

7. Ibid.; *P&M,* pp. 36-37.

8. *P&M,* pp. 157-58, 289.

9. *P&M,* pp. 172-73, 277.

10. Charles Francis Adams, ed., *Familiar Letters of John Adams and his Wife, Abigail Adams, during the Revolution* (New York, 1876), p. 215.

11. *P&M Suppl.,* pp. 55, 118.

12. Hester Dorsey Richardson, *Side-Lights on Maryland History with Sketches of Early Maryland Families* (Baltimore, 1913), 2:185-86, with illustrations of heirlooms.

13. Elizabeth Bordley Gibson *Biographical Sketches of the Bordley Family* (Philadelphia, 1865), p. 105.

14. *Selected Papers* 1:126-27.

15. Nicholas B. Wainwright, *Colonial Grandeur in Philadelphia: The House & Furniture of General John Cadwalader* (Philadelphia, 1964), pp. 1-2, *et passim.*

16. *P&M,* pp. 175, 322.

17. Gibson, *Biographical Sketches,* p. 105.

6

In the Shadow of His Father

Rembrandt Peale, Charles Willson Peale, and the American Portrait Tradition

————◆◉◆————

LILLIAN B. MILLER

D
URING his lifetime, Rembrandt Peale lived in the shadow of his father, Charles Willson Peale (fig. 36). In the years that followed Rembrandt's death, his career and reputation continued to be eclipsed by his father's more colorful and more productive life as successful artist, museum keeper, inventor, and naturalist. Just as Rembrandt's life pales in comparison to his father's, so does his art. When we contemplate the large number and variety of works in the elder Peale's oeuvre — the heroic portraits in the grand manner, sensitive half-lengths and dignified busts, charming conversation pieces, miniatures, history paintings, still lifes, landscapes, and even genre — we are awed by the man's inventiveness, originality, energy, and daring. Rembrandt's work does not affect us in the same way. We feel great respect for his technique (he was a better painter than his father technically); we take pleasure in some truly beautiful paintings, such as *Rubens Peale with a Geranium* (fig. 37), and we respond intellectually and psychologically to such penetrating characterizations as his *William Findley* (fig. 38). We are impressed by Rembrandt's sensitive use of color and atmosphere and by his talent for clear and direct portraiture. However, except for that brief moment following his return from Paris in 1810 when he aspired to history painting, Rembrandt's work has a limited range: for the most part, simple half-length or bust-size portraits devoid of accessories or complicated allusions. It is the narrow and somewhat repeti-

tive nature of his canvases in comparison with the extent and variety of his father's work that has given Rembrandt the reputation of being an uninteresting artist whose work comes to life only in the portraits of intimate friends or members of his family.

Despite their limitations, Rembrandt Peale's portraits, especially those forceful and elegant likenesses painted when he returned from England in 1803 (figs. 38, 39), call for a reevaluation of his artistic reputation. Ironically, however, such an effort must once again place Rembrandt in comparison with his father, since Rembrandt's paintings of the period reflect the elder Peale's artistic instructions and basic approaches to portraiture. Although many influences contributed to Rembrandt's achievement, including those he encountered in England during his 1802–03 visit and his own intrinsic talent, keen eyesight, and sensitive response to color and atmosphere, his father's ideas about art generally and portraiture in particular help explain many of Rembrandt Peale's artistic practices before he encountered the Parisian art world. In many ways, Charles Willson Peale's teaching contributed to the success of his son's work.

It was inevitable that Rembrandt should have been influenced by his father. He was first introduced to paint and canvas as well as to works of art in his father's studio, and he began the practice of portraiture under his father's tutelage. He grew up in a household dominated by the various artistic projects in which his father was engaged: portraits, miniatures, transparencies, moving pictures. He was surrounded by artists, all of whom were taught by his father — his father's pupils, his uncle James, his sister Angelica Kauffman, and his elder brother Raphaelle. His father's treasured book, the Reverend Matthew Pilkington's *Dictionary of Painters* (1770), became the family "bible" and provided fascinating reading for an impressionable boy convinced that artists occupied a very special social position. Listening to his father reminisce about his early friendship with such renowned painters as John Singleton Copley and Benjamin West, and about his visits to the London studios of such great artists as Sir Joshua Reynolds, Francis Cotes, and Joseph Wilton, and observing him function in his museum and in the Philadelphia community, Rembrandt must have become even more impressed with the social rewards of the artist's life. If his father had not walked with kings and emperors, as had the artistic characters portrayed by Pilkington, the elder Peale could count among his friends equally eminent leaders of the American republic: George Washington, Thomas

Jefferson, Benjamin Franklin, Alexander Hamilton, and Governor Mc-
Kean, among all those others whose portraits could be studied in the
family's art gallery.

Rembrandt's affection for his father undoubtedly reinforced his re-
ceptivity to Charles Willson Peale's lessons in the art of portraiture. In
turn, the elder Peale offered loving support to this talented son, for whose
future he had great ambitions. He created numerous opportunities for
the young man to develop as an artist and provided him with sitters
to paint, pictures to copy, money for travel to London and Paris, and
constant advice tempered by large amounts of praise. "My heart," he
wrote to Rembrandt on his son's return from Paris in 1810, "has always
been panting for your safety, success, and happiness."[1] Until his death
in 1827, the elder Peale continued to provide guidance and support to
Rembrandt; and long after his father's death, Rembrandt continued
to draw upon the ideas and practices that his father had inculcated.[2]

Charles Willson Peale's art reflected the fundamentals of the British
portrait tradition that he had absorbed in the 1760s when he had studied
painting in the London studio of Benjamin West. This tradition also
structured Rembrandt's work. In their adaptation of the British portrait tradition to American conditions, both Peales contributed to the
development of a national portrait style, one that simplified the British
model and so departed in many important ways from it.

We do not know much about Charles Willson Peale's English experiences except what we are able to piece together from a pocket diary
of expenses that he kept during his London stay and a few letters to
his patrons.[3] Peale probably attended informal life classes at St. Martin's Lane Academy, precursor to the Royal Academy School. The trans-
planted Philadelphia artist Benjamin West, a director of the school, sent
his students to study there, as did the eminent British portraitist Sir
Joshua Reynolds. Peale also may have drawn from casts in the duke
of Richmond's collection in Whitehall, which was freely available. Not
far from London, Hampton Court contained paintings from the royal
collection which Peale may have studied; the walls of London's Found-
ling Hospital included a gallery of paintings by Thomas Hudson, William Hogarth, Joseph Highmore, Allan Ramsay, and Reynolds; old
pictures frequently were auctioned in the public auction rooms, and
in Benjamin West's private picture gallery hung paintings and drawings by the great masters along with West's copies.[4] Although he was
in London for less than three years, Peale absorbed both visually and

intellectually the prevailing world of art; he acquired not only techniques, but also ideas.

When Peale first made his appearance in West's studio in 1767, London artists and connoisseurs, inspired by their encounters with classical and Renaissance art, were excitedly debating new ideas about directions and possibilities of the art of painting. One of the leading contributors to this aesthetic ferment was West, recently returned from Rome and already gaining recognition as a practitioner of fashionable Italian styles based on the examples of Raphael, Michelangelo, Correggio, and Titian. From these Italian masters, West had absorbed such artistic practices as subtle modelling, muted colors, clarity of form, and nearly invisible brushwork. Young and bold, West was ambitious for large commissions, and particularly for subjects demanding literary imagination and knowledge of classical models. With such large canvases as *Agrippina Landing at Brundisium with the Ashes of Germanicus* (1766; copy, 1770, Philadelphia Museum of Art) or *The Departure of Regulus* (1767, Collection of Her Majesty Queen Elizabeth II), West not only gave new impetus to large-scale history painting, but in doing so, became an important force in the London art world.

West taught his pupils some simple but important lessons. Accepting the contemporary conviction that Florentine draftsmanship was superior to Venetian color, he emphasized the importance of drawing. "Correctness of outline," he later wrote to Peale, "and the justness of character in the human figure are eternal . . . all other points are in a degree subordinate and indifferent — such as colour, manners and customs." In drawing, the artist should confine himself to the antique; when painting, however, he should take nature as his model. Light and shadow, West lectured, were in constant motion, and the painter must always be concerned with effectively using chiaroscuro to represent the illusion of reality.[5]

From Sir Joshua Reynolds, too, whose studio he visited, Peale must have discovered the importance of chiaroscuro, for Reynolds was "masterly" in his "control of the pattern of light and shade over the whole area" of the canvas.[6] And from the British portraits he was able to study, Peale learned how to introduce into a painting such conventions of British eighteenth-century portraiture as the curving tree, straight pillar, landscape cutout, crossed legs, and accessories that indicate occupation or familial relationships (fig. 33).

Peale also visited the studios of Francis Cotes (1726–70), rival to Reynolds, and Allen Ramsay, an artist whose poses were generally more natural and intimate than those of conventional British portraitists.[7] Cotes, too, emphasized design and draftsmanship, with results that Alastair Smart calls "superb."[8] Like Reynolds, Cotes painted portraits in the Grand Manner, giving much attention to costume and accessories, and landscape backgrounds. From both Cotes and Reynolds, and perhaps from others, Peale learned how to present three-dimensional form on a flat canvas and how to use perspective to move into the canvas to indicate distance and space (fig. 40).

Along with technique and style, Peale absorbed from West and Reynolds and other London artists a philosophy of aesthetic idealism, the belief that even while he took nature as his model, the artist should not confine himself to mere imitation. He should, instead, as Reynolds later lectured in his Third Discourse, direct his efforts to reproducing "the more perfect ideas of beauty fixed in his mind." Rather than "seeking praise by deceiving the superficial sense of the spectator," the artist, said Reynolds, "must endeavor to improve [mankind] by the grandeur of his ideas." The intellectual content of art ennobled it, separated the artist from the mere mechanic, and produced those "great efforts in an instant which eloquence and poetry . . . are scarcely able to attain."[9]

Aesthetic idealism persisted into the nineteenth century. In 1809, when Rembrandt was on his way to Paris to continue his artistic studies, West wrote to the elder Peale that he hoped Rembrandt would not waste his "genius" on portraits, but would "ever bear in mind, that the art of painting has powers to dignify man, by transmitting to posterity his noble actions, and his mental powers, to be viewed in those valuable lessons of religion, love of country, and morality."[10]

Since spiritual, moral, and national themes were the stuff of history, history painting, which required the greatest mental effort, was regarded in the eighteenth and early nineteenth centuries as the highest realm of artistic excellence. Even to be "a good face painter," West lectured his students, "a degree of the historical and poetical genius was requisite." The artist, West emphasized, "must strive for fame by captivating the imagination." To succeed, the artist required knowledge of "the science of painting," by which West meant not simply technique, but also acquaintance with the compositions and artistic practices of the Renaissance masters.[11]

Charles Willson Peale's response to these ideas was immediate and longstanding: he never relinquished the hope of eventually creating a significant history painting.[12] Although he was forced, when he returned to Annapolis, to limit his ambitions to portraiture, the major artistic interest of his Maryland patrons, he made the most of such limitations. The urban gentry of the city and Eastern Shore planters were eager to commission portraits in the British manner. For them Peale created a group of large full-length pieces, frequently consisting of more than one person, which in their elaborate costumes and accessories showed how much he had absorbed from his English experiences (figs. 26, 27, 31). With their pale flesh tones, but strong color in dress and accessories, and their emphasis on a deep chiaroscuro, these early paintings reveal Peale's debt to both West and Reynolds. The concern of these artists with draftsmanship is reflected in Peale's tendency to outline features before painting — at first with charcoal, later with paint, a practice that resulted, as he later wrote, in "a minuteness of lines, and pains taking," but that also contributed to the faithful likenesses much prized by his American sitters.[13]

His full-length Annapolis and early Philadelphia portraits and conversation pieces also reveal how impressed Peale had become with Grand Manner portraiture such as he had studied in Cotes's and Reynolds's studios and at the exhibitions of the Society of Artists of Great Britain, in which he also exhibited.[14] One of his earliest efforts, painted actually while he was still in London, followed this convention: a full-length symbolic portrait of William Pitt (fig. 7), in which he combined costume, accessories, background and pose to establish Pitt's status in the British libertarian tradition and to symbolize the Great Commoner's defense of the colonies. Portraits in the Grand Manner became Peale's substitute for the history paintings which he believed impossible to execute without recourse to old master and classical models. Before and during the Revolution, Peale was able to create a large body of such works on either private or public commission.

Like Reynolds, Charles Willson Peale was interested not in the psychological condition of his sitters, but in character as it was revealed in externalities that could be read by the eye rather than probed with the mind (fig. 41). Also like Reynolds, Peale had a particularly sharp eye. The strong naturalistic style he developed on his return to America was as much the result of good vision as it was of theory.[15]

Thus, strong emphasis on chiaroscuro, good draftsmanship, and rich colors became the elements in the British portrait tradition that Peale brought back to America along with conventional eighteenth-century poses, compositions, and aesthetic ideas. Not all of these were adaptable to American conditions. Here were no "Greesian and Roman statues," no "works of a Raphael and Corregea"—with all of which "a good painter of either portrait or History" must be well acquainted. All that Peale had, as he explained to his friend and patron John Beale Bordley, was an "enthusiastic mind" and "a good Eye" and, "like Rembrandt," a "variety of Characters to paint." Nature, after all, he was forced to conclude, "is the best Picture to Coppy."[16]

In settling for good draftsmanship, Peale remained convinced that the main concern of the portraitist should be to obtain a reasonable likeness, a concern his American patrons shared. In 1788 he proudly related to a correspondent "a favorable anecdote" which occurred when he painted the portrait of Thomas Johnson (Hammond-Harwood House, Annapolis). He had placed a looking glass so that the old gentleman could watch the picture while he was working on it. "When it was nearly finished," Peale wrote, "[Johnson] put his hand on his cap, and exclaimed in some surprise that he felt his Cap on his head, yet that he could not see it, when in fact, he only see the portrait."[17]

Since Peale could not duplicate for his children the opportunities he had enjoyed in London, he had to modify the lessons he had learned in West's studio. When conditions seemed favorable to the founding of such new organizations as the Columbianum (1794) and later, in 1805, the Pennsylvania Academy of the Fine Arts, he did attempt to introduce life classes (in the former) and study from casts (in the latter). Occasionally, his children were able to examine copies of great paintings in the studios of British visitors such as Robert Edge Pine or in the private collections of such wealthy Philadelphians as William Hamilton or John Swanwick (whose collection actually was housed in Peale's gallery for some time); but these were transitory and short-lived artistic experiences, especially in the lean years following the Revolution during which Rembrandt developed his artistic talents.[18]

For teaching purposes, Peale had to rely on his few sculptured busts, his small collection of engravings, and his own gallery of portraits of eminent Americans. He was able to teach his children drawing, which included line, chiaroscuro, and perspective, and how to mix pigments. Color, however, was not his forte, and his emphasis on drawing tended to exaggerate the still-life quality of the objects and people rendered, freeze them in space, and emphasize thought over feeling, the conceptual over the sensuous. Engravings, also, confirmed the tendency to linearity as did casts, which the chaste and dignified coloristic patterns of Peale's gallery portraits did little to correct. Designed to exhibit the great men of the nation in republican simplicity and virtue, these bust portraits in oval frames (fig. 42) became models for the kind of portraits Rembrandt painted in 1805 at fifty dollars each, hoping thereby to establish his reputation (fig. 38).

Limited commissions or portraits painted on speculation did not provide Rembrandt the opportunity to attempt full-length portraits in the Grand Manner such as his father had produced in the years following his return from England. Whether Rembrandt actually could paint such complicated works even if commissioned to do so, however, is a question. Certainly he displayed artistry at a very early age, as testified by his *Self-Portrait at age 13* (1791, private collection), and by the remarkable *Rubens Peale with a Geranium* (fig. 37). But these were fairly simple busts or half-lengths, requiring no special training in anatomy or composition or complicated drapery.

Possibly these were the kind of lessons the elder Peale hoped Rembrandt would obtain in England when he sent him to London with his brother Rubens in 1802 to exhibit the mastodon and at the same time to strengthen his painting skills.[19] Rembrandt remained in England for only seventeen months, much of which time was spent carting the skeleton of the mammoth around the provinces. During the short period he spent in London, Rembrandt did begin studies with West, who introduced him to the American artist Washington Allston and to Sir Thomas Lawrence, but Rembrandt seems to have had little to do with either man. He painted two likenesses in London for his father's gallery — one of Robert Bloomfield the poet (unlocated) and the other of the scientist Joseph Banks (fig. 44), his only work that suggests, in its free treatment, "elaborate penciling around the eyes, eyebrows, and mouth, and squiggles of viscous paint in the hair," a distinct English influence, as Dorinda Evans has pointed out.[20]

Rembrandt sent two portraits to the exhibition of the Royal Academy in 1803, an unknown subject in chalk and a self-portrait holding a tooth of the mastodon (unlocated). We can surmise that this was either a bust portrait like the *Banks* or a half-length like that of his brother. Presumably he sketched for a while from casts at the Royal Academy but was refused admission to the life class (which constituted official enrollment) because of an undescribed "trick practiced on Mr. West," president of the academy.[21] As a result, until he went to Paris in 1810, Rembrandt seems never formally to have studied anatomy, either at an academy or, later, in the Medical College of the University of Pennsylvania where classes in anatomy were offered.

In 1805, casts of full-length figures were imported to Philadelphia by the newly organized Pennsylvania Academy of the Fine Arts, but casts were not an adequate substitute for the live body, as Rembrandt would later discover when he finally was able to draw from the nude in Paris.[22] Together with his limited experience with the great paintings of the Renaissance, which might have served as compositional models,[23] Rembrandt's limited knowledge of anatomy, the influence of the bust portraits hanging in his father's gallery, and perhaps, also, lack of commissions contributed to his eschewing portraiture in the Grand Manner and concentrating on small-scale canvases.

Rembrandt may also have been influenced to concentrate on this kind of portraiture by the success experienced by Gilbert Stuart with the bust portrait — paintings, as E. P. Richardson has described them, "without movement or background."[24] Making no great demands on the artist's imagination or education in connoisseurship as did the large scale and complicated backgrounds of portraits in the Grand Manner, the Stuart-type portrait was favored not only by American artists but also by American patrons for its simplicity and clarity — and also for its cheapness. For the most part Rembrandt's portraits follow Stuart's pattern: heads looking either right or left, with few accessories of background or costume except for the back or arm of a chair and an occasional curtain, simple pictures that emphasize naturalistic representation and reveal a sensitivity to character and position.

If Rembrandt did not return to the United States with knowledge or skill in Grand Manner portraiture or history painting, he did acquire some useful lessons about color. Impressed with the coloristic practices of London painters, and perhaps also with Stuart's successful performance in this respect, on his return Rembrandt undertook the study of chemistry at the University of Pennsylvania. His innovations much impressed his father, who after having experienced difficulties with his pigments — especially with a fading lake red — when he first returned to America in 1769, was thereafter particularly concerned with color and frequently cited his improvement in color as a touchstone for his improvement in art. In 1805, for instance, the elder Peale waxed enthusiastic about a painting, possibly a study for *The Exhumation of the Mastodon* (fig. 66), not only because it demonstrated "a neater pensil" but because it showed his "better knowledge of Colours and the judgment ripened by observation on what has been done by the most noted artists." Especially significant, however, were Rembrandt's experiments with pigments and oils. "[They] opened my Eyes," Peale wrote to his English correspondent John Hawkins, "and I realy expect to paint much better pictures than I have ever done before." Rembrandt's "fondness of Chimstry," Peale was convinced, would acquire for him "a great name as a Colourist of the first grade."[25]

Both the elder Peale and Rembrandt were well acquainted with Leonardo da Vinci's *Treatise on Painting* (1802 edition), and in Rembrandt's copy of the book (Redwood Library and Athenaeum, Newport, R.I.) one of his most emphatic pencil lines was placed against the passage recommending painters to "colour and dress their figures with the brightest and most lively colours; for if they are painted of a dull or obscure color, they will detach but little and not much be seen, when the picture is placed at some distance; because the colour of every object is obscured in the shades" (p. 165). Rembrandt's pursuit of pigments, then, and clear color (which temporarily succeeded when he discovered encaustic painting techniques in Paris in 1810), is understandable in the light of his father's concerns and his own reading.[26]

Charles Willson Peale was also captivated by the use of light in paintings: how it both revealed form and illuminated images, how it could be used compositionally—as "the management of light"—and how it could be used symbolically (fig. 45). Rembrandt's interest in light may be seen in the deep chiaroscuro of one of his very first paintings—the 1791 *Self Portrait*—while a flooding of light and composed shadows emphasize the rich coloring of his *William Raborg* (fig. 43), a portrait that in many respects—in such small details as ring, letter, buttons, as well as in such larger considerations of "dignity and pleasing effects"—reveals clearly how much Rembrandt had absorbed from his father's teaching.[27] Light and color not only enhance but also create the power of such works as his 1805 portrait of Thomas Jefferson (fig. 39); and his interest and mastery of these elements would develop greatly over time, as the beautiful and vivid portraits of *Mr. and Mrs. Koch* illustrate (figs. 46, 47).

Peale's concern that portraits emphasize the dignity of the sitter—a characteristic he very much missed in his son Raphaelle's portraits and the absence of which he blamed for Raphaelle's failure to obtain commissions[28]—derived from a didactic attitude toward art and life that

Rembrandt absorbed and reflected in his own work along with the fundamentals of the elder Peale's art education. A picture, Rembrandt lectured in language reminiscent of his father's, must be addressed to the sober mind, and not to "*wild imagination*." Like Charles Willson Peale, Rembrandt accepted the principle of "naturalism": "Painting . . . must possess the forms, the colours, and the finish of Nature, of which the eye is the sole judge," he wrote. Along with good eyesight, Rembrandt stressed an understanding of the laws of chiaroscuro and light, knowledge of the chemistry of color and of perspective "that shall seem to divest the Canvas of its flat and tangible surface," and a capacity for execution "that shall happily imitate the texture of all known bodies, and especially give to flesh its diversified hues of health and beauty." He echoed his father's insistence that a portrait should present an individual in his most cheerful and attractive state, and insisted that although the eye was "the sole judge," it was the "cultivated eye" of which he spoke, the eye "that can appreciate the touches that remark the expression of thought."[29]

Such an emphasis on the role of the intellect reflected the eighteenth-century theory of the ideal more than nineteenth-century romanticism, and brought Rembrandt Peale closer to his father's generation than to his own. Some of Rembrandt's best portraits combine clear likeness with the kind of classical idealism the elder Peale had given to his 1795 portrait of Washington (New-York Historical Society): a combination of particularity of image and a recognition of the meaning of the individual in public, or universal, terms, an image that is timeless and therefore iconic. Rembrandt's two portraits of Thomas Jefferson demonstrate this iconic quality (1800, White House, Washington, D.C.; fig. 39).

Although Rembrandt later deviated from naturalism, his most artistically accomplished works of any period are strongly marked by it, as, for example, his 1812 portrait of his father (fig. 36) or his 1834 portrait of his brother, *Rubens Peale* (fig. 48). His portraits are very real images of recognizable individuals, and in artistic technique — although not in variety, imagination, or scale and complexity — they frequently surpass similar works in his father's oeuvre. The clarity of drawing he later responded to in French neoclassical art was a reinforcement of lessons his father had inculcated in him since childhood. He admitted as much later in life when he wrote in his "Reminiscences" of the necessity for beginning artists to "learn to draw everything before their eyes, with accuracy and facility."[30]

Along with a crisp naturalistic style, Rembrandt's work is marked by meticulousness of execution and graceful line (as in *Samuel Buckley Morris,* fig. 49), strong sense of character (as in *Judge Moses Levy,* fig. 50), and intense concern with painterly techniques, as in the beautifully rendered textures of his portrait of his wife *Eleanor Short Peale* (ca. 1810, Amherst College). Throughout his long career, his major strengths derived from a well-trained eye rather than imagination, a deficiency recognized by his father when he wrote to Benjamin West in 1815, "Rembrandt has painted some originals of a large size, he is very successful in Colouring. In composition I cannot say so much for him, but he may yet improve, as he possesses literary talents and some gen[i]us in poetry."[31] However, "his talent of catching strong character," as the architect Benjamin Henry Latrobe reported to Thomas Jefferson, his love of light and color, his strong draftsmanship, and his careful concern with artistry and the profession of the artist mark him as his father's son and, at the same time, earn for Rembrandt Peale a very high place in the roster of American nineteenth-century artists.[32]

NOTES

This chapter was originally published in the *Pennsylvania Magazine of History and Biography* 110 (1986): 33–70. The author is grateful to Carol Hevner for conversation, advice, and generous sharing of information.

1. Charles Willson Peale to Rembrandt Peale, Philadelphia, November 19, 1810, P-S, F:IIA/49F4–7.

2. For Rembrandt's appreciation of his father and his artistic achievements, see Rembrandt's article, "Charles Willson Peale. A Sketch by His Son," *The Crayon* 1 (1855): 81–83.

3. *Selected Papers* 1:51–70; also see p. 47.

4. Dorinda Evans, *Benjamin West and His American Students* (Washington, D.C., 1980), p. 44; Ellen G. Miles, introduction to *Thomas Hudson, 1701–1779. Portrait Painter and Collector. A bicentenary exhibition* (London, 1979), n.p.

5. Benjamin West to Charles Willson Peale, London, September 19, 1809, published in *The Portfolio* 3 (January 1810): 8–13, in *Selected Papers* 2:1218–22. Also see Evans, *Benjamin West and His American Students,* p. 21, for quote of West to Constable: "Always remember, sir, that light and shadow never stand still"; and p. 22, for his advice to students, "Draw from the Antique, paint from nature. Study the masters but copy nature."

6. Ellis Waterhouse, *Reynolds* (London, 1973), p. 11.

7. For Peale's visit to Reynolds's and Cotes's studio, see Charles Willson Peale to John Beale Bordley, London, March 1767, in *Selected Papers* 1:47–51.

8. Alastair Smart, *Introducing Francis Cotes, R.A. (1726-1770)* (Nottingham University Art Gallery, 1971), n.p.

9. Sir Joshua Reynolds, *Discourses on Art* (New York, 1961), pp. 43, 44 (Third Discourse).

10. Benjamin West to Charles Willson Peale, September 19, 1809.

11. John Galt, *The Life of Benjamin West,* ed. Nathalia Wright (Gainesville, Fla., 1960), 2:94; Evans, *Benjamin West and His American Students,* p. 22.

12. See chap. 10.

13. Charles Willson Peale to John Dickinson, Philadelphia, March 22, 1799, in *Selected Papers* 2:239-40.

14. For catalogues, see F:IIA/2C1-E5.

15. Ellis Waterhouse, "Foreword," in *Sir Joshua Reynolds, P.R.A.* (Plymouth, England, 1973), n.p.; Waterhouse, *Reynolds,* pp. 9-10.

16. Charles Willson Peale to John Beale Bordley, 1770-71, in *Selected Papers* 1:86; Charles Willson Peale to John Beale Bordley, Annapolis, November, 1772, in *Selected Papers* 1:126-27.

17. Charles Willson Peale to Christopher Richmond, Philadelphia, October 22, 1788, in *Selected Papers* 1:543.

18. In his "Reminiscences" for *The Crayon* 1:22-23, Rembrandt described the Swanwick Collection as well as copies of paintings and engravings he had seen when a boy in the home of banker Robert Morris and in the studio of British artist Robert Edge Pine. Later, in 1803 and again in 1811, he had the opportunity of examining the Stier Collection before it was returned to Holland.

19. Charles Willson Peale to Edmund Jenings, Philadelphia, June 22, 1802, P-S, F:IIA/26B5-6.

20. Evans, *Benjamin West and His American Students,* p. 142.

21. C. Edwards Lester, *The Artists of America: A Series of Biographical Sketches of American Artists* (New York, 1846), p. 206; Rembrandt Peale, "Reminiscences," 1:290.

22. Rembrandt never dismissed the usefulness of casts for the artist. In his "Lecture on the Fine Arts" (1839), he urged the careful preservation of *"admirable* and *authentic* casts, executed under the responsible professors in Europe. Casts such as we already possess [in the Pennsylvania Academy]" (p. 29; F:VIB/21).

23. Later, in 1828, Rembrandt traveled to Italy to make copies of the great paintings of the Renaissance for a gallery he hoped to open in Philadelphia upon his return. He also used Renaissance paintings as models for some of his "fancy pieces." See John Mahey, "The Studio of Rembrandt Peale," *American Art Journal* 1 (Fall 1969): 20-40.

24. E. P. Richardson, *Gilbert Stuart, Portraitist of the Young Republic, 1755-1828* (Providence, R.I., 1967), pp. 31-32. Richardson points out how few full-lengths Stuart painted on his return to America other than the Lansdowne portrait of Washington. In America, Richardson writes, Stuart "abandoned the large scale and rich backgrounds of his London style" (p. 20).

25. Charles Willson Peale to John I. Hawkins, December 17, 1805, P-S, in *Selected Papers* 2:915.

26. Later in life, Rembrandt attributed his interest in color to a Venetian paint-

ing he had seen in John Swanwick's collection while still a schoolboy (*The Crayon* 1:23).

27. Charles Willson Peale to Benjamin West, Philadelphia, September 11, 1815, P-S, F:IIA/56B5-8. Rembrandt's interest in a deep chiaroscuro was strengthened by his reading; in his copy of Leonardo's *Treatise,* he marked the passage giving advice about the ways in which objects placed between lights and shades have "greater relievo" than those placed "wholly in the light or in shadow" (p. 188).

28. See Charles Willson Peale to Benjamin West, September 11, 1815, P-S, F:IIA/56B5-8.

29. Rembrandt Peale, "Lecture on the Fine Arts," ms. at the National Academy of Design, pp. 15–16. Also see p. 24, where Rembrandt discusses portraits that "exemplify a Moral." His later attempts at imaginative compositions in such paintings as *The Roman Daughter* (1812, National Museum of American Art) or *The Court of Death* (1820, Detroit Institute of Arts) were a reflection of the didactic impulse generated by his father's insistence that art convey moral lessons and be, as Rembrandt himself put it, "expressions of thought."

30. *The Crayon* 1:22.

31. Charles Willson Peale to Benjamin West, September 11, 1815.

32. Benjamin Henry Latrobe to Thomas Jefferson, May 19, 1811, Library of Congress: Thomas Jefferson Papers. F:VIA/2C11–D4.

7

Lessons from a Dutiful Son

Rembrandt Peale's Artistic Influence on His Father, Charles Willson Peale

———◄◈►———

CAROL EATON HEVNER

> Duty to parents and gratitude to preceptors are virtues which
> no one was ever deficient in, that prospered and was happy.[1]

FOR Charles Willson Peale's second son, Rembrandt (1778–1860), mastery of his chosen vocation of artist was the linchpin of his identity. From his earliest studies, he diligently worked at honing his skills and devising improved artistic methods and execution. Such accomplishments were a means of uniting with his father, of deepening his parent's love and respect while, perhaps, also representing an understandable attempt to surpass him.[2] Charles had, in fact, acknowledged to Thomas Jefferson that Rembrandt's improvements and success in his work were "of infinite pleasure" to him: "As a fond parent," he wrote, "I wished to have kept him in my Bosom, his talents have endeared him to me — and in parting with him I shall part with a friend and counsellor on all occasions."[3] The interest, assistance, and sharing which existed between Charles and his son may be seen within the context of their dedication to the ideal of familial duty, respect, and responsibility, an ideal very much a part of the time and place in which they lived, as well as one particularly dear to Charles with his large multigenerational family. As early as 1792, he wrote to a friend, "I have laboured to instruct my children to be industrious and careful that they may help themselves and be useful members of the community — and as I have several, some amongst them will be able to assist me."[4] In

1812, he wrote to Rembrandt, "It shall be my earnest study to do everything in my power to produce now and in future a perfect harmony amongst all my children," and "You know my anxiety to serve each and every one of my children."[5]

In many ways, the shape of Rembrandt's career revealed his respect for and assimilation of his father's ideals and pursuits. Rembrandt saw his vocation as socially useful, and his painting, writing, and museum projects were carried out with an eye to the education and refinement of his audience. Rembrandt was a young man eager for responsibility, and Charles's desire to help him was surely reinforced by his observation that his son was, like himself, an individual who craved order and system and applied himself with energy and intensity. Although Charles believed that Rembrandt had married too early and so limited his freedom and educational possibilities, Rembrandt's marriage may be seen not so much as rebellion on the young man's part as a need to have his own supportive nuclear family.[6] His father, however, remained optimistic; he wrote to his daughter Angelica, "It will require time for [Rembrandt's] merrits to be known, but in the end he will I doubt not find his genious rewarded. he must encounter some difficulties for a time, as he has a family to support. The Profession is honorable, and if he gives such portraits as I know he can produce, he will before he arrives at my age, be wealthy."[7] Charles wished his son both artistic and financial success, and in the opening years of the century, Rembrandt's work promised both.

The portraits which Charles watched his son produce at this time clearly stimulated and challenged the elder artist. "Rembrandt has rekindled my desire of devoting as much time, as I can possible spare from the Museum, to the pensil, which till of late I had almost laid aside," he wrote to his former teacher, Benjamin West.[8] As Rembrandt's works increasingly began to exhibit a strong naturalistic character and painterly refinement, the father could pay him no greater compliment than to attempt to emulate him. While the purpose of this chapter is to explore the particular ways in which Rembrandt's development as an artist between 1804 and 1822 affected the character and quality of Charles Willson Peale's late work, it is clear that Rembrandt's artistic strengths and predilections strongly registered on his father's consciousness long before 1804.[9] Rembrandt's innate grasp of naturalism and three-dimensionality, as well as his ability to create vivid images, may be seen as early as 1795 in his life portrait of *George Washington* (fig. 51) or in his portrait of his younger sibling, *Rubens Peale with a Geranium* (fig. 37). It should be noted, however, that during these years, despite his announced intention, Charles had not totally withdrawn from painting, nor was his development as an artist in decline or arrest. In fact, two particularly accomplished and important works from his hand date to 1795 — *The Staircase Group* (fig. 75), painted for the museum, and the portrait of his brother, *James Peale Painting a Miniature* (fig. 52). Charles's ability to be creatively influenced by his son's work was, indeed, a function of his own artistic vitality, although his interest and involvement with painting seem to have waxed and waned in relation to available time and the amount of artistic activity surrounding him.

In 1795, for example, an artists' organization, the Columbianum, was founded in Philadelphia, giving rise to at least a short-lived optimism about the practice and support of the arts in the city. Charles's resurgent interest in painting in 1805 may certainly be attributed, in some part, to his involvement with the founding of the Pennsylvania Academy of the Fine Arts and with it the establishment of the art community on a firmer footing. In 1807, Charles wrote to Robert Fulton in New York of his excitement about the exhibition at the Academy of Fulton's collection, which included a number of dramatic works by Benjamin West. "I am delighted with your collection of Pictures," he wrote, "several of them are wonderful works of art. We shall now feel the Pulse of the Citizens of Philada: with the effect of a grand Exhibition."[10] The growing professionalism of the artistic establishment in Philadelphia with the annual exhibitions at the Pennsylvania Academy from 1810 through the 1820s provided, in fact, an ongoing stimulus for Peale.

From 1804, the specific influence of Rembrandt on Charles can be documented. Having led a peripatetic existence since his return from London in the fall of 1803, Rembrandt was happy to settle down in Philadelphia in July 1804 in a painting room partitioned off by his father in the space below the Long Gallery of the statehouse, in which Peale's Philadelphia Museum was then housed. Business, however, proved slow, and late in December, father and son left for Washington in search of "Some business." In his diary Charles wrote that he "hoped by [Rembrandt's] Painting the likenesses of some of the Public officials . . . [and] by exhibiting the portraits [he] may excite the desire of some of the members of Congress to employ him."[11] Rembrandt did, in fact, paint three fine portraits, *Thomas Jefferson* (fig. 39), *Albert Gallatin* (Independence National Historical Park Collection, Philadelphia) and *William*

Findley (fig. 38). The likeness of *Gilbert Stuart,* also done at this time, was apparently a joint effort with Charles (fig. 53).

These portraits, all placed in the Philadelphia Museum, were of a somewhat different artistic character from those executed for the museum by his father which, despite their verisimilitude, reveal a strong sense of decorative linearity and a cameolike format which often tended to immobilize the subjects. Rembrandt's *Thomas Jefferson* broke with this neat, often elegant, linearity. The image is remarkable in its frank revelation of the toughness, intelligence and careworn character of the president. One sees a strained face of mottled colors and unkempt hair that falls into a large fur collar. The paint is loosely handled; yet, in its forcefulness and careful scrutiny, the whole is profoundly dignified. In contrast to Charles's portraits, Rembrandt's works of 1805 are strongly particularized characterizations revealing an interest in the anatomical vagaries of the sitter. In none of these portraits is there a geometric basis for the individual features or the heads; in none of them does linearity override the more painterly and optically based depiction of form. Charles clearly did not overlook Rembrandt's mastery, for he wrote to John DePeyster in March 1805 that the *Jefferson* was on exhibition at the museum "at the head of the room."[12]

The Stuart portrait, on the other hand, appears from the extant documentation to have been begun by Charles on January 3, 1805.[13] Since Rembrandt annotated it as his work in his copy of the catalogue for the 1854 auction sale of the Philadelphia Museum, it seems logical to assume from both this fact and the evidence of the painting itself that the work was completed by Rembrandt when his father returned to Philadelphia ahead of him.[14] Rembrandt also wrote to William Dunlap in 1834, "[The portrait] was begun by my father in one sitting and finished by me in two other sittings at Washington."[15]

The Peales had known Stuart from his residence in Philadelphia between the fall of 1794 and the fall of 1803, when he moved to Washington. An artist of international reputation and often dazzling ability, Stuart readily obtained commissions and competed with the Peales in more than his famous depiction of the first president. His problematic and prodigal personality hardly met Charles's standards of personal behavior, and, for his part, Stuart apparently found Peale provincial and moralistic. Still, Stuart's painting room was one of the first stops father and son made on their arrival in the capital. Charles noted in his journal, "We visited Mr. Stewart where we were amused by him and his paintings all the morning."[16] Stuart's studio was, undoubtedly, the best place to take the artistic pulse of Washington. Although Stuart commented that the portrait taken of him for the Peale museum made him look clownish, his family thought it a good likeness. If lacking in elegance, it was not lacking in dignity. Stuart created paintings which, at their best, were strong delineations of individual character painted with a beautifully fluid technique and clarity of color. Many of Rembrandt's early works painted between 1795 and 1808 exhibit a sensitivity to color and surface handling that reveals close attention to Stuart's style and technique. That there was contact between these two artists is documented in a letter of 1806 in which Rembrandt noted, "You [Stuart] have freely explained to me some of the principles of the Art, which have assisted me much." Some of these principles involved the use of light and color and obtaining a greater sense of three-dimensionality:

> My last and greatest improvement I have effected by following the advice of Sir Joshua [Reynolds], to study by lamplight, the effects of which delight me by the precision of the lights, beauty of the shadows and richness of the reflections. It seems to favor the manner which I have heard you say principally distinguished you from Mr. West, in producing the effect of projection, instead of depending merely on the accuracy of the outline.[17]

Rembrandt's portrait of *John Miller* from this time demonstrates how he put these lessons into practice (fig. 54). It is a portrait that possesses a strength and presence emanating from Rembrandt's increasing ability to create a three-dimensional vision, grasp the likeness, and produce a believable visual match with reality. The portrait reveals its subject both psychologically and physically. This strongly realized naturalistic style would leave its mark on Charles. The period between 1805 and late 1808 was a time when Rembrandt's portrait career in Philadelphia was at its peak both in terms of the demand for his work and the quality of the works produced.

Charles frequently expressed pride in his son's professional prospects. For instance, in May 1805, he wrote to his daughter Angelica, "Rembrandt is now full of business, . . . last week he began and finished almost compleatly four pictures, his colouring is rich and natural, and all his portraits strikingly like, so that we may hope and expect, his merits will be extoled from one end of the continent to the other as soon as his Pictures are seen."[18] Shortly after, he wrote to Benjamin Henry Latrobe of the effect Rembrandt was having on his own work: "My Son

Rembrandt has opened my Eyes to some important methods of producing fine pictures — he is astonishingly improved, and still I hope &
believe improving. we might work togather with a great deal of satisfaction and not unprofitable to each other."[19] Charles also boasted to Jefferson
of his improvements:

> It can scarcely be believed that I should now paint much better than
> when I was much younger & in constant practice. but my judgement is
> ripened; I produce a better effect, which is of greater importance than
> a neat Pensilling. and I have more knowledge of colouring than I had
> 30 years past. one other reason in proof of the possibility of my improve-
> ment, is having the talents of my Son Rembrandt, who is a Philosopher,
> a Chimest and a persevering young man, and daily conversing on the
> art; on the pigments and compounding those of affinity, and finding the
> best oils &c — with the modes of execution practiced by the best Masters,
> Antient as well as Modern, striving thus to get light, and which I flatter
> myself will raise my Son to great eminance in his profession, it would
> be strange if I could not also improve, when it is an object with me to
> prove that acquirements is attainable at any period of life.[20]

During the years 1806–08, Charles created his unusual and impressive
Exhumation of the Mastodon (fig. 66). Designed as an enhancement to the
mammoth materials in the Philadelphia Museum, this was an ambitious painting with a multitude of figures in action, an atmospheric landscape rich in color, and a scientific device of enormous proportions as
a centerpiece. It was a challenging composition and called for an artist
who was secure in his artistic skills, a fact Peale readily admitted to his
friend, John Hawkins.

> I thought [it] would be a tryal which should determine whether I should
> paint another picture. I got togather such painting apparatus as were
> meerly a shift — but after I brough[t] the picture into some forwardness
> I found it less difficult work than I expected, and instead of burning my
> Pensils, I ordered a fine Mahogany *Easel* to be made, and every other
> article relating to the Art of the best and most convenient form &c deter-
> mining to shew more talents at 65 than when at the age of 40 yrs. This
> proves that it is not the bodily but the mental powers which is most im-
> portant to constitute the Painter.[21]

Charles's museum portraits at this time reveal an enhanced sense of
projection and a greater sense of anatomical definition accented with
a careful use of light. Earlier trademarks of his style, such as the al-

mond shaped black-rimmed eyes, have been modified. Charles wrote to the American ambassador to France, John Armstrong, "[Rembrandt] has taught me to paint a more natural portrait than I could do at the best time of my life."[22] These changes in Charles's style may be readily seen by comparing his first museum portrait — that of the revolutionary hero *Baron DeKalb,* (1781–82) (fig. 55) — and even his more sophisticated portrait of *John Adams* of ca. 1791–94 (Independence National Historical Park Collection, Philadelphia) to his 1807 portrait of the American poet and diplomat *Joel Barlow* (fig. 56).

In 1807 Rembrandt, who according to his father was becoming "pale and feeble" from too much concentration on his painting, was eager to leave Philadelphia to study in France. His father believed, "His portraits would excite admiration in any part of Europe. His pictures are highly finished equall to Flemish, and the colours are such that time cannot change them."[23]

Moreover, Rembrandt's virtues of "Enthusiasm & judgement, his taste, Industry, and perseverance," which encouraged him to pursue the "mysteries of Chymistry for the discovery of perfect & durable materials," would result, his father was confident, in his "ultimate success." As Charles wrote to Jefferson, "[He] has given me such a system of art as will enable me to execute Works of greater harmony & duribility than ever."[24]

Thus, even prior to Rembrandt's intensive period of European study between 1808 and 1810, the younger artist had made a significant impact on his father's practice and style of painting.[25] Charles wrote to his daughter Angelica in Baltimore in June 1808 about his portraits of *Zebulon Montgomery Pike* (Independence National Historical Park Collection, Philadelphia), *William Bartram* (fig. 57), and *Angelica Kauffmann* (unlocated) which he had just completed, indicating that in finishing these works Rembrandt's "system of colouring" was "all important, for I never painted with so much ease, nor have I ever in my best time equaled some of these pieces."[26] The portrait of his botanist friend William Bartram does, in fact, show Peale in top form. It is a strong likeness, revealing a grasp of anatomical structure and a fine sense of light and texture. The reflection of light in the subject's blue eyes and the decorative and symbolic accent of the branch of jasmine give the portrait a sense of liveliness and grace. It balances the poetic and genteel qualities often found in Peale's early works with a naturalistic rigor and substance gleaned from the influence of Rembrandt. Charles was, in fact, ready to compete with his son, and wrote to him that he was feeling very proud of his recent work. "I tell you this to put you on your mettle, for if you do not improve very fast I shall overtake you."[27]

Charles endeavored to assist Rembrandt financially on both his 1808 and his 1809–10 Parisian trips by commissioning portraits of European cultural, scientific, and political leaders for the Philadelphia Museum. The seven portraits with which Rembrandt returned in 1808 were advertised in the newspapers as "the commencement of a New series of Portraits (of a different size) for the Museum."[28] Before Rembrandt left again in 1809 to continue his studies, Charles "engaged him to paint for the Museum 50 additional Portraits to be had in different parts of Europe"; for this commission, Rembrandt was to receive five thousand dollars.[29] While this large number of portraits was never completed, the moral and financial support that such a commission represented was extremely significant. As Charles wrote to his friend Hawkins in London, "Giving Rembrandt the means of improving his talents in this work is a very important affair to him, indeed he says 'the Emperor could not do more for him.'"[30]

The stylistic character of the portraits produced during Rembrandt's Parisian period did not so much diverge from his pre-Paris works as enhance their characteristics of three-dimensionality, depth of color, and attention to anatomical detail. The study of anatomy often became particularly rigorous in Rembrandt Peale's work after his Paris experience, however. In his best works after 1810, naturalism and anatomical conceptualization are held in balance, but in his less successful works the abstract application of anatomical detail is apt to become rigid. This was a problem that Charles never seemed to face. While he clearly picked up a greater accuracy in anatomical detail from Rembrandt, he never permitted the forms to override his expressive intention. His was always a lighter, more genial hand. Rembrandt's use of color, however, certainly gained in depth from his French studies. As Lois Fink has noted, it is from this time that "his use of pigment expresses a sensuous richness."[31]

Rembrandt wrote home enthusiastically of his experiments with the encaustic medium in which beeswax was used as a binder for pigment. With this ancient technique, revived by French neoclassical painters, he believed he had found the perfect medium to ensure both brilliancy and durability of tints. He found it especially good for rendering flesh.[32] Charles also embraced encaustic enthusiastically, utilizing it for a number of family portraits. He wrote to Rembrandt in August 1811, "The portrait of Sophonisba will be one of my best, it appears to me that a great advantage in encaustic painting in particular is to paint very light, and in finishing to glaze down to the true tints which give a richness not to be acquired in any other mode."[33] Both artists seem to have eventually dropped the technique, apparently because its durability was not what they had expected. Rembrandt does not even mention it in his manual of painting procedures, "Notes of the Painting Room."

During the first two decades of the nineteenth century, Charles continued to credit his son's methods and inspiration. Letters from this period document Rembrandt's continual sharing of professional information with his father, particularly on systems of coloring or "palettes." For example, in 1815 Charles wrote,

> I have carefully preserved your table of mixed flesh tints with a description of the colours used with your remarks on the use of them, several tints in the various parts of the face. This course I will follow until you may find leisure to give me your more simplified mode by a table of like form.[34]

In a letter to Rembrandt in 1816, he revealed how anxious he was to test his careful application against the works of other artists. There were, in fact, many artists whose work he could compare against his own at this time. In 1815, for example, Thomas Birch and Gilbert Stuart exhibited at the Pennsylvania Academy of the Fine Arts, and Thomas Sully showed sixteen paintings.[35] Late in 1815, Charles was ready to exhibit the portrait of his daughter Sybilla, a picture painted with "Rembrandt's colours."[36] Charles's portrait of his third wife, *Hannah Moore Peale,* also dates from this time, and is particularly notable for its subtle handling of light and color and its tender veracity (fig. 58). In executing this portrait, Charles seems to have been experimenting with his son's suggestion to use a large magnifying glass. He did not find the method particularly successful, but it seems quite clear that this portrait was indebted to Rembrandt in other ways. *Hannah,* in fact, bears a striking formal resemblance to one of Rembrandt's most successful and powerful works—his 1812 portrait of his father, *Charles Willson Peale,* painted shortly after his return from Paris (fig. 36). These portraits make a strong pair and fully testify to Rembrandt's artistic influence on Charles Willson. Both images are strictly frontal with shading on the right-hand side of the face and a pocket of light focused behind the right shoulder. Compositionally, the oval sweep of Hannah's linen echoes the arm, palette,

and brushes of Charles. Both portraits are highly naturalistic, mapping
out the details of the faces of the seventy-one-year-old painter and his
sixty-one-year-old wife. While the sense of volume and anatomical structure is more pronounced in Rembrandt's work, the portrait of *Hannah*
is well articulated and three-dimensional. The portraits also match each
other in their exploration of character. Charles appears handsome, determined, genial but indomitable; Hannah's long oval weathered face,
surrounded by a warm light, is peaceful and controlled, her soft hazel
eyes and rosy lips are kind and delicate touches accenting her chiseled
features.

Similarly composed, but less psychologically revealing, is Charles's
portrait of Rembrandt of 1818 (fig. 59). His letter to his son describing
the work is a mixture of technical comments and personal hopes:

> But your portrait has undergone an important change. In the beginning
> you know it was with a gloomy background. I have made it a *Profetick
> Picture* on the Dark side (left) I have made a thick wood. The depth of
> the B. [burnt] umber and Blue has a good effect here, on the right in
> the horizon a lightening up, emblematical that the evening of your days
> will be brighter than on former times — the orange color takes off the sal-
> low tint of the face. The upper part of the ground is the same as it was,
> I have not touched it, and the light grey tint beneath which is the warm
> horizon & distant mountain, and in the middle distance below a river
> & cascade. The green & orange tints improves the picture considerably.[37]

How seamlessly Charles was ultimately able to wed Rembrandt's lessons to his own sensibility is evident in his 1818 portrait *Angelica Peale
Robinson and Her Daughter Charlotte* (fig. 60). A portrait replete with
Charles's characteristic tenderness and delicacy, it also reveals a depth
and range of light and color as well as an anatomical scrutiny and sense
of three-dimensionality reminiscent of the vibrant naturalism of the
French artist, Jacques Louis David, whose portrait of 1810 by Rembrandt
hung in the Philadelphia Museum (Pennsylvania Academy of the Fine
Arts).[38]

Charles's landscape painting was also shaped by Rembrandt's hints
and methods. In a letter of 1816, Charles referred back to 1811 when Rembrandt had painted his large landscape of *Harper's Ferry* (private collection), commenting, "I wish I had treasured up your observations on
Landscape painting; by noting down what you gave me at the time you
was painting harpers ferry." He told his son, however, that he was busy

studying the various types of foliage and had just finished twelve small landscape views and was about to make a few more in a larger format with the aid of a drawing machine.[39] "Within a short time," he wrote to Jefferson, "I have studied effects I have seen in Landscape which I had not noticed before."[40] In 1818, he wrote to Angelica, "Your brother Rembrandt has given me a system of . . . mixtures for landscape painting which will render that kind of painting much more pleasing and easy of execution."[41]

Rembrandt's successful history painting, *The Court of Death* (1820), initially earned a significant amount of money and notoriety. Large, serious and accomplished, although certainly not inspired, it was a work his father admired in its intention and its effect. Not only had he posed for one of the figures, but also he had made a sketch of it which he sent to Jefferson (private collection):

> When I made my sketch from the picture the latter figure was not painted in, as may [be] seen by the enclosed slight drawing. It is a very rude and imperfect performance, and is only meant to give an Idea of the Design, The Painting is powerful in its effect, the drawing and coloring fine.[42]

Despite his unnecessary disclaimer on the quality of his drawing, Charles was serious in his attention to this work; on July 23, 1820, he wrote to Rembrandt that he was planning to copy it in a 2'8" by 3'5" format. This was never done, however, because Rembrandt apparently objected to it.

> Seeing that you are apprehensive that my copying your Court of death may be a disadvantage to you which assuredly I would not suffer, I hasten to inform you that I have dropped that Idea of making a Coppy, altho' I would like such a subject to be before me in my painting room here.[43]

Rembrandt's forays into history painting from 1811 to 1820 were a point of pride and possibly of inspiration to Charles. One might, in fact, speculate that it fueled his desire to execute his own masterpiece, *The Artist in His Museum* (1822, fig. 61). In this self-portrait, Peale, who not only gestures but actively lifts the curtain, shows himself in a pose suggestive of control and proprietorship. Roger Stein has justly noted the emblematic character of this work and its obvious parallel to both the Van der Myn portrait of *Charles Calvert, 5th Lord Baltimore* (fig. 6) and Peale's own portrait of *William Pitt* (fig. 7).[44] *The Artist in His Museum* also parallels Stuart's full-length Lansdowne portrait of *George Washington* (1796, on loan, National Portrait Gallery, Washington, D.C.), a reference that Peale may have chosen in order to define himself as a founding father in his own world of natural science and in the documentation of American heroes. Certainly, the rich red curtains and black frock coats in each painting create a strong visual parallel.

While the emblematic character of Charles's painting is undeniable, it is also interesting to view the self-portrait in the light of Rembrandt's essay in the Philadelphia *National Gazette* on October 28, 1820, entitled "Original Thoughts on Allegorical Painting." Here Rembrandt sets himself against contrived symbols, personifications, and allegories, and champions the easily readable and immediately expressive. He stresses "going directly to the heart," to the feelings, and states that the artist can communicate best through accuracy of delineation, the force of his figures, the reality of his coloring, and the animation and propriety of his expression. All these elements are operative in *The Artist in His Museum.* Charles has a penetrating gaze as he beckons the viewer to enter into this long space and examine the displays more closely. The pose of the figure farthest in the distance suggests contemplative assessment and rational scrutiny as he gazes forward, arms folded in front of his body. The figure closest to the viewer is, on the other hand, emotive and surprised as she faces outward with her hands raised in amazement, her dress illuminated by the light flooding in from the windows to the right. Between these two figures are a man and a boy — a father and son, most likely. They seem to occupy neither extreme of the other figures, but rather seem to move more slowly through the exhibit. The gesture of the father echoes that of Peale, who saw himself as a father figure in so many ways. The man and boy may also be regarded as participants in the universal life cycle, an idea important to Peale.

To bring the life cycle closer to the subject of this essay, one might conclude by realizing how pleasing to Charles the mutual duty of father and son must have seemed, as they shared each other's knowledge and passion for painting. While their relationship was not always smooth, and as with most parents and children, they often did not agree, yet their respect for and interest in each other's work seems to have created a particular bond between them. The ability to render a "better effect," to use more durable materials and techniques, to enhance three-dimensionality and anatomical definition, to achieve an enhanced naturalism, an increased sense of opticality, and a rich and natural coloring were all lessons that Charles specifically credited to Rembrandt.

The blossoming of Charles Willson Peale's late style was a function of his talent as well as of his desire to master a more sophisticated painting style in greater harmony with the developing expertise of American artists in general. It was, however, also a function of his vital spirit and his lifelong interest in self-improvement and ongoing accomplishment. When Rembrandt wrote of his father's death at age eighty-six, he added that he died "not of old age, but by an affection of the heart, induced by over exertion."[45] Charles seemed to his son incapable of merely fading away. In turn, Charles recognized the debt he owed to Rembrandt for reawakening his interest and enthusiasm in painting and sharpening his painterly skills. In a letter presenting to his son the skeleton of the mammoth as a gift for his Baltimore museum, he reminisced on the "labours [they] had together getting the skeleton . . . and putting the bones in their proper situations." The gift of this skeleton, however, was given "in consideration of the value I have received by the aid you have given me in a system of colouring for the portraits and landscape painting, and also for your dutiful conduct toward me."[46]

NOTES

1. William Mavor, L.L.D., *A Father's Gift to His Children: Consisting of Original Essays, Tales, Fables, Reflections, etc.,* 2d ed. (London, 1805): 1:18.

2. Charles Willson Peale to Angelica Peale Robinson, October 29, 1805, P-S, in *Selected Papers* 2:904.

3. Charles Willson Peale to Thomas Jefferson, February 7, 1807, February 21, 1808, Library of Congress: Thomas Jefferson Papers, in *Selected Papers* 2:1003, 1063.

4. Charles Willson Peale to George Walton, Esq., January 15, 1793, P-S, F:IIA/17F13–14.

5. Charles Willson Peale to Rembrandt Peale, September 17, 1812, P-S, F:IIA/51E11–14; Charles Willson Peale to Rembrandt Peale, July 27, 1812, P-S, F:IIA/51D5–11.

6. Rembrandt's mother, Rachel Brewer, died in 1790, when he was twelve years old. Charles Willson Peale remarried late in 1791, and Charles insisted that his children call his new wife "Mother." What influence the early death of his natural mother had on Rembrandt's sense of family can only be surmised.

7. Charles Willson Peale to Angelica Peale Robinson, September 3, 1804, P-S, in *Selected Papers* 2:750.

8. Charles Willson Peale to Benjamin West, December 16, 1807, P-S, in *Selected Papers* 2:1052.

9. These dates represent, on the one hand, the beginning of documents that detail the influence of Rembrandt on his father and, on the other hand, the completion of Charles's autobiographical painting *The Artist in His Museum* (fig. 61), which

he described as "a lasting monument to [his] art" and which reveals many of the influences attributed to Rembrandt.

10. Charles Willson Peale to Robert Fulton, November 15, 1807, P-S, in *Selected Papers* 2:1047.

11. P-S, in *Selected Papers* 2:783.

12. P-S, in *Selected Papers* 2:816.

13. Charles Willson Peale to Raphaelle Peale, Rubens Peale, and Sophonisba Peale, January 30, February 1, 1805, P-S, in *Selected Papers* 2:795.

14. Collaborative work by father and son on a portrait was more the exception than the rule. On this trip, however, both men were painting and assisting each other. In 1808, Charles Willson Peale finished a portrait of *Elizabeth Bordley* (private collection), which Rembrandt had begun but had not been able to finish before leaving for France (*P&M*, p. 87).

15. Rembrandt Peale to William Dunlap, December 27, 1834, in *Magazine of American History* 5 (1880): 129. This letter was written in response to Dunlap's request for information on the Peales for his *History of the Rise and Progress of the Arts of Design in the United States* (New York, 1834), 2:50–58.

16. *Selected Papers* 2:786.

17. Rembrandt Peale to Gilbert Stuart, March 24, 1806, in George C. Mason, *The Life and Works of Gilbert Stuart* (New York, 1879), pp. 71–72, quoted in *Selected Papers* 2:948–49.

18. Charles Willson Peale to Angelica Peale Robinson, May 24, 1805, P-S, in *Selected Papers* 2:841

19. Charles Willson Peale to Benjamin Henry Latrobe, July 21, 1805, P-S, in *Selected Papers* 2:869.

20. Charles Willson Peale to Thomas Jefferson, December 24, 1806, Library of Congress: Thomas Jefferson Papers, in *Selected Papers* 2:992–93.

21. Charles Willson Peale to John I. Hawkins, April 3, 1807, P-S, in *Selected Papers* 2:1010; also see Charles Willson Peale to John I. Hawkins, December 28, 1806, P-S, in *Selected Papers* 2:996, 1036.

22. Charles Willson Peale to John Armstrong, April 20, 1808, P-S, in *Selected Papers* 2:1074–75.

23. Charles Willson Peale to Angelica Peale Robinson, August 2, 1807, P-S, in *Selected Papers* 2:1025; Charles Willson Peale to John I. Hawkins, October 25, 1807, P-S, in *Selected Papers* 2:1035–36.

24. Charles Willson Peale to Thomas Jefferson, February 21, 1808, Library of Congress: Thomas Jefferson Papers, in *Selected Papers* 2:1063–65.

25. Rembrandt sailed from Baltimore to France on April 7, 1808, arriving in Paris in June. He returned to New York in October, but made a second visit to Paris in the fall of 1809, this time accompanied by his family. He remained there until October 1810.

26. Charles Willson Peale to Angelica Peale Robinson, June 16, 1808, P-S, in *Selected Papers* 2:1087.

27. Charles Willson Peale to Rembrandt Peale, June 26, 1808, P-S, in *Selected Papers* 2:1093.

28. Charles Willson Peale to Joel Barlow, April 2, 1809, P-S, in *Selected Papers*

2:1188. These were the portraits of *General John Armstrong* (Independence National Historical Park Collection, Philadelphia), *Count Rumford (Benjamin Thompson)* (American Academy of Arts and Sciences, Boston), *Dominique-Vivant Denon* (Pennsylvania Academy of the Fine Arts, Philadelphia), *Jean-Antoine Houdon* (Pennsylvania Academy of the Fine Arts, Philadelphia), *Abbé René-Just Haüy* (private collection), *Georges Cuvier* (Mütter Museum, College of Physicians, Philadelphia), and *Jacques-Henri Bernardin de Saint-Pierre* (Corcoran Gallery of Art, Washington, D.C.).

29. Ibid.

30. Charles Willson Peale to John I. Hawkins, May 4, 1809, P-S, in *Selected Papers* 2:1200.

31. Lois Marie Fink, "Rembrandt Peale in Paris," *Pennsylvania Magazine of History and Biography* 110, no. 1 (January 1986): 76.

32. "Original letters from Paris," *The Portfolio* 4, no. 3 (September 1810): 276, 278. On September 10, 1810, Rembrandt presented a paper on his particular formulation of this method to the Institute of France, an event that surely must have pleased his father.

33. Charles Willson Peale to Rembrandt Peale, August 27, 1811, P-S, F:IIA/50D11–13; *P&M*, p. 192.

34. Charles Willson Peale to Rembrandt Peale, September 10, 1815, P-S, F:IIA/56A13–B4.

35. Anna Wells Rutledge, comp., *Cumulative Record of the Exhibition Catalogues of the Pennsylvania Academy of the Fine Arts, 1807–70* (Philadelphia, 1955), pp. 28, 217, 219–22.

36. Charles Willson Peale to Rembrandt Peale, February 20, 1816, P-S, F:IIA/56G6–8.

37. Charles Willson Peale to Rembrandt Peale, August 9, 1818, P-S, F:IIA/61A6–8.

38. Charles Willson Peale to Angelica Peale Robinson, January 15, 1818, P-S, F:IIA/60C13–D1.

39. Charles Willson Peale to Rembrandt Peale, December 27, 1816, P-S, F:IIA/58F12–14.

40. Charles Willson Peale to Thomas Jefferson, August 9, 1816, Library of Congress: Thomas Jefferson Papers, F:IIA/57F9–14.

41. Charles Willson Peale to Angelica Peale Robinson, July 24, 1818, P-S, F:IIA/61A2–5.

42. Charles Willson Peale to Thomas Jefferson, July 3, 1820, Library of Congress: Thomas Jefferson Papers, F:IIA/64D8–9.

43. Charles Willson Peale to Rembrandt Peale, July 23, 1820, P-S, F:IIA/64F5–6.

44. See chap. 11.

45. Rembrandt Peale, "Reminiscences, Charles Willson Peale, A Sketch by His Son," *The Crayon* 1, no. 6 (February 1855): 83.

46. Charles Willson Peale to Rembrandt Peale, August 9, 1818, P-S, F:IIA/61A6–8.

8

"Good Chiefs and Wise Men"

Indians as Symbols of Peace in the Art of Charles Willson Peale

———◆———

CHARLES COLEMAN SELLERS

C HARLES Willson Peale was the irrepressible optimist of the American Revolution. He confidently expected that with liberty achieved, the nation would set new standards changing the world — ideals of reason and nature derived from the more romantic of the French philosophers, of whom Rousseau appealed to him the most. His museum of natural history, conceived in 1784 and begun in 1786, was intended both to advance science and educate the masses. An understanding of natural history, he believed, would lead to wise use of natural resources, healthy living, and longer life. Above all, it would teach a lesson of peace among men and nations, and he never tired of decrying that man alone, of all the animals, preyed upon his own species. Moreover, the mere contemplation of nature's beauties influenced the mind toward reverence and love for all creatures. He stressed this point in opening his series of lectures on natural history in 1800:

> An instance of this is in the memory of many of my hearers. The chiefs of several nations of Indians, who had an hereditary enmity to each other happened to meet unexpectedly in the Museum in 1796; they regarded each other with considerable emotion, which in some degree subsided when, by their interpreters, they were informed that each party, ignorant of the intention of the other, had come merely to view the Museum. Never having before met, but in the field of battle, where the recollection of former scenes of bloodshed only roused the spirit of revenge, no room

was left for the feelings of the social man. — Now, for the first time, finding themselves in peace, surrounded by a scene calculated to inspire the
most perfect harmony, the first suggestion was, — that as men of the same
species they were not enemies by nature, but ought forever to bury the
hatchet of war.

  After leaving the Museum they formed a treaty so far as their powers
extended, and wishing the white people to be witnesses of the sincerity
of their intentions, at the request of the Secretary at War, I supplied them
with a room. — Sixty-four chiefs of eight or ten nations met; they heard
a speech sent by General WASHINGTON, recommending peace. — Their
orators spoke, and they departed friends. [1]

The date of that unique council was Friday, December 1, 1796. The
museum was then in the Hall of the American Philosophical Society
on what is now Philadelphia's Independence Square (fig. 62). A regularly scheduled meeting of the Society was held that night, but its minutes say nothing of the proceedings of the warriors earlier in the day.
For that, one must go to the papers of the president and secretary of
war, where the incident loses some of Peale's cherished moral, but none
of its drama. A powerful confederacy of tribes armed and encouraged
by the British had twice defeated the "Legion" of the United States: Gen.
Josiah Harmar had been beaten back ingloriously; Arthur St. Clair's
army had been erased in a bloody rout. Anthony Wayne marched next,
out to the west of Lake Erie, American territory still held by the British Fort Miami.

The story of the council at the museum begins with another council
of Indian chiefs outside Fort Miami on the night of August 19, 1794.
Wayne was nearby, at a place where much of the forest had been lev-
eled by some tremendous storm of the past. The Miami warrior Little
Turtle, who had led the tribes to victory over St. Clair in 1791, was now
advising caution, even overtures for peace. But Blue Jacket of the Shawnee, who had fought under Little Turtle, then spoke for an immediate
night attack and was ready to lead it. [2] The final decision was for an
attack the next day, and it was made with Blue Jacket at the head of
the whole force and a young warrior, Tecumseh, leading the Shawnees.
The Battle of Fallen Timbers was a stand-up fight of about sixteen hundred Indians and British volunteers against Wayne's thousand. [3] But
Wayne's cannon and cavalry broke their line and furiously pursued it.
The tribesmen fled to the fort but found its gates closed against them.
Nothing could have told them more clearly that they were now, and
would be in future, at the mercy of the Americans.

By the turn of the year, chiefs and warriors were coming to "Mad Anthony's" camp at Greenville in Western Ohio seeking terms. Wayne reported to the secretary of war on February 12, 1795, that "the infamous Blue Jacket" had "come with a crowd of Shawnee and Delaware warriors, bearing a flag and suing for peace."[4] His tone changed after three weeks in camp. It was then "the famous Blue Jacket" with whom he was dealing.[5] In their talks, Blue Jacket had shown a paper, signed by Sir John Johnson, 1784, certifying him as "War Chief." Wayne countered by showing an American officer's commission with its engraved decorations and, noting the light in the other's eye, ordered his efficient quartermaster general, Colonel O'Hara, to add engraved commissions to the list of requisites for the coming ceremonies.[6] Wayne himself was receiving propitiatory gifts, some of which he passed on to Peale's museum for public display:

> A Large Indian Mantle, made of a Buffaloe's skin and ornament[ed] with Porcupine quills;
> A Pipe of the Sack nation of Indians who reside at the junction of the Tyger and Missouri Rivers. This nation, it is said, are able to send out 10,000 warriors;
> A Chipewas Pipe, and a Pipe of Peace of the Hickapoos, Piankashaws and Kaskaskie, natives of the Mississippi and Missouri, which was passed through and was smoked by the several Tribes of Indians previous to the treaty of Peace, lately concluded with them by General Wayne Presented by General WAYNE.[7]

That treaty had been signed on August 3, 1795. Ninety-one chiefs — Wyandots, Delawares, Shawnees, Ottawas, Chippewas, Potawatomies, Miamis, Kickapoos, Kaskaskias, Weas, and Eel River Tribe — made their marks below "Mad Anthony's" bold signature. Lands were ceded in return for $20,000 and payments to follow every year in perpetuity.[8] The chiefs, to whom face-to-face reassurances meant much, were invited, at their own request, to visit the Great Father in Philadelphia, to give and be given final words of trust and respect.

President Washington's Indian policy could now be extended into the northwest. It was centered upon the encouragement of settled living and agriculture, with American agents going out as missionaries of "husbandry."[9] Wayne's treaty specified that, whenever requested, annual gifts to the Indians could take the form of tools and domestic animals. The treaty did contain some seeds of further conflict — or so Wayne's young aide-de-camp, William Henry Harrison, would in time decide — but for the nonce all hopes for a permanent peace were high.

Concluding arrangements took time and a year went by before the official visitations were made. On October 3, 1796, three parties set out from Detroit on the long journey to Philadelphia.[10] The first to arrive walked into the office of Dr. James McHenry, secretary of war, on November 20. McHenry reported to the president:

> The Indian Chiefs named Mus-qua-cu-nokan or Red pole, Wey-a-pur-sen-waw, or Blue Jacket, She-me-jum-ne-sa or Soldier, Asi-me-the, and Muc-ca-ti-wa-saw or Black chief, stiling themselves the representatives of the Wyandots, Delawares, Shawanoes, Ottawas, Chipwas, Putawatimes, Miamis, Eel River, Weas, Kickapoos, Piankashaws, and Kaskaskias have informed the Secretary of War in a talk delivered by Red pole at the War Office on the 20th inst: that they had come a great way to see their Father the President; that they had long listened to the British; that they had discovered their error; that they had made peace with the fifteen fires (meaning the United States) and in future would only listen to their great Father the President; that they were now waiting till they could hear what advice he could give them, which they would follow; and that they would on their part try to keep the path open between their people and the people of the United States. That finally, they wished to hear the President's advice as soon as possible, having a great way to go to get to their nations.
>
> To this Blue Jacket added, that what had been spoken by Red pole was the sense of all the warriors present. That he rose to mention this and give a particular proof of his own sincerity by delivering to his great Father the commission he had received a long time ago from the British; that he now broke it, and would hereafter serve faithfully the United States.[11]

The president's short speech of good advice, November 29, was a plea for the industrious, "comfortable" life of the farmer, urging friendship between men and nations. At the end, with an approving word for Blue Jacket's surrender of his British title, he gave each warrior a handsomely engraved commission as an American chief, in "proof of [his] esteem and friendship."[12] All through that week they were feasted in four separate parties at their Great Father's table, the guests at the first [party], on Monday the twenty-eighth being the Shawnees' Red Pole—"Principal Chief"—and Blue Jacket, together with three Potawatomies, five Chippewas, and two interpreters.[13]

The unexpected encounter in Philosophical Hall occurred in the midst of these excitements, on Thursday, December 1, and at the intertribal peacemaking council on the next day. The news of it was printed a week later in Benjamin Franklin Bache's *Aurora* of December 8, heading the column filled by Washington's last annual message to Congress before his retirement from office:

A singular circumstance took place a few days ago in this city. Several chiefs of the Creeks, Cherokees, and other nations of Indians, now here upon an invitation of the President of the United States, met accidentally at Peale's Museum. They shewed evident surprise at the recontre, and were remarkably shy of each other at first. They by degrees, however, through the Intervention of the interpreters, became more reconciled to each other, and at last entered into conversation. Some of the chiefs were from tribes hostile to others, but in this first interview they made such progress towards a reconciliation, that they agreed to meet again at the Museum, and the chiefs from the following tribes did assemble, and after a sitting of some hours, concluded a pact of peace and friendship.

The following is a list of the tribes represented.

Creeks, Cherokees, Choctaws, and Chicasaws, all southern Shawnee, Wyandots, Delawares, Miamis, Chippewas, Kickapoos, and other of the north western Indians.

The conference was opened by a message from the President, encouraging them to make up their differences. The Indians were so struck with the singular manner of their meeting, that they expressed their persuasion, that the Great Spirit must have brought them thus together for the purpose of reconciliation, an opinion which will probably secure the permanency of their friendly union.

There is a religious note also in the message which the secretary of war brought on behalf of Washington. The words, dated December 1, 1796, are McHenry's and are preserved in his papers at the William L. Clements Library, University of Michigan. He spoke in the poetic imagery of the council fire:

Brothers

The president of the United States, your father, who loves you as his Children, has heard the request which some of you have made to him, and agreed that you should all meet in one assembly, to strengthen before me, as a solemn witness, that chain of friendship which ought to connect you together, and which he wishes may continue like the sun always bright.

The great Spirit whom your father the President and the people of the United States adore, requires from men of every colour and language that they should live in peace and love each other. Nations which engage in war and forsake this path are sure to be hurt, though they should kill a great many of those they fight against, for war is a fire that burns the large trees as well as the small ones.

To avoid this terrible fire, good Chiefs and Wise men, whenever a dispute or difference happens between the people of their respective nations, will meet and try to have it settled in a peaceable manner; and rather than go to War will give up something to which they think they have a right.

By observing this line of moderation and strictly performing all its promises, a nation may avoid a War that might cost it more lives and property than the thing about which they quarrelled was worth.

Your father the President wishes, if any of you have differences to settle, to remember this rule; and recommends it to you, to hold fast the Chain of friendship, which now unites you in peace, and which he wishes never to see broken.

Brothers, you will now proceed to business.

Proceed to business they did, with Red Pole as principal orator. No transcript of his words was made, and we have only a memorandum of McHenry's to attest his genuine zeal for peace:

Red pole

Thinks their young men cannot be effectually restrained while they are obliged to go to a distance for their powder &c — The traders should be obliged to reside at the Indian vill[ages] so that the young men should have no excuse to go to a distance and that the chiefs might always know where they went.[14]

Red Pole and Blue Jacket, both signers for the Shawnees at the Treaty of Greenville, had been to the fore in everything up to this final conference on tribal relations, and it was in their portraits that Peale determined to perpetuate the story and its moral. He might have painted them for the museum gallery, but decided instead upon a series of wax sculptures illustrating the races of mankind, each life-size and each in characteristic native dress. There were ten in all — sachem and the war chief, a "Carib, or Native Indian of Guana — South America," a native of the "Oonalaska Island on the north west coast of America," natives of Kamtschatka, of the Sandwich Islands, of Otaheite, of the Gold Coast of Africa, a Chinese laborer, and a Chinese mandarin.[15] When the work was completed and announced in the papers of August 1797, the figure of Red Pole stood also as a monument to departed worth. On his return journey, camping on an island near Pittsburgh, Red Pole had contracted pneumonia and died. Dr. Nathaniel Bedfore, Pittsburgh's best physician, and two other doctors had been hurried to his side in vain.[16] At McHenry's order and as holder of an American chief's commission, he had been given a soldier's burial in old Trinity churchyard under a commemorative stone that still stands outside the present cathedral:[17]

MIO-QUA-COO-NA-CAW

OR

RED POLE

PRINCIPAL VILLAGE CHIEF OF THE

SHAWNEE NATION

DIED AT PITTSBURGH. 28th OF JANUARY

1797

LAMENTED BY THE UNITED STATES

Peale published the epitaph in his newspaper announcement of the figures, adding a tribute to Red Pole's "excellent speech at a Grand Conference held at the Museum in Philadelphia on the 2d of December 1796."[18] When George Washington, a private citizen once more, visited Philadelphia in the autumn of 1798, he was invited to see the sculptures at the museum. What he said or thought of the Indians is not recorded, although the Peales always remembered how, in passing the full-length painting of Raphaelle and Titian Peale, the trompe l'oeil portrait now at the Philadelphia Museum of Art (fig. 75), he had "bowed politely to the painted figures which he afterwards acknowledged he thought were living persons."[19]

As for the tribes who brought their own affairs into order there in the midst of Peale's scientific classification of nature, the newspaper reports name Creeks, Cherokees, Chickasaws, and Chocktaws in addition to those from the northwest. There had been treaties with the Creeks and Cherokees not long before, and a Creek delegation left for home at about the same time as Red Pole. It would seem, therefore, that the former British allies from the north were coming to new terms with the southern tribes. Peale's recollection of 1800 that they "had never before met but in the field of battle," may not be entirely accurate, as the newspaper report of their being simply "remarkably shy of each other" suggests.

Friction had developed among the signers to the Treaty of Greenville; and though this could hardly have entered into the conference at the museum, it does appear in the aftermath of the making of the portraits in wax. Wayne had explained the matter to McHenry when the Indians were leaving Detroit:

> Among whom is the famous Shawanoe Chief *Blue Jacket,* who, it is said had the Chief Command of the Indian Army on the 4th of November 1791 against Genl. St. Clair, *The Little Turtle* Miama Chief who also claims that honor, & who is his rival for fame & power — & said to be daily gaining ground with the Wabash Indians — refuses or declines to proceed in Company with *Blue Jacket:* he possessed the spirit of litigation to a high degree, possibly he may have been tampered with by some of the speculating land jobbers.[20]

Little Turtle was in Philadelphia in 1797 when the wax figures of Red Pole and the despised Blue Jacket first came to public view. The Turtle, who had presented a case for peace before Fallen Timbers, was still its advocate, and to keep him so he had been awarded a small pension. When, at this same time, McHenry brought him to Gilbert Stuart to have his portrait painted to hang in the War Office, there is a strong implication that the rivalry with Blue Jacket had something to do with it. The portrait of Little Turtle, destroyed by fire, is now known only through prints made from it (fig. 63)[21] and remembered, too, in an anecdote of the moment. Sittings to Stuart were always lively, and here there was a bantering Irishman with whom the Indian kept up a battle of wits as well as language differences allowed. The Turtle, however, sensed that he was receiving a kind of immortality as the picture matured, becoming silent and sedate. The Irishman claimed victory. When that idea reached him through the interpreter, Little Turtle struck back. "He mistakes, I was just thinking of proposing to this man to paint us both on one board and there I would stand face to face with him and blackguard him eternally."[22]

Also on the Philadelphia scene in 1797 there was another chief, once greatly feared but now interested in peaceful accommodation. This was Joseph Brant, Thayendanegea of the Mohawks, holder of a captain's commission in the British army, who had led the warriors of the Iroquois in a terrible raid and massacre during the Revolution. Afterward, he had been a leader in holding the northern tribes to British allegiance and in St. Clair's defeat, 1791. But now his power had been broken, and the Adams administration, threatened only by war with France, had no interest in him. He became nonetheless something of a social lion — entertained, rather curiously, at the dinner tables of American sympathizers with France. He met the French exiles and diplomats with whom Peale also associated — freedom-fighter Kosciuszko and the historian Comte de Volney — one with his passion for national liberties, the other seeking a common understanding for all mankind. Both had interviews with Brant and Little Turtle, their fame and that of the chiefs remembered together.[23] Volney was an admirer of the museum, and Peale would always treasure his words as he first came through its door. "This is the Temple of God! Here is nothing but Truth and Reason!"[24]

Not many persons could have seen Captain Brant as an advocate of peace, but at least he was living proof of Peale's belief that only education was needed to bring the red man to a level equal to that of the white. Brant, well read, widely traveled, thoroughly literate and urbane, could hold his own very well in any company of gentlemen. Romney's portrait of him, painted in England, stresses the soldier. Peale's for the museum gallery is characterized by gentleness and an upward, searching look apparently intended to symbolize the aspirations of his race (fig. 64).

Ten years later, the Louisiana Purchase and the return of the explorers Lewis and Clark had put a new edge on the American expansionist spirit; perhaps sensing this fact, Peale again slanted a museum exhibit toward peace and brotherhood. President Jefferson had made the museum a depository for some of that expedition's scientific materials, and the explorers themselves made gifts. Peale explained to the president, on January 29, 1808, what use he had made of one of them:

I completed a wax figure of Capt. Lewis and placed it in the Museum. My object in this work, is to give a lesson to the Indians who may visit the Museum, and also to show my sentiments respecting wars, the figure being dressed in an Indian dress presented to Capt. Lewis by Comeawait, Chief of Shoshone Nation [fig. 65], who was suspicious that Capt. Lewis meant to lead him into an ambuscade with his enemies. The figure has its right hand on its breast and the left holds the *Calmut* which was given me by Capt. Lewis. In a tablet I give the story in a few words, and then add, "This mantle, composed of 140 ermine skins, was put on Capt. Lewis by Comeawhait, their Chief. Lewis is supposed to say, 'Brother, I accept your dress. — It is the object of my heart to promote amongst you, our neighbors, peace and good will — that you may bury the hatchet deep in the ground never to be taken up again — and that henceforward you may smoke the *Calmut* of Peace and live in perpetual harmony, not only with each other, but with the white men, your brothers, who will teach you many useful arts.' Possessed of every comfort in life, what cause ought to involve us in war? Men are not too numerous for the lands we are to cultivate; and disease makes havoc enough amongst them without deliberately destroying each other — If any differences arise about lands or trade, let each party appoint judicious persons to meet together and amicably settle the disputed point." Such I believe to be the sentiments of our friend Lewis, and which he endeavored to instil in the minds of the various savages he met with in his long and hazardous tour. I am pleased when I can give an object which affords a moral sentiment to the Visitors to the Museum.[25]

A year later, General Harrison would conclude his treaty with the tribes who had met at Greenville — Shawnees excluded — a land grab of massive proportions that would precipitate new warfare and lead on to his triumph at Tippecanoe. Peale by that time had retired to his farm, and his son Rubens, more businessman than moralist, had taken over the museum with an emphasis on entertainment rather than instruction.

Captain Brant is still to be seen, alert and hopeful, in the portrait gallery at Independence National Historical Park, but Red Pole, Blue Jacket, and Lewis with his ermine mantle and pipe of peace have vanished. The Peale collections were scattered in the mid-nineteenth century, the wax figures apparently destroyed in one of the fires that wiped out the Barnum museum enterprises in New York and Philadelphia.

NOTES

This chapter was originally published in the *American Art Journal* 7 (1975): 10–18.

1. *Discourse Introductory to a Course of Lectures on the Science of Nature* (Philadelphia, 1800), pp. 39–40 (F:IID/3).

2. Benjamin B. Thatcher, *Indian Biography* (1932; rpt. New York, 1845), 2:257; Richard C. Knopf, ed., *Anthony Wayne, A Name in Arms: Soldier, Diplomat, Defender of Expansion Westward of a Nation; The Wayne-Knox-Pinckney-McHenry Correspondence* (Pittsburgh, Pa., 1960), p. 9.

3. *Ohio Archaeological and Historical Quarterly* 15 (1906): 444–45; Knopf, ed., *Wayne Correspondence*, pp. 295–96.

4. Knopf, ed., *Wayne Correspondence*, p. 390.

5. Ibid.

6. Ibid., pp. 390, 414.

7. *Claypoole's American Daily Advertiser* (Philadelphia), June 18, 1796.

8. Charles J. Kappler, ed., *Indian Treaties, 1778–1883* (1904; rpt. New York, 1972), pp. 44–45.

9. Bernard C. Steiner, *The Life and Correspondence of James McHenry, Secretary of War under Washington and Adams* (Cleveland, 1907), pp. 175–76, 261–62.

10. Knopf, *Wayne Correspondence,* p. 532.

11. Washington Papers, Library of Congress.

12. John C. Fitzpatrick, ed., *The Writings of George Washington* (Washington, D.C., 1931–44), 35:302.

13. Fitzpatrick, ed., *Writings of Washington,* 35:302n; list of Indian guests (Washington Papers, Library of Congress).

14. McHenry Papers, William L. Clements Library, University of Michigan, Ann Arbor.

15. *Claypoole's American Daily Advertiser,* August 12, 1797.

16. Stephen Quinon, "The Old Indian Burying Ground," *Western Pennsylvania Historical Magazine* 3 (1921): 207–09; C.W.W. Elkin, "Remarks on Some Old Cemeteries of the Pittsburgh Region," *Western Pennsylvania Historical Magazine* 38 (1965): 106.

17. Interment later moved to the chancel of Trinity Church (now Cathedral); *Pennsylvania Magazine of History and Biography* 4 (1880): 123.

18. *Claypoole's American Daily Advertiser,* August 12, 1797.

19. Rembrandt Peale, "Reminiscences," *The Crayon* 3 (1856): 100.

20. Knopf, ed., *Wayne Correspondence,* p. 532.

21. Thatcher, *Indian Biography* 2:269; Frederick W. Hodge, ed., *Handbook of American Indians North of Mexico* (Washington, D.C., 1912), 1:771, with illustration.

22. Calvin M. Young, *Little Turtle (Me-she-kin-no-qua). The Great Chief of the Miami Indian Nation* (Greencastle, Ohio, 1917), p. 147.

23. Ibid., pp. 145–47.

24. *Dunlap and Claypoole's American Daily Advertiser,* December 30, 1795.

25. Library of Congress: Jefferson Papers, in *Selected Papers* 2:1055–56.

9

Charles Willson Peale

The Portraitist as Divine

————◄◉►————

DAVID STEINBERG

IN the sixteenth century, the ancient idea that some poets possess
a special relationship to the divine was newly associated with artists as part of a widespread movement to improve their social status. This notion of the *divino artista* took the form of both legends of
artists destined to greatness from birth and tales of extraordinary assistance in specific acts of creation. Such conceptions of the artist under-
went a variety of transformations up to the nineteenth century, when
the modern notion of original genius in the arts was codified.[1]

During the mid-1780s in Philadelphia, Charles Willson Peale painted
an elaborate self-portrait composition that included his daughter Angelica Kauffman Peale and a portrait of his wife Rachel Brewer Peale,
now in the Bayou Bend collection of The Museum of Fine Arts in Houston
(fig. 71). The date of 1782–85 proposed by Charles Coleman Sellers implies a link between the uninscribed canvas and the opening in late 1782
of Peale's newly expanded picture gallery, "ornamented with the portraits of a great number of worthy Personages."[2] For Peale, the pros-
pect of increasing his professional status as well as his base of patronage
by having his own face appear among those worthies may have provided the specific impetus to create this uncommissioned work.[3]

The depicted attributes of palette, pencil (as the paintbrush was called
prior to the nineteenth century), and effigy of Rachel on the adjacent
easel identify Peale as a portraitist. Engaged in the act of painting, he
might be looking at the model herself. The disposition of primary and

cast shadows supports this suggestion. While the faces of father and daughter indicate a light source to the right of the picture, the lighting on Rachel's head from the opposite direction proposes the fiction that the model is to be found on the other side of the picture plane. Alluding to Rachel's presence but showing only her effigy, Peale portrayed himself painting her from life. To those aware of the relationship between the figures, the composition defines Peale as a devoted husband.

The representation of Angelica hinders a straightforward identification of her as the father's daughter. With raised left forearm and index finger making a conventional sign for the idea of heaven, she manifests a higher affiliation. The logic-defying configuration of her other hand complicates this divine linkage. On the picture plane, the tips of Angelica's right thumb and first finger align with the left and right edges of the artist's pencil, creating the impression that she but varies his act of holding. When considered in spatial terms, however, her first fingertip does not actually touch the handle; rather, it extends behind. For this finger to grip in conjunction with her thumb, her hand would have to supinate almost ninety degrees from its depicted position. The pencil end extended past her first finger forestalls a proposal that she grasps the handle from above. The deftly foreshortened hand at the pencil's center indicates that Peale painted unequivocal manual contact when he chose to. Alternatively, he presented Angelica's thumb and first finger so that they image an inexplicable contact.

The collaboration between Peale and Angelica relates the painting to images of supernatural aid to the artist in the moment of creation.[4] Jan Gossart's panel of ca. 1520 depicting an angel guiding Saint Luke's hand offers a lucid formulation of this conventional imagery in pictorial terms (fig. 100). In giving his daughter such a part in his picture, Peale continued the iconographic tradition that had developed around the Swiss-born painter Angelica Kauffmann (1741–95; fig. 101), whom he had known in London, and after whom he named his daughter.[5] In Rome, for example, the reference to the cosmopolitan artist as "the divine Angelica" alluded to her heavenly eponym. The alphabetically organized special exhibition catalogue for the Society of Artists in 1768, which included Peale as an exhibitor, effectually invoked Angelica as the muse of the show by listing her first and, uniquely, by Christian name alone.[6] At least nominally angelic, Angelica Kauffman Peale manifests some divine identity in the Houston canvas.[7]

Partly due to the greater status accorded to *logos* and to literary arts, pictures representing divine collaboration with writers are more common than those showing such assistance to artists.[8] For this reason, it is not surprising that Peale found a source for his composition in an allegorical portrait of an author, *Colley Cibber, Esq.* by Jean-Baptiste Van Loo, now known only from an engraving of 1758 by Edward Fisher (fig. 102).[9] As in the Houston canvas, creator and finger-raising child encounter the same tool. Having discerned Van Loo's allusion to divine inspiration, Peale adapted this imagery to his self-presentation as a painter. By rendering the contact between figure and pencil in nonrational terms, he emphasized the mysterious character of interaction with the divine.

A picture-in-a-picture, Rachel's effigy possesses a vivacity equivalent to the figures in the enveloping space. Although the canvas on the easel is tilted both laterally and longitudinally, Rachel's bust is not foreshortened. This spatial anomaly has its psychological equivalent in the direct eye contact the bust makes with the beholder. By this device, Peale compared the portrait bust to life itself. Such mythical creations as the animated clay figures of Prometheus anticipate the role that Peale established for the bust of Rachel in his painting.[10] This motif was a staple of Anglo-American poetry of the eighteenth century devoted to the painter's art;[11] among contemporary American paintings, the treatment of the theme in the Houston canvas appears to be unique.

In composing his picture of divine animation, Peale combined the pictorial type of supernatural collaboration with a type of double portrait composition that featured an artist next to a portrait of a female family member, usually his wife. Dirck Jacobsz's portrait of his parents exemplifies this tradition early in its history (fig. 103).[12] Using the device of equivalent vivacity, such paintings enabled artists to celebrate their illusionistic skills as well as to define their identity in terms of kinship ties. The magical conception of artistic creation to which these double portraits allude is essential to the meaning of the Houston canvas.

A verse from Peale's London notebook of 1767–69 attests to his early interest in divine collaboration:

> Such Beauty in every Feature
> And only the Effect of Nature
> Reason and sense in Such Perfection
> And not Borrow'd from Education
> How ye. Youths can ye. avoid the Tem[p]tation?
> Can there be a Nobler theme

Ugly to her is Fancy's Queen
Such Excellence by a Painters Pensil
They can ne'r attain, and to Excell
Unless some Divine Should Aid
Such Beauty has the Lovely Maid[13]

In this meandering panegyric, Peale sought to declare the beauty of a particular, unnamed woman. Challenging other youthful artists to create portraits which either match or surpass her appearance, Peale introduced the image of divine aid for the artist's pencil. Only with such intervention, so his apology for the limitations of the painter's art went, could one do justice to, or improve upon, her beauty.

One of the earliest known references to painting in Philadelphia demonstrates the conventional nature of the link between female beauty and divine assistance to the portraitist. The painter under discussion was the Swedish immigrant Gustavus Hesselius (1682–1755), father of John Hesselius (1728/29–78), who initiated Peale into the mysteries of the painter's art. In a letter of 1733, James Logan commented on his daughters' estimate of the limits of the elder Hesselius's work: "Our girles believing the Originals have but little from nature to recommend them, would scarce be willing to have that little (if any) ill treated by a Pencil the Graces never favour'd."[14] For Logan, the influence of the sister goddesses of antiquity who dispense charm and beauty is conspicuous in its absence.

In contrast to this gentleman's confident use of the classical allusion, the practicing artist at the outset of his career does not appear to have been so sure how one depicted beauty. Peale only ventured to refer to a successful painting of the object of his attentions as a hypothetical proposal. Even if such a portrait were to be created, he did not address the questions of which divine was "some Divine," why it would offer aid, or how it would manifest itself.

In 1772, Peale confessed his lack of mastery in such areas of speculation: "A good painter of either portrait or History, must . . . account for every beauty, must know the original cause of beauty — in all he sees — these are some of the requisites of a good painter, these are more than I shall ever have time or opportunity to < Study > know."[15] The impulse to cross out "Study" and replace it with "know" suggests that he believed that the comprehension of beauty lay beyond booklearning. Although Peale may have heard of such works of English aesthetics as Francis Hutcheson's *An Enquiry into the Original of Our Ideas of Beauty and Virtue* (1725) and Daniel Webb's *An Inquiry into the Beauties of Painting* (1760), he

did not seem to believe that, even if he were familiar with their arguments, they could bring him any closer to understanding the issues surrounding the perception and creation of beauty. The association of
beauty and divinity has long been a central tenet of Western aesthetics,
yet Peale's first versified evocation of divine efficacy stands isolated from
a developed intellectual context.

The mystery of depicting beauty was not the only problem of the
portraitist that Peale considered in terms of divine collaboration. In a
poem written less than two years after he returned from London, he
turned his attention to the remarkable phenomenon of portraits appearing to convey the feelings of their sitters. Bearing the title "On a Picture of Mrs. Peale, Drawn by her Husband, August 1770," the poem
was published anonymously in the *Maryland Gazette* for April 18, 1771.[16]
At the time, *Mrs. Peale* was probably on view in the painter's room in
Annapolis.[17]

> WHEN PEALE his lovely ARRIA drew,
> Like *Rubens* erst by love impell'd,
> Nature, to Love and Genius true,
> Herself the glowing Pencil held.
> Yes! plastic Nature could alone,
> These warm and Speaking Features give,
> Or else she taught her genuine Son,
> To bid the breathing Canvas live.
> The Rose & Lilly's mingled Dye,
> And ev'ry mere external Charm,
> A While may please the vacant Eye,
> But can no feeling Bosom warm.
> Give ME, depictur'd warm from Life,
> Each soft Emotion of the Mind,
> Give me the MOTHER and the WIFE
> As here in beauteous ARRIA join'd.

Some two weeks prior to this publication, Peale included the poem
in a letter to John Beale Bordley. His casual report, "These lines was
found pin'd to Rachels portrait," leaves the matter of authorship un-
resolved; yet the question preceding his cordial close, "Who do you sus-
pect to be the auther?" has the ring of feigned naiveté and implies that
Bordley did not need to look very far for an answer.[18]

Peale's fictional poet-viewer conjoins the *topoi* of divine collaboration
and animation, attributing the creation of the "breathing" *Mrs. Peale* to
the plastic Nature of the artist. According to the division of divine labor

posited by English Neoplatonists of the seventeenth century, God does not guide each earthly action. Rather, at the Creation, He instituted under Him an operative force to execute "that Part of his Providence which consists in the Regular and Orderly Motion of Matter." As envisioned by the third earl of Shaftesbury (1671–1713), plastic Nature is an animating and inspiring power immanent in man.[19] Well suited to the varieties of deist thought, this concept naturalized some aspects of the divine, and posited a quasi-divine Nature.[20] In his personification of plastic Nature, the implicitly male poet-viewer of the *Maryland Gazette* figured a female who influenced Peale's creation by either holding his pencil or teaching him. With an indeterminacy befitting the description of a divine force at work, the poem juxtaposes ordinary acts without resolving which of them was the real means of interaction.

While the poet-viewer presented the imagery of divine collaboration in contemporary terms, the context in which he set the living painting motif clarifies its identity as a rhetorical device. Plastic Nature effected a network of feeling that extended from the emotion-filled artist to the beholder, who experienced a variant of the artist's emotions. *Mrs. Peale* seemed to be a "breathing Canvas" to the poet-viewer because of its power to engage him. Transferring the aura of mystery from a portrait that moves to a portrait that moves its beholder, he reformulated the ancient *topos* in terms of the power of sympathy, a popular arena for speculation in the eighteenth century.[21]

The similar words "lovely" and "love" in the opening lines of the poem bridge the concern with beauty presented in the London notebook poem and the interest in affect demonstrated by the poet-viewer. In *De Arte Graphica*, with which Peale was familiar, Charles Alphonse Dufresnoy referred to beauty's capacity to inspire emotion in terms of its influence on the practicing artist:

> When first the orient rays of beauty move
> The conscious soul, they light the lamp of love,
> Love wakes those warm desires that prompt our chace,
> To follow and to fix each flying grace.[22]

This sequence, which culminates in the artist's desire to represent the object of his perception and affection, may be considered a prelude to the scenario set forth by the poet-viewer.

The concept of earthly love occasioning divine intervention in the creation of art has a sacred antecedent in legends that Saint Luke's piety determined his receipt of heavenly guidance for his painting of the *Virgin and Child.* [23] According to the *Maryland Gazette,* plastic Nature came to the aid of a loving artist, just as she had assisted Rubens one and a half centuries earlier when he had painted his wives. [24] Earlier writers had also posited a correlation between a portraitist's feelings and the engagement of the divine in his work. In *The Painting of the Ancients,* Franciscus Junius elaborated a tale that he had read in Pliny the Elder that exemplifies this theme:

> As for the particular nature of the Artificers, it hath ever been so, that the livelinesse of great spirits cannot containe it selfe within the compasse of an ordinary practice, but it will alwayes issue forth, whilest every one doth most readily expresse in his workes the inward motions of his most forward mind: so doe we also finde that the bravest Artists have spent their labour most prosperously about such things as they did much delight in by a violent driving of their passion, or else by a quiet guiding of their Nature. *Pansias,* being exceedingly in love with his countrey-woman *Glycera,* left a most famous Picture, knowne every where by the name of *Stephanopleces,* that is, a woman Garland-maker; and this hath ever been esteemed his best worke, because hee was enforced thereunto by the extremitie of his Passion. [25]

Referring to artists as "great spirits" and to "a quiet guiding of their Nature," Junius represented the process whereby Pansias's love influenced his painting in terms that resemble the religio-physiological force plastic Nature. His own compelling account enabled Junius, who never saw the *Stephanopleces,* to assert that it was Pansias's best work. Beginning with a similar notion of successful portrait creation, the poet-viewer of the *Maryland Gazette* went on to define the quality of *Mrs. Peale.*

In the consideration of superficial portraiture which fails to move, the synecdochic "feeling Bosom" of line twelve represents an ideal beholder of portraits. The poet-viewer introduces his voice for the first time in the following line ("Give ME . . .), suggesting both his identification with this empathic approach to pictorial experience and distance from the insensibility demonstrated by "the vacant Eye." Moved by his successful encounter with *Mrs. Peale,* he declares his appetite to see a range of emotion represented ("Give ME, depictur'd warm from Life / Each soft Emotion of the Mind"). This multivalent passage also suggests his desire for the painting to affect him ("Give ME . . . / Each soft Emotion of the Mind"). [26]

Peale's invention of a fictional poet-viewer not only provided a means

for him to puff his work anonymously; the voice of the author also offered visitors to his painting room and readers of the *Maryland Gazette*
an exemplar of viewership. Pairing poem and painting, Peale sought
to cultivate an audience that would engage in an emotive relationship
with his portraits and would judge art by its capacity to move them.[27]
The painter was well aware of the high value that European art theory
placed upon the movement of the passions in the experience of art. While
this was commonly understood to be the goal of history painting, the
highest ranked genre, Peale applied this standard to his own art of portraiture. In this regard, *Mrs. Peale* anticipated the public function of
Rachel Weeping (fig. 30), which set forth the effigy of Rachel as an exem-
plary mourner, and had its own poem published on it at the time of
the gallery opening in 1782.[28]

Peale complemented his interest in reception with an attempt to understand his own act of creation. Toward this end, he thought in terms
of both the occasional and the durational forms of the *divino artista* legend.
Plastic Nature is "to Love and Genius true." Love is the condition which
prompted her engagement; genius provided the medium through which
she acted. As Peale stated in his autobiography, "It has been said, and
generally is an adopted opinion that Genius for the fine arts, is a particular gift, and not an acquirement. That Poets, Painters &c are born
such."[29] Although he attributed this belief to third parties and a general
climate of opinion, he does not contradict the received wisdom to which
he refers.[30] The reference to gifts that the genius received at birth thus
accords with the conception of the *divino artista* as one born with remarkable powers, although the fatalistic notion of predestination to greatness is absent from Peale's definition.

On balance, the artist's genius is just as important to the poem's account of the successful creation of Mrs. Peale's portrait as the collaboration with plastic Nature. By definition, plastic Nature is immanent in
all creatures; yet, according to the poem, only an individual's genius
lets her express herself fully. Peale's genius thus distinguished his production from the works of artists who, although they might paint loved
ones, were not endowed with comparable gifts.

The Houston painting lends itself to explication according to the *Maryland Gazette* poem. According to this text, Angelica may personify plastic Nature. While the poem does not personify genius, its identification
of Peale with that divine gift raises the possibility that in his painting,
he intended Angelica to be an allegorical representation of Genius. In

either case, the painting portrays Peale as a divine artist. His creation of an effigy that is virtually alive becomes evidence of his successful emulation of the Creator.

The Houston painting's dual status as a pictorial experience in its own right and as an exposition of ideas about the creation of affective portraiture complicates its interpretation. For example, while the bust of Rachel may demonstrate the role of emotion in the conception and reception of a portrait, the other two portraits offer themselves for consideration in the same terms. This situation challenges the viewer to gauge his or her own emotional response to the figures of Peale and Angelica, raising questions about Peale's feelings for himself and his daughter, as well as about the role of plastic Nature in the creation of these effigies. A similar complication arises in terms of the viewer's definition of his or her own role in relation to the canvas. When looking at the bust of Rachel, he or she may identify with the feelings of the poet-viewer when he beheld *Mrs. Peale,* and thereby recreate some form of Peale's experience of love when he beheld his wife. Yet if, as suggested earlier, the figure of the artist has been depicted looking at Rachel, then the Houston canvas continually evokes her presence on the viewer's side of the picture plane, and invites an identification with Rachel.

No mention of the Houston canvas appears in Peale's papers or museum catalogues.[31] Although it is a highly personal picture, representing ideas that he had considered for over a decade, it is difficult to imagine that he did not bother to exhibit this ambitious representation of the means and ends of success in portraiture. Some of his contemporaries may have found its subject matter obscure. Perhaps the depiction of Angelica's relationship to her father's pencil was misunderstood as an example of bad painting. Most important, however, the presentation of the portraitist as divine had the potential to be perceived as politically incorrect, for Philadelphia in the 1780s presented a climate of reception in which some men asserted with great fervor that "all men are created equal."

NOTES

I would like to thank Alexander Nemerov for sharing his ideas about the interpretation of pictorial conventions.

1. Ernst Kris and Otto Kurz, *Legend, Myth, and Magic in the Image of the Artist,* trans. Alastair Laing and Lottie M. Newman (New Haven, Conn., and London,

1979; originally published as *Die Legende vom Kuensteer: Ein historischer Versuch*, Vienna, 1934). See the chapter *"Deux artifex—divino artista."* Ideas about the divinely inspired artist arose after the Quattrocento, according to Martin Kemp, "From "Mimesis" to "Fantasia": The Quattrocento vocabulary of creation, inspiration and genius in the visual arts," *Viator* 8 (1977): 347–98.

2. *P&M*, p. 159; *Pennsylvania Packet*, November 14, 1782, in *Selected Papers* 1:373. A date as late as ca. 1788, based upon an estimate of the age of Angelica (b. 1775), has been proposed by David B. Warren, *Bayou Bend: American Furniture, Paintings and Silver from the Bayou Bend Collection* (Houston, Texas, 1975), p. 139.

3. Although it is likely that *The Peale Family* (fig. 28) was on view in the new gallery, that painting does not depict Peale's face.

4. In this regard, see David Warren's observation that "Angelica, who painted well as a little girl, reaches like a playful muse to guide her father's brush" (*Bayou Bend*, p. 139).

5. Peale recounted his memories of Angelica Kauffmann in his autobiography. The relevant passage is reprinted in *CWP*, p. 64.

6. Abbé Peter Grant to John Morgan, August 31, 1765, quoted in Arthur S. Marks, "Angelica Kauffmann and Some Americans on the Grand Tour," *American Art Journal* 12 (Spring 1980): 23; *A Catalogue of the Pictures, Sculptures, Designs in Architecture, Models, Drawings, Prints &c. which the Society of Artists of Great-Britain have the honour to exhibit to his Majesty the King of Denmark at their room in Spring-Garden*, September 30, 1768, p. 3. In this regard, see also Benjamin West's portrait drawing of Angelica whose mask on a chain signifies Imitation and presents her as an allegorical figure of Painting (fig. 101).

7. Angelica's status as both a youth and a female made her a favorite object of her father's interest in allegory. In the reception that he planned for Washington at Grey's Ferry in 1789, Peale built a triumphal arch and cast his daughter as a figure of Victory: "As Washington passed under [the arch], Mr. Peale's daughter Angelica an exceedingly beautiful girl in her fourteenth year—who was placed in the centre—was to crown the Hero with a wreath of laurel" (Titian R. Peale, MS biography, P-S, p. 133).

8. The *locus classicus* is Caravaggio's *St. Matthew Composing His Gospel* (1602, destroyed, formerly Kaiser-Friedrich-Museum, Berlin).

9. In the modern literature, the status of Cibber's daughter as his Muse was noted in Edgar Wind, "The Sources of David's *Horaces*," *Journal of the Warburg and Courtauld Institutes* 4 (1941): 137. This composition is often cited as the prototype for Hogarth's *David Garrick and his Wife* (1757, Windson Castle), but a source that comes closer to capturing the irony of the interaction between writer and Muselike figure is Philippe Mercier, *The Letter Writer* (probably 1740s, Iveagh Bequest, Marble Hill, Twickenham) reproduced in E. M. Johnson, *Francis Cotes* (London, 1976), fig. 87. In addition to providing Peale with a model, the Fisher engraving may also have given George de Marees the idea to cast his daughter as a personification of Painting in *The Artist with his Daughter Maria Antonia* (1760, Alte Pinakothek, Munich), reproduced in Ludwig Goldscheider, *Five Hundred Self-Portraits* (Vienna and London, 1937).

10. Prometheus is discussed in "The Envy of the Gods," Kris and Kurz, *Legend*.

11. The American literary expression of this commonplace may be considered to begin with George Berkeley's "America or the Muse's Refuge, A Prophecy," of 1725/26, which recalls the era in Europe "When heavenly flame did animate her clay." The theme continues in "To Mr. Smibert on the sight of his Pictures," of 1730, which refers to portraits as "Crowds of new Beings [who] lift their dawning Heads." Both are reprinted in Henry Wilder Foote, *John Smibert, Painter* (Cambridge, Mass., 1950), pp. 30, 54–55. "EXTEMPORE: On seeing Mr. WOLLASTON'S Pictures in Annapolis," published in the *Maryland Gazette* of 1753, exhorts the reader to "Behold the won'drous Power of Art! / That . . . makes the lifeless Canvas Breathe." (rpt. in Wayne Craven, *Colonial American Portraiture* [Cambridge, Mass., 1987], p. 371). "Upon seeing the Portrait of Miss **** by Mr. West" of 1758 declares of West's painting, "Both Guido's judgement and skill confess / Informing canvas with a living soul" (in *American Magazine and Monthly Chronicle for the British Colonies* 1, no. 5 [February 1758]: 237–38).

12. For examples in the English tradition, see *Thomas Beach and His Sister Frances* (1770, Capt. J.H.P. Brain), reproduced in Elise S. Beach, *Thomas Beach: A Dorset Portrait Painter* (London, 1934), facing p. 32; and *Benjamin West and his Wife* (1806, Pennsylvania Academy of the Fine Arts). Because Peale could not have seen either of these pictures, both having been painted after he left England, with the West painted later than the Houston canvas, it seems likely that Peale knew some similar prototype.

13. Memorandum book, P-S, in *Selected Papers* 1:53, 56. Presumably, the second person "ye. youths" of line 5 reappears as the third-person "they" in line 9.

14. James Logan to William Logan, May 31, 1733, in Frederick B. Tolles, "A Contemporary Comment on Gustavus Hesselius," *Art Quarterly* 17, no. 3 (Autumn 1954): 271.

15. Charles Willson Peale to John Beale Bordley, November 1772, P-S, in *Selected Papers* 1:127.

16. The headnote and epigraph preceding the poem are reprinted in *CWP*, p. 93.

17. The title of the poem yields a working title for the unlocated painting (*Mrs. Peale*) and also identifies its subject matter (Mrs. Peale). Because of this overt pairing of poem and painting, Charles Coleman Sellers associated *Mrs. Peale* with the early work that Peale described in a letter of August 23, 1823, to his son Rembrandt as "my picture . . . of your mother looking on her naked child who sleeps, a picture I painted about 1772, which was much admired and handsome verses wrote on it" (P-S, F:IIA/69B4–5). This remembrance was prompted by his copying the work into his *Staircase Self-portrait* (unlocated, 1823). Sellers also linked these references with the painting that Peale copied in 1771 for Edmund Jenings: a "piece of Mrs. Peale and Child . . . an attempt of a Tender Sentiment" (see *P&M*, pp. 162–64). Peale to Edmund Jenings, April 20, 1771, in *Selected Papers* 1:96–97.

The analysis of *Mrs. Peale* presented in this essay refers only to the effigy of Rachel; despite the poem's reference to two roles ("the MOTHER and the WIFE"), it mentions no pictorial content other than Peale's "lovely ARRIA." The possibility should be raised that *Mrs. Peale* and Rachel "looking on her naked child who sleeps" were two different pictures, and that the former, like the bust in the Houston canvas, depicted Rachel alone. Perhaps the verses that Peale referred to in 1823 for the mother and child picture are now lost, or at a distance of some fifty years, he mistakenly associated the *Maryland Gazette* poem with his mother and child picture. In this context, it should be noted that Charles Coleman Sellers later revised his belief that the *Maryland Gazette* poem, the original of the picture in the *Staircase Self-portrait,* and Jenings's copy were all connected with a single painting. Instead, he referred to two mother and child pictures: the earlier was the subject of the *Maryland Gazette* poem and copied for Jenings; the later was the painting copied into the *Staircase Self-portrait.* He also associated this second painting with a *Maryland Gazette* poem of 1773 (see *CWP,* pp. 92–93, 105–06). For the poem of 1773, see note 27.

18. April 5, 1771, P-S, in *Selected Papers* 1:93.

19. Ralph Cudworth, *True Intellectual System,* quoted in Ernst Cassirer, *The Platonic Renaissance in England,* trans. James P. Pettegrove (New York, 1953), p. 140. For Shaftesbury's attribution of creativity to plastic Nature, see ibid., p. 166.

20. Bassanio's speech from *The Merchant of Venice,* which served as the epigraph for the *Maryland Gazette* poem, similarly confounds a distinction between mortal and divine accomplishment. Upon seeing Portia's portrait, he exclaims: "What find I here? Fair Portia's counterfeit! What demi-god hath come so near creation?" In the *Maryland Gazette,* "Arria" was substituted for "Portia."

21. James Engell, *The Creative Imagination, Enlightenment to Romanticism* (Cambridge, Mass., and London, 1981).

22. *The Art of Painting,* trans. William Mason (York, England, 1783; rpt. New York, 1969), p. 6. Peale was familiar with the Wills translation of 1754.

23. Ernst von Dobschuetz, *Christusbilder, Untersuchungen zur christlichen Legende* (Leipzig, 1899), p. 278.

24. For the fame of Rubens's portrait of his second wife Helena Fourment (Gulbenkian Collection, Lisbon) in mid-eighteenth-century Britain, see Aileen Ribeiro, *The Dress Worn at Masquerades in England, 1730 to 1790, and Its Relation to Fancy Dress in Portraiture* (New York, 1984), pp. 144–57.

25. *The Painting of the Ancients, in three Bookes . . .* (London, 1638; rpt. Westmead, England, 1972), pp. 48–49. Pansias is mentioned in both Lib. 21, Cap. 3 and Lib. 35, Cap. 40 of Pliny the Elder's *Natural History.*

26. The relationship between viewing portraits and experiencing emotion is explored in E. H. Gombrich, "The Mask and the Face: the perception of physiognomic likeness in life and in art," in *Art, Perception, and Reality* (Baltimore and London, 1972), pp. 1–46, esp. 35ff.

27. The dedication of the *Maryland Gazette* poem of July 8, 1773, "*To Mr. CHARLES PEALE, on his exquisite and celebrated picture of beauty, addressing itself to insensibility,*" suggests that some members of his public perceived the intent of Peale's pictorial and poetic efforts at education.

28. In "A Death in the Family," *Bulletin, Philadelphia Museum of Art* 78, no. 335 (Spring 1982): 3–13, Phoebe Lloyd discusses the importance of showmanship in Peale's conception and exhibition of *Rachel Weeping.*

29. A(TS): 37.

30. "Now there are proofs of men, that show an equal readiness to acquire knowledge in whatever may be thought difficult. Perhaps their minds may be compared to a fine soil, in which everything will grow that is sown therein. But remember,

cultivation is *absolutely necessary*" (ibid). The subsequent discussion of the training of St. George Peale, which is the dramatic focus of *The Peale Family,* elides the notion that different people, like soils, have different capacities. Sellers misinterprets this passage in his assertion that "Peale . . . differed from the world's opinion in believing art to be more a matter of understanding and practice than of innate qualities of mind" (*P&M,* p. 9). Rather, Peale believed that both were necessary.

31. The provenance of the Houston canvas is incomplete. It is thought to have been bought in the 1854 museum gallery sale by Angelica's grandson George Rowan Robinson, but it does not appear in the sales catalogue (see *P&M,* p. 159).

10

Charles Willson Peale as History Painter

The Exhumation of the Mastodon

———————◆———————

LILLIAN B. MILLER

B
ETWEEN 1806 and 1808, Charles Willson Peale painted his first history painting, *The Exhumation of the Mastodon* (fig. 66). In many ways a summary of Peale's various interests in the art and science of his day, the work captures accurately, colorfully, and certainly humanly, the intellectual and cultural environment that influenced Peale's development as a painter, naturalist, and museum entrepreneur. Until recently, the painting has been regarded as either "an amusing record of the Museum" or an example of "the amplification of American self-portraiture . . . [merging] with . . . genre painting." Even when it has been recognized as a history painting, its meaning has been relegated to autobiography, its two subjects — the "digging" and "the tangible reality of the large family group" — becoming "complementary expressions of Peale's self-conception."[1]

Although accurate as far as they go, these interpretations seem to me to miss the full meaning of the painting and, therefore, its significance for Peale and American art history. From its initial conception in 1804 when Peale first mentioned the maturing of his "design," his intention was to paint "a large historical, emblematical Picture," in which the portraits of his children would be introduced.[2] Two years later, when he "resumed" his painting, he was convinced that it was "by much the most important work that [he had] done."[3] Through the fall of 1806 and winter of 1807, the painting completely obsessed him. From morning to night he worked at his easel, though it was difficult to paint by lamplight. News of the work's progress filled his correspondence with family members and friends, until in triumph he could proclaim in 1808, "[I have] never painted with so much ease, nor have I ever in my best time equaled some of these pieces."[4] His success proved, he insisted, that age did not necessarily impair an artist's skill: "It is not the bodily but the mental powers which is most important to constitute the Painter."[5]

Peale's concern with his age and his long absence from "the Pallet" is understandable. He was sixty-five years old in 1806 and had devoted almost his entire painting career to portraiture. How could an artist thus trained manage the architectonics required to create a history painting in the grand style? He himself questioned whether this was not a foolhardy attempt, and when he began his labors, he cushioned himself against disappointment by calling his plan merely "a tryal."[6]

Peale's desire to do a history painting reflected not only the high premium placed on that kind of work by eighteenth-century artists and connoisseurs, but also the hold that history painting had on the American artist's imagination. Like Copley, Trumbull, and the many American students of art who maintained a steady pilgrimage to West's studio during the late eighteenth and early nineteenth centuries, Peale, too, fell under the spell of neoclassical aesthetics, the rules of which were later to be so firmly laid down by Sir Joshua Reynolds in his *Discourses on Art* (1769–91).[7] As a neophyte in West's studio in 1767–69, Peale had quickly learned that ideal works with a historical theme or subject represented the highest artistic expression, while portrait painting, the study of which constituted his initial purpose in coming to London, seemed to be a lower and more limited artistic pursuit. If, as a result of prevailing conditions in America, Peale had been unable to fulfill his hopes up to now, he never lost sight of his earlier aspirations.[8] Certainly, the experiences of studying West's "elegant" historical paintings or watching the master depart for the queen's palace with his much admired neoclassical painting *Agrippina Landing at Brundisium* (1768, Yale University Art Gallery) tucked under his arm must have impressed upon him the value of such works.[9] And when in 1785, West sent him a drawing of *Agrippina and Her Children in the Roman Camp* (fig. 67), perhaps in acknowledgment of Peale's help in providing him with descriptions and sketches of uniforms, Indian clothing, and scenery for his projected American Revolution series, Peale was even more forcibly reminded of that earlier occasion in West's studio and of the painting's meaning for West's career, for the *Agrippina* had launched West on his successful course as court painter to George III. Continuing correspondence with West and constant reminders of West's success as a history painter increased his sense of frustration at being unable to carry on such a work in America. In 1793, for example, he wrote to West that the absence of a market for "good works with the pencil" made him "loose all [his] relish for painting."[10] Differentiating between ideal works and portrait painting — commissions for which he seems to have had in plenty — he was also, of course, apologizing to his master for his lack of significant artistic achievement. Therefore, when in 1806 — forty years after his initial exposure to neoclassical aesthetic theory — Peale saw the opportunity to fulfill his aspirations, he seized upon it with enthusiasm. The time was propitious and his theme clear, and as an artist, he believed that he was technically prepared to embark on the much longed for artistic adventure.

The story of *The Exhumation of the Mastodon* begins in 1801, on the morning when Peale climbed onto the diligence stage in Philadelphia and headed for New York City. accompanied by his twenty-three-year-old son Rembrandt, already a professional portraitist; a young professor of chemistry at the University of Pennsylvania, Dr. James Woodhouse; and museum aide Jotham Fenton, a skilled naturalist who helped Peale in preserving and stuffing his animal skins for exhibition in the museum. It was, Peale wrote in his diary, a pleasant journey to New York.[11] Arriving on July 30, the group rested for a day and the following morning took passage on the "fast sailing and very comfortable" sloop *President Jefferson* — an aptly symbolic name, given Jefferson's scientific enthusiasms and personal support of the expedition's aims. The sloop was headed up the Hudson River to Newburgh, and although it rained and the berths were hard, making sleep almost impossible, the members of the small party maintained their exuberance. Both Charles Willson Peale and Rembrandt were so impressed by the scenery that they made watercolor sketches of the landscape along the Hudson (American Philosophical Society).[12] This was Peale's second visit to the town, but the most important, for on this trip he was to take up "from a Morass the Mammoth bones," a discovery which as late as 1852 remained unsurpassed in the "intense interest" it excited.[13]

To understand the significance of Peale's effort, we must see it in the context of eighteenth-century paleontology or geology. The eighteenth-century scientist believed that God had created the universe in a great spasm of primordial energy, a supreme act of creation as described in Genesis. Since the world was created by God, the original act was perfect; in turn, the perfection of the world and of nature revealed God's existence. Lines which Peale excerpted from Fettiplace Beller's *Injured Innocence,* a poetic drama of 1732, and which he placed over the south door of his museum, give us a good summary of the major beliefs of his scientific circle:

> The book of Nature open —
> — Explore the wond'rous work
> A solemn Institute of laws eternal
> Whose unaltered page no time can change,
> No copier can corrupt.[14]

Two words sum up eighteenth-century cosmology: *eternal* and *unaltered.* From this belief in the world's perfection followed other corollaries: that the earth, for instance, was always the same, from its first creation to the present; that it was stable and eternally durable; that it was full — that is, complete — containing within it all the variety and ingenuity of creation, from the microscopic to the large, in a great chain of being that was orderly, observable, and indestructible. Peale frequently enjoyed quoting from James Thomson's *The Seasons* (London, 1726–30):

> How wond'rous is this scene! where all is form'd
> With number, weight, and measure! all designed
> For some great end . . . each moss
> Each shell, each crawling insect, holds a rank
> Important in the plan of him who form'd
> This scale of beings: holds a rank which lost
> Would break the chain and leave behind a gap
> Which nature's self would rue.[15]

Since the concept of an orderly chain of being was accepted as a matter of faith, the task facing the eighteenth-century scientist was to search for "missing links." There were, as Peale wrote in his museum catalogue, "some chasms in this connecting chain."[16] These were the undiscovered, unexplored parts of nature. The fact that they had not been found did not mean that they did not exist. Rather, most eighteenth-century scholars believed that the entire chain still survived. No species of animal had become or could become extinct. As Jefferson wrote in his *Memoir on the Discovery of Certain Bones:* "If one link in nature's chain might be lost, another and another might be lost, till this whole system of things should evanish by piecemeal." Therefore, in the "economy of nature" nothing ever disappeared; nature, said Jefferson, never "permitted any one race of her animals to become extinct"; nature never "formed any link in her great work so weak as to be broken."[17]

By 1801, when Peale began to dig for mastodon bones, this belief was already being challenged by such French zoologists and naturalists as J.B.A.P. Monet de Lamarck and Étienne Geoffroy Saint-Hilaire, and in Philadelphia by the young Dr. Benjamin Smith Barton, who questioned whether species were constant, permanent, and unchanging, and whether there was a chain of nature or absolute dependence of one species on another.[18] Nevertheless, despite the challenges, the belief in the interdependence of species underlay the excitement over the discovery of the mammoth bones, for the mammoth was viewed as another link in the chain, and it was thought that knowledge about this huge animal must eventually add to the understanding of God's great plan of creation.

Peale's wonderful find and his mounted skeleton also became important in determining the outcome of the argument as to whether or not the American *incognitum* was a species of elephant or a totally different species. If an elephant, how could one explain its northern habitat? If an unknown species, then was it still alive and creating havoc somewhere in the western or northern wilderness? If extinct, then man's belief in the "economy of nature" and God's great plan for the universe had to be reordered, for how could God create a species unable to survive? As Peale wrote in his autobiography many years later in describing his efforts at piecing together the bones of this huge skeleton, "By perseverance he [Peale] hoped to accomplish an object which would enlighten the whole world with the knowledge of what kind of animal the mammoth, so called, could be."[19]

Although the long-range scientific results of Peale's discovery were to be the most important, there were also some immediate consequences of significance for the time. The mammoth was considered an American species, "an Antique Wonder of North America," as Peale called it in an advertising broadside, or the "American Miracle," as it was reported in the *Times* of Charleston, South Carolina, on March 5, 1802. As such, it was associated with the history of the land and its ancient Indian legends as told by an imaginary Indian in Peale's fanciful words:

TEN THOUSAND MOONS AGO, when nought but gloomy forests covered this land of the sleeping Sun, long before the pale men, with thunder and fire at their command, rushed on the wings of the wind to ruin this garden of nature . . . a race of animals were in being, huge as the frowning Precipice, cruel as the bloody Panther, swift as the descending Eagle, and terrible as the Angel of the Night.[20]

As an American species, the mammoth proved that life in America did not degenerate, as the French naturalist the Comte de Buffon claimed. In his *Notes on Virginia* (1787), Jefferson had actively discredited Buffon's theory, and Peale also dismissed it as "ridiculous." Now, however, their rejection of the French scientist's ideas was confirmed by the discovery of the gigantic bones.[21] A matter of national pride, the mastodon also suggested the great western wilderness that constituted the American landscape at the beginning of the nineteenth century. Two decades hence, that wilderness would become a positive cultural value, the theme of artists and writers who, seeking an American past in which they could root their art, found it not in the ruins of civilization as in Europe, but in the promise of future prosperity embodied in the pristine forests and unsettled plains of the American West.

Given, then, the widespread acceptance of these ideas, it is understandable why the discovery of mastodon bones would arouse such great excitement. It is also clear why, for a man such as Peale, engaged in developing the first important scientific museum in the United States and anxious to make it successful both as a repository of scientific information as well as a public educational institution, the recapturing of these bones from the muck of time (so to speak) and reconstructing them into a skeleton as true to life as possible, were such important and historically significant events that the scene could become the subject of a history painting.

Why a history painting? Why didn't Peale conceive of his painting simply as a genre scene that told an interesting story and described an unusual discovery? The answer, I believe, is that Peale did not regard this as merely an interesting story. In his mind, it was a heroic drama, full of struggle and travail, replete with both human and cosmic significance and containing within it those elements of awesomeness and fear that defined the sublime — an essential ingredient of eighteenth-century history painting. "The subject," he wrote to his daughter Angelica, was "grand, nay awful," made so "by the appearance of tremendous gust coming on." The "gust" was the threat of an impending thunderstorm which, if it had occurred, would have reduced, literally, all his efforts to mud. Peale was well aware of the sublime nature of storms. Earlier, on his way to Newburgh, he and his fellow travelers experienced a "gust" at Dunderberg that "astonished" them "with the sublimity of the scene." Twenty years later in his autobiography, he recorded how Rembrandt had exclaimed, "how awfully grand!"[22]

In the autobiography, Peale described the actual exhumation of the bones in similarly epic terms, noting the long and frustrating — often "hopeless" — labor involved not only "to keep the morass, that is the marle from overwhelming them," but to maintain the battle against the elements. As in all great epic tales, there was a moment of surcease from "their fatigues" when the party climbed "a steep mountain . . . from the top of [which] they could see all the country below, which appeared like a fine garden."[23] But then the battle resumed, as Peale approached a new morass:

> The aspect was the grandest he had ever seen. It was a clear and bright sunny day. the contrast the greater when near the morass of an immense size; of many miles extant, it was covered with lofty trees, whose tops obscured the sun from the bodies and limbs below, and caused a solemn darkness beneath, the eye could not penetrate the depth of extent; it was dark and solemn to the utmost extent of the word, the whole surface of the morass was covered with bodies of large trees, the limbs of which had moldered into the soil, it seemed by the magnitude of the trees fallen, as well as of those standing to be in this state for thousands of years."[24]

It was in these labors and the tedious work that followed in assembling the bones, many of which were broken or decayed, that Peale found the meaning of his painting: courage in the face of overwhelming odds, perseverance in a task with a socially useful purpose, and a concern for what he called posterity, the future generations who would benefit from the enlightenment his work would bring. To Peale, this was a theme that equaled the great themes of classical history and also seemed especially appropriate to American republicanism, for the courage it honored was called forth by civilian rather than military goals. Not civil strife, but civil harmony was the inevitable result of understanding God's great design for the universe, according to Peale. If men would only come to realize "their reciprocal dependence," Peale lectured, they would "learn how to cultivate the arts of peace." By making his countrymen aware of the wisdom of "the divine Architect" and of the interdependency of plant and animal life through a painting expressing God's cosmic design, Peale believed that he was "sowing the seed of Virtue" and influencing Americans to act "benevolently" in their social relations.[25]

It was particularly important to Peale's undertaking that the subject of his work convey a moral message. "Subjects that have not a virtuous tendency" should be eschewed in art, he wrote to Jefferson, no matter how meritorious a painting's execution.[26] Peale was not alone in his insistence that art serve didactic purposes. The morality of a work of art was an important precept in the eighteenth-century "system of rules" that governed aesthetic matters. A few years later, Peale would be reminded of it — if, indeed, he needed such a reminder — by a letter from West in which the master wrote:

> The art of painting has powers to dignify man, by transmitting to posterity his noble actions, and his mental powers, to be viewed in those invaluable lessons of religion, love of country, and morality; such subjects are worthy of the pencil, they are worthy of being placed in view as the most instructive records of a rising generation.[27]

Thoroughly indoctrinated in such ideas, Peale understood that of all the various branches of painting, history, which displayed the human nature of great men in action, provided the most sublime subject matter. He also was aware that the central theme of these paintings usually emanated from the moral efforts of a hero, whether it was Regulus returning to certain death in order to keep his word, or Wolfe dying at Quebec for the sake of empire (1770, National Gallery of Canada). He may not actually have read Reynolds's prescription that the subject of history painting must be "generally interesting" and mark "an instance of heroick action, or heroick suffering," but he was surely influenced by the prevailing assumptions that underlay Reynolds's *Discourses*. Moreover, by the time Peale came to paint his grand work, West had succeeded in laying to rest criticism of his effort in the *Wolfe* to combine historical truth of costume and scenery with ideal truth of form by way of "quoted" or borrowed compositions, grouping, and expression. Peale's decision to commemorate an incident in his own lifetime, then, followed the trend established by West and brought to a high art by Copley, of painting contemporary history subjects and endowing newsworthy events with the moral significance of classical legends.[28]

From the beginning of his studies in London, Peale had to recognize that he could not aspire to the lofty rank of history painter. When he wrote to one of his patrons, Charles Carroll, Barrister, that he hoped to undertake the "Study of History Painting" by "Copying of good Painting," Carroll immediately dampened his enthusiasm. History painting, Carroll wrote to his protégé,

> I Look upon as the most Difficult Part of the Profession and Requires the utmost Genius in the artist   few arrive at a High Point of Perfection in it And indeed in this Part of the world few have a Taste for it and very few can go thro' the Expence of giving that Encouragement that such an artist would Desire.[29]

Agreeing with his patron, Peale determined to study miniature painting instead, but he never totally abandoned the idea of becoming a history painter. He watched West at work, learned how to paint large oil portraits as well as miniatures, practiced the art of sculpture, and learned the technique of mezzotint engraving. He also studied whatever paintings were available to the public in English private collections, read treatises on art, and watched popular portraitists at work. In London he was able to effect a compromise between portraiture and history painting that for a long time seemed to satisfy both the desire to do something in the Grand Manner and the necessity to earn a living by his art in America.

Peale's compromise lay in the tradition of the heroic or allegorical portrait, or, put another way, in an attempt to make the portrait carry the burden of history painting by including in it storytelling symbols and emblematic elements that would elevate it beyond portraiture by the expression of a significant theme. Since Elizabethan times, the allegorical portrait had served historical purposes for English courtiers and royalty.[30] By the end of the seventeenth century, and particularly by the middle of the eighteenth, when English painting began to feel the full impact of continental practices, the heroic portrait, usually reserved for royalty and highly placed personages, became popular among wealthy individuals — full-length standing figures in formal poses, garnished by dramatic cloud contrasts, classical architecture and statuary, Roman columns denoting strength and firmness, billowing velvet curtains, and rich furnishings. In the mid-eighteenth century, British Whigs introduced a collection of symbols to promote their political position, and soon these symbols became the stock-in-trade of designers and artists working for a Whig clientele.[31] The emphasis of British neoclassical art on such idealizations and symbols met Peale's own interest in placing his art at the service of his country. The results were portraits replete with easily legible symbolism designed to propagandize the American cause or point to politically liberal conclusions.

Peale's paintings in this style are well known.[32] Beginning with the miniature *Bordley Brothers* (fig. 19), in which the two young sons of his patron John Beale Bordley are portrayed sharing an open book and guarded by the bust of the Roman goddess of wisdom, Minerva, and moving on to the more elaborate *William Pitt* (fig. 7), with its paraphernalia of classical symbols dedicated to liberty and its meaning for Britain and America, Peale executed three more important portraits in this vein: *John Beale Bordley* (fig. 5); *Washington at Princeton* (fig. 33) and its many replicas and variants; and *Conrad Alexandre Gérard* (fig. 74).

After the American Revolution and a few years of furious participation in radical politics, Peale abandoned heroic portraiture, partly because of personal disappointments and partly because he no longer received large public commissions. Having lost his conservative clientele through his involvement in revolutionary politics, he rejected politics altogether, along with ideologically created symbols and political allegory. In England, he had absorbed the Renaissance precept that art should imitate nature; when he found himself back in America without classical statuary or historical art to imitate in order to achieve "ideal" nature, Peale increasingly turned to nature itself as a model. Quite early in his career he wrote to Bordley that his paintings fell "far short" of the excellence of the masters because he had neither the time nor opportunity to become "well acquainted with the Gresian [*sic*] and Roman statues to be able to draw them at pleasure by memory, and account for every beauty." He went on to say, however, "As I have variety of Characters to paint that I must as Rambrant did make these my Articles and improve myself as well as I can while I am providing for my support."[33]

Peale did just that. He taught himself the art of landscape painting and perspective by inventing a perspective machine and by painting scenes for the Annapolis theater. His *Nancy Hallam as Imogen in "Cymbeline"* (fig. 40) demanded the kind of scope in size and perspective that he would eventually use in the *Exhumation*, although in this painting he did not have to concern himself with organizing a schema that would successfully unite a number of figures in space. He experimented with family groups and double portraits in which he faced the necessity to create a sense of group harmony or domestic affection through his placement of figures in space, as in the charming *Mr. and Mrs. James Gittings and Granddaughter* (fig. 68). During and immediately following the Revolution, public commissions to prepare transparencies and triumphal arches for celebrations and, in particular, his moving pictures (now lost), increased his capacity to compose large-scale pictures containing a number of figures within landscape, to create designs on a number of planes, and to organize disparate storytelling elements in the manner of history painting.

It is interesting that although Peale conceived of his history painting in 1804, he did not begin it until 1806,[34] the year following the establishment of the Pennsylvania Academy of the Fine Arts. That very year, a building was constructed for the academy and casts of classical statuary obtained. A list of statuary to be purchased for the academy, in Peale's handwriting, makes it clear that Peale was familiar with the well-known Greek and Roman statues which for generations had provided learning models for English and continental art academies. The availability of these classical casts in the Pennsylvania Academy, along with some Dutch paintings, which had recently been imported by a Philadelphia merchant; the presence in Philadelphia of panoramists such as William Winstanley and English-trained landscapists such as George Beck, Francis Guy, and William Groombridge; the influence of Rembrandt Peale's interest in history painting and especially Rembrandt's new color system; the possibility of once again taking his place in an academic art world; and perhaps the desire to improve his museum exhibitions so that the institution would be accepted as an adjunct to a National College—all of these factors, it seems to me, stimulated Peale to pick up his pencil once again and make the attempt at working out on canvas the grand "design" he had envisioned in 1804.[35]

In assembling the elements that would be included in his painting, Peale was very much aware of the problems of design inherent in creating a large historical work. Later, in 1822, when faced with the problem of composing a self-portrait for his museum, he wrote to Rembrandt of the need for his design to be "expressive" in order to "bring forth into public view, the beauties of Nature and art."[36] Peale also was well trained in academic procedures. Thus, he collected sketches of many of the figures and accessories he planned to introduce into the painting before beginning the large canvas. At the time of the exhumation, in 1801, he had sketched in his diary his conception of a great Chinese wheel that would be turned by boys treading its built-in steps; as the wheel turned under such power, the buckets would dip into the morass to bring up the water, making it possible to dig for the bones buried beneath the mud.[37] This sketch gave him his central focus and the triangular construction around which the rest of the composition could be organized. He also took sketches of his children not only to perpetuate the likenesses of his beloved family, but more important, to symbolize posterity—his own posterity—who were, in effect, the intellectual beneficiaries of his great discovery. To illustrate this point clearly, he painted little Sybilla Miriam pointing upward as she explains to her younger sister Elizabeth the divine meaning of the event. Included among the family portraits was even the family dog, a loyal member of the clan. Peale had good precedent for including family portraits in his large work; Benjamin West had clearly done so in his *William Penn's Treaty with the Indians* (fig. 69) in order to "give that Identity which was necessary in such a novel subject."[38]

Peale derived the formal composition of his painting from a number of sources, although many aspects of the design seem to have been of his own devising. The little children resemble Agrippina's in posture; the classical bas-relief of family members was also undoubtedly suggested by West, either in the *Agrippina* or more likely *Penn's Treaty,* which by this time was probably one of the most popular paintings in late eighteenth-century America, and by 1806, already an icon, its familiar figures having been reproduced on textiles, ceramics, medals, and currency. From *Penn's Treaty* and also *The Death of General Wolfe* perhaps came the idea of a central group engaged in the main activity, surrounded by observers whose presence commented on the theme. In *Penn's Treaty,* for instance, the observers are an Indian woman with children in the right corner, Philadelphia merchants on the left;[39] in the *Exhumation,* the principal observer other than the members of the family was Alexander Wilson, whose book on American ornithology was published in 1808, the year in which Peale probably added his figure to the near-completed canvas. Since Wilson had derived much of his information about birds from the specimens in Peale's museum, Peale probably considered him close to being a family member, although still outside the main circle; therefore, he included him in the painting in the role of the naturalist who would realize the scientific implications of the discovery and obtain knowledge from it, just as Wilson had from Peale's stuffed birds in the museum: alien yet related intellectually.

In contrast to West's painting, Peale's work contains two separate groups, divided by the line of earthworks that outlines the pit in which the workers are laboring. The two groups of active workmen and passive observers represent the two kinds of energy at work here — physical and intellectual, and their separation within the canvas's space, as well as in dress and posture, is meaningful. Peale connects the two groups by means of his outstretched arm which points to the newly discovered bone and, in effect, brings the viewer's attention back to the drawn image.

One critic of Peale's paintings has remarked on the absence of interaction among the members of the central group and between them and other groups of observers standing around the pit.[40] To some extent, this is in the nature of neoclassical history painting, the composition of which frequently took the form of a relief, with figures standing parallel to the picture plane as immobile as the statues from which their forms were derived. Peale, too, had recourse to classical statuary — the newly arrived casts, the absence of which up to now had presumably inhibited him from taking on a large-scale work. The casts, I believe, explain the posture of some of the workmen and more prominent characters. Their classical allusions, if accepted, contribute to the painting's meaning. For instance, the Apollo Belvedere probably provided Peale (as it had Benjamin West in his figure of the Indian chief in *Penn's Treaty*) with the model for his most important character — himself. Every history painting featured a central hero engaged in a dramatic activity. Peale may have been egotistical in making himself the hero of his painting, but I think his was an intellectual decision; he was the artist-naturalist-educator engaged in a valiant effort to extricate from the earth a symbol of geological time before it was destroyed by the relentless force of the elements. That he modeled himself after the Apollo must have also amused him, for Apollo was not only the mythological god of poetry and music, both of which Peale had great affection for, but also the symbol of the wisdom of the oracle (and, incidentally, of manly beauty!). Surely Peale must have enjoyed the appropriateness of the association, especially since such eighteenth-century virtues as harmony, orderliness, balance, and rationality were also associated with Apollo.[41]

The Venus de Medici provided Peale with one of his more amusing figures — that of his dead second wife Elizabeth DePeyster Peale, shown to the left scolding little Titian Ramsay Peale, while pointing to the oncoming storm. Betsy's plumpness had been a frequent source of family humor, and Peale must have delighted in the possibility of associating her with the Venus. The cast, however, accounts for the awkward position of Betsy's arm as she grabs Titian with it. Antinous Capitoline was used, I believe, for the standing figure of James Peale and the Farnese Hercules for Alexander Wilson, in order to suggest the strength of the naturalist's intellect in contrast to the slightness of his physique. The Torso Belvedere and possibly the figures in the *Laocoön* group helped Peale to draw the workers laboring to unearth the precious bones.

In other respects, Peale's painting conforms to the academic rules governing history painting. His grouping of characters lays out and defines the spatial limits of the canvas. Light and the reflection of the blue sky in the blue water of the pit connect the elements within the painting visually as well as intellectually, representing as they do God's presence in both heaven and earth and the illumination that accompanies understanding of God's plan. The light also falls upon Peale as the enlightened expounder of nature's laws and on the sketch of the bone, man's re-creation of what was to be found in nature.

Peale's painting is placed within nature. The pit represents man's invasion of nature's secrets; the machine, the method whereby those secrets are revealed. Peale was not opposed to machinery, nor did he view it as a desecration of nature's garden. Rather, he was fascinated by the idea of invention and regarded technological innovation as man's intelligent use of natural resources for facilitating work and easing life's pains. Throughout his career, he adopted and improved such inventions as the polygraph, the physiognotrace, the windmill, the steam bath, and fireplace to that purpose. His Chinese wheel in the painting was, in his mind, an ingenious contraption that took advantage of nature's laws to solve a labor problem.

Around Peale, the hero, circulate the forces of nature which man cannot control — the Catskill Mountain rainstorm that threatened to destroy the entire effort. The frightened horses responding to the storm heighten the dramatic tension of the scene, contrasting with calm and rational man who continues his pursuit of knowledge whatever the risks. Realism and symbolism merge here, but the storm gave Peale the opportunity to paint a symbolic sky and sublime cloud effects, as well as to experiment with lighting, in which he was always interested.[42]

Despite its great interest, Peale's painting, in the long run, does not completely achieve the grand effect that he believed his theme demanded. That later generations have mistaken his history painting for an amusing genre piece indicates his ultimate failure to realize his perceived goals.

What Peale could not do was to generalize the entire picture so that it would become something more than an assemblage of portraits. He followed all the rules, but the rules themselves were not sufficient to ensure a coherent picture in which the disparate elements would be unified and details subordinated to the dramatic whole. His method of utilizing casts and observing "what has been done by the most noted talents" reflected the lessons he had learned in West's studio and Reynolds's advice in his Sixth Discourse;[43] but what Reynolds really meant when he urged young artists to imitate the great masters was that they should absorb by such study the principles that had made their work great. Peale had few such works available for study in America. Copies of West's copies of old masters, a few of West's paintings, a few engravings from West's and other English painters' works, and his plaster casts, together with forty-year-old memories of fine works that he had seen in London — these served as his models.[44] Hopefully, he believed these would suffice. That they did not suggests the difficulties experienced by early nineteenth-century American artists who, removed from the academies and galleries of Europe, were forced to depend on the printed image or text for guidance.

Peale made a few other attempts at history painting. Between 1818 and 1820, he worked on a *Retreat Across the Delaware, 1776,* now lost, which was intended "to represent some of the horrors of War."[45] In his second attempt at a biblical subject (the first having been his copy as a student of West's *Elisha Restoring to Life the Shunammite's Son* [fig. 17]), Peale allowed himself "some liberty" in the copy of Charles Catton's *Noah's Ark* (fig. 70) in which he substituted animals from his museum for some in the original, notably the American buffalo for an elk on the left.[46] After he had successfully completed the *Exhumation,* he was stimulated to finish a family group portrait which he had begun thirty-five years earlier (fig. 28). His improvements, he believed, lay in creating a more unified design "sufficient to tell the object" and in making his figures more "distinct." To give it the semblance, however, of a historical painting, he decided to "make a key to it with some historic fact that give [*sic*] rise to the design of the piece."[47]

In one of his last paintings, *The Artist in His Museum* (fig. 61), in which he returned to heroic portraiture, Peale painted what was probably his masterpiece. *The Artist in His Museum* expresses Peale's increased sense of history as well as the meaning of his life. In a rational, geometric design, he demonstrates the relationship among the members of the animal kingdom, the cosmic view of creation that informed the *Exhumation,* the feeling for posterity and the sense of the past that made him in the present a conductor between the two. As he draws open the curtain to that past — symbolized by the collection of animal and human portraits — he is at once the artist exhibiting the sources of his inspiration and the teacher raising the veil of ignorance from a dimly lit foreground to an illuminated background of knowledge, where posterity in the shape of a small boy is centered.

Just as the *Exhumation* associated the meaning of Peale's museum with nature, and *Noah's Ark* was, as he wrote, "a Museum in itself,"[48] so this self-portrait made the museum the central subject. To Peale, the whole world was "a museum in which all men are destined to be employed and amused."[49] The painting becomes Peale's paradigm of that world, its orderliness symbolized by the even row upon row of specimens arranged according to the Linnaean system of classification of species, and by the parallel rows of revolutionary portraits — the men whose images were to influence posterity by reminding future generations of republican virtues and character. The busts of representative men facing them from the cases to the right universalize the lesson (fig. 72).

Peale's museum expressed the importance that the eighteenth century placed on education and intellectual efforts;[50] as Peale wrote to Jefferson, the belief "that the attainment of Happiness, Individual as well as Public, depends on the cultivation of the human mind."[51] If that world seems to us conservative, with its faith in stability, design, and completeness — an unchanging world order — it was not necessarily a world opposed to change and innovation. And if Peale's emblems of that world consisted of historical and archaeological artifacts, such as fossils and portraits of dead heroes, this did not mean that he thought only in terms of the past.[52] On the contrary, Peale was constantly aware of his obligations to the present and future generations; his sense of the continuity of all life — past, present, and future — is exemplified in his *Self-Portrait with Angelica and a Portrait of Rachel* (fig. 71), in which Angelica takes the brush from her father's hand in a gesture that was as "emblematical" as it was playful.

Peale's world was a happy and optimistic one, marked by order and intelligibility. By the time he died in 1827, it was changing. He already had to agree with his son Rembrandt that perhaps species could become extinct — an admission that opened up the worrisome question of what happened to the great chain of being when such a gap occurred.

Whether he was ready to accept the catastrophist theory that accounted for such phenomena by positing the possibility of a series of mighty convulsions, as Abraham Davidson believes,[53] is not clear from his papers. What is clear from them, however, and from the evidence of his paintings, is that in all ways Peale was an eighteenth-century thinker and artist. As such, he was convinced that all experience was symbolic and didactic, particularly the experience of nature and art. The naturalist and the artist were symbolic presences who, whether they raised the curtain of the past to the present as in *The Artist in His Museum* or expounded the principles of creation to posterity as in *The Exhumation of the Mastodon,* showed the viewer where America was and to what limits it could aspire. Through the work of the artist and scientist, teachers of the meaning of experience, Peale believed that Americans would come to realize their glorious future, to which he — the eternal optimist — pointed the way.

NOTES

This chapter was originally published in the *American Art Journal* 13 (1981): 47–68. A briefer version of this essay was presented at a symposium "The Versatile Mr. Peale," organized by the Friends of Independence National Historical Park on April 11, 1980, in Philadelphia.

1. E. P. Richardson, *Painting in America: The Story of 450 Years* (New York, 1956), p. 119; John Wilmerding, "Peale, Quidor, and Eakins: Self-Portraiture as Genre Painting," in *Art Studies for an Editor: 25 Essays in Memory of Milton S. Fox* (New York, 1975), pp. 291–92; Abraham Davidson, "Charles Willson Peale's *Exhuming the First American Mastodon:* An Interpretation," in ibid., p. 63.

2. Charles Willson Peale to Mrs. Nathaniel Ramsay, September 7, 1804, P-S, in *Selected Papers* 2:751–53.

3. Charles Willson Peale to John Hawkins, August 28, December 28, 1806, P-S, in *Selected Papers* 2:1087–91.

4. Charles Willson Peale to Angelica Peale Robinson, June 16, 1808, P-S, in *Selected Papers* 2:994–98.

5. Charles Willson Peale to John Hawkins, March 28, 1807, P-S, in *Selected Papers* 2: 1008–11. See also Charles Willson Peale to Benjamin West, December 16, 1807, P-S, in *Selected Papers* 2:1052–54.

6. Charles Willson Peale to John Hawkins, March 28, 1807. See also C. W. Peale to Benjamin West, December 16, 1807, in which he wrote, "I still doubted my abilities of making a tolerable picture."

7. See Joshua Reynolds, *Discourses on Art,* ed. Robert R. Wark (San Marino, Calif., 1975), pp. 52, 70.

8. The idea that Peale's view of "painting as a craft rather than as an art, and as a means of support for his family rather than as an intellectual endeavor . . . insulated him later from the elevated theories of Benjamin West and Joshua Reynolds in the eighteenth century and from the romantic visions and impractical experiments of his son Rembrandt in the nineteenth" has been generally expressed but, in my opinion, is not true. Peale could practice a temporary "pragmatism," but underneath his seeming acquiescence to reality, it seems to me that he continued to aspire to more lofty achievements. See Louise Lippincott, "Charles Willson Peale and His Family of Painters," in *This Academy. The Pennsylvania Academy of the Fine Arts, 1805–1976* (Philadelphia, 1976), pp. 76, 77.

9. In his autobiography written sixty years later, Peale recollected (speaking in the third person), "Mr. West painted in the time that Peale was with him, the landing of Agrippa with the ashes of Germanicus, Elisha restoring to life the Shunamite's son; Angelica and Medoro, and the return of Regulus to Carthage. This was his first picture that he painted for the King, and the writer remembers his going to the Queen's Pallace to show his Majesty the drawing, a first sketch." Peale also remembered that the sketch was so small that the queen had to bend down to examine it while it rested on a chair. Peale's memory may have telescoped the events. The subject of the *Regulus* was suggested by the king at this meeting, so West could not have carried a sketch of that picture to the palace. Perhaps West brought along his sketch of the *Agrippina* to show the king, perhaps the finished painting (A(TS): 95. See also Robert C. Alberts, *Benjamin West. A Biography* (Boston, 1978), p. 87; Allen Staley, "Benjamin West's *The Landing of Agrippina at Brundisium with the Ashes of Germanicus,*" *Bulletin, Philadelphia Museum of Art,* 61, nos. 287–88 (Fall 1965/Winter 1966): 13.

10. Charles Willson Peale to Benjamin West, May 28, 1793, P-S, in *Selected Papers* 2:47–48.

11. Charles Willson Peale, Diary 19, in *Selected Papers* 2:351.

12. Peale's interest in landscape painting as a unique art form and not simply as an element within a portrait continued to increase after this experience. In 1805, while on his honeymoon with the third Mrs. Peale, he pleased himself by painting two landscapes which were "well deserving of frames" (private collection), and he indicated that he would like to paint more if time permitted. He also at this time was still contemplating an "allegorical" picture, perhaps the design of the *Exhumation* (Charles Willson Peale to Rubens Peale, October 14, 1805, P-S, in *Selected Papers* 2:896–97).

13. See Arthur Barneveld Bibbins, "Charles Willson Peale's Painting, 'The Exhuming of the First American Mastodon,'" *Bulletin of the Geological Society of America* 18 (1907), p. 652. See also Whitfield J. Bell, Jr., "A Box of Old Bones. A Note on the Identification of the Mastodon, 1766–1806," *Proceedings of the American Philosophical Society* 93, no. 2 (May 1949).

14. Undated memorandum, Peale-Sellers Papers.

15. See Charles Willson Peale, *Discourse Introductory to a Course of Lectures* (Philadelphia, 1800); *CWP,* pp. 225, 283, 461. The concept of a chain of being extends back to the Renaissance, but in eighteenth-century America it carried different meaning. Notably, it was less static in its implications and no longer included a definition

of a hierarchical society. Rather, as Herbert Leventhal has pointed out, its "primary purpose and use . . . was . . . to 'order' nature itself" (*In the Shadow of the Enlightenment: Occultism and Renaissance Science in Eighteenth-Century America* [New York, 1976], pp. 258-59).

16. Charles Willson Peale and A.F.M.J. Palisot de Beauvois, *A Scientific and Descriptive Catalogue of Peale's Museum* (Philadelphia, 1796).

17. Thomas Jefferson, *Notes on Virginia*, in *The Works of Thomas Jefferson*, ed. P. L. Ford (New York & London, 1904), 3:411, 427; Thomas Jefferson, "A Memoir on the Discovery of Certain Bones . . . ," *Transactions of the American Philosophical Society* 4 (1799): 255-56. See also John C. Greene, *The Death of Adam. Evolution and Its Impact on Western Thought* (Ames, Iowa, 1959), pp. 101-02.

18. See Lamarck and Geoffroy to Charles Willson Peale, in *Science*, n.s., 19, no. 490 (1904): 798-99; published also in *Selected Papers* 2:141-45; Benjamin Smith Barton, *A Discourse on Some of the Principal Desiderata in Natural History* (Philadelphia, 1807), p. 20.

19. A(TS): 311. See also Charles Willson Peale to Thomas Jefferson, January 12, 1806, P-S, in *Selected Papers* 2:920-22, wherein Peale indicates that he asked Dr. Caspar Wistar to examine the mammoth and elephant skeletons and compare them. For further discussion of the distinction between elephant and mammoth bones, see William Hunter, "Observations on the bones found near the river Ohio," *The American Museum* 5 (February 1789): 152-55; Greene, *The Death of Adam*, pp. 89-117; Bell, "A Box of Old Bones," pp. 169-77.

20. Broadside, P-S, reproduced in Sellers, *Mr. Peale's Museum*, p. 146. Also see the *Philadelphia Gazette, and Daily Advertiser*, December 24, 1801.

21. Sellers, *Mr. Peale's Museum*, p. 103.

22. Charles Willson Peale to Angelica Peale Robinson, September 13, 1806, P-S, F:IIA/39D5; A(TS): 288.

23. A(TS): 297-98.

24. Ibid., pp. 301-03.

25. Charles Willson Peale, "A Walk with a Friend in the Philadelphia Museum, 1805-1806," Ms., Historical Society of Pennsylvania; Peale, *Discourse Introductory*, pp. 6, 9, 42-43. Also see Charles Willson Peale to the Representatives of the State of Massachusetts in Congress, December 14, 1795, Massachusetts Historical Society, Boston, Theodore Sedgwick Collection, in *Selected Papers* 2:136; Daniel J. Boorstin, *The Lost World of Thomas Jefferson* (Boston, 1963), pp. 173-85.

26. Charles Willson Peale to Thomas Jefferson, July 3, 1820, P-S, F:IIA/64D8-9.

27. Benjamin West to Charles Willson Peale, September 19, 1809, *The Port Folio* 3 (1810): 8-13, in *Selected Papers* 2:1218-23.

28. For Reynolds, see *Discourses*, p. 57. West's and Copley's achievements in extending the range of subjects for history painters are best analyzed in Edgar Wind, "The Revolution of History Painting," *Journal of the Warburg Institute* 2 (1938): 116-27; Charles Mitchell, "Benjamin West's 'Death of General Wolfe' and the Popular History Piece," ibid. 7 (1944): 20-33. Peale kept referring to his paintings as "interresting" and "valuable." See, for example, Charles Willson Peale to Rubens Peale, September 16, 1806, P-S, in *Selected Papers* 2:983-85; Charles Willson Peale to Thomas Jefferson, November 26, 1806, P-S, F:IIA/39E10; Charles Willson Peale

to Benjamin West, December 16, 1807, P-S, in *Selected Papers* 2:1052–54; A(TS):296.

29. Charles Carroll, Barrister, to Charles Willson Peale, October 29, 1767, Maryland Historical Society: Charles Carroll Papers, in *Selected Papers* 1:70–71.

30. See Roy Strong, *The English Icon* (London, 1969), pp. 29–41.

31. Frank H. Sommer, "The Metamorphoses of Britannia," in *American Art: 1750–1800. Towards Independence,* ed. Charles F. Montgomery and Patricia E. Kane (Boston, 1976), pp. 40–49. Peale's familiarity with stock Whig imagery may be seen not only in his revolutionary paintings, but in the "emblematical ensigns" he designed for the Newburyport Stamp Act demonstrations as early as 1765, and the battle flags he painted for militia companies (Charles Willson Peale, Diary 1, P-S, in *Selected Papers* 1:38–45, 51–70; *Virginia Gazette,* February 23, 1775).

32. For full descriptions and explanation of these paintings, see *P&M,* pp. 37, 38, 86, 173, 226–28; *P&M Suppl.,* pp. 55, 63–64.

33. Charles Willson Peale to John Beale Bordley, November 1772, P-S, in *Selected Papers* 1:126–28.

34. In 1805, Peale began an allegorical picture once again, but he could never find the time to grind his colors. See Charles Willson Peale to Rubens Peale, October 14, 1805, P-S, in *Selected Papers* 2:896–97; Charles Willson Peale to Hannah Moore Peale, October 5, 1805, P-S, in *Selected Papers* 2:892–93.

35. "Lists of Casts in Academy," n.d., in "Papers Relating to the Founding and History of the Pennsylvania Academy of the Fine Arts," Pennsylvania Academy of the Fine Arts Archives. See also Nicholas Biddle to Charles Willson Peale et al., November 20, 1805, in which Biddle lists the casts he is sending to the Academy, Pennsylvania Academy of the Fine Arts Archives; Anna Wells Rutledge, comp., *Cumulative Record of Exhibition Catalogues. The Pennsylvania Academy of the Fine Arts, 1807–1870* . . . (Philadelphia, 1955), p. 1. Also see Charles Willson Peale to John Hawkins, August 28, 1806, P-S, in *Selected Papers* 2:980–82, for an expression of Peale's sense that the market for art was picking up in Philadelphia and that his museum might be "attached to that great Seminary," a national college, being planned by Congress.

36. Charles Willson Peale to Rembrandt Peale, July 23, 1822, P-S, F:IIA/67D3.

37. See *Selected Papers* 2:358n.

38. Quoted in Charles Coleman Sellers, "The Beginning: A Monument to Probity, Candor and Peace," in Pennsylvania Academy of the Fine Arts, *Symbols of Peace: "William Penn's Treaty with the Indians"* (Philadelphia, 1976), n.p. West's letter was dated February 2, 1805.

39. Anthony N.B. Garvan, "The Consequence: The Social Impact of Benjamin West's Painting," ibid., n.p.; Ann Uhry Abrams, "Benjamin West's Documentation of Colonial History: *William Penn's Treaty with the Indians,*" *Art Bulletin* 64 (March 1982): 59–65.

40. Clive Bush, *The Dream of Reason. American Consciousness and Cultural Achievement from Independence to the Civil War* (London, 1977), p. 82.

41. The Apollo Belvedere was a popular classical model for eighteenth-century English painters such as Allan Ramsay, Joshua Reynolds, Henry Fuseli, and John Flaxman, as well as Benjamin West, all of whom fell under the influence of Johannes Winckelmann's enthusiasm for Greek art. While studying in London, Peale seems to have absorbed West's "conventional acceptance of classical antiquity," as

David Irwin has described it, which accounts for his conviction once back in America that he could not create history painting without such examples before him (David Irwin, *English Neoclassical Art, Studies in Inspiration and Taste* [London, 1966], pp. 31–75).

42. See Charles Willson Peale to Rubens Peale, September 16, 1806, P-S, *Selected Papers* 2:983–85. "The Effect of the storm is good," Peale wrote, "it forms a fine contrast to the sunshine about the Wheel and buckets &c."

43. Charles Willson Peale to John Hawkins, August 28, P-S, in *Selected Papers* 2:980–82.

44. Peale was familiar with engravings of West's *Regulus Returning to Carthage, Hannibal Swearing Perpetual Enmity to the Romans, Daniel Interpreting the Handwriting on the Wall,* and *Erastatus the Physician Discovers the Love of Antiochus for Strastonica,* among other engravings taken from West's paintings. He also knew prints taken from Francis Wheatley's *Rural Benevolence, Rural Sympathy,* and *Howard Visiting and Relieving the Distressed in Prison* (Charles Willson Peale to John Dickinson, March 22, 1799, P-S, in *Selected Papers* 2:239–41; John Dickinson to C. W. Peale, April 29, 1799, P-S, F:IIA/22D7–10).

45. Charles Willson Peale to Thomas Jefferson, August 21, 1819, P-S, F:IIA/62F5–6; Charles Willson Peale to Charles Peale Polk, January 9, 1820, P-S, F:IIA/63F1–3.

46. Charles Willson Peale to Titian Ramsay Peale, December 25, 1819, P-S, F:IIA/61B12–14.

47. Charles Willson Peale to Angelica Peale Robinson, September 8, 1808, P-S, in *Selected Papers* 2:1129–33; Charles Willson Peale to Rembrandt Peale, September 11, 1808, P-S, in *Selected Papers* 2:1133–44.

48. Charles Willson Peale to George Bomford, May 1, 1819, P-S, F:IIA/62D6.

49. Charles Willson Peale, *Introduction to a Course of Lectures . . . November 16, 1799* (Philadelphia, 1800), p. 19.

50. The most complete analysis and summary of the aims and progress of Peale's museum may be found in Sellers, *Mr. Peale's Museum,* esp. chap. 5.

51. Charles Willson Peale to Thomas Jefferson, January 1, 1819, P-S, F:IIA/61E12–13.

52. Bush, *The Dream of Reason,* p. 80.

53. Davidson, "Charles Willson Peale's *Exhuming the First American Mastodon,*" pp. 64–67.

II

Charles Willson Peale's Expressive Design

The Artist in His Museum

------◆------

ROGER B. STEIN

Although I am friendly to portraying eminent men, I am not
friendly to the indiscriminate waste of genius in portrait painting; and I do hope that your son will ever bear in his mind,
that the art of painting has powers to dignify man, by transmitting to posterity his noble actions, and his mental powers,
to be viewed in those invaluable lessons of religion, love of
country, and morality; such subjects are worthy of the pencil,
they are worthy of being placed in view as the most instructive
records of a rising generation.
— Benjamin West to Charles Willson Peale, 1809[1]

ANY work of art is a moment in the life of its culture, but some cap-
ture that moment with a special richness and complexity. The
large-scale self-portrait by Charles Willson Peale of 1822, entitled *The Artist in His Museum* (fig. 61), is such a work. A self-conscious
cultural statement, it stands at the end of the amply documented life of
a major artist and crystallizes in its particular ways some of the shapes
of American culture at a crucial point of transition, just as Peale and his
world were giving way to a new "romantic" America.

In an obvious sense, all portraits are cultural and historical documents,
biographical statements about the life of an individual. This is especially
true of a self-portrait, since the artist is shaping the materials of his or
her own life and externalizing them, making them publicly available on

the canvas. Over the course of his lifetime, Charles Willson Peale painted a number of self-portraits, of which at least eighteen are known. These include the earliest, 1762–63, when he was first trying his hand as painter (unlocated); a miniature done in 1765 after his visit to Copley's studio in Boston (unlocated); a clay bust done in London, where he spent twenty-five months studying, beginning in February 1767 (unlocated, but see fig. 28); a small portrait of 1777–78, when he was serving in the Pennsylvania militia with Washington's army (American Philosophical Society); a conversation piece group portrait with his growing family begun in the early 1770s (fig. 28), and another wherein we find him posed as painter with his first wife and daughter in the 1780s (fig. 71); a head with raised spectacles in 1804, when he took up palette and brush again after an interval of six years spent working on his museum (fig. 77); and finally, an important group of seven self-portraits including *The Artist in His Museum* done (between 1821 and 1824) in the last decade of his life. Although undoubtedly some of these self-portraits were relatively private acts, for his own instruction or for family and friends, *The Artist in His Museum* of 1822 was a direct response to a public commission.[2]

The museum, which Peale had founded in the 1780s and to which he had devoted a large proportion of his enormous energies over almost forty years, had finally become in fact, as it had always been in intent, a public institution; and the trustees of the newly incorporated Philadelphia Museum in their meeting of July 19, 1822, had asked the eighty-one-year-old artist "to paint a full length likeness of himself for the Museum."[3] He responded with alacrity and set to work immediately, and his energetic efforts over the seven weeks it took him to complete this huge 103½ by 80 inch canvas are richly recorded in a wealth of documents — letters to relatives and friends, a retrospective autobiographical account, and, finally and most important, the evidence of the completed work itself — all of which can define for us (as they did for Peale himself) the web of relations between the artist and his world, between a particular self and the culture in which he was such an involved participant.

The autobiographical act of self-definition is at one and the same time an act of public-relatedness, an attempt to locate oneself personally and pictorially within one's times and for the largest possible audience. Peale's completed painting was hung initially in the museum and, after 1878, on the walls of the Pennsylvania Academy of the Fine Arts. It has appeared in many exhibitions, and the image has been reproduced in countless books, articles, and catalogues on American art and culture. This familiarity and popularity is itself testimony to the painting's function as a public image — comparable in kind, if not quite in degree, to Gilbert Stuart's Athenaeum portrait of Washington or, more nearly, to Asher Durand's *Kindred Spirits* — a double portrait of Thomas Cole and William Cullen Bryant — a shared and sharable cultural re-presentation of a man in his time and place.

The Emblematic Portrait

The historical archaeology required to understand Peale's 1822 cultural statement demands not only that we dig up, identify, and label the constituent parts presented to us but also that we reconstruct the vision, focusing our attention on how and why the parts are related on the canvas. Peale himself was unmistakably clear on the primacy of the pictorial organization as he worked out the conception and execution of the painting. The task was not merely to gather around the figure separate elements, associated in some random way with his public experience as founder of the museum. On July 23, only four days after the trustees acted, Peale wrote to his son Rembrandt:

> My next object in writing, is to try your invention of a composition of a large whole-length portrait — The Trustee's at their last meeting, directed me to make a whole length Portrait of myself for the Museum, which I have promised to perform without delay — and I have bought canvas. . . . I think it important that I should not only make it a lasting monument of my art as a Painter, but also that the design should be expressive that I bring forth into public view, the beauties of Nature and art, the rise & progress of the Museum.[4]

The first task, thus, was compositional: how to give shape to the only requirement — that the work be a full-length portrait. Beyond this, the task was not merely to make the work his best artistic effort but that "the Design should be expressive," that in the organization of images the formal pattern should be itself a mode for shaping meaning.

This idea crops up again and again in his letters. By August 4 the prepared canvas is before him, and he writes to another son, Rubens, "[I am] studying the composition. The design which I have thought best, as simply shewing that I have brought subjects of Natural History into view, is by representing myself putting a curtain aside to shew the Museum."[5] Or after the work was completed, he writes to Thomas Jefferson of the commission, beginning, "I have made the design as I have conceived appropriate."[6] In all cases, Peale's first attention is to composition and "Design," the mode of organizing meaning on the canvas. Where and in what attitude to place the figure, what the "scene" was to be, what particular elements to include and for what reasons of time and individual significance, how to solve problems of perspective, what sources might be useful as examples (Rembrandt suggested a Thomas Lawrence portrait currently on exhibit in New York)[7] — all these questions followed from or were subsequent to the problem of design. In simplest terms, this emphasis of Peale's reminds us that a painting is a construction in a two-dimensional space, a patterning of elements on the canvas, and that even the clearly powerful ego satisfaction involved in representing oneself publicly must, to the painter, be controlled by the pictorial need to map the constituent parts in a meaningful series of relationships on the canvas.

This truism of pictorial practice must not be seen as an alien technical matter to the historian of culture, for Peale's decision that "the Design should be expressive" offers us a cultural clue to the understanding of his intellectual, scientific, and aesthetic universe. The design of the painting, we shall ultimately suggest, is coterminous with the design of Peale's universe. The form and shape of the painting are not merely means to convey meaning; they are themselves bearers of meaning, and the student of culture cannot separate the constituent elements from the "Design" without missing the way in which Charles Willson Peale's painting re-presents its culture. As for the second repeated note in Peale's emphasis on "Design" — that its function is to "bring forth into public view the beauties of Nature and art" — that also suggests not only a subject matter, "Nature and art," but a mode of making them available to the viewer, the full understanding of which depends ultimately upon our recapturing the dynamics of Peale's particular version of Lockean epistemology.

Two cases in point should make initially clear Peale's focusing of the biographic data, the source material of his life as founder and director of the museum, around the needs of "Design" and bringing forth of "the beauties of Nature and art." The commission clearly indicated that the setting for the portrait should be the museum itself, which after its earliest years in his house on Lombard Street in Philadelphia and then in Philosophical Hall had been located since 1802 in the second floor of the State House, the building we know as Independence Hall. The Long

Room, a 100-foot chamber running the length of the building, was the obvious setting since it housed the larger share of the museum's exhibits. Peale employed his drawing machine to establish the perspective lines of the room. He set his son Titian "at work to fill it up with his water colors, and he has nearly finished an admirable representation," he writes in his letter of August 4 to Rubens. But even a brief comparative glance at the sketch (fig. 72) and the finished painting (fig. 61) indicates that Peale has altered "reality" to meet the needs of his design. The perspective has been opened up into the foreground at the base of the painting. The cabinets between the windows on the outside wall to the right, which contained cases of insects, minerals, and fossils, a group of landscape paintings, a series of busts above, and the organ case (visible about halfway down the room in the sketch), have all been displaced by the partially hidden skeleton of the mastodon and other animals, brought in from quite another room in the building, as museum visitors would have quickly recognized.

Into the big space at the lower left opened up by Peale's manipulation of the perspective, he has introduced the dead turkey on a taxidermist's chest. This turkey was one of the specimens that Titian, now serving as manager of the museum, had brought back from the Long expedition to Missouri (1819), to be stuffed and included in his father's collection.[8] The documentation of elements in the painting to their sources in Peale's life is an almost endless task, for the work is richly associative, and the turkey is one particular choice that Peale made to fill the space which the widening of the perspective had produced.

However, understanding its biographical source does not explain the larger significance of the turkey within the painting for Peale and his culture; and beyond its value as a separate object lies its dynamic function within the design in bringing forth the beauties of nature and art. Its foreground role for the viewer is as a still life, *nature morte,* but it is dead nature that will be transformed within the space of the canvas and the museum into an artistically framed object in one of the cases behind it, to be revitalized by the beauty of art in several senses. Our perception of this is part of the complex spatial interplay, a cognitive game that Peale controls to define for the viewer the significance of each separate object within the world of the artist and his museum.

The first important clue to Peale's method lies in his notion of the kind of portrait he has created. The convention within which Peale was working becomes explicit in his unpublished third-person autobiography:

> Peale thought as he was required to make this Portrait, that he would
> not make a picture such as are usually done in common Portraits, and
> having made some studies he determined to have the light received from
> behind him, and putting himself in the attitude of lifting up a curtain
> to shew the Museum—emblematical that he had given to his country a
> sight of nature history in his labours to form a Museum.[9]

By defining this special portrait as "emblematical," Peale illuminates his
method in this work and underlines his allegiance to a long tradition.

The emblem is an Italian Renaissance creation—a pictorial image
with a verbal commentary that interprets it and creates meaning by explicating the often complex and frequently arbitrarily organized visual
image or images. The visual thus comes to stand for some idea not because it illustrates its subject perceptually, in a narrative or realistic or
discursive or psychologically expressive manner, but through our acceptance conceptually of the wittily contrived arbitrary pattern. Andrea
Alciati and Cesare Ripa were the progenitors of a century or more of
emblem books, gatherings of such witty and learned images and texts.
Linked initially to heraldic devices and, in the seventeenth century, to
poetic conceits ("Make me, O Lord, thy Spinning Wheele compleate,"
intoned the Puritan poet Edward Taylor), the emblem tradition flourished equally in southern and in northern Europe, where the engraved
Dutch versions far outshone in aesthetic quality their often visually crude
Italian sources. Emblems became part of the visual language of history
painting and portraiture as well, even long after the visual image had
lost its explicit verbal commentary. The cultural audience for whom
they were created could be depended upon to understand that a column
in a portrait stood for firmness and steadfastness, a dog for fidelity, a
Phrygian cap for liberty, a figure with snakes in its hair for discord. In
the emblematic portrait the conceptual controls the perceptual, asks
us to know the value of its subject through these images, which sur-
round it and stand for attributes, ideas, and values of the sitter. The
emblematic portrait requires the viewer's knowledge of a system of meanings and his or her active engagement to create intellectual coherence
and meaning out of the images so arranged—rather, that is, than merely
perceiving persons in their living space at a particular moment in historical time.[10]

The importance of this tradition to Charles Willson Peale and to
American portraiture in general is easy to overlook, given the emphasis
in American art history until recently on limners and likenesses, on the
strength of the "realistic" tradition of linear treatment, on rather vague

notions of an American "pragmatic" tradition as a reaction against an equally vaguely defined European "aristocratic" tradition. Even the crucial discoveries and suggestions by Waldron Phoenix Belknap and others of the mezzotint and print sources of eighteenth-century American portraits have been on the whole reduced to searches for solutions to formal problems. By focusing on the technical problems facing untrained provincials of placing the figure in space, most scholars have largely overlooked the possible conceptual significance of colonial adaptations and perhaps wrongly assumed that the Americans were ignorant of or denied the emblematic tradition.[11]

Yet despite the fact that Charles Willson Peale was the creator of a multitude of stunningly simple portraits focusing almost exclusively on the figure or on the figure in a generalized landscape background, we need to recall Peale's thorough familiarity with the emblematic tradition. At several points he attributed his inspiration to becoming a portraitist to seeing the large full-length emblematic portrait of *Charles Calvert, Fifth Lord Baltimore* (fig. 6), now attributed to the Dutch artist Herman Van der Myn, which in the eighteenth century hung in the Annapolis statehouse. Although it was sadly deteriorated until recently, one can still make out in this emblematic portrait the distant ancestor (reversed) of *The Artist in His Museum*. The figure stands before the elegantly raised drapery with his baton of authority gesturing into the background, at his back a covered table, and beyond that an Indian with bow. The deep space defines a coastline with ships on the horizon, standing for the maritime present of the colony, while the Indian defines the interior wilderness and savage past of America. The middle third of the canvas groups together emblems of colonial authority and the white man's aristocratic power: his hat, his sword, the gathered flags, his elegant embroidered waistcoat echoed in the embroidered Baltimore heraldic device on the figured drapery of the table. On the floor at his feet, by contrast, we find what seem to be images of Indian authority — a shield, arrows, and a ceremonial sword. Political and social power relations are thus defined by the spatial location of particular emblematic elements grouped in an intellectually coherent though arbitrary order around the controlling figure.

If this public image offered to Peale one noble example of the possibilities of the grand style of emblematic portraiture — and one that Peale did not forget[12] — his two years in England offered him the opportunity to study other emblematic portraits, to know Joshua Reynolds and see his work in that vein and to hear him argue, at least informally, for the grand style. This meant for Reynolds, as it did for others, adaptation and imitation of classical elements and drawing upon the emblematic tradition.[13] The consequences of this became clear when Peale returned to America in March 1769 with his most traditional effort at an emblematic portrait: the large 8 by 5 foot oil painting and the mezzotint engraved version of a portrait of William Pitt (fig. 7).

The Whig parliamentary leader and spokesman for the colonial cause had not had time to pose for the American, who had been commissioned by Edmund Jenings to paint Pitt's portrait for the gentlemen of Westmoreland County, Virginia. Peale chose to depict him not in contemporary dress, as William Hoare had done, nor in the robes of state, as Copley and West would later do in their death scenes of the earl of Chatham. Instead, Peale drew upon Joseph Wilton's statue of Pitt dressed as a Roman, in toga and tunic, and surrounded Pitt with a wealth of emblems to locate him politically for his American audience as the spokesman for colonial liberties. Hoping to achieve fame and financial reward for the work, he completed in London the mezzotint engraving of it to bring home with him; he struck off at the same time a broadside to accompany the mezzotint. "The Principal Figure," the broadside explained, "is that of Mr. Pitt, in a Consular Habit, speaking in Defense of the Claims of the American Colonies, on the Principles of the British Constitution."[14] It went on to point to verbal elements in the work—the Magna Carta in Pitt's hand, the banner placed between the heads of Sir Philip Sydney and Hampden (whom he identified) on the sacred altar of liberty, which reads *"Sanctus Amor Patriae Dat Animum"*—and to supplement these, as emblematists frequently did, with quotations from other intellectually related sources (in this case, from Montesquieu). The view of Whitehall, an elegant architectural backdrop (traditional in such portraiture), is identified in the broadside for its political relevance to the emblematic program. He further identifies and explicates complex emblematic groupings like that of the shadowy Indian—we recall in the Calvert portrait the use of the Indian—sitting beneath the statue of British Liberty with Phrygian cap, who is "trampling under Foot the Petition of the Congress at New-York."

> An Indian is placed on the Pedestal, in an erect Posture, with an attentive Countenance, watching, as America has done for Five Years past, the extraordinary Motions of the British Senate—He listens to the Orator,[15] and has a Bow in his Hand, and a Dog by his Side, to shew the natural *Faithfulness and Firmness of America.*

1. Unknown, attributed to John Hesselius, *Daniel of St. Thomas Jenifer*, ca. 1760–70. Oil on canvas, 49½ x 39½". *National Portrait Gallery, Smithsonian Institution, Washington, D.C.*

2. Sir Joshua Reynolds, *Charles Carroll of Carrollton*, ca. 1763. Oil on canvas, 30 x 25″. *Yale Center for British Art, Paul Mellon Collection, Yale University, New Haven, Connecticut.*

3. Charles Willson Peale, *Margaret Tilghman (Mrs. Charles) Carroll,* ca. 1770. Oil on canvas, 50 x 40". *Mount Clare Museum, Baltimore.*

4. Charles Willson Peale, *Charles Carroll, Barrister,* ca. 1770. Oil on canvas, 49½ x 38". *Mount Clare Museum, Baltimore.*

5. Charles Willson Peale, *John Beale Bordley,* 1770. Oil on canvas, 84½ x 58½".
National Gallery of Art, Washington, D.C. Gift of the Barra Foundation, Inc.

6. Herman van der Myn, *Charles Calvert, Fifth Lord Baltimore*, ca. 1730.
Oil on canvas, 106 x 67⅛". *The Peale Museum, Baltimore.*

7. Charles Willson Peale, *William Pitt*, 1768. Oil on canvas, 95¼ x 61¼".
Westmoreland County Museum, Montross, Virginia; replica, Statehouse, Annapolis, Maryland.

8. Charles Willson Peale, *Thomas Ringgold,*
ca. 1770. Watercolor on ivory, 1⅜ x 1⅜".
Washington College, Chestertown, Maryland.

9. Charles Willson Peale, *Thomas Ringgold,* ca. 1773. Oil on canvas,
30 x 25⅛". *The Baltimore Museum of Art. Friends of the American Wing Auction Fund.*

10. John Hesselius, *Charles Carroll, Barrister,* ca. 1760. Oil on canvas, 30 x 25″. *Private Collection.*

11. John Singleton Copley, *Francis Wentworth (Mrs. Theodore) Atkinson*, 1765. Oil on canvas, 51 x 40″. *Collection of The New York Public Library, New York City. Astor, Lenox and Tilden Foundations.*

12. Charles Willson Peale, *Judge James Arbuckle of Accommac*, 1766. Oil on canvas, 48 x 36½". *Private collection.*

13. Charles Willson Peale, *Mrs. James Arbuckle and Son,* 1766. Oil on canvas, 48 x 36¼". *Private collection.*

14. Matthew Pratt, *The American School*, 1765. Oil on canvas, 36 x 50¼".
The Metropolitan Museum of Art, New York City. Gift of Samuel P. Avery, 1987.

15. Benjamin West, *Charles Willson Peale*, 1767–69. Oil on
canvas, 28¼ x 23". *Courtesy of the New-York Historical Society, New
York City. Gift of Thomas J. Bryan, 1867.*

16. Benjamin West, *Pylades and Orestes*, 1766. Oil on canvas, 39½ x 49¾". *Tate Gallery, London.*

17. Charles Willson Peale after Benjamin West, *Elisha Restoring to Life the Shunammite's Son*, 1767. Watercolor on paper, mounted on canvas, 16 x 24". *Private collection.*

18. John Singleton Copley, *Young Lady with a Bird and Dog (Mary Warner)*, 1767. Oil on canvas, 48⅛ x 39¾". *The Toledo Museum of Art, Toledo, Ohio. Gift of Florence Scott Libbey.*

19. Charles Willson Peale, *Matthias and Thomas Bordley*, 1767. Watercolor on ivory, 3⅝ x 4¼″. *National Museum of American Art, Smithsonian Institution, Washington, D.C. Museum purchase/gift of Mr. and Mrs. Murray Lloyd Goldsborough, Jr.*

20. Charles Willson Peale, *Little Girl with a Toy Horse,* 1768. Oil on canvas, 36 x 28″.
The Bayou Bend Collection, The Museum of Fine Arts, Houston. Gift of Miss Ima Hogg.

21. Charles Willson Peale, *Rachel Brewer (Mrs. Charles Willson) Peale,* ca. 1769. Watercolor on ivory, 2¼ x 1¹³⁄₁₆". *The Metropolitan Museum of Art, New York City. Gift of Mr. J. William Middendorf II, 1968.*

22. John Singleton Copley, *Sarah Gray (Mrs. Samuel) Cary,* ca. 1769. Watercolor on ivory, 1⅜ x 1³⁄₁₆". *Private collection.*

23. John Singleton Copley, *Samuel Adams*, 1770–72. Oil on canvas, 50 x 40 ¼".
Courtesy, Museum of Fine Arts, Boston. Deposited by the City of Boston.

24. Francis Cotes, *Thomas and Isabel Crathorne*, 1767. Oil on canvas, 52½ x 59½". *The Henry E. Huntington Library and Art Gallery, San Marino, California.*

25. Sir Joshua Reynolds, *Mr. and Mrs. Godfrey Wentworth*, 1763. *Yale University Art Gallery, New Haven, Connecticut.*

26. Charles Willson Peale, *The Johnsons of "Rose Hill,"* 1772. Oil on canvas, 48 x 58½".
The Trustees of the C. Burr Artz Library, Frederick, Maryland.

27. Charles Willson Peale, *The John Cadwalader Family*, 1772. Oil on canvas,
51½ × 41¼″. *Philadelphia Museum of Art. Cadwalader Family Collection: Purchased with
funds contributed by Pew Memorial Trust & gift of an anonymous donor.*

28. Charles Willson Peale, *The Peale Family Group*, ca. 1772–1809. Oil on canvas, 56½ x 89½". *Courtesy of The New-York Historical Society, New York City.*

29. Charles Willson Peale, *Benjamin and Eleanor Ridgely Laming*, 1788. Oil on canvas, 42 x 60¼". *National Gallery of Art, Washington, D.C. Gift of Morris Schapiro.*

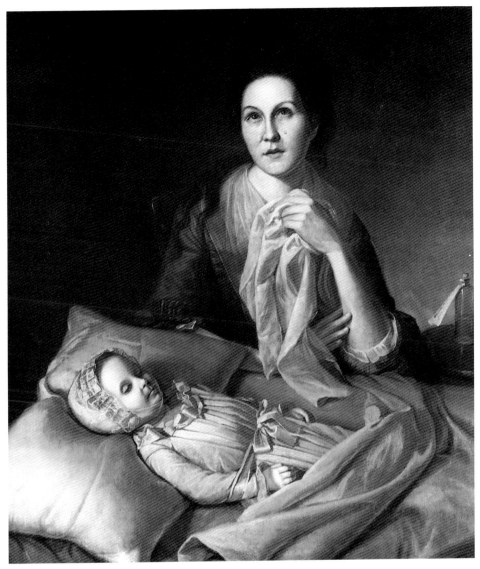

30. Charles Willson Peale, *Rachel Weeping*, 1772. Oil on canvas, 37⅛ × 32¼″. *Philadelphia Museum of Art. Given by the Barra Foundation, Inc.*

31. Charles Willson Peale, *The Edward Lloyd Family,* 1771. Oil on canvas, 48 x 57½". *The Henry Francis du Pont Winterthur Museum, Delaware.*

32. Charles Willson Peale, *Richard Bennett Lloyd*, 1771. Oil on canvas, 48 x 36⅛".
The Henry Francis du Pont Winterthur Museum, Delaware.

33. Charles Willson Peale, *George Washington at the Battle of Princeton*, 1779. Oil on canvas, 94 x 59″. *Courtesy of the Pennsylvania Academy of the Fine Arts, Philadelphia. Gift of Maria McKean Allen and Phoebe Warren Downes through the bequest of their mother, Elizabeth Wharton.*

34. Charles Willson Peale, *Henrietta Maria Bordley*, 1773. Oil on canvas, 23 ⅝ x 19". *Honolulu Academy of Arts. Purchase, Academy funds, and Gifts from Robert Allerton, 1972.*

35. Charles Willson Peale, *Ann Proctor*, 1789. Oil on canvas, 22 ½ x 18". *Hammond-Harwood House, Annapolis, Maryland.*

36. Rembrandt Peale, *Charles Willson Peale*, 1812. Oil on canvas, 29¾ x 24½". *Historical Society of Pennsylvania, Philadelphia.*

37. Rembrandt Peale, *Rubens Peale with a Geranium*, 1801. Oil on canvas, 28¼ x 24″. National Gallery of Art, Washington, D.C. Patrons' Permanent Fund.

38. Rembrandt Peale, *William Findley*, 1805. Oil on canvas, 23½ x 16½". *Independence National Historical Park Collection.*

39. Rembrandt Peale, *Thomas Jefferson*, 1805. Oil on canvas, 28 x 23½". *Courtesy of The New-York Historical Society, New York City.*

40. Charles Willson Peale, *Nancy Hallam as Fidèle in "Cymbeline,"* 1771. Oil on canvas, 50 x 40½". *The Colonial Williamsburg Foundation.*

41. Charles Willson Peale, *John Dickinson,* 1770. Oil on canvas, 49 x 39″. *Historical Society of Pennsylvania, Philadelphia.*

42. Charles Willson Peale, *Thomas Jefferson*, 1791. Oil on canvas, 24 x 20″. *Independence National Historical Park Collection, Philadelphia.*

43. Rembrandt Peale, *William Raborg*, 1797. Oil on canvas, 36 x 27″. *Courtesy of the Pennsylvania Academy of the Fine Arts, Philadelphia. Gift of Brigadier General and Mrs. Edgar P. Owens.*

44. Rembrandt Peale, *Sir Joseph Banks*, 1803. Oil on canvas, 23 ½ x 19 ½ ". *Academy of Natural Sciences, Philadelphia.*

45. Charles Willson Peale, *James Peale by Lamplight*, 1822. Oil on canvas, 27 x 36". *Founders Society. The Detroit Institute of Arts.*

46. Rembrandt Peale, *Jacob Gerard Koch,* ca. 1814. Oil on canvas, 34 x 29". *The Los Angeles County Museum of Art. Purchased with Funds Provided by Mr. and Mrs. William Preston Harrison Collection, Mary D. Keeler Bequest and Dr. Dorothea Moore.*

47. Rembrandt Peale, *Jane Griffith (Mrs. Jacob Gerard) Koch,* ca. 1814. Oil on canvas, 34 x 29″. *The Los Angeles County Museum of Art. Purchased with Funds Provided by Mr. and Mrs. William Preston Harrison Collection, Mary D. Keeler Bequest and Dr. Dorothea Moore.*

48. Rembrandt Peale, *Rubens Peale*, 1834. Oil on canvas, 24 x 20". *Wadsworth Atheneum, Hartford, Connecticut. William B. and Mary Arabella Goodwin Collection.*

49. Rembrandt Peale, *Samuel Buckley Morris,* 1795. Oil on canvas, 26 x 22". *Independence National Historical Park Collection, Philadelphia.*

50. Rembrandt Peale, *Judge Moses Levy*, ca. 1807–08. Oil on canvas, 29 x 24½". *Collection of the Montclair Art Museum, Montclair, New Jersey.*

51. Rembrandt Peale, *George Washington*, 1795. Oil on canvas, 21 x 17". *Historical Society of Pennsylvania, Philadelphia.*

52. Charles Willson Peale, *James Peale Painting a Miniature,* 1795. Oil on canvas, 30 x 25″. *Mead Art Museum, Amherst College. Bequest of Herbert W. Pratt '95.*

53. Charles Willson Peale and Rembrandt Peale, *Gilbert Stuart*, 1805. Oil on canvas, 23½ x 19½". *Courtesy of The New-York Historical Society, New York City.*

54. Rembrandt Peale, *John Miller,* 1805–07. Oil on canvas, 27 x 25″. *Private collection.*

55. Charles Willson Peale, *Johann, Baron DeKalb*, 1781–82. Oil on canvas, 22 x 18″.
Independence National Historical Park Collection, Philadelphia.

56. Charles Willson Peale, *Joel Barlow*, 1807. Oil on canvas, 24 x 20". *Diplomatic Reception Rooms, United States Department of State, Washington. Gift of Mr. and Mrs. Joel Barlow, 1970.*

57. Charles Willson Peale, *William Bartram*, 1808. Oil on canvas, 23 x 19". *Independence National Historical Park Collection, Philadelphia.*

58. Charles Willson Peale, *Hannah Moore (Mrs. Charles Willson [3]) Peale*, 1816. Oil on canvas, 24 x 20″. *Courtesy, Museum of Fine Arts, Boston. Gift of Mrs. Reginald Seabury Parker in memory of her husband.*

59. Charles Willson Peale, *Rembrandt Peale,* 1818. Oil on canvas, 27 x 20 ⅞".
National Portrait Gallery, Smithsonian Institution, Washington, D.C.

60. Charles Willson Peale, *Angelica Peale Robinson and Her Daughter Charlotte,*
1818. Oil on canvas, 30 x 24⅞". *Private collection.*

61. Charles Willson Peale, *The Artist in His Museum*, 1822. Oil on canvas, 103½ x 80".
Courtesy of the Pennsylvania Academy of the Fine Arts, Philadelphia. Gift of Mrs. Sarah Harrison (The Joseph Harrison, Jr., Collection).

62. William Birch, *Back of the State House Philadelphia*, 1799. Engraving, 8⁸⁄₁₀ × 11²⁄₁₀″. *Philadelphia Museum of Art. George W. Elkins Collection. Given by Mrs. Walter C. Jenny in memory of her late husband, former Justice of the Museum.*

63. Unknown, from a portrait, since destroyed, by Gilbert Stuart, *Little Turtle (Michiniksa)*, 1797. Lithograph. *Smithsonian Institution, National Anthropological Archives, Bureau of American Ethnology Collection, Washington, D.C.*

64. Charles Willson Peale, *Joseph Brant (Thayendanegea),* 1797. Oil on canvas, 25½ x 21¼". *Independence National Historical Park Collection, Philadelphia.*

65. C.B.J. Fevret De Saint-Memin, *Captain Meri-wether Lewis in Shoshone Costume*, 1807. Watercolor on paper, 6¼ x 3¾". *Courtesy of the New-York Historical Society, New York City. Gift of the heirs of Hall Park McCullough, 1971.*

66. Charles Willson Peale, *The Exhumation of the Mastodon*, 1806–08. Oil on canvas, 50 x 60½". *The Peale Museum, Baltimore.*

67. Benjamin West, *Agrippina with Her Children Going Through the Roman Camp,* 1785. Pen and ink, wash, body color, 16½ x 23″. *Private collection.*

68. Charles Willson Peale, *Mr. and Mrs. James Gittings and Granddaughter,* 1791. Oil on canvas, 40 x 64″. *The Peale Museum, Baltimore.*

69. Benjamin West, *William Penn's Treaty with the Indians*, 1771. Oil on canvas, 75½ x 107¾".
Courtesy of the Pennsylvania Academy of the Fine Arts, Philadelphia. Gift of Mrs. Sarah Harrison (The Joseph Harrison, Jr., Collection).

70. Charles Willson Peale after Charles Catton, Jr., *Noah and His Ark,* 1819. Oil on canvas, 40 ¼ x 50 ¾ ". *Courtesy of the Pennsylvania Academy of the Fine Arts, Philadelphia. Collections Fund.*

71. Charles Willson Peale, *Self-Portrait with Angelica and a Portrait of Rachel,* ca. 1782–85. Oil on canvas, 35⅜ x 27⅝". *The Bayou Bend Collection, The Museum of Fine Arts, Houston.*

72. Titian Ramsay Peale, *Interior of Peale's Museum,* 1822. Ink and water-color sketch on paper, 14 x 20 ¾". *The Detroit Institute of Arts. Founders Society Purchase, Director's Discretionary Fund.*

73. Charles Willson Peale, *Benjamin Franklin*, 1789. Oil on canvas, 36 x 27″. *Historical Society of Pennsylvania, Philadelphia.*

74. Charles Willson Peale, *Conrad Alexandre Gérard,* 1779. Oil on canvas, 95 x 59⅛". *Independence National Historical Park Collection, Philadelphia.*

75. Charles Willson Peale, *Staircase Group*, ca. 1795. Oil on canvas, 89 × 39½". *Philadelphia Museum of Art. George W. Elkins Collection.*

76. Raphaelle Peale, *Venus Rising from the Sea — A Deception,* 1823. Oil on canvas, 29 x 24″. *The Nelson-Atkins Museum of Art, Kansas City, Missouri. Nelson Fund.*

77. Charles Willson Peale, *Self-Portrait (With Spectacles)*, ca. 1804. Oil on canvas, 26 x 22". *Courtesy of the Pennsylvania Academy of the Fine Arts, Philadelphia. Henry D. Gilpin Fund.*

78. Peale's Museum, Golden Pheasants. *Museum of Comparative Zoology, Harvard University.*

79. Titian Ramsay Peale, *Dusky Wolf Devouring a Mule Deer Head,* 1820.
Watercolor on paper, 7½ x 9¼″. *American Philosophical Society, Philadelphia.*

80. Peale's Museum, Ticket to the Museum, 1788. Engraving. *Peale family descent to Elise Peale Patterson de Gelpi-Toro.*

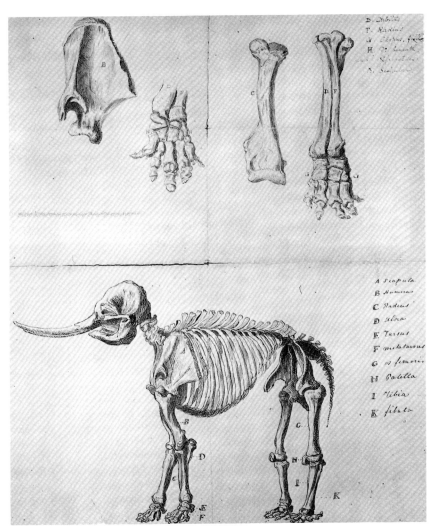

81. Rembrandt Peale, *Working Sketch of the Mastodon*, 1801. Ink and watercolor on paper, 15 3/16 x 12 3/4 ". *American Philosophical Society, Philadelphia.*

THIS FIGURE

Represents a machine for using the Steam Bath.

It was made by Mr. Peale, the proprietor of the Mufeum. The four fides, (which are covered with linen, oiled and painted) are fo connected by folding hinges, that it may be folded up and carried about very conveniently :

A, fhews the pipe by which the fteam enters the machine.

B, the opening of the pipe.

C, the tube from the machine to

D, the tea-kettle in which the water is heated.

E, the feat on which the perfon fits.

F, a piece of cloth lined with oiled cloth, having a hole through which the perfon puts his head and draws it clofe about his neck by a ftring; there are alfo fhort fleaves to put one's hands out occafionally. A tin cover for the tea-kettle fhould be made for the purpofe ; lined with cork that it may fit accurately, and having a hole in its top communicating with the tube, as feen in the figure— The fpout fhould be ftopped that none of the fteam may efcape through it.

82. Drawing and description of the vapor bath, in Henry Wilson Lockette, *An Inaugural Dissertation on the Warm Bath* (Philadelphia, 1801). *American Philosophical Society, Philadelphia.*

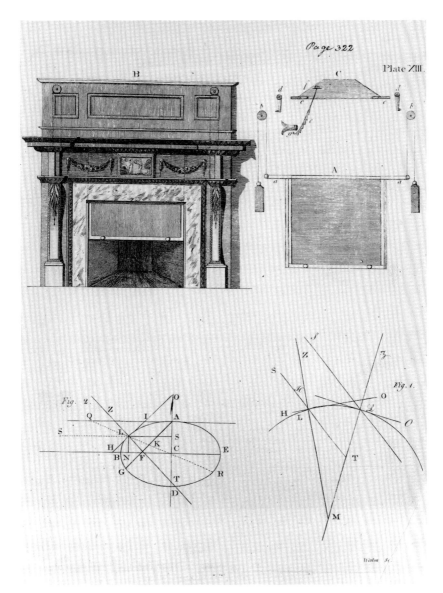

83. Charles Willson Peale and Raphaelle Peale, The Peales' Fireplace Design, 1797. Engraving after an unlocated drawing. *American Philosophical Society,* Transactions *o.s. 5 (1802): plate XIII.*

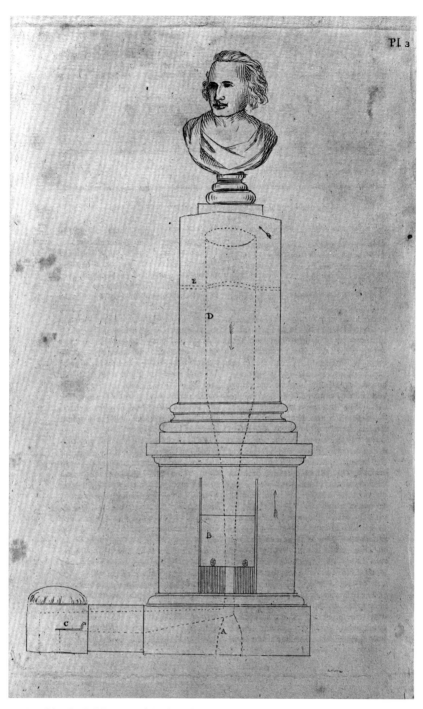

Pl 3

84. Charles Willson Peale's "Smoke Eater." The Weekly Magazine, *2, 25 (July 21, 1798): 353-54.*

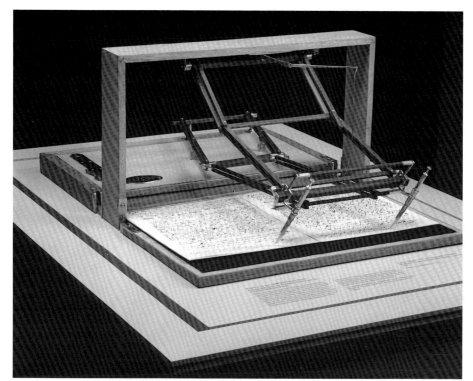

85. Charles Willson Peale, Polygraph. *Prints collection, Manuscripts Division, Special Collections Department, University of Virginia, Charlottesville.*

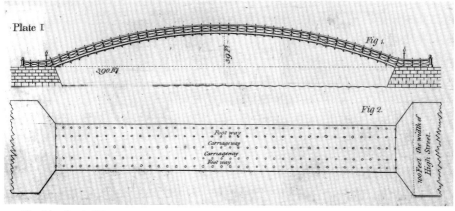

86. Charles Willson Peale, Design for a Bridge over the Schuylkill River in *An Essay on Building Wooden Bridges* (Philadelphia, 1797). *American Philosophical Society.*

and orchards, that on the north side is an old orchard of about 70 Trees it is so far from the House & much out of sight, it is always pillaged & little good [?] from it, that by the barn and other Houses I [?] for my own use, that I might give the fruit to my friends without giving umbrage to my Tennant. When I chuse to send apples to the Market I shall then let him gather & sell them & receive ⅓ the profit. you may think that I have given him too little of this sort of fruit, there are many apple Tree's scattered over different parts of the farm. My wood for firing & fences are along the East side about the skirts of that Meadow, also a strip joining Mr C⅐'s Wisters on the south. If I ever sell any part of this farm it will be the 10 ac[?] on the north, which road divides from the other fields, then leaving me 6 or 7 fields, some of which are large enough to be divided again.

The Sketch before us is taken just within the Gate leading from Germantown. It was my intention to pass over all my sketches with Ink on the spot, in which case they might have been better done, but to postpone doing them & writing my letter, some opportunity of sending might be lost, and I am just able to do this sort of business with this pain in my side, I have been bled, since I began to write in the morning — and find some relief from it. In this view imagine that you see a beautiful Meadow on your right.

The Tennants House seems to terminate the lane, from thence it turns up a gentle declivity to the Mansion, of which you see the Top of a Red roof on the left over the hill. formerly a road went over this hill at the dotted lines — The present road is much better, for you reach the house on the side of 2 stories, the back part is only one story. The common water course is on the edge of the meadow on the right and the dotted line is a ditch to which I have a flood-gate to let the water on the meadow at Pleasure. The Tennant house is white, south east.

This Sketch was the first I made when I set out, but after I had reached the Gate, on seeing the Top of my [?] I conceived that the one above would be preferable, but as little trouble attends the making them you get both, this being so much nearer the [?] I have marked the ends of some [?] between the windows, from these I intend to make a Piazer extending round the south end. at the X is a fine spring running out of a Rock — at this I shall make a spring House & perhaps a mill, embracing the churning of Butter, grinding my tools, beating Hommony, washing cloaths, grinding paints, coarse grinding of feed for cattle &c &c from this spot within my own ground I have so full a fall of water, but if I [?] a mill at [?] by the permission of Mr Cha Wistar to make a tail race through his meadow I shall get 5 feet fall in addition, this would certainly be desirable but it will be attended with greater expence, and therefore I am yet in doubt on the subject, more especially as 10 feet is quite sufficient for the above purposes, yet should I wish to embrace spinning & carding work & cotton the latter is important. The Clump of Tree's at the end of the Tennant House are the weeping willow, they are so indifferently drawn that I think it necessary to mention it—they [?] a charming shade to the House.

87. Charles Willson Peale, Sketches of Belfield, in Charles Willson Peale to Rembrandt Peale, 1810. *American Philosophical Society, Philadelphia.*

the House. I have fences to make round this House for a Garden &c. all & such things
29. help to give value to the place, and comfort to those whom I employ to aid me in farming

This View is taken at a [...] the [...]
house a small Distance, by which you see
the roof of the Mansion over the Garden fence
which of boards on a Stone Wall. The Barn
and one of the Barracks on the West. the
Coach House near the Center, Spring house
on the East side and the Bath House below
it. There is 4 large Popplers (Tulip Tree) which
crosses the Road, and the Lumbardy Poppler
a row of them on your right hand, just
about the Bath House is a small fish pond
with about 200 Catfish which I brought
from the falls of Schuylkill, in the month
of May we can always get a supply of them
and they may be carried a considerable distance
alive [...] tubs with clover to keep them from
crowding each other with their sharp spines.

I ought to have told you that I find the soreness of my side abated considerably, and I have but
little doubt that I shall be wholly recovered before I finish this letter. I shall be very much
mortified should it miscarry, because I know these sketches will give you considerable amusement, as they will exercise your Judgment to connect the whole together in order to
have a comprehensive & correct Idea of the Place which I have chosen to spend the remainder of my days. yet I am apprehensive that it will require all your knowledge of perspective and drawing to understand them so slightly [...] rude are the lines, with my [...]
and not done either in the Designs [...] manuscript, with any previous Study, but straight
forward as my Idea's occurred at the time of execution. But to go on my next Sketch will be
just beyond the Popplers, near the corner of the fence of the yard.

In this view the stone steps at the End of the
house is seen which lead to [...] in front of the
Garden, the Garden pails are on a stone wall
on which grows Creepers, now in full bloom
they are a fine crimoson [...] flowers in Clusters
and an abundance of humming are daily suching
the honey. Green Gages, Damsons & quinces all
along this wall & beneath rose bushes, you may
discover a long Roof which has shelters for Bee
hives, conveniently situated to get their food from
the flowers of the Garden. a House between the
Coach House & Mansion we call the smoke-
house is so much covered with that elegant
Creeper that it can scarcely be seen, I intend
to convert it into a Wash House & raise a small
Story over it for the purpose of a smoke-house
If I have enough stone but when I raise the
[...] Story it will be dashed with white mortar
[...] appearance more decent — and then the
Creeper must be removed because they ruin
the roofs of such houses as they are suffered to
grow on. The 2 end windows of the Mansion, a window near the Garden, one window & a Door leadi
and took the partition down I made a door leading to the Balcony, because I thought it necessary to have on
large room in a Country House here many of family portraits are placed. The room with it on this
[...], I am now writing in, & have your [...] Portrait, the last you painted in my left hand, and when i
get to a period, or changing my paper, or thinking what I shall next write on, I cast a look
on it & think what I shall dictate to amuse you, and then the thought of your long absen
intrudes — But the great object for which we are separated, the pleasure which you will hav
in making acquaintance with the first men in Europe, your raising [...] a Portrait Painte
and withall your increase of knowledge generally — all these things help to [...] me for your
long stay abroad. I am at this minute looking for Rubens to bring here a Gentleman who [...]
your letter, whom I have heard praises your Portraits up to the Skies. I long to see him, I [...]

88. John Woodside, *Lemon Hill,* 1807. *Historical Society of Pennsylvania, Philadelphia.*

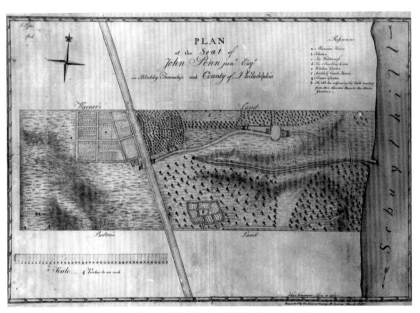

89. John Nancarrow, Plan of the Seat of John Penn, 1787. *Historical Society of Pennsylvania, Philadelphia.*

90. *The Woodlands,* in William Birch, *The Country Seats of the United States of North America* (Philadelphia, 1808). *Historical Society of Pennsylvania, Philadelphia.*

91. Jane Bradick, *View of the West Front of Monticello and Gardens,* 1825. *Thomas Jefferson Memorial Foundation.*

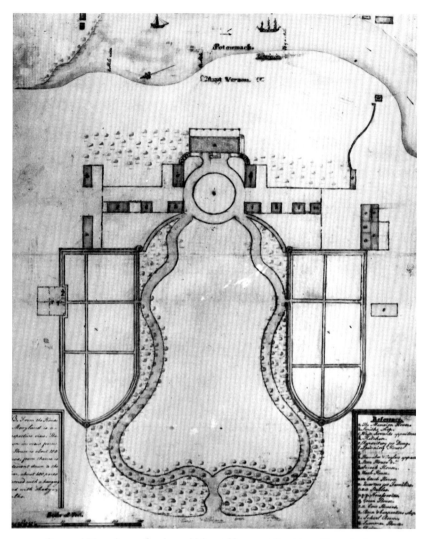

92. Samuel Vaughan, *Gardens of Mount Vernon*, 1787. *Mount Vernon Ladies Association.*

93. Charles Willson Peale, *View of the Garden at Belfield*, 1815–1816. Oil on canvas, 28 x 36½". *Private Collection. Photograph Courtesy of Kennedy Galleries, Inc., New York City.*

94. Charles Willson Peale, *Belfield Farm,* 1815–20. Oil on canvas, 10¾ x 15⅝". *Detroit Institute of Arts. Gift of Dr. and Mrs. Irving Levitt.*

could the dead feel any interest in Monu-
-ments or other remembrances of them, when, as
Anacreon says ΟΛΙγη δε κεισομεσθα
κονις, οςεων λυθεν]ων
the following would be to my Manes the most
gratifying.
On the grave a plain die or cube of 3.f without any
mouldings, surmounted by an Obelisk
of 6.f. height, each of a single stone:
on the faces of the Obelisk the following
inscription, & not a word more
          Here was buried
          Thomas Jefferson
Author of the Declaration of American Independance
          of the Statute of Virginia for religious freedom
     & Father of the University of Virginia.
because by these, as testimonials that I have lived, I wish most to
be remembered. _____ to be of the coarse stone of which
my columns are made, that no one might be tempted
hereafter to destroy it for the value of the materials.
my bust by Ciracchi, with the pedestal and truncated
column on which it stands, might be given to the University
if they would place it in the Dome room of the Rotunda.
on the Die of the Obelisk might be engraved
          Born apr. 2. 1743. O.S.
          Died _____

95. Thomas Jefferson, Sketch for his own tombstone, n.d. *Massachusetts Historical
Society.*

96. Cornelia Jefferson Randolph, att., A Garden Seat by Mr. Jones from Chambers's Kew, ca. 1820. *Thomas Jefferson Papers, Manuscripts Division, Special Collections Department, University of Virginia Library.*

97. A reconstruction of Peale's transparent Triumphal Arch, 1783–84, Drawing by Lester Hoadley Sellers based on description in Peale's *Autobiography*. *American Philosophical Society, Philadelphia.*

98. Hugh Reinagle, *View of Elgin Gardens on Fifth Avenue*, ca. 1811. *Eno Collection, Miriam & Ira D. Wallach Division of Art, Prints and Photographs, The New York Public Library. Astor, Lenox and Tilden Foundations.*

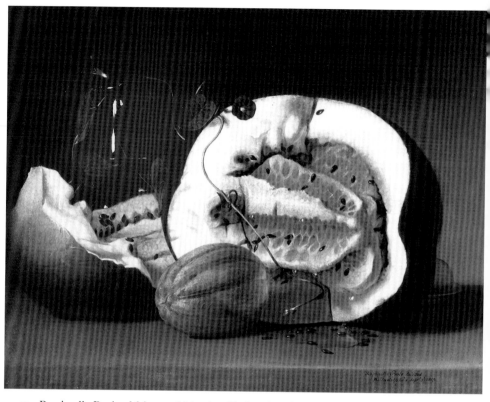

99. Raphaelle Peale, *Melons and Morning Glories*, 1813. Oil on canvas, 20 ¾ x 25 ¾". *National Museum of American Art, Smithsonian Institution, Washington, D.C.*

100. Jan Gossart called Mabuse, *Saint Luke Painting the Madonna,* ca. 1520. Tempera on panel, 9½ x 11¾". *Kunsthistorisches Museum, Vienna.*

101. Benjamin West, *Angelica Kauffmann,* ca. 1763. Crayon, pen and ink on paper, 6 x 4 ¾". *Friends Historical Collection, Swarthmore College, Swarthmore, Pennsylvania.*

Colley Cibber, Esq.
late Poet-Laureat.

102. Edward Fisher after Jean-Baptiste Van Loo, *Colley Cibber and His Daughter*, 1758. Engraving. *The Henry E. Huntington Library and Art Gallery, San Marino, California.*

103. Dirck Jacobsz, *Jakob Cornelisz van Oostsanen Painting a Portrait of His Wife*, ca. 1550. Oil on wood panel, 24 $\frac{7}{16}$ x 19 $\frac{7}{16}$". *The Toledo Museum of Art, Toledo, Ohio. Gift of Edward Drummond Libbey.*

The point is quickly clear: The interplay of word and image within the portrait and of broadside and picture more fully make this a rich emblematic commentary on the current political crisis. As an independent work of art, the painting and its mezzotint must be judged awkward performances, spatially crowded and rhetorically stilted. The existence of the elaborate broadside guide to the work suggests Peale's didactic intention in assisting his potential audience to read the emblematic program. Sales of the mezzotint were small, however, despite Pitt's political appeal and Peale's emblematic clarity. He did, however, complete a second version of the large-scale portrait for the sophisticated politicians of the Annapolis statehouse.[16]

Peale's 1770 portrait of his friend John Beale Bordley (fig. 5) suggests both his persistence in the emblematic mode and his sensitivity to his native American context. The painting was a sequel to the *Pitt* portrait and intended for the same patron, Edmund Jenings; it is almost as large (84½ by 58½ inches), similar in structure, with the figure gesturing toward the statue that holds the Phrygian liberty cap and, in this case, also the scales of justice. Where Pitt holds the Magna Carta, Bordley leans on the book which notes in Latin that the laws of England have been changed, and at his feet is a ripped sheet with the legible inscription "Imperial Civil / Law-Summary / Proceeding," an angry counterpart of the *Pitt,* where Liberty tramples underfoot the petition of the Congress at New York. But the contrasts are equally striking. A curving tree trunk replaces the Doric column of the *Pitt,* and the setting is rural America rather than urban London or Rome, for Bordley represented the agricultural gentry of a prosperous America. His "altar" is a large rock; and the peach tree, the house under construction in the background (Bordley's own, at Wye Island on Maryland's Eastern Shore, was of a different construction), the sheep and pack driver—all thus emblematize the rural wealth of America now in danger of forfeiture by British colonial policy.[17]

Peale even took care that in fulfilling his patron's desire for native American material, it would function beyond the merely topographical. He placed a flowering jimsonweed—named, he writes Jenings, "from Jamestown (Virginia), where they were found in abundance on the first settling of that place"[18] — at the foot of the statue, mentioning to Jenings that it was known to cause madness and violent death to those who ate it. As Charles Sellers rightly emphasized, such a choice was no accident but "a warning similar to the rattlesnake's banner, 'Don't tread on me,'

that to devour the American plant [itself a visual pun on plantation?]
will lead to madness and death."[19] In the jimsonweed, the historical past
becomes present, and American natural history is turned to political
purposes. Peale had learned well the emblematic mode of portraiture.
From copying Old World usages he began to refashion it partially to
native American purposes.[20] In *The Artist in His Museum* some fifty years
later, he would set a similar gesturing figure into a context that would,
by the canons of Reynoldsian imitation, combine the beauties of nature, which the Bordley portrait emphasized, with those of art — an art
freed from the directly imitative neoclassicism of statues and columns
and altars and togas. The exterior of Whitehall would be exchanged
for the interior of Independence Hall, but the mode of relating the component parts of the picture would still be essentially that of the emblematic portraiture he had learned as a young man.

In the years after 1770, Peale's portraits were less complex, and there
was less demand for full-scale emblematic portraits. The outlet for his
emblematic inclination lay rather in a range of patriotic purposes. The
political and military struggles of the war for independence had their
conceptual and aesthetic counterpart in a national search for an adequate system to express and propagandize the emerging United States
of America. In his later autobiography, Peale noticed that as early as
1765 he had helped to make "emblematical ensigns" as a part of the Newburyport, Massachusetts, public protest against the Stamp Act, and in
1775 he was called upon to design an emblematic flag for the Baltimore
Independent Company as the colonies prepared for war.[21] In the later
years of the war, Peale made frequent emblematic contributions to the
development and popularization of a national public iconography, and
this persisted after the war as well. He designed and decorated triumphal arches to celebrate the birth of the French dauphin in 1782, which,
with all its coats of arms, sunbursts, and wreaths of laurel, included
also a panel with the words:

> MARIA ANTONIETTA, *QUEEN OF FRANCE*
> No emblems here the Tablet grace;
> What Pencil can her Emblem trace?
> Let Beauty, Wit, and Worth advance,
> And joining form the Queen of France.[22]

The poetic denial underlines the point, for the emblematic had always
involved a shifting combination of verbal and visual components, de-

pendent for its achievement upon the conceptual completion of the incomplete pattern within the mind of the viewer-reader rather than merely a literal, perceptual recognition of the empirical world.

It is unnecessary here to detail Peale's repeated excursions into the emblematic for political purposes: sometimes relatively simple transparent paintings, sometimes elaborate programs on triumphal arches, theatrical performances for Washington's procession northward toward his inauguration, or other kinds of emblematic displays ending—not always successfully!—in fireworks. The evidence of these activities has been amply documented by Charles Coleman Sellers,[23] but the importance of these activities needs clarifying. In the first place, they remind us that artistic activity in the eighteenth century was rich, by no means limited to what we now call the "fine arts" of painting, sculpture, and architecture. English court masques from the time of Inigo Jones on, Dresden court parades, waterworks and fireworks—like those for which Handel wrote music—and the arrangement of gardens at Stowe, Stourhead, and Versailles typically drew upon the emblem tradition and the leading artists of the day to shape and execute their vision.[24] One thus needs to feel the continuity between Peale's pictorial activities and these other efforts.

In the second place, Peale's efforts were part of a search for American national emblems, an aesthetic contribution to a process of national self-definition that involved the reinterpretation and adaptation of traditional emblems and the creation of new ones to define the emerging nation. Finally, one must insist that if the emblematic tradition had its origins in a sophisticated courtly tradition—clearly in the eighteenth century and perhaps especially, though by no means exclusively, in Peale's America[25]—it had been translated as well into popular terms for a larger audience. If the Pitt mezzotint and broadside were rather elaborately verbal, the triumphal arches were not, and the emblematic could be found in cartoons and broadsides, on currency and newspaper mastheads, as well as in portraits, on the pediments of public buildings, and in collections of poetry and prose from Ben Franklin's broadsides to Barlow's *Columbiad*. Although scholars of American art history in its early years have tended to emphasize the native (that is, realistic, hardline) qualities of American art, the larger American audience during Peale's lifetime was also more or less familiar with reading experience emblematically.[26] Thus one returns to Peale's portraiture with a clear sense that our reading of these works in emblematic ways is not a hermetic

and anachronistic mode of analysis imposed upon the works, but a recapturing of the late eighteenth- and early nineteenth-century cognitive modes that Peale shared with his patrons, whether gentlemen or
the wider republican audience he increasingly sought.

The emblematic portrait of a public figure was by no means Peale's
special province. Benjamin Franklin had been probably the first national
hero thus treated, from Fragonard's 1777 apotheosis on. (The Fragonard
image had its origins in a verbal motto — in this case, Turgot's "*Eripuit
coelo, fulmen sceptrumque tiranis.*") Peale's first Franklin portrait was a copy
of the David Martin "thumb" portrait, with the bust of Newton behind
the table (American Philosophical Society, Philadelphia). Then, after
a smaller head-and-shoulders oval portrait and mezzotint (Pennsylvania
Academy of the Fine Arts, Philadelphia), he produced his 1789 half-length
of the aged Franklin seated, abstracted in thought at a desk, with lightning illuminating a group of buildings in the background, an inkstand
at the lower right, a lightning rod in his hand to the left, and between
them a sheaf of papers with a long inscription defining the electrical
principle that makes necessary the lightning rod (fig. 73). It is, thus,
a carefully balanced pictorial statement, verbal as well as visual, of the
sublime action of natural forces that calls into being human thought,
the verbal articulation of ideas and principles, and the invention of means
to come to terms with nature. Peale had abandoned the toga-draped
figure and classical gods in attendance — as Benjamin West did not in
his post-1800 version of Franklin, with *putti* — but he still organizes the
empirical world emblematically to create a portrait the meaning of
which is a function of the viewer's intellectual recognition of a pattern
of significance.[27]

Of all the American national heroes subject to emblematic treatment,
surely George Washington is the most important, from the Revolution
on to the decades after his death, which saw an outpouring of graphic
mourning pictures, apotheoses, and statues from Canova's ill-fated North
Carolina version to the notorious Horatio Greenough Olympic *Washington* for the national capitol. Peale had five separate sittings with Washington from 1772 to 1795. In most of the works produced out of these
opportunities, the background is empty or a simple landscape, without
curtains, columns, and other conventional accessories, as Sellers points
out. But Sellers rightly singles out the 1779 sitting, the result of which
was what he calls a "court painting in the finest sense,"[28] that is, an emblematic portrait (fig. 33). Peale the designer here drapes the fallen Hes-

sian flags of Trenton to the right, the British flags of Princeton to the left, a version of the American flag in the sky above, two cannons emphasizing the two battles. The raw landscape contains a train of marching prisoners and barren trees — not only, one suspects, a realistic temporal clue but also an emotional statement from Peale, who hated war and conflict and searched always for harmony. Nassau Hall stands on the horizon — again, not only as an index of location but also as an image of the seat of learning that could produce intellectual harmony.[29]

This public portrait, though commissioned for the chamber of the Supreme Executive Council of Pennsylvania, spent most of its early years in Peale's possession, in the 1780s in his first portrait gallery on Lombard Street. After 1802, when Peale moved into the former statehouse, the portrait remained there (even though the government had removed to Harrisburg) on one of the end walls of the Long Room next to the equally large-scale 1779 emblematic portrait of the French minister in America, Conrad Gérard, with its statues of America and France entwined in flowers (fig. 74).[30] These portraits are not visible in either Titian's sketch or the finished canvas of *The Artist in His Museum*. Their absence suggests that perhaps they had been crowded out of the Long Room by the ever present need for more space for newly acquired objects in the museum, or else that Peale chose to "remove" them from the wall in the final picture, perhaps to avoid their drawing the viewer's attention too clearly or forcefully to that perspectival focal point or to avoid their competing as separate emblematic statements within the total pattern of the picture. A third, equally intriguing possibility is that these large portraits are hung at the other end of the Long Room, that is, behind where we as viewers are standing. We cannot finally know Peale's reasoning on this particular issue, in the absence of documentary evidence, but we can point to the several grounds here upon which Peale's choice to exclude the Washington and Gérard might be based, grounds that clearly did shape his decisions more generally in this picture: historical (the "actual" situation of the Long Room in 1822), pictorial (the formal need to create a coherent, visually satisfying design), emblematic (the relation of parts to a total program of meaning), and epistemological (the relation of the viewer outside to the view within the canvas).

The portraits that are visible on the walls in *The Artist in His Museum* are not large-scale emblematic portraits of the type we have been discussing, but head-and-shoulders works, mostly without background, in what came to be the standard museum format of about 22 by 19 inches, mounted in uniform oval gilt frames. The design within Peale's museum in the 1822 self-portrait of the artist lay not in the isolated significance of individual portraits but in the pattern of the whole, in the use of the portraits within a total program, in the role they play in bringing "into public view the beauties of Nature and art." In *The Artist in His Museum* individual heads are not recognizable, though it seems likely that the military one closest to us, in the upper left-hand corner, is that of the Baron de Kalb (fig. 55). If so, this is particularly appropriate, for Peale's portrait collection began, in at least one version of the history of the museum, with the Kalb portrait, completed only two months before the general's death after the battle of Camden in 1780.[31] The argument about the function of the object to denote the museum's origin is reinforced spatially by the placement directly below him, in the vertical strip of the doorway under the eagle, of another such object, the Allegheny paddlefish, with its inscription: "With this article the Museum commenced, June 1784." As Peale's portrait gallery of the 1780s expanded into the more comprehensive museum housed in the statehouse, the portraits came to function as instances of measuring past and present military heroism, public and private merit — in politics, natural philosophy, and even longevity (age itself as a human merit and standard). The collection focused primarily on national figures, but because Peale was an international *philosophe* in attitude, it included as well some French and German heroes, such as Lafayette, Baron Cuvier, and Alexander von Humboldt. Peale's printed guides to the paintings offered biographical précis with pointed indications of the public merit and moral character of these individuals, and the collection thus becomes a visual expression of the age's concern with biography.[32]

Peale's preoccupation with biography was shared by Jeremy Belknap, author of *American Biography,* and the collections of the Massachusetts Historical Society (founded in 1791) and other groups; indeed, it stretched back at least as far as Book II of Cotton Mather's *Magnalia* as a series of Plutarchian standards from the past for the emulation of the present and future. Another reminder of the prevalence of this attitude and expressive mode appeared two years after Peale's *Artist in His Museum* in young Samuel F. B. Morse's famous portrait of Lafayette, done during his triumphal return tour of the United States in 1824 (City Hall, New York City).[33] The French hero stands on a classical balcony with the portrait busts of Washington and Franklin, his American counterparts, displayed on the balustrade behind him. The setting sun that illuminates the scene is not only an allusion to Lafayette's age; it suggests as well the dying of the great heroic age.

Indeed, the literary heroes of the romantic era would be defined largely in other terms: not as models of republican emulation but as unaccommodated individuals, frequently set off in isolation from or at odds with the national experience. Rip Van Winkle, Arthur Gordon Pym, and Ahab come quickly to mind. Hester Prynne is problematically so — her daughter, Pearl, will become the heroine of the future only after she is humanized and loses her specifically emblematic status, as her mother never fully can. Fenimore Cooper, in whose writings, as in those of Irving and Bryant, one finds frequent allusions to "emblems" (which, we would argue, should not be translated into the later — and different — "symbol"), is transitional, as creator both of Harvey Birch and *The Pilot* and of the stiff formal and social heroes and heroines of his romances. If Natty Bumppo of *The Deerslayer* (1840) is the new unaccommodated hero, we must remember that he "grew," in Cooper if not in his own life chronologically, out of the emblematic hero of *The Prairie* (1827), whose first appearance against the garish sunset sky is the vernacular equivalent of Morse's *Lafayette.* The gap that separates the old man of 1827 on the bluff in the open vastness of the rural West from the old gentleman in small clothes raising the curtain of his museum in Philadelphia in 1822 is an important one, to which we need to return.

For the present, though, we can reenter the Long Room with a firmer sense of the emblematic tradition within which Peale frequently worked — not as an occasional aberration or an unfortunate European heritage that sometimes tainted his "Americanness" as an artist, but as a substantial part of Peale's and his generation's way of seeing and knowing, their cognitive equipment, and their way of visually and verbally shaping their understanding of their universe. During the 1820s Peale had a renewed interest in painting self-portraits: in three half-lengths, he shows himself with a palette or brush "in the character of a painter," in another with a mastodon bone as a public lecturer. The commission to do the large-scale *Artist in His Museum* produced initially and rapidly another half-length in which he tried out in a preliminary way his unusual scheme for backlighting the head.[34] The task, in the final work, was to fill in that space, to articulate in the painting with the emblematic mode fully at his command the meaning of the museum. We need, then, to examine that space, for only after we have understood the contribution and role of the elements chosen for inclusion therein to Peale's conceptual universe will we be fully prepared to define precisely how the figure functions within the painting to organize meaning, to "bring forth into public view, the beauties of Nature and art, the rise and progress of the Museum."

The Beauties of Nature

The history of Peale's museum, the growth of its collection, its absorption of Peale's energies to the point where he abandoned painting almost completely during the years 1798–1804, and the connection of the activities and achievements of the museum to those of other institutions and individuals, cooperatively and competitively, is a story that has often been told. Similarly, the strains and tensions between the museum's scientific and didactic purposes or between the Peales' roles as curators and cataloguers and their roles as artists and promoter-showmen — these also are well known. What must concern us here is the significance of the elements Peale selected from that long and complex story for inclusion within the picture, so that we may understand how his choices function to make the design of *The Artist in His Museum* "expressive."

One choice, implied in the commission, is so obvious as to be easily overlooked: Peale's decision to show "the beauties of Nature" indoors, within the museum walls, rather than in their original outdoor setting. In this painting, Peale has studiously eliminated the exterior world, not only by enclosing us within the perspectival lines of the Long Room, but also by arranging what we do see to reinforce that sense of enclosure. The turkey from the Long expedition is, we have noted, limp and dead, awaiting taxidermic transformation into a piece of museum statuary. The cases along the left wall offer us views of other birds; they barely give us a glimpse of the natural setting that the Peales painted on the walls of those cases to locate the birds and animals within their habitats for the museum visitor.

Clearly this was a choice; Peale's interest in "Nature" was not confined to its role within the museum. A number of his portraits had included landscape settings. During his 1801 boat trip up the Hudson in search of the mastodon bones, he had excitedly sketched view after watercolor view of the passing scenery as the boat moved toward Newburgh,[35] and the key pictorial record of that venture, the 1806–08 "Mammoth Picture," was a painting with an outdoor setting. As he approached his official retirement in 1810, Peale purchased land in the suburbs of Phila-

delphia near Germantown and established Farm Persevere, later Belfield. Here he not only carried on agricultural experiments in consulta-
tion with Thomas Jefferson and other gentleman farmers and scientific
agriculturists, but also, like Jefferson at Monticello, laid out an elaborate emblematic garden with statues, walkways, grottoes, and pedestals
with appropriate mottoes — a complex program modeled upon English
gardens of the first half of the eighteenth century. Belfield is important in our present context because Peale consciously eliminated it from
The Artist in His Museum. In Titian's sketch, Peale's Belfield landscapes
(figs. 93, 94) are clearly visible in the right foreground, but these emblems of his life of rural retirement have been excluded from the final
work, their place taken by the table, the curtain, and the skeleton of the
mastodon.[36]

Comparison of Titian's preliminary watercolor with Peale's final painting makes clear that Peale has redesigned the exhibition space of the
Long Room for pictorial purposes. He has preserved the regularity of
his perspective lines on the left, even though he has opened them up
at the base. But instead of contrasting these to the predominantly vertical lines and illuminated box forms of the outside window wall on the
right, as we see them recorded in the watercolor, he has draped the curtain on that side, confining the strong light primarily to the area in front
of the curtain and filling in the lower half of the foreground with the
pile of bones and the table. Behind them stands the skeleton of the mastodon, with the intertwined heads of the llama, deer, and other quadrupeds vaguely visible between the mastodon's legs. In thus arranging his
material, Peale gave up the possibility of juxtaposing the more purely
geometrical and rectilinear design of the museum to the soft curves of
the black-dressed central figure of himself, and offers us instead in the
museum space a counterpoint of light gridded pattern on the left and
the dark and murky irregular shapes on the right.

The overall patterning is reinforced by the artist's sensitive treatment
of color and detail.[37] The deep red of the damask curtain is brighter
in intensity on the left side, and the gold-fringed bottom of the curtain
is confined also to the left half, where it is carefully related in hue and
placement to the band of gilt that frames the two rows of portraits. Indeed, the little decorative band that separates the portraits from the four
rows of bird cases below is a stylized gold and red fan pattern, which
specifically echoes in two dimensions both the red and gold color and
the lacy pattern of the curtain and its fringe. The other strong gold note

in the picture is the Quaker lady, placed directly under the vertical line from which hangs a golden gas lamp. Color links her with the left side, though her hands are raised in a gesture of wonder at the vision across the room. She is looking at the mastodon.

Clearly, all of this formal evidence bespeaks a carefully premeditated arrangement of the design of the painting. Peale controls the viewer's perceptual experience by reorganizing the museum space. In the conceptual patterning, the emblematic significance of the two sides of the picture, he found the appropriate pictorial language for expressing the meaning of the museum.

This was indeed part of an ongoing process for Peale, and by no means an isolated pictorial problem. There is considerable evidence that over the years, in the constant arrangement and rearrangement of the museum from one location to another and as new materials were added, Peale was especially sensitive to spatial arrangement as a mode of shaping meaning and — equally important — the visitor's perception of meaning. He took pride in the "elegant appearance" of the Long Room, the rows of gilt-framed portraits, the cases "neat without being gaudy," the framed catalogue, which "makes a beautiful division" of the shelves from end to end of the room.[38]

The significance of his aesthetic pride comes clear in his introductory lecture on natural history of 1799. He contrasted the modern awareness of the earth with that of the ancients, who "had to remember all creation as it were in a Mass; jumbled together." The modern mind, in possessing a system of classification and arrangement, gains "possession of the master key of a grand Pallace by which we can step into each of the apartments, and open any of the Cabinets, to become acquainted with their contents."[39] Peale's architectural metaphor here is not merely decorative. The linguistic equation of mental processes with spatial arrangement is a central clue to reading the architectural arrangement of Peale's museum and its eventual crystallization in *The Artist in His Museum*. It is Peale's mode of using space to mirror, and in turn to replicate, the parity he believed to exist between the order of the natural universe and that at least potentially within the human mind itself.

Hence the importance of reading the museum not merely as a collection of objects but as shaped space. Others have emphasized Peale's sense of pictorial design in the museum. Sellers links the museum to Peale's interest in moving pictures — "a new kind of painting," in Peale's words.[40] We may note that Peale's placement not only of identifying labels but also of discursive statements, mottoes, and biblical injunctions at strate-

gic points again bespeaks the visual-verbal emblematic habit. The words
not only label or duplicate the visual; they offer a running counterpoint,
and the musical metaphor becomes literal in the organ concerts held
regularly in the Long Room or the anthems that became part of even
the printed version of Peale's lectures, for the aim of learning was, for
him, the recognition of the harmony of the universe.[41] Even the 1802
admission ticket to the museum had an arrangement of birds on the
left side, an American bison to the right, the paddlefish and crustaceans
at the base and at the top, and in the middle of a sunburst that looks
back to centuries of pictorial icons of deity, the open book, plainly inscribed "Nature," with a scroll below: "Explore the wondrous work" (see
fig. 80).[42]

When Peale reopened the museum in its earlier Lombard Street location in the fall of 1797 after a bad recurrence of the yellow fever epidemic in Philadelphia, he tried to reassure potential visitors of the salu-
brious location of the spot and emphasized how "the works of Nature"
were "so well calculated to delight the mind and enlarge the understanding," as if these mental processes were needed, implicitly, as a bulwark
against the irrational assault of diseased nature.[43] Three years later, at
the University of Pennsylvania, in his introductory lecture to a series
on "The Science of Nature," he makes clear that its purpose is "that of
manifesting by those works the goodness and wisdom of the Creator,
in making every being in the best form to ensure its happiness, obtaining its support, with its connections and dependence toward the support of other beings; — In short, to display by visible objects the harmony of the universe."[44] Peale's teleological premises were, of course,
not his alone, but shared with his generation and all those who believed
in the great chain of being. Not only do individual works give evidence
of a benevolent creative power. We behold them in their interconnected-
ness, and that is made known to our consciousness not by an act of faith
but through God's — and after Him, Peale's — "displaying" them to us.
Earlier in the lecture he had envisioned for his audience the kind of
museum space he had in mind:

> Let us suppose we have before us a spacious building, with a suite of
> rooms several hundred feet in length, even the length of one of the squares
> of our city, in which are arranged specimens of all the various animals
> of this vast continent, and of all other countries; — these in high preser-
> vation, under glass to secure them from injury. — Let us suppose them
> classically arranged, so that the mind may not be confused and distracted
> in viewing and studying such a multitude of objects.[45]

The elements of the design of both the museum and its avatar, the 1822 painting, are already there in his suppositions of 1800. The Long Room itself extended some hundred feet across the front of the statehouse, located at the spatial center of the urban civic core of Philadelphia, an experiential index of its conceptual centrality to human life. Within the museum the arrangement was to be governed by the need to order human perception and understanding. The epistemological model is Lockean. The creator is known not through innate ideas or through faith, but through the mind's rational processing of the sense data of visible objects presented in such a way as to ensure clear discrimination of the signs, without confusion or distraction.

Finally, as many have pointed out, Peale's insistence that the objects be "classically arranged" is the clue that his ordering principle is that of Linnaean biology. He acknowledged that indebtedness again and again in his lectures. Linnaeus (1707–78) had "opened the book of nature to a wondering world" and had traveled "to acquire knowledge, *that* knowledge be defused into classical arrangement, which will be admired for ages," as he put it in 1813.[46] Such an arrangement, Peale insisted at the end of his 1800 lecture, is not his own idiosyncratic preference. The arrangement is Linnaean, he said, "not because I have chosen it, but because the world has proved that Linnaeus had judiciously adopted it."[47] The order exists in the world, it is not imposed upon it. Linnaeus's classificatory system of orders and genuses, the *classes* of creation, is, in Peale's estimation, an observation and ordering of the truth of the visible universe. Lockean empiricism posited the reality of the phenomenal world, that things are not merely outward signs of the noumenal, or manifestations of the essential; Lockean epistemology had also located the problem of knowing within the human mind, that tabula rasa registering and ordering the sense data, "simple ideas," which it received from the visible universe.

Linnaeus's Lockean premises are clear in the introduction of his *Systema naturae,* published in English translation in London in 1806: man "is able to reason justly upon whatever discovers itself to his sense; and to look with reverence and wonder, upon the works of Him who created all things."[48] "Sense" is the organ of perception; reason the discriminating power of the mind to sort and judge. The object in nature "discovers itself" — that is, it makes itself available through the senses — to that perceiving and reasoning mind which, once it has performed those acts, may "look with reverence and wonder, upon the works of Him who created all things."[49] One must insist upon the specific dynamics of the

Lockean epistemology here because it is ultimately recapitulated in Peale's *Artist in His Museum* in the tiny figures in the background. The man sees, as the birds in the cases discover themselves to his sense; the father and son with a book reason justly upon the significance of the arrangement visually available in the cases and verbally ordered in rational sequences in the catalogue in the child's hand, while the lady closest to us stands with hands raised in a gesture of wonder (her Quaker religion implies the "reverence"). The visual sign system in the picture is an exact replication of the underlying Lockean/Linnaean epistemology.

Linneaus's statement had gone on to make even clearer the theological implication: "That existence is surely contemptible, which regards only the gratification of instinctive wants, and the preservation of a body made to perish." Mere sensory stimulation was not enough, though the emphasis is not on the traditional body-soul split but on the decay of nature. Linnaeus concludes: "It is therefore the business of a thinking being to look forward to the purposes of all things; and to remember that the end of creation is, that God may be glorified in all his works." No Westminster catechism here, no decision, as Thoreau was to wryly put it, that men "have somewhat hastily concluded that it is the chief end of man here to 'glorify God and enjoy him forever.'"[50] The point of empiricism was not transcendence out of the natural world; it was circular, to know God through his works.[51]

In the 1799 lecture, Peale recorded for his audience a moment in his own experience that reinforces the point in these Lockean religious terms:

> Never shall I forget my disagreeable sensations, when a naturalist, my friend, demanded of me, why I called a toad, ugly? — My conscience instantly smote me for presuming to depreciate the works of *Divine Wisdom;* and from that moment became convinced, that everything is beautiful in its kind; and I have now a continued pleasure in the contemplation of many things which once appeared disgusting and terrible to me.[52]

This is no ecstatic moment, no mystical awakening as a transparent eyeball, no transcendental longing of the moth for the star. Its closest analogue is not Emerson or Kant or Poe but Jonathan Edwards in his description of the effects of grace as a "new sense" upon the Lockean self in his "Personal Narrative":

> After this my sense of divine things gradually increased . . . the appearance of every thing was altered. . . . And scarce any thing, among all the works of nature, was so sweet to me as thunder and lightning; formerly, nothing had been so terrible to me.[53]

Edwards's sense of deity is more direct and powerful, and Peale's more mediated, but it is a matter of the degree to which the movement from sense to understanding leads on to passionate feeling within a common set of Lockean premises, not of kind. They share the perceptual recognition of the order of God's universe, the recording of feelings which move from disgust and terror to delight and pleasure in contemplation, from the perceptual to the conceptual and thence to an aesthetic recognition of the order and beauty of the visible creation. For Peale and his Quaker lady, this recognition has an aesthetic label not part of Edwards's theological vocabulary. It is the perception of the sublime.

But the perception of the sublime, located in the vision of the mastodon on the right side of the painting, can be fully understood only in the context of its counterpart in the beautiful order, "classically arranged," on the left-hand side behind the Quaker lady. Peale's usage of "classical" may seem at first rather odd to our ear, since the arrangement of the cases, portraits, and even the bench is notably lacking in pediments, triglyphs, Ionic pilasters, and the like, though such were the decor of the Assembly Room below, where the Declaration of Independence was signed.[54] Peale is using the term adjectivally in a strict scientific sense, as pertaining to *classus,* the Linnaean mode of identifying objects through their relationships to others of a similar kind, according to sexual differentiation and observable characteristics. Linnaeus's approach was empiricist, dependent upon clear seeing; but it was also based upon a static conception of the universe rather than a dynamic one. Linnaeus had regularized the species empirically into clearer groupings, though the idea of a fixed number of species, unvaried since the Creation, none added, none disappearing, goes back to Aristotle and was part of the heritage of eighteenth-century classifiers and theorists of species, in America as well as in Europe. In this sense, one may say that Peale's notion of "classical" arrangement has not completely lost its ancient Greek connotations.[55] Furthermore, insofar as "classical" is not aesthetically merely a matter of decorative orders but of an attitude toward space, an emphasis on harmonious proportion and balance, then this idea, especially in its Renaissance revival through vanishing-point perspective, is clearly operative in the Peale museum and the Peale picture, from the initial work of his "drawing machine" in the watercolor sketch of the room to its remaining elements in the final painting, especially in the deep perspective space to the left.

The regularity of the perspectival system on the left frames the cases of birds, visibly arranged in their Linnaean classes, thus pulling together the several senses of the term *classical*. Although only vaguely sketched in the painting, the progression is readable to the viewer in the painting as well as in Titian's sketch: from the top rank of raptors (the vultures, hawks, owls — signalized for us in the eagle), to the colorful songbirds in the second rank, and on down to the ducks and the penguins and pelicans of the lower orders of birds on the bottom rank. In the museum, as we have earlier noted, the cases were distinguished with descriptive labels through a numbering system keyed to a printed guidebook (apparently largely ignored by most visitors). In "Walk with a Friend in the Philadelphia Museum," Peale moved methodically from case to case labeling and commenting. On the toucan, for example, he warned his friend,

> [It] furnishes a striking instance of our incapacity on a slight view of judging of the utility of the forms we often meet with that appear strange. But on a closer view we find the perfection of the works of Creation; in providing suitable organs for the support and also happiness of each individual being; each species being fitted to fill their various stations allotted them in the grand scale of Nature, and the more we inspect into her ways, the more we shall have abundant cause to lift up our hearts and minds in love and admiration to the great first cause![56]

Brief perceptual recognition of the forms, taxonomic identification, is not enough; one needs a "closer view" (which obviously its static position in a museum case affords) that allows us to see and to understand the *telos* of each creature and its place in the great chain of being — verbally here, the "scale of Nature," and visually, its location in the grid of museum space.

Most of the birds are simply too small or too sketchily painted to operate for the viewer as individual emblems leading the mind eventually through perception to love and admiration for the great First Cause. Surely the problem of scale (in this second, more particular sense) was itself one reason why Peale eliminated the cases on the opposite wall from the final picture. The minerals and fossils and insects required at certain points mounted microscopes to see and hence to understand their significance, and if the "great scale of Nature" needs to be perceived from the lowest to the highest order, from the fossil past to the available present, from the tiniest insect to the largest carnivore, the painter who operates within these Lockean premises has still to define these relationships and make available their meanings within the visual capacities of paint on canvas and the perceptual capacities of the human viewer.

Peale's recognition of this restriction is available to us in his softened focus on some of the objects and his highlighting of others. The natural order of the birds is also knowable to us through his representative selection of the turkey boldly placed in the left foreground. The turkey, as a western expedition specimen, extends our understanding in complex ways. Alive it had roamed the woods, dead it will be aesthetically transformed, reborn through the magic and restored through the science of taxidermy, and funneled from the open space of our world into its place within the beautiful grid of the Linnaean system. But clearly the American wild turkey had further significance as Peale's 1822 choice for the avatar of the Linnaean world. It was already a national emblem, a clear alternative to the bald eagle placed conspicuously directly above it. Franklin, as is well known, preferred it to the rapacious eagle as the national bird; and there may be an unconscious irony, in the "great scale of Nature," in placing above the raptors portraits of *Homo sapiens* — many of whom are military heroes. But the turkey was already identified with American rural experience. One year after the painting, Fenimore Cooper would make the traditional "turkey shoot" an important scene in the Christmas festivities of Templeton in *The Pioneers.*[57] In 1825 Titian's drawing of the turkey, which he had brought to his father's museum, was engraved for inclusion in the Charles Lucien Bonaparte supplement to Alexander Wilson's *American Ornithology,* published in the same year. John James Audubon, who had also worked briefly on the Bonaparte supplement, went to Florida, where it is likely his own original painting of the wild turkey was completed. By the middle of 1826, Audubon was in England to arrange for the printing of his greatest contribution to American natural history and American nationalism, the elephant folio *Birds of America.* Audubon chose for the first plate of this serial publication the wild turkey and sent the first group of five plates to his wife in the United States in March 1827.[58] The point is clear enough: Charles Willson Peale's emblematic choice of the turkey in *The Artist in His Museum* was part of a nationalistic celebration of the vitality of the American wilderness.

Unlike the eagle placed above, which is assertive if not quite defiant, the turkey is not yet hierarchically posed within the painting.[59] But even bowed in death, awaiting transformation, as an American species with rich connotations identifying it with American experience, it functions within the picture as part of the American nationalist's response to Buffon and those European naturalists who had underestimated North America's contributions to natural history, some in fact arguing that species degenerated in scale and longevity in the New World. The nationalistic argument in terms of species is well known. It was articulated and documented in the learned journals of the day; Jefferson had argued it in his 1785 *Notes on Virginia;* Peale's notes and lectures on natural history, including the "Walk with a Friend," contain many passages contradicting Buffon's charges. Indeed, the argument was sufficiently well known that Washington Irving had used it as deadpan humor in the introductory chapter of *The Sketch Book* (1819).[60] One must not overstate Peale's own position. He was an internationalist, not a narrow or strident nationalist, and the museum included portraits of Humboldt, Cuvier, and Buffon, and specimens from the whole world. But the harmony of the universe that he sought obviously could not be understood by ignoring the special contributions of the new nation and the old earth of this hemisphere.

All of which points us inevitably toward the mastodon on the right side of *The Artist in His Museum,* which clarifies this argument in important ways. The jawbone and leaning leg bone in the right foreground pictorially balance the turkey to the left. They offer us an initial emblematic comparison — of the American past to the American present, a movement from the "beautiful" order of the classically lit cabinets and portraits to the dark and obscure "sublime" of the prehistoric past. Two highlights fall on the teeth of the jawbone and on the painter's palette, to which the leg bone directs our vision, and beyond the partially visible mounted skeleton of the mastodon (itself a work of nature completed by art, the missing bones having been carved of wood by William Rush) we can make out a llama, a deer, an elk, and a bear dimly visible between the legs.[61]

There is a possible biographical joke inherent in the jawbone: Peale was sketching human dentures in letters to friends in these weeks during which the picture was in process,[62] indefatigably trying to improve the human condition through developing more effective false teeth; but the function of the jawbone to the scientific community was clear. Osteological evidence had led Cuvier to define the American find as a "mastodonte," a prehistoric ruminant (like the deer and llama of the present?) rather than a carnivore as Peale and others had originally thought.[63]

Thus the bones locate meaning scientifically, temporally, nationally, and spatially within the picture.

Verbal evidence about the mastodon is scattered throughout the Peale papers. Peale's first exposure to the bones had been as Philadelphia artist, commissioned in 1783 to make drawings of the Morgan collection of bones for the visiting German physician Charles Frederick Michaelis. These drawings include one of a jawbone which Cuvier studied and reproduced in his 1806 *Annales.* [64] This experience has frequently been cited as another germ of Peale's museum, and thus its appropriate foreground place in a painting depicting the "rise and progress" of the museum, with the palette placed strategically above. Among the wealth of verbal materials on the mastodon we may single out here the most complete account, Rembrandt Peale's *Historical Disquisition on the Mammoth, or Great American Incognitum,* published in London in 1803 when Peale's son was exhibiting there one of the two skeletons they had exhumed two years earlier. Rembrandt's ninety-page pamphlet was available for sale and was displayed in framed cases on the wall of the museum for all to read (if they had the energy!) while gazing in wonder at the original evidence.

The pamphlet was dedicated to his father, who had placed the "Mammoth — the first of American animals, in the first of American Museums." Rembrandt emphasized at the outset the violent agitation of the earth's surface and quoted Cuvier at length on the contrast between the order of present nature and the disorder and confusion of the fossil past: "These traces of desolation have always acted on the human mind." For Cuvier as well as for the Americans, it was not merely the facts but their effects upon the perceiving consciousness that were at issue. With obvious nationalistic relish, Rembrandt quoted Buffon's earlier allusion to the "pretended MAMMOTH, a fabulous animal, supposed to inhabit the regions of the north where are frequently found bones, teeth, and tusks resembling those of the elephant," and then went on to point out Buffon's "several errors." To Buffon's distress at the idea that any race might become extinct, Rembrandt countered, "We are forced to submit to concurring facts as the voice of God — the bones exist — the animals do not!" He identified the word "mammoth" explicitly with the American finds "as a term well appropriate to express its quality of supereminent magnitude," and told his readers of the skeleton in the Philadelphia Museum, "where it will remain a monument, not only of stupendous creation, and some wonderful revelation in nature, but of the scientific zeal, and indefatigable perseverance, of a man from whose private exertions a museum has been founded, surpassed by few in Europe, and likely to become a national establishment, on the most liberal plan." Taxonomy bends before the perception of sublime creation, the bones are identified with his father's scientific zeal, and both linked to the museum as an American national achievement.[65]

The *Disquisition* moves on to describe narratively the exhumation of the bones, then to engage questions of theory and comparative evidence, and ends by moving from scientific discourse to the legendary American Indian traditions concerning the mastodon. Fact gives way to myth, rational osteological discrimination to the sublime rhetoric of the Indian orators in the American wilderness. Noting that another form of Indian legend could be found in Jefferson's *Notes on Virginia,* Rembrandt concludes that whatever caused the destruction of the species also destroyed "those inhabitants from whom there might have been transmitted some satisfactory account of these stupendous beings, which at all times must have filled the human mind with surprise and wonder."[66] Our background figures in *The Artist in His Museum* thus do more than replicate Lockean epistemology; they form part of the drama of historic time: the man examines the present directly, the father and son study the past through the achievement of a written system of classification, the Quaker lady re-experiences in the museum the "surprise and wonder" felt by those who lived in the prehistoric past.

One further visual-verbal constellation is needed to understand fully the place and function of the mastodon within the 1822 painting, and that is Peale's earlier pictorial celebration of the great event that brought it to the museum. The 1806–08 "Mammoth Picture," as Peale himself referred to it, is well known today as *The Exhumation of the Mastodon* (fig. 66). The work is familiar to students of American art and American culture more generally, though it is hard to categorize, for it is at one and the same time a history painting commemorating a great American event; a realistic genre piece of the digging up of the bones from John Masten's marl pit, with accurate depictions of the apparatus and the process, including such details as the tempting jug that held the reward to any besogged worker who came across a new bone; a group portrait of Peale's family and friends, not all of whom were there at the Masten farm (including Peale's deceased second wife Elizabeth as well as his current third wife, Hannah); and, obviously, a landscape as well, with the threat of a thunderstorm that all feared would wipe out the scientific efforts. The work has also been perceptively discussed as a unique combination of all of these and more: a harnessing together of disparate elements to create a nontemporal unity that defines a relation between the chain of being in nature (understood in terms of catastrophist geological theory) and in Peale's personal history (dramatized in the extended family portrait). Abraham Davidson's argument demonstrates how Peale brought space and time together to create what is in our terms a conceptual unity of meaning.[67]

For our purposes, thus, it is important to recognize the "Mammoth Picture" as emblematic in both conception and execution. As early as 1804, he had described in a letter a "large historical, emblematical Picture, in which I shall introduce the Portraits of my children."[68] But it is equally important, in terms of *The Artist in His Museum,* to understand the contribution of the "Mammoth Picture" to the argument about the relation between pictorial design and natural history. If the role of the mastodon in Peale's intellectual universe and his museum was to excite wonder by its vast size, its obscure origins, its links to an earlier mythic past now disappeared, and yet at the same time to serve as a prehistoric link in the great chain of American being, it had multiple functions to perform. The American past was to be made available for the use of the present, our "heritage" in the American land clarified in this era of political experimentation. The structure and pattern of natural history was to be filled out, within which arguments about extinct versus still existing species (as Thomas Jefferson believed), or about Peale's "mammoths" versus Cuvier's "mastodontes," could be argued by reasonable men.

At the same time this creature offered to viewers aesthetically the experience of the sublime — clarified increasingly in the eighteenth century as a term to describe overwhelming size, indefiniteness, obscurity, and evidence of the unmediated power of deity (the Noachic origins of catastrophist geological theory ensuring the harmony here of religion and science). As Edmund Burke had redefined the aesthetic of the sublime in Lockean terms more as a psychological process of perceivers than as a quality of objects, the sublime meant the experience of awe — with security (without such a security of vantage point, awe and wonder could turn into pure fear and terror). That point had been made clearly enough by Peale's friend Jefferson in his two early statements of the sublime in the *Notes on Virginia* (1785): the excursus on the Natural Bridge and that on the confluence of the Shenandoah and Potomac rivers at Harpers Ferry in the Blue Ridge Mountains.[69]

The great achievement of Peale's "Mammoth Picture" in these terms is the way in which it finds a pictorial design to express these very different implications of his natural history discoveries. In its place in the museum in the mammoth room, it offered answers to frequent visitors' questions about the process of the exhumation and how it was carried out. It also brought the outdoor world and the experience of nature indoors, as a necessarily scaled-down version of the habitat backgrounds which the Peales painted behind their other stuffed specimens.[70] The painting organizes our understanding of nature in special ways. The dark and murky foreground puts us on the brink of the marl pit, where this recovery of the sublime past is taking place. The dark right triangle to the lower left of the picture matches an equally dark one to the upper right, wherein the natural sublime is manifest in the present. The crack of lightning and the dark and turbulent skies (to which the second Mrs. Peale directs the attention of the child Titian) threaten the work in process, and on the hillside behind the scaffolding the two frightened horses run wild.[71]

But the central point to be made about the "Mammoth Picture" is that our experience of the natural sublime — whether of the prehistoric past in the pit below or of the vital present in the landscape beyond — is controlled and ordered by the geometric and rational design of the well-lit middle distance, which binds the dark triangles and gives constructive unity to the composition. The scattered workers of the lower left crystallize into the near frieze of the Peale family and others in a band across the far side of the pit, and the great pyramidal construction of the waterwheel organizes and grids the whole, in easily read two- and three-dimensional geometric patterns. The formal design of the canvas is Peale's way of dramatizing the triumph of human rational order over the sublime. As Peale wrote, his brother James stands with hands out "in an action of wonder at the exploring work,"[72] but James's gesture is carefully contained within two arms and a cross support of the central pyramid and contrasts to the quiet meditation of the isolated figure of Alexander Wilson to the left in front of the regular triangular prism of the wooden equipment tent. As these figures indicating the range of human response foreshadow the figures in *The Artist in His Museum,* so does the design of the canvas express Peale's earlier sense of how to bring the sublimity of the mastodon and our sublime experience of nature within Enlightenment rational modes of thought, how to perceive and then to reconstruct pictorially the harmony and order of the universe. Peale believed that order existed, that the bones would contribute to rather than shatter our conceptual image of the great chain of being — a chain which the buckets and wheel, with their human motive force inside, make visually manifest. (The wit of this was surely not lost on Peale, however descriptively accurate his depiction may have been of the millwright's device.)[73] In an alternative expression of catastrophist theory, Peale would copy in 1819 Charles Catton's painting of *Noah and His Ark* (fig. 71) as an explicitly biblical statement, emphasizing again the harmony of created beings around the patriarch (Peale the museum director was himself seventy-eight at that time) rather than the catastrophic convulsion of the deluge that had buried the mastodon in the marl pit.

What finally needs emphasizing is that Peale's sense of design is ultimately pictorial. Within the exhumation scene, Peale and his artist sons Rembrandt and Raphaelle hold the life-size drawing of the bones; in a larger sense, the "Mammoth Picture" itself reduces the multiple functions of the mastodon to pictorial unity through the expressive design of a canvas of which he is at once creator and, inside it, the gesturing artist-director-scientist-entrepreneur. The lines from here to *The Artist in His Museum* are clear and direct. In their basic dynamics they are not, we may note, Peale's alone, for they echo those of his friend Jefferson in the sublime passages in the *Notes*. Jefferson had proceeded topographically from the ordered world of natural creation in Virginia to confront two sublime spectacles. Trying to bring these experiences under control, he had moved from rational statement and measurement through an agitated prose that reflected the sudden "avulsions" of the earth under the effects of the deluge, which produce dizziness, strain, and headache upon the narrative consciousness. Order was restored through the aesthetic organization of the scene into "picture," as the eye moved from "fore-ground, . . . inviting you, as it were, from the riot and tumult roaring around, to pass through the breach and participate in the calm below. Here," says Jefferson, in that crucially ambiguous phase, "the eye ultimately composes itself."[74] As with Peale in the "Mammoth Picture," the sublime is brought under control aesthetically through ordering the landscape and giving it pictorial design. Peale's aesthetic strategy is thus part of a shared vision.[75]

We return thus to the right side of *The Artist in His Museum* with a clearer sense of the implications of Peale's choices here: to dramatize the sublime, by contrast to the ordered beautiful classification of the left side of the picture, as an obscure, partially glimpsed image of immensity. It is available for the wonder of the Quaker lady but only partially for us. The osteological evidence of jawbone and femur is visible in the foreground, but the fully reconstructed skeleton remains behind the half-lifted curtain under the control of the artist-director-entrepreneur of the museum. Natural history has been transformed into pictorial emblem in the new mode — not as Phrygian cap or garlanded statue or togated gesturing figure; American natural history itself now serves emblematic purposes.

It was the function of the emblem to teach, to transform an image into an object of contemplation from which we were to learn. Peale's museum was centrally didactic in intent. His own lectures in 1799 and 1800, to which we have referred earlier, were part of that process. We may conclude our discussion of the role of natural history in Peale's universe and in his paintings by catching the formulation of his young colleague John Godman, Rembrandt Peale's son-in-law, who lectured at the museum in the 1820s.[76] In 1829 Godman argued thus to his audience:

> We desire, as far as practicable, to solicit your attention to the study of nature through some of her most interesting works; to excite your wishes to become acquainted with the living beings scattered in rich profusion over the earth, to call forth your admiration at the endless variety of form, the singular contrivance, the beautiful adaptation, the wonderful perfection exhibited throughout animated nature, and thence to win your observation to their habits and manners, the benefits they confer upon mankind, their relations to each other, and their subordination in the system of the universe. . . . The enlightened student of nature can never forget the omnipresence of Deity — it is everywhere before his eyes, and in his heart — obvious and palpable; — it is a consciousness, not a doctrine; a reality, not an opinion, identified with his very being, and attested to his understanding by every circumstance of his existence.[77]

Godman's lecture is worth quoting at length, because it captures dramatically the didactic impulse of the museum and the perceptual process so alive in the progression of verbs — which it asked of visitors. From soliciting the attention to exciting the wishes to calling forth their admiration and thence to winning their observation the language is undiluted Locke. When in the second part Godman wants to insist upon the theological function of enlightenment knowing, he must make clear that it is not only "before his eyes"; it is "in his heart." This is not yet, we must make clear, the romantic triumph of heart over head, but rather an integration of knowing within the self: "a consciousness, not a doctrine." What Godman's rhetoric understands is that Lockean epistemology located the problem of knowing not in objects, however skillfully arranged and labeled and described, nor in some dogmatic credo, some "doctrine," but in consciousness itself. It is this that Jefferson was grasping for in his Harpers Ferry passage, when he said that "here the eye ultimately composes itself,"[78] although his specific phrasing teeters on the edge of romantic solipsism. And it is in these terms that Peale's *Artist in His Museum* needs finally to be understood, not merely as one of the last in a long series of emblematic portraits, nor as the exemplification of a doctrine or set of ideas about American natural history as it was gathered in the museum, but as a shaping of consciousness, a way of seeing, a mode of cognition.

The Picture as Aesthetic Strategy

The Artist in His Museum calls attention to itself as a picture, and we must come to terms with this, the ultimate shape of his expressive design. In this respect also, as with its role as portrait and as a visualization of his ideas on natural history, the operative context is important. *The Artist in His Museum* is a gallery picture, a type of painting with a long tradition, especially in northern Europe, in which is depicted a room filled with works of art, with various people posed in relation to one another and to the collection of art objects. Madlyn Millner Kahr, who has documented the genre, comments,

> The most obvious effect of a gallery picture is to immortalize a collection as an expression of the personality of the collector. Since many of the pictures, however [in the sixteenth- and seventeenth-century works she discusses] do not reflect real collections at all, or else take liberties with collections that existed, the artist's personality may have come into play more forcefully than the patron's.[79]

As Kahr points out, these paintings were commissioned as a means of ennobling the patron and emphasizing his status as an aristocratic lover of beauty and the liberal arts, for these works and the world depicted within the paintings were to be appreciated not just for their craft, as the work of artisans, but as exemplifications of the arts of the mind. The painter, in carrying out the commission, was thus associated and concomitantly "ennobled," his craft in copying and organizing the work (the *disegno externo*) put to the higher purpose of celebrating art as an expression of nobility of mind (the *disegno interno*).

The utility of this pictorial tradition to Charles Willson Peale in carrying out the commission of the Philadelphia Museum trustees should be readily apparent. On the one hand, Peale immediately saw the task as a portrait of himself in the museum displaying its exhibits, the "beauties of Nature and art." It was the trustees' clear intent to honor the collector; to Peale it offered an opportunity to display and to elevate the status of his collection. The unity of the painting is not simply descriptive, as a realistic view of a particular place, but conceptual, a selection and reorganization of elements of the collection to create a mental image of the order and harmony of the universe as Peale understood it. Peale's palette and brush are visible on the table, and the taxidermist's box suggests the craft involved in mounting the natural specimens; but the emphasis of the picture — visually focused for us by Peale's careful backlighting of his head (an innovation in this portrait of which he was especially proud) — is on the mental harmony, the *disegno interno,* that the picture creates and emblematizes.

However, the limitations of the European tradition for the American painter are equally significant. Unlike Velásquez or Rubens and David Teniers II, Peale was not a dependent artisan seeking to ennoble his profession and himself through royal or aristocratic patronage, but a polymathic citizen seeking to engage the interests of the American public. Although institutional control of the museum had passed from Peale to a public board of trustees, Peale's patron had always been the public. Unlike his European predecessors, the painter in the picture as well as the painter of the picture was the collector and not his servant or hireling. This is clear if we compare Peale to his artistic contemporary in England, Johann Zoffany. In the *Tribuna of the Uffizi* (1772–78), Zoffany wittily brought together elegant aristocratic British cognoscenti around a selection of the artistic riches of Florence and placed them all in complex relation in one gallery of the Uffizi; in *Charles Townley and his Friends* (1782) he gathered into one ideal room the classical statuary that the pictorially isolated figure of Townley had collected for his own contemplation and for the limited pleasure of a select group of connoisseurs.[80] By contrast, Peale's efforts, in the museum and in the picture, were directed not at ennobling the collector at the expense of an envious populace but at bringing the beauties of nature and art into public view. The pictorial evidence is clear: the gesturing figure in *The Artist in His Museum* lifts the curtain and invites us in. We seem to have easy entrance into the picture.

And that carries us to the third consideration about the gallery paint-ing and its significance for the Peale picture: it focuses our attention on Peale's links to the Dutch and Flemish tradition of northern Euro-pean painting. What particular access Peale had to this special kind of painting, in originals or copies or in engraved versions, is at present not fully clear. It is clear that seventeenth-century northern paintings were available in America during Peale's lifetime and perhaps especially in the Philadelphia area. The Joseph Bonaparte collection in Borden-town, New Jersey, contained examples of Dutch and Flemish work; Robert Fulton's collection included similar work, as did other contem-porary American collections and exhibitions at the Pennsylvania Acad-emy and elsewhere within Peale's circuit. The proliferation of still-life painting among the extended Peale family (including brother James and his progeny) for several generations clearly implies a familiarity with the Dutch and Flemish tradition, and Raphaelle especially was a prac-titioner of trompe l'oeil or "deception" pieces in the Dutch manner. Other contemporary Philadelphia artists shared these interests. William Birch and his son Thomas, a specialist in seascapes, borrowed Dutch formulas in that mode, and in 1824 Charles Willson Peale visited the Washington studio of Charles Bird King, another practitioner of Dutch-inspired trompe l'oeil and *vanitas* still lifes, and commented on seeing there also landscapes and "emblematical" pieces (see, for example, *Poor Artist's Cup-board* [ca. 1815, Corcoran Gallery of Art, Washington, D.C.]). Although the story is still incomplete, the evidence of Philadelphia's familiarity with the seventeenth-century northern tradition is clear. Besides, the issue, with respect to *The Artist in His Museum,* is not of mechanical "in-fluence" of one or more particular "sources" but of relationships of vi-sion and affinities of intention and execution.[81]

The aim of the Peale picture, like that of Peale's museum, was public accessibility, but accessibility of a special kind: "that the Design should be expressive that I bring forth into public view, the beauties of Nature and art, the rise and progress of the Museum." The Lockean empiricist in him was convinced that the truth of the harmony and order of the universe was available to the rational mind through the experience of sense data as these are received and ordered by consciousness. Obviously for the painter in him as well, retinal impressions were primary, the necessary means for shaping within the mind through emblem, natural classification, and aesthetic theories of the sublime and beautiful some conceptual unity of meaning. But the pictorial strategy for bringing his material "into public view" was still an open question.

Peale's answer was to make the process of seeing self-consciously part of the expressive design of the canvas, to call our attention to our visual experience, rather than to make his picture a transparent window into the universe. In this, his work bespeaks its northern heritage, for, as Svetlana Alpers succinctly puts it,

> Northern artists, far longer and more persistently than those in the South, trusted to the flatness of the working surface; . . . the flatness of the surface of Northern art was not killed off by perspective. . . . As an image of the world, Northern art is more often like a mirror than a window. This is as true of Van Eyck as it is of Vermeer. The common denominator between both aspects (flatness of working surface and mirror) is the absence of the maker or viewer, clearly posited in space and located in time, that is central to the creation of Italian art. Northern art, it might be argued, moved from the eye of God (Van Eyck's mirror in the *Arnolfini Wedding*) to the optical lens like a reflecting eye (the world cast into the surface of the canvas as in Vermeer).[82]

It is true that Peale developed his picture from a perspectival drawing worked out with his "machine," which his son Titian then filled in with narrative details; but at a later stage he altered the vanishing point perspective, bending it out awkwardly (by Italian Renaissance standards) to accommodate other needs of the picture and thus calling attention to both perspective and the painting itself as pictorial constructions. When contrasted to the huge figure of the artist, the diminutive scale of the background visitors — especially when these figures are placed against the bent perspectival grid of the cases — feels exaggerated to our eyes, more like looking through an optical instrument than a direct experience of the world. Clearly the "actual" dimensions of the Long Room, one hundred feet from end to end, created the problem, but there were other possible ways to compensate; Peale's solution feels particularly northern. It is true that the lines of the floorboards carry the eye from our viewer's space through the picture to the background spectators, and the blurring of objects as we look back or into the murky shadows to the right reinforces the experience of perceptual movement into deep space, but Peale cuts against this through the device of the curtain, which forces us back to the surface of the canvas and makes us aware of the picture plane.

The curtain is central to an understanding of the painting, its meaning, and its significance as an experienced art object. The curtain's function is metonymic. It has lost its simple, essentially static function in countless portraits as "drapery" on one side of the figure offering contrast of texture and a suggestion of elegance (balancing sometimes a view on the other side), and becomes instead dramatic in several senses. Peale's lifting of the curtain places him in the pictorial role of director (the visual pun was surely intentional),[83] admitting us the audience to a show in his theater, the Peale museum. The language is precise: Peale was the theatrical entrepreneur of his museum, and a master of special effects (transparencies, fireworks, organ interludes, lecture-demonstrations), and always had to tread a fine line between science and showmanship — between attracting audiences to the museum with oddities and instructing them in Linnaean classification.[84] The gesture of the director is not agitated or melodramatic but graceful and elegant, as we follow the line from his calf upward through the Hogarthian S-curve, the line of beauty which he so frequently employed. It is a movement befitting an introduction to rational entertainment; and the drama he offers us here looks rather static (the figures, and perhaps especially the stylized Quaker lady, seem like parts of a tableau), for the drama that Peale offers us through the senses is finally acted out in the human mind.

Yet in a more immediate sense the curtain here, as in any theater, defines the boundary between inside and outside, between the constructed world of art and artifice, and life. Our stage language is not only responsive to the thespian side of Peale and to the rich theatrical life of urban Philadelphia, where Peale lived and worked through most of his adult life (rural Belfield was just an interlude). It is also responsive visually, both to the new popular genre of paintings of theatrical scenes in the eighteenth century throughout Europe (especially of the new bourgeois theater), and to the consequent emphasis, within these paintings on a relatively shallow stage on which the figures play their parts on the canvas.[85] In *The Artist in His Museum,* Peale's stage is — at least theoretically — deep, but the curtain focuses our attention self-consciously on the picture plane behind which we are permitted to see certain staged tableaux or dramas. The origins of this pictorial strategy are, again, Dutch and Flemish bourgeois interiors of the seventeenth century, with their mirrors and doorways and half-pulled curtains allowing us to move around and through pictorial space without ever losing our sense that it is an artfully constructed space, not a window into the "real world." At one extreme, these paintings overtly play with the borderline itself. Trompe l'oeil devices place certain objects outside the ostensible "picture," though these objects turn out to be painted; or, in window scenes of young ladies or niches containing still lifes, curtains are hung on rods over them, which seem to have been raised to allow us to view the people and objects behind. (Of course, small paintings were in fact frequently protected by such curtains when not being viewed, which doubles the punning.)[86]

One final point about the curtain: Peale's explicitly dramatic image makes clear the other metonymic usage that he shares with his northern European forebears. In theatrical terms a stage curtain is also a "canvas," and although the deep red flowered fabric here looks more like damask, the visual pun remains and its intent is clear: the curtain in the painting, now partially lifted, is parallel to and, at least at the top, ambiguously close to the picture plane. It thus doubles our awareness of "picture." It is not only the borderline between life and art; it is itself a painted replication of the canvas that is Peale's pictorial surface.

What, then, are the implications for meaning of this complex aesthetic and epistemological system of the Peale picture? *The Artist in His Museum* self-consciously transforms nature into art in and through the painting. Immediately contiguous to our space as viewers in the world lies the brilliantly lit untransformed jawbone of the prehistoric predecessor, a fragment of ancient nature. Behind it are two other fragments with the light of the outside world separating them from the jawbone. On the other side lies inanimate dead present nature, the turkey awkwardly framing with its body the tools of taxidermic transformation, just as the socket curve of the mastodon femur echoes the painter's palette on the table above it. Between these emblems of nature and art, of past and present, near the surface of the canvas stands the artist-scientist-director, who has the capacity to transform nature into art: to reanimate the turkey into an artistically alive exhibit in a framed case, artfully to reconstruct the whole skeleton of the past (the missing pieces re-created by William Rush) out of the fragments available to us in "life." The artist and his curtain do indeed stand at the juncture of life and art, between the raw and the cooked, as it were.

Beyond the curtain we can see the effects of such transformation under the Enlightenment aesthetic of Peale: nature's creatures framed in cases by art for human visitors, outstanding examples of whose species are also arrayed in the row of portraits above, differences of scale carefully balanced right and left (missing from the picture on the far right, we have noted, are the smallest-scale objects with their attendant microscope). Differences of sex, age, and aesthetic response to the sublime and the beautiful are also carefully balanced, facing right and left, with the man educating the boy moving out toward us, the viewers, who are being educated by looking in. The formal patterning of the epistemological process has all the elegant order of an eighteenth-century dance — and all the quiet wit of the age of which *The Artist in His Museum* was one of the last expressions.

Charles Willson Peale was not a naturally humorous person and could be at times rather sententious and grave. As for "the word witt," he wrote to his daughter Angelica in 1813, "I have never loved the character of witty persons. . . . They do not always consider whether a saying might not hurt the feelings of another, and in my opinion, one ounce of good nature is of more *real value* than a pound of witt, nay of 1000."[87] Such a statement speaks both to Peale's kindness and to his moral desire to assist his fellow human beings. Though it dissociates him from the age's propensity toward vicious and cutting wit, barbed humor, it does not deny that as artist he was capable of that verbal and visual play with reality, that enlightening twist of our vantage point on experience, which is a measure of true wit in the finest sense.

Peale's wit in *The Artist in His Museum* is a conscious exploration of the boundaries between life and art, between nature and science, between the visual and verbal, between the simple ideas of the senses and the complex organization of the mind. In the cognitive games he plays in the painting, he continues and extends the epistemological inquiries not only of Locke and his philosophical followers but also of Leeuwenhoeck and his microscopes, Hoogstraten and his painted perspectival boxes, Jan de Heem and his extraordinary trompe l'oeil *natures mortes,* Vermeer and his pearly drops of partly focused sunlight on a blue gown. While West, Copley, Allston, and Vanderlyn explored the Italian and French heritage of the grand style, Peale the northerner wittily dramatized the complex dynamics of human consciousness. In this process, as Jefferson said, "The eye ultimately composes itself."

Aftermath

When completed in September 1822, *The Artist in His Museum* was judged a success by those who saw it,[88] and that judgment has, on the whole, been sustained over time, though with less enthusiasm and perhaps less understanding as assumptions changed and as later generations lost the contexts within which the painting worked. The pictorial events in the following year serve as a kind of coda, recapitulating in their different ways the nature of Peale's achievement. The first, a work Peale did for the Baltimore Peale's Museum (under the management of his son Rubens) was another large painting of himself, the *Staircase Self-Portrait*. The canvas no longer exists—it was probably burned in a fire in 1865—but the description of the work makes clear that it was an extension and elaboration of the problems Peale had engaged in *The Artist in His Museum*, combining these with his most successful explicitly trompe l'oeil experiment, the *Staircase Group* (ca. 1795, fig. 75) of his sons Raphaelle and the first Titian Ramsay. Like that earlier work, which had always been a great attraction at the Philadelphia museum, the new self-portrait blurred the distinction between the world and art through the device of steps (some constructed in wood which was then carpeted, some on the painted surface of the canvas) that lead the viewer from our world into the work of art. In the 1823 painting, Peale was seen standing outdoors on steps leading upward into the museum. As the painter gathered emblems of his life and work around the figure (it was precisely at this moment, Sellers's biography reminds us, that Peale acquired the Van der Myn *Lord Baltimore* painting [fig. 6]),[89] he recalled the famous story of the Greek painter Apelles and the birds pecking at the painted grapes, for it reinforced his own purpose. "I mean to make the whole a piece of deception if I can," he wrote to Rubens on August 5, 1823.[90] The term "deception," in one of its significations at this time, meant precisely that kind of trompe l'oeil still life for which seventeenth-century Dutch practice had offered models to him, to Raphaelle, and to Charles Bird King. Peale's attention was clearly focused on the work of art not as a description of the world but as a self-referential act of pictorial wit. His glee a month later at his own triumph was undiluted: "What is extraordinary, every one is deceived by some part of the picture. The truth is that I had determined from the commencement of it to make as much as I could in it to deceive the eye of the critical observer."[91] The triumph of the picture plane as illusionistic surface was complete. The wit of the artistic game had no concomitant ill effects; it had harmed no one.

The second event was more complex and more problematic, in the same terms. In 1822 or 1823 (the date is uncertain) Raphaelle Peale produced his most famous work, *Venus Rising from the Sea—A Deception*, formerly known as *After the Bath* (fig. 76). The work is justly celebrated today as a brilliant early American example of trompe l'oeil still life and as a figure painting, for the cloth napkin partially hides the body of a woman, based upon Valentine Green's 1772 engraving, *Venus Rising from the Sea,* after the painting by James Barry.[92] This "deception" has been explained within the Peale family tradition as a pictorial joke that Raphaelle played upon his peppery wife, the redoubtable Patty Mac-Glathery, its function "simply to turn upon Patty the laughter of the children and the boarders" when (like Apelles' birds) she discovered that the cloth napkin hiding the indecent nude was all a painted surface.[93] But a more careful look at the biographical situation and our pictorial context suggests another plausible possibility: that the little Raphaelle Peale work should be understood as a brilliant parody of the values his father expressed in *The Artist in His Museum.*

Consider the evidence: Raphaelle, the oldest of the Peale children who lived beyond infancy was surely the most continuously troubling to Peale. He was brilliant, erratic, a ventriloquist, theatrical assistant to his father, and the leading family practitioner of that visual ventriloquism, silhouette-making. At his best Raphaelle was an extraordinarily talented painter in oils, the finest American practitioner of that least consequential of genres (by eighteenth-century Reynoldsian standards): still life. But Raphaelle's artistic energies were limited. Through most of his later years he was seriously ill, most probably traceable to arsenic and mercury poisoning of his system as a result of his work as a taxidermist for the Peale museum, the effects of which were called "gout" at the time.[94] He also relied upon alcohol at times, perhaps to deaden the pain of his illness, and was periodically incapacitated and even on occasion suicidal, whether at home in Philadelphia or, increasingly, in his restless wanderings through the southern states while he left Patty at home to manage their large family and boarding house.

To Charles Willson Peale, Raphaelle was the prodigal son who never reformed. His father's deep love of this errant son was coupled with constant admonitions, the record of which stretches through the Peale correspondence and includes such pseudo-public statements as Peale's 1812 *Essay to Promote Domestic Happiness,* the directness of whose relation to the Raphaelle-Patty situation must have been painfully obvious and publicly humiliating to his son and daughter-in-law.[95] The *Essay* ended with the story of the prodigal son, but alas, Raphaelle's story was never to have such a happy ending; he died of his illness in 1825, his great promise as an artist only partially fulfilled in a scattering of works over the years.

When this life of unfulfilled promise is put against the constant admonitions and equally constant disappointments of that inescapable public eminence, his father, publicly summarized in *The Artist in His Museum,* Raphaelle's strategy in *Venus Rising from the Sea — A Deception* becomes clearer. Using the same Dutch pictorial language of "deception," Raphaelle reverses the curtain gesture of his father, who is bringing into public view the beauties of nature and art; instead, he uses his pictorial art to hide "nature" in the shape of a nude woman. And barely visible around the edges of this deception piece are the shapes which he has copied out of his father's 1817 portrait of him "in the character of a painter." Where the face would have been hangs the napkin.[96] *Venus Rising From the Sea — A Deception* is thus the opposite of a public portrait of the artist. The psychological implications of such a literal self- and father-destroying act are intriguing, though they are difficult to prove; quiet acceptance of the humiliation, not public rage against the impossible expectations that his father's life posed for him, was the decorous expectation of the Peale family and the only seemingly justifiable response to the old man's kind concern. (The family apparently turned the blame on the overburdened Patty, implying that she had driven him to drink.)

What is not speculation is the pictorial evidence: that in everything from the differences in scale of the two works (the museum portrait is 103½ by 80 inches, in contrast to Raphaelle's 28 by 23 inch canvas) to the inversion of the public world and the suppression of the grand manner and the public emblems of the classical world of Venus, in the shift from a man dressed in old-fashioned clothes to the unclothed woman, or from public family entertainment to private burlesque show, from self-advertisement to self-denial or self-obliteration — in everything but the shared artistic sense that the role of the painted canvas is to dramatize the triumph of the artist to reveal or to conceal, in varying degrees, "life," Raphaelle Peale's *Venus Rising From the Sea — A Deception* is a mordantly witty covert parody of what his father was trying to accomplish in *The Artist in His Museum.* The artistic enactment of Lockean epistemology had been turned back upon itself. The extraordinarily skillful revelation of the shapes and textures of the observable world become in Raphaelle's picture a mask for the inner thoughts and feelings of the artist.

Shifts in culture and consciousness are not brought about by two paintings, however richly contextualized, although such shifts should be readable in single works. *The Artist in His Museum* is the end of a tradition, a summary of a world in process of radical transformation. It was only three years after Peale completed his magnum opus that John Trumbull and Asher Durand came across the little landscapes of Cole in the window of a New York shop, and the publication of Fenimore Cooper's *Spy* (1821) and his *Pioneers* (1823), the first of the Leatherstocking tales, bracket the Peale picture by a year each way. By 1827, in *The Prairie,* Cooper was to dramatize the American adventure into space in starkest terms. The encounter with "Nature" moves from the rational confines of the Peale museum into the sublime space of a conceptually defined midwestern America (Cooper had not visually experienced the prairies), and the lone indecorous Natty Bumppo articulates his version of a dynamic and instinctive romantic naturalism in counterpoint with Dr. Obed Batt, a laboriously drawn parody of the scientific rationalism of Peale's Philadelphia world. In search of his own version of the mastodon, the Vespertilio Horribilis, Obed Batt fails to recognize his own ass: "'The image of the Vespertilio was on the retina,' the astounded enquirer into the secrets of nature observed, . . .' and I was silly enough to mistake my own faithful beast for the monster.'" Cooper's implicit critique here of the limits of Lockean epistemology when men have fixed mental images is clear. He goes on, in deadpan commentary: "From that moment the world has heard no more of the Vespertilio Horribilis Americanus, and the natural sciences have irretrievably lost an important link in that great animated chain which is said to connect earth and heaven, and in which man is thought to be so familiarly complicated with the monkey."[97] One hopes that Charles Willson Peale did not hear this, for the implications of Cooper's remark would do much to shatter the design that the Philadelphia artist had so carefully constructed in his museum.

NOTES

This chapter is a slightly revised and shortened version of the original which appeared in *Prospects: An Annual of American Cultural Studies* 6 (1981), 139–85. I am grateful to Jack Salzman, editor, and to the Cambridge University Press for permission to reprint it here.

1. Quoted in William Dunlap, *History of the Rise and Progress of the Arts of Design in the United States,* ed. Frank W. Bayley and Charles Goodspeed (Boston, 1918), 1:92–93; see also *Selected Papers* 2:1218–23.

2. See the full descriptive account in *P&M,* pp. 158–63.

3. Quoted in ibid., p. 160.

4. Charles Willson Peale to Rembrandt Peale, July 23, 1822, P-S, F:IIA/67D3.

5. Charles Willson Peale to Rubens Peale, August 4, 1822, P-S, F:IIA/67D6–8.

6. Charles Willson Peale to Thomas Jefferson, October 29, 1822, Library of Congress: Thomas Jefferson Papers, P-S, F:IIA/67F6–14.

7. This portrait (107 by 69½ inches) of Benjamin West was commissioned by the American Academy of Fine Arts. West is shown in his robes as president of the Royal Academy, standing full length with drapery behind and to the right of him and gesturing to the viewer's left at a small version of Raphael's *Death of Ananias* on an easel while lecturing on "The Immutability of Colors." Completed by Lawrence after West's death in 1820, it reached the AAFA in New York in 1822, where Rembrandt Peale saw it. It is now owned by the Wadsworth Atheneum, Hartford, Conn. A copy attributed to Rembrandt Peale is unlocated.

8. This particular bird may be the one that went to the Peabody Museum at Harvard. For an illustration, see Edgar P. Richardson, Brooke Hindle, and Lillian B. Miller, *Charles Willson Peale and His World* (New York, 1983), p. 116. See also Jessie J. Poesch, *Titian Ramsay Peale, 1799–1885 and His Journals of the Wilkes Expedition,* American Philosophical Society, *Memoirs* 52 (1961): 47, and Sellers, *Mr. Peale's Museum,* p. 242.

9. A(TS): 446.

10. For the Renaissance tradition of emblems, see Mario Praz, *Studies in Seventeenth Century Imagery,* 2d ed. (Rome, 1964); and Rosemary Freeman, *English Emblem Books* (London, 1948). For a recent critique from the point of view of German scholarship, which modifies Freeman's emphasis on the "arbitrariness" of the emblem, see Peter M. Daly, *Literature in the Light of Emblem* (Toronto, 1979), esp. pp. 1–102. My own conviction is that the emblematic mode was a continuing one in American art, from the seventeenth century well into the nineteenth. For an early American case, see Roger B. Stein, "Thomas Smith's Self-Portrait: Image/Text as Artifact," *Art Journal* 44 (Winter 1984): 316–27.

11. For one recent exception to this pattern, see Roland E. Fleischer, "Emblems and Colonial American Painting," *American Art Journal* 20 (1988): 2–35.

12. One year after he painted *The Artist in His Museum,* Peale saw the already deteriorated *Lord Baltimore* again on a trip to Annapolis, and by offering to do six portraits of Maryland governors for the statehouse, he gained ownership of the painting. He took it to Philadelphia for cleaning, and it was still in his studio when he died in 1827. After many years at the Pennsylvania Academy of the Fine Arts, the painting was finally returned in 1957 to Peale's Museum in Baltimore, the institution founded by his son Rembrandt, for which Peale had originally destined it (*CWP,* pp. 33–34, 410, 480.).

13. Did Peale hear Reynolds's First Discourse before the new Royal Academy on January 2, 1769, two months before he returned to America? Reynolds recommended to young students "an implicit obedience to the *Rules of Art,* as established by the practice of the great MASTERS. . . . That those models, which have passed through the approbation of ages, should be considered by them as perfect and infallible Guides, as subjects for their imitation, not their criticism" (*Seven Discourses*

Delivered in the Royal Academy by the President [1778; rpt. London, 1971], p. 13). That Peale had listened to this or similar advice is clear from the "imitation" in the Pitt portrait discussed below. For Reynolds's use of the emblematic, see E. H. Gombrich, "Reynolds's Theory and Practice of Imitation," in his *Norm and Form: Studies in the Art of the Renaissance* (London, 1966), pp. 129–34. Ronald Paulson, in his brilliant discussion of continuities and change in the emblematic tradition, locates Reynolds as a transitional figure, moving away from the manipulation of shared emblematic understanding and usage to a more generally associative expressive usage; see Ronald Paulson, *Emblem and Expression: Meaning in English Art of the Eighteenth Century* (London, 1975), esp. pp. 80–94. In what follows, I would want to locate Peale also within the transition, while insisting on his intermittent use of the specifically emblematic.

14. *P&M,* pp. 172–73.

15. Peale has already noted that Pitt "makes a figure of Rhetoric"—that is, that even his posture stands emblematically for a specific traditional quality. In addition, Frank H. Sommers III has suggested that the figure is an allusion to Brutus, the Roman martyr, thus enriching its emblematic significance ("Thomas Hollis and the Arts of Dissent," in *Prints in and of America to 1850,* ed. John D. Morse [Charlottesville, Va., 1970], pp. 151–55). For the classical pictorial context, see the Brown University exhibition catalogue, *The Classical Spirit in American Portraiture* (Providence, R.I., 1976).

16. *P&M,* p. 273. For John Singleton Copley's response to the copy of the mezzotint which Peale sent to him in Boston, see *Letters and Papers of John Singleton Copley and Henry Pelham, 1739–1776,* ed. Guernsey Jones (Boston, 1914), pp. 100–01.

17. *P&M Suppl.,* pp. 55–56; *CWP,* pp. 83–86; for the specific meaning of this painting, see chap. 5.

18. *P&M Suppl.,* p. 55.

19. *CWP,* p. 86.

20. For a discussion which demonstrates that the Schuylkill River background in Peale's portrait of John Dickinson, done in the same year as the Bordley portrait, is politically emblematic, see Karol Ann Lawson, "A New World of Gladness and Exertion: Images of the North American Landscape in Maps, Portraits, and Serial Prints Before 1820" (Ph.D. diss., University of Virginia, 1988), chap. 5.

21. *P&M Suppl.,* pp. 11, 14, *CWP,* p. 111; Charles Willson Peale to John Pinckney, January/February 25, 1775, P-S, in *Selected Papers* 1:138–39.

22. *Selected Papers* 1:369.

23. See esp. *P&M Suppl.,* pp. 9, 16–33, 40–41, 47–48.

24. The exhibition of *The Splendor of Dresden: Five Centuries of Art Collecting* (National Gallery, Washington, D.C.; Metropolitan Museum of Art, New York; Museums of San Francisco, 1978–79) made the point by devoting one section to court festivities; the section on the Electoral Kunstkammer, dating to 1560, with its combination of pictures, statues, tools for gardening and the chase, mineral specimens, and scientific instruments, suggests another distant source for the arrangement organized in the background of *The Artist in His Museum.*

25. Hogarth is a notable case in point; see the literature on him by Ronald Paulson, Frederick Antal, and others.

26. The newspaper accounts of Peale's transparent paintings, triumphal arches, and the like — in some cases the only sources for this occasional work, since it has disappeared, as it was intended to — are clear in their "emblematical" labeling of these activities. See the quotations cited by Sellers in *P&M Suppl.; Selected Papers* 1:354, 361, 367, 370.

27. For the Peale Franklin portraits, see *P&M,* pp. 80–83; for the larger context, see Charles Coleman Sellers, *Benjamin Franklin in Portraiture* (New Haven, Conn., 1962).

28. *P&M,* p. 225. Although here and elsewhere Sellers is content with a very general usage of the term "symbolism" to characterize those aspects of Peale's work which extend meaning beyond denotation of the observable world, it seems to me especially important to insist on the distinction between emblem and symbol during Peale's lifetime, for it was precisely then that the codifications of emblematic meaning and the world view they shaped were being challenged by Schiller, Coleridge, and other romantic theorists.

29. Peale had close intellectual and political connections at the time with President John Witherspoon (Independence National Historical Park Collection) and the astronomer David Rittenhouse of Princeton (University of Pennsylvania), whose portraits he took (*P&M,* pp. 181–82, 252–53). Peale's 1783 revision of his 1779 *Washington,* in which he includes the death of General Mercer (Princeton University; *P&M,* pp. 234–35), echoes in some ways his former teacher Benjamin West's *Death of Wolfe* (1771). Copley's *Death of Chatham,* and *Death of Major Peirson* (1782–84), completed just as Peale was finishing his new *Washington,* also focus on the death of a hero, as do John Trumbull's *Death of General Warren* and *Death of Montgomery* (1786).

30. *P&M,* p. 86; *CWP,* pp. 175–77. The view of Independence Hall in the background of the *Gérard* portrait made it inevitably part of an inside-outside game for visitors to the Long Room.

31. Jessie J. Poesch, "A Precise View of Peale's Museum," *Antiques* 78 (October 1960): 344; *P&M,* pp. 114–15.

32. *Historical Catalogue of the Paintings in the Philadelphia Museum, Consisting Chiefly of Portraits of Revolutionary Patriots and Other Distinguished Characters* (1813).

33. For Peale's response to the Lafayette visit, see *CWP,* pp. 414–18, and *P&M Suppl.,* pp. 47–48.

34. *P&M,* pp. 160, 162, 163.

35. *P&M Suppl.,* pp. 33–34; eight of them are reproduced in *CWP,* plates VIII–IX; see also *Selected Papers* 2:323–27.

36. The description of Peale's Germantown farm may be found in Jessie J. Poesch, "Mr. Peale's 'Farm Persevere': Some Documentary Views," American Philosophical Society, *Proceedings* 100 (December 1956): 545–56; see also Jessie J. Poesch, "Germantown Landscapes: A Peale Family Amusement," *Antiques* 72 (November 1957): 434–39. Peale's manuscript letterbooks, Belfield daybook, and autobiography (P-S) contain the records of the estate. See also *Selected Papers,* vol. 3. For a discussion of the garden, see chap. 14.

For Jeffersonian parallels, see Frederick D. Nichols and Ralph E. Griswold, *Thomas Jefferson, Landscape Architect* (Charlottesville, Va., 1978); and E. M. Betts, ed., *Thomas Jefferson's Garden Book,* American Philosophical Society, *Memoirs* 22 (1944).

For English eighteenth-century sources, from an emblematic point of view, see Paulson, *Emblem and Expression,* esp. pp. 19–34; and John Dixon Hunt and Peter Willis, *The Genius of the Place: The English Landscape Garden, 1620–1820* (New York, 1975).

37. See Richardson, Hindle, and Miller, *Charles Willson Peale and His World,* p. 105; also plate 75. A good color version of the painting accompanies Louise Lippincott's useful "Charles Willson Peale and His Family of Painters," *In This Academy: The Pennsylvania Academy of the Fine Arts, 1805–1976* (Philadelphia, 1976), p. 78.

38. Ms., Charles Willson Peale, "Walk With a Friend in the Philadelphia Museum," Historical Society of Pennsylvania, F:IID/27E4–29D12.

39. Ms. lecture, "The Theory of the Earth. Linnaean System of Animals and Moral Reflections on Man," Academy of Natural Sciences, Philadelphia, F:IID/3.

40. *CWP,* p. 331; see also Sellers's entire chapter 24 for useful information on the organization of the museum.

41. See *CWP,* p. 467, for an example.

42. This is one version; variants exist. See the reproductions in Charles Coleman Sellers, *Charles Willson Peale* (Philadelphia, 1947), 2:270. Sellers, in *Mr. Peale's Museum,* discusses the organ (p. 196), the tickets, and the source of the Book of Nature emblem (pp. 15, 154, 218); biblical mottoes (pp. 216–20) were apparently — at least in part — the deist's strategy to draw into the museum a sectarian Christian audience.

43. Quoted in *CWP,* p. 284. Charles Brockden Brown made Philadelphia during the yellow fever epidemic the setting for his *Arthur Mervyn; or Memoirs of the Year 1793* (Philadelphia, 1798).

44. *Discourse Introductory to a Course of Lectures on the Science of Nature . . . Delivered . . . November 8, 1800* (Philadelphia, 1800), p. 48.

45. Ibid., p. 32.

46. Peale, "Walk with a Friend," cited in Clive Bush, *The Dream of Reason: American Consciousness and Cultural Achievement from Independence to the Civil War* (London, 1977), p. 79.

47. *Discourse, 1800,* p. 48.

48. Linnaeus's work was translated by William Turton and published in 7 volumes between 1802 and 1806 as *A General System of Nature.* This passage is quoted in Bush, *Dream of Reason,* p. 196. See *Selected Papers* 2:630n for Peale's ownership of Turton's work.

49. Ibid., p. 197.

50. Henry David Thoreau, *Walden,* chap. 2.

51. Cf. Emerson in "Nature": "A fact is the end or last issue of spirit. The visible creation is the terminus or circumference of the invisible world" (chap. IV, "Language"). One should not overemphasize the differences between Locke and the transcendentalist strain. It is Edgar Allan Poe who is the real enemy of Lockean empiricism.

52. *Introduction to a Course of Lectures on Natural History Delivered . . . November 15, 1799* (Philadelphia, 1800), p. 14. In *Selected Papers* 2:266.

53. *Jonathan Edwards: Representative Selections,* ed. Clarence H. Faust and Thomas H. Johnson (New York, 1962), pp. 60–61.

54. See Irma B. Jaffe, *Trumbull: The Declaration of Independence* (New York, 1976),

pp. 67–73 and plates. Note also that the specifically classical forms of the busts in the Long Room, visible in the Titian Peale sketch, have been eliminated from the final painting. They are identified in Poesch, "Precise View," pp. 344–45.

55. On Linnaeus, see especially James L. Larson, *Reason and Experience: The Representation of Natural Order in the Work of Carl von Linné* (Berkeley, Calif., 1971), and Frans A. Stafleu, *Linnaeus and the Linnaeans: The Spreading of Their Ideas in Systematic Botany, 1735–1789* (Utrecht, 1971). On the American scene, Daniel Boorstin's *The Lost World of Thomas Jefferson* (New York, 1948), is still useful. See esp. chap. 1, "Nature as the Work of Art."

56. Peale, "Walk with a Friend."

57. James Fenimore Cooper, *The Pioneers,* chap. 17. Visual renderings of this popular Cooper scene include Tompkins H. Matteson (1857, New York State Historical Assn., Cooperstown) and William Walcutt (ca. 1850, National Museum of American Art, Washington, D.C.).

58. Poesch, *Titian Ramsay Peale,* pp. 46–47, and Sellers, *Mr. Peale's Museum,* p. 242. The Titian plate of the turkey is reproduced in color in the modern reprint of Alexander Wilson's *American Ornithology,* entitled *American Bird Engravings* (New York, 1975); the Audubon wild turkey is the first plate in *The Original Watercolor Paintings by John James Audubon for The Birds of America,* intro. Marshall B. Davidson (New York, 1966). For further details on the engraving of Audubon's work, see Waldemar H. Fries, *The Double Elephant Folio: The Story of Audubon's Birds of America* (Chicago, 1973), pp. 11, 14, and *passim.*

59. Compare the eagle in this painting with the slightly different stance of the pair in the Titian drawing and Peale's drawings of eagles in his 1812–24 sketchbook (*P&M Suppl.,* p. 111), and both with Wilson's version in the 1808–14 *American Ornithology* (*American Bird Engravings,* plate 76), which was itself the model for Audubon's plate in the later *Birds of America* (plate 1 in Davidson edition). Cf. the comment and illustration in Sellers, *Mr. Peale's Museum,* p. 89. Audubon mentions seeing Wilson drawing this eagle in Philadelphia on a visit there, and the engraving of his own eagle was completed in 1828 (Maria R. Audubon, *Audubon and His Journals* [New York, 1960], 2:203, 295). The eagle in *The Artist in His Museum,* like that in Wilson, is "white-headed," while the pair in Titian's sketch appear not to be. Peale noted in his 1813 "Walk with a Friend" that the *Falco leucocephalus,* the white-headed eagle, is improperly called the bald eagle and that it "does not get the dress of a white head and tail until the fifth year of its age." The version in our painting is a somewhat flattened, stylized bird, with its white plumage — the plumage chosen by Wilson and Audubon and familiar to us in the national emblem. The salmon-colored blur under the eagle in the picture echoes the color of the fish in the Wilson plate, which may have served in part as a model, though the disposition of the body and wings is somewhat different.

Two further biographical notes: Peale was especially fond of an eagle kept in a wire cage on top of Philosophical Hall, when the museum was there, which was tame enough for him to handle (Sellers, *Peale,* 2:62–63); second, one may notice the whimsical visual similarity between the white-headed or bald eagle in its dark feathers and its bald-headed master in his dark coat with long tail. This visual wit seems reinforced by the darkly but specially lit head of the turkey and by a contrasting pun on the right side of the picture: the immense femur of the mastodon contrasted to the elegantly silhouetted calf of the old man. Further evidence of visual puns, especially by Raphaelle Peale, will be discussed below.

60. For a useful summary of the early national argument, see Ralph N. Miller, "American Nationalism as a Theory of Nature," *William and Mary Quarterly,* 3d ser. 12 (1955): 74–95; for Jefferson's *Notes on Virgina,* see the well-indexed edition of William Peden (Chapel Hill, N.C., 1955). Irving speaks, in "The Author's Account of Himself," of his delight in going to Europe to see "the gigantic race from which I am degenerated."

61. In the ms. "Walk with a Friend," Historical Society of Pennsylvania, Peale drew special attention to the American elk, "not known by Buffon," and to be differentiated from the moose, and also to the *Cervus virginiansus:* "Its well turned and delicate limbs, stately carriage and smooth skin, render it the Admiration of most foreigners that visit the Museum."

62. See, for example, Charles Willson Peale to Dr. Hasfield, August 26, 1822, P-S, F:IIA/67E4-5.

63. Whitfield J. Bell, Jr., "A Box of Old Bones: A Note on the Identification of the Mastodon, 1766–1806," American Philosophical Society, *Proceedings* 93 (May 1949): 177.

64. Ibid., pp. 169–77.

65. Rembrandt Peale, *An Historical Disquisition on the Mammoth, or Great American Incognitum, an Extinct, Immense, Carnivorous Animal, Whose Fossil Remains Have Been Found in America* (London, 1803), pp. iv–v, 4, 9, 10, 15–16; also in *Selected Papers* 2:544–81.

66. Ibid., p. 91.

67. Abraham Davidson, "Charles Willson Peale's Exhuming the First American Mastodon: An Interpretation," in *Art Studies for an Editor: 25 Essays in Memory of Milton S. Fox* (New York, 1976), pp. 61–70. For the argument on the work as a history painting, see chap. 10.

68. Charles Willson Peale to Mrs. Nathaniel Ramsay, September 7, 1804, P-S, in *Selected Papers* 2:753; also see *P&M Suppl.,* p. 37. Davidson recognizes a link between the mastodon painting and the Pitt portrait, but obscures the connection by mislabeling and misunderstanding the process as "symbolism" (Davidson, "Peale's Exhuming," p. 63).

69. Jefferson, *Notes,* pp. 19, 24–25. These passages were well known to Americans and to foreign visitors such as Brissot de Warville, the comte de Volney, Richard Cobden, and Augustus John Foster. Rembrandt Peale did a watercolor sketch of Harpers Ferry ca. 1811 (Peale Museum, Baltimore); then turned it into an oil painting (Walker Art Center, Minneapolis), and then into a lithograph for public consumption about 1827. Herman Melville could count on general public knowledge of the reference, when he likened the leap of the great white whale to the Natural Bridge (*Moby-Dick,* chap. 133). See Wilbur H. Hunter, "The Peale Family and Peale's Baltimore Museum," *Pennsylvania Magazine of History and Biography* (1965): 318.

70. Another, larger landscape (now unlocated) from a different point of view also hung in the same room (*P&M Suppl.,* pp. 34, 36). For Peale's vivid diary account of the exhumation and the difficulties encountered, with a sketch of the works, see Sellers, *Mr. Peale's Museum,* pp. 131–37; *Selected Papers* 2:308–79.

71. The wild-steed motif as index of the sublime was to become a familiar one. George Stubbs had already used it frequently in England in his horse-lion confrontations (see Basil Taylor, "George Stubbs: 'The Lion and Horse' Theme," *Burlington Magazine* 107 [1965]: 81–86). Thomas Cole used it in his otherwise bucolic *View of the Catskills: Early Autumn* (1837, Metropolitan Museum of Art, New York). It became a popular folkloric image as well. See George Kendall, "A Superb Wild Horse," in *Humor of the Old Southwest,* ed. Hennig Cohen and William B. Dillingham (2d ed., Athens, Georgia, 1975), pp. 92–93. Melville captures it in his image of the white steed of the prairies, land alternative to Moby-Dick in the famous "Whiteness of the Whale," chap. 42. It has, of course, biblical origins in Revelation 6, which Benjamin West explored in a variety of pictorial ways.

72. A(TS): 371; quoted in Davidson, "Peale's *Exhuming,*" p. 62; the autobiography also has an extended account of the exhumation process.

73. It is worth noting in this respect that both the technology of the wheel pump and the artistry of the picture have precursors, extending back at least to the woodcuts of the sixteenth-century metallurgist Agricola. See Herbert C. Hoover and Lou H. Hoover, trans., *De Re Metallica, from First Latin Edition of 1556* (rpt. New York, 1950), esp. book VI with its plates. I am grateful to my former colleague Bert Hansen for calling this to my attention.

74. Jefferson, *Notes on Virginia,* p. 19.

75. It needs to be compared with the pyramidal order in the middle ground that John Singleton Copley establishes in *Watson and the Shark* (1778), equally an imposition of human geometric control over the experience of the sublime confrontation between shark and helpless Watson in the foreground — though there are differences, especially in the background. See my "Copley's *Watson and the Shark* and Aesthetics in the 1770s," *Discoveries and Consideration: Essays in Early American Literature and Aesthetics Presented to Harold Jantz,* ed. Calvin Israel (Albany, N.Y., 1976), pp. 85–130. These three Enlightenment strategies for bringing the sublime under control in the middle distance are not, we must insist, instances of American "pastoral" in the loose way that Leo Marx's less perceptive followers have used his insights in *The Machine in the Garden.* For the generation of Copley, Jefferson, and Peale, the issues and their aesthetic expression are rather different.

76. See Sellers, *Peale* (1947), 2:355–56; for Godman's discussion of the mastodon, see John Godman, *American Natural History* (Philadelphia, 1826), 2:204–52.

77. John Godman, *Addresses Delivered on Various Public Occasions* (Philadelphia, 1829), pp. 110, 128–29. I quote it from the suggestive chapter on "Philadelphia Science and the Artist-Naturalist" in William H. Truettner, *The Natural Man Observed: A Study in Catlin's Indian Gallery* (Washington, D.C., 1979), p. 68. Truettner's study is helpful for locating Peale in relation to the next — and finally very different — generation.

78. Jefferson, *Notes on Virginia,* p. 19.

79. Madlyn Millner Kahr, "Velásquez and Las Meniñas," *Art Bulletin* 57 (June 1975): 225–46, at p. 239. Readers are referred to Kahr's article for its perceptive insights and for the wealth of illustrations of northern European gallery pictures with which Velásquez's work is linked. My attention was initially called to this kind of "source" for *The Artist in His Museum* by Patrick Stewart, Jr., in his critical review

of my first brief comments on the painting in "Structure as Meaning: Towards a Cultural Interpretation of American Painting," *American Art Review* 3 (March–April 1976): 66–78; and ibid. 3 (September–October 1976): 49–55.

80. Both works are discussed and illustrated, with special reference to emblematic strategies, in Paulson, *Emblem and Expression,* pp. 138–48, 152–58.

81. The Bonaparte collection is frequently noted in the literature of American art history; Peale's sketch of the academy walls displaying Fulton's collection, in a letter of November 15, 1807, is reproduced in *P&M Suppl.,* p. 107. Lillian B. Miller, *Patrons and Patriotism: The Encouragement of the Fine Arts in the United States, 1790–1860* (Chicago, 1966), mentions numerous northern European works in collections; and the published catalogues of the American Academy of Fine Arts, the National Academy of Design, and the Pennsylvania Academy of the Fine Arts contain considerable raw data (though of course attributions to particular artists are open to question). For the Peale family and still life, see esp. Charles H. Elam, ed., *The Peale Family,* exhibition catalogue (Detroit Institute of Art, 1967); and William H. Gerdts and Russell Burke, *American Still-Life Painting* (New York, 1971), chap. 2; for Peale's comment on King, see Andrew J. Cosentino, *The Paintings of Charles Bird King, 1785–1862* (Washington, D.C., 1977), p. 80. For three recent works that emphasize the Dutch impact, see H. Nichols B. Clark, "A Taste for the Netherlands: The Impact of Seventeenth-Century Dutch and Flemish Genre Painting on American Art 1800–1860," *American Art Journal* 14 (Spring 1982), 23–38; H. Nichols B. Clark, *Francis W. Edmonds: American Master in the Dutch Tradition* (Washington, D.C., 1988); and Sarah Burns, *Pastoral Inventions: Rural Life in Nineteenth-Century American Art and Culture* (Philadelphia, 1989).

82. Svetlana Alpers, "Is Art History?" *Daedalus* 106 (Summer 1977): 5. The idea and implications of this have subsequently been more fully developed in Alpers's *The Art of Describing: Dutch Art in the Seventeenth Century* (Chicago, 1983).

83. The visual pun is not an unusual pictorial event. Within the Peale family, Raphaelle was the most frequent practitioner.

84. This balancing is mirrored in the movement of the museum itself from the Lombard Street residence to Philosophical Hall, with a great parade (*CWP,* pp. 264–65), from thence to the statehouse; eventually, part of it went to P. T. Barnum's American Museum. On the continual tension between science and showmanship, see Sellers, *Mr. Peale's Museum, passim.*

85. The work of Jean-Baptiste Greuze was fashioned after the conventions of the new drama and aesthetically justified by Diderot. Along with works by the Scot David Wilkie (*Blind Fiddler,* 1806), Greuze's work served as model and inspiration for John Krimmel's shallow-staged genre pieces in Philadelphia in the second decade of the nineteenth century. See Patricia Hills, *The Painter's America: Rural and Urban Life, 1810–1910* (New York, 1974), pp. 2–9.

86. Two examples shown in the *Splendors of Dresden* exhibition were the Vermeer, *Girl at a Window Reading a Letter* (ca. 1658) and the Gerard Dou, *Still-Life with Candlesticks and Pocket Watch,* nos. 553 and 559 in the catalogue.

87. Quoted in *CWP,* p. 474*n*10.

88. *P&M,* pp. 161–62.

89. *CWP,* p. 410.

90. Ibid.

91. *P&M*, p. 162, contains the gathered evidence on this lost work. Trompe l'oeil devices to emphasize Peale's role as artist (also involving Raphaelle) can be traced back to as early as 1787, when Peale sculptured a life-size self-portrait in wax for his Lombard Street Museum (See Sellers, *Mr. Peale's Museum*, pp. 30–31, for an account of this "deception").

92. For the earlier scholarship on this painting, see Gerdts and Burke, *American Still-Life Painting*, pp. 30, 31, and William H. Gerdts, *The Great American Nude: A History in Art* (New York, 1974), p. 45; for the related Charles Bird King, *Environs of Italy*, see Cosentino, *King*, p. 99, and the colored plate, p. 100; and Gerdts and Burke, *American Still-Life Painting*, pp. 51–53.

For the most recent analysis, see Dorinda Evans, "Raphaelle Peale's *Venus Rising From the Sea:* Further Support for a Change in Interpretation," *American Art Journal* 14 (Summer 1982): 63–72; William H. Gerdts, "A Deception Unmasked: An Artist Uncovered," *American Art Journal* 18 (1986): 4–23; and Phoebe Lloyd, "Philadelphia Story," *Art in America* 76 (November 1988): 154–71, 195–203, esp. 164–67. For an overview of Raphaelle's work in context, see also the catalogue of the National Gallery of Art exhibition by Nicolai Cikovsky, Jr., et al., *Raphaelle Peale Still Lifes* (Washington, D.C., 1988).

The recent work makes clear that one version of the painting, now lost, was exhibited at the Pennsylvania Academy in May of 1822, before his father received the commission for *The Artist in His Museum* (Evans, "Raphaelle Peale's *Venus*," p. 69); but Gerdts and Lloyd are agreed that the painting we know is a second version which should be dated 1823 (Lloyd, "Philadelphia Story," p. 201n38), after the completion of *The Artist in His Museum*.

93. *CWP*, p. 420. Sellers points out in *Mr. Peale's Museum*, p. 246, that in 1822–23 the popular Philadelphia competitor of the Peale museum with its scientific fare, the Washington Museum at Second and Market streets, was exhibiting paintings including Adolph Wertmüller's *Danaë and the Shower of Gold*. This notorious nude, a succès de scandale (see Gerdts, *Great American Nude*, pp. 39–41, 44–45) that the elder Peale deplored, may also have been in Raphaelle's consciousness when he created his inverted image of the Danaë, the covered nude "after the bath."

94. This diagnosis was first argued in Lloyd, "Philadelphia Story." Her subsequent research with Gordon Bendersky, M.D., seems to confirm the diagnosis and etiology of Raphaelle's illness. This makes the presence of the dead turkey draped over the taxidermical instruments in *The Artist in His Museum* potentially a particularly poignant or ironic personal family symbol.

95. Charles Willson Peale, *An Essay to Promote Domestic Happiness* (Philadelphia, 1812); Peale could not resist using teleology at Raphaelle's expense: "How wonderful, beautiful, and wise is the divine work of creation! Each individual creature, made with forms and capacities, best calculated to fill its station and relation with other beings" (p. 19). He ended with Luke 15: "For thy brother was dead, and is alive again; and was lost, and is found" (p. 24).

96. Evans ("Raphaelle Peale's *Venus*," p. 72) and Lloyd ("Philadelphia Story," pp. 165 and 165n32) both dismiss the earlier suggestion (*CWP*, p. 485n5 and *Suppl.*, pp. 75–76) that Raphaelle painted his *Deception* over a replica or copy of Charles

Willson Peale's 1817 portrait of Raphaelle, an error which I repeated in the original version of this essay.

97. James Fenimore Cooper, *The Prairie: A Tale* (New York, 1950), pp. 77, 78. As Henry Nash Smith points out in his introduction (p. vii), Edwin James's account of the Long expedition of 1819–20, on which Titian Ramsay Peale served as assistant naturalist, was one of Cooper's sources for both the descriptions of the territory and his parody of scientific rationalism.

12

The Waning of
an Enlightenment Ideal

Charles Willson Peale's Philadelphia Museum
1790–1820

———◈———

SIDNEY HART AND DAVID C. WARD

O N April 24, 1794, Charles Willson Peale (fig. 77) "respectfully"
informed the public that "he should bid adieu to Portrait Painting" and he recommended his artist sons Raphaelle and Rembrandt to those desiring portraits. Peale did continue to paint to the
end of his life, but his hitherto prodigious output of commissioned portraits dwindled to a yearly handful of portraits of his family, special
friends, and the occasional notable American or European.[1]

Peale did not, however, abandon his active role in the cultural life
of Philadelphia and the new nation; if anything his withdrawal from
painting was followed by a period of increased activity and creativity
in which he worked to establish and improve the organizations that would
support and advance the artistic, scientific, and intellectual needs of
Americans. Among scientists, he was a bulwark of the American Philosophical Society, faithfully attending meetings, contributing prize essays and papers, and serving as one of the society's officers. In the arts,
Peale was instrumental in efforts, first with the aborted Columbianum
and later successfully with the Pennsylvania Academy of the Fine Arts,
to establish a permanent institution to improve, promote, and exhibit
the work of American artists. Overshadowing all these—and a multi-
plicity of other activities—was Peale's most important contribution to

Philadelphia's, and indeed America's, culture: the establishment and operation of the Philadelphia Museum or, as it was familiarly known, Peale's museum. As Peale explained in his announcement of his retirement from an artistic career: "It is his fixed determination to encrease the subjects of the Museum with all his powers, whilst life and health will admit of it" (fig. 80).[2]

The museum began as an offshoot of Peale's efforts to run a portrait gallery to display his paintings. A chance remark from a friend that the public might also pay to see some natural history specimens that Peale had on hand ultimately led to the creation of a museum housing collections of art, science, natural history, and technology. Peale was receptive to the idea of expanding a portrait gallery into a museum not simply because such a museum might produce revenue. Beyond the necessity to make money and support his large family was Peale's drive to make the museum one of America's preeminent cultural institutions — a drive that followed logically from his world view, a view that grew out of his career as an artisan and artist and reflected eighteenth-century Enlightenment and republican ideas about order, harmony, and civic virtue.[3]

This chapter will examine Charles Willson Peale's attempts to obtain government support for his museum between 1790 and 1820. For Peale, government support for educational and cultural institutions was essential for an enlightened, republican society. However, the changing nature of American culture in the first years of the nineteenth century made Peale's efforts problematical and ultimately fruitless. We will argue that Peale's museum was an institution arising out of the ideals of the eighteenth-century Enlightenment; that its continued existence into the nineteenth century as an educational institution was hampered by changing cultural and intellectual values that focused on the specific and specialized rather than the general and universal; that these changing values precluded continued local and state government support; and that Peale's opportunity to obtain national support was blocked by a political ideology — Jeffersonianism — that rigidly circumscribed the area of society into which the national government would intervene. Existing studies of Peale's museum have been both presentist and ahistorical in their explanations of why Peale was unable to obtain government support and ensure the long-term survival of his museum. By placing the museum in the ideological and political context of the early nineteenth century, we will suggest another hypothesis — namely, that Charles Willson Peale, a man of the eighteenth-century Enlightenment who believed in unity and harmony, found himself in conflict with the ideals of the new century, in which the universal and general categories of the Enlightenment would be broken down into distinct and separate spheres of thought and action. In terms of Peale's greatest creation — his Philadelphia Museum — this meant, as he feared, the absence of government support; his museum would not be a permanent institution for posterity but would last little more than twenty years after his death.

In its philosophy, organization, and arrangement, Peale's Philadelphia Museum embodied much of the spirit of the eighteenth-century Enlightenment. The basic tenets of the Enlightenment's cosmology were all demonstrated in graphic display. The Linnaean classification of species indicated the order, harmony, and regularity of nature and also testified to man's ability to perceive its complexities and present them in a systematic way. The species were also displayed as links in a great chain of being that depicted a static universe of ascending life forms from the simplest organism to man. Peale conceived of his museum and its displays as a "world in miniature" in which life in its variegated but ultimately harmonious forms would be on view. Peale had "no doubt" that his "assemblage of nature . . . when critically examined" would be "found to be a part of a great whole, combined together by unchangeable laws of infinite wisdom."[4]

It is worth noting that Peale seriously considered displaying the embalmed corpses of eminent men to show the highest level attained in the natural world. When this proved unworkable, a substitute was found in his portraits that lined the walls, significantly displayed *above* the natural history specimens. The harmonies of the mechanical world were also represented in displays of the latest technology. In addition to the fascination of watching intricate and complicated mechanisms working harmoniously, viewers could realize from the inventions that progress had been made, and would continue to be made, in the material conditions of mankind through the application of man's rational powers to solve or ameliorate the problems of living, a key tenet of Enlightenment thought (fig. 72).[5]

In its organization and operation, Peale's museum was democratic and popular, reflecting the proprietor's ideological and political views. During the American Revolution, Peale had been a radical republican who in his art and actions supported the colonial cause and the democratization of American culture and society. He served as a soldier in the

militia and as a member of Philadelphia's political committees and societies. These groups actively promoted and supported the most radical
ideas and policies of the American Revolution, including the Pennsylvania constitution of 1776. His commitment to republican ideology and
democratic polity was well known. As heir to both the Enlightenment
and the American Revolution, Peale believed that improvement in knowledge led necessarily to improvement in character and that republics
could survive only with an educated and virtuous citizenry.

Peale's major justification in seeking state support for his museum
was predicated on the republican concept of civic virtue. In his memorial to the Pennsylvania legislature in 1795, he defined his museum as
an educational institution and then pointed out what for the legislators
surely would be a well-known republican formulation: "In a country
where institutions all depend upon the virtue of the people, which in
its turn is secured only as they are well informed, the promotion of
knowledge is the First of duties." For men such as Peale, the American
Revolution provided the opportunity to create an intellectual and cultural renaissance, and perhaps even a secular millennium, in which ignorance and superstition would give way to reason and truth. Only Peale's
fear of the still strong influence of organized religion kept him from calling his museum a "Temple of Wisdom." But the museum's function,
nonetheless, would be to educate and teach virtue to the public by demonstrating the benevolence of the creator and the order, harmony, and
beauty of his creation. It was a matter of faith to the proprietor that
"nothing which human invention has yet found out, can so forcibly impress sentiments of piety, and a reverence for the supreme Creator" as
a well organized museum.[6]

In dramatic contrast to traditional European practice, the museum
was open to the public without restriction, except for the payment of
an admission fee of twenty-five cents; additional fees were sometimes
imposed for special exhibits, such as the mastodon display, and events
such as lectures and concerts. In Peale's museum, again unlike the state-
run museums and collections in Europe, specimens and artifacts were
not hidden in drawers or storerooms, accessible only to the learned and
privileged. Rather, Peale's overriding goal was to disseminate knowledge to as wide an audience as possible. Peale (and his workers) were
expert taxidermists, adept at preserving and displaying animal specimens (fig. 78). Peale was a pioneer in the use of the habitat group in
which animals were displayed in a lifelike manner in realistic settings

made to duplicate nature as closely as possible (fig. 79). The clear intention was to attract the eye of interested laymen, so that they would learn more about the natural world. Peale did not assume knowledge and expertise about what was displayed so he added labels and descriptions to the exhibits in order to facilitate the public's education; to further inform and orient the visitor, Peale published *A Guide to the Philadelphia Museum,* which he distributed free of charge. The scholar, too, was not neglected, since Peale's expert taxidermy and display of natural history specimens, all arranged in the best scientific and taxonomic order, were calculated to facilitate scientific observation and analysis; the museum was frequently used by science classes at the University of Pennsylvania as well as by prominent individual scientists such as Alexander Wilson and Benjamin Smith Barton. Peale's intention, besides universal education, was also to make his museum a public institution in a democratic state. In his mind, this meant that he had to compel "the unwise as [well] as the learned to feel the importance of a well organized Museum, before . . . [he could have] any pretention or expectation of getting any aid from our Public bodies."[7]

The museum soon became highly popular among not only Philadelphians but also all Americans and foreign visitors, achieving its founder's goal of involving large numbers of people in a democratic cultural and intellectual experience. One indication of the museum's national (and indeed international) popularity and renown was the range and extent of the individuals who donated specimens and artifacts to it. Peale received items from such disparate people as local Pennsylvania artisans and farmers and the most eminent scientists in the United States and Europe. Geographically, items came to the museum from the settled areas of the east coast but also from the frontier regions of North America, South America, the Pacific islands, and the Orient. It was this far-flung network of donors, acting independently and voluntarily, that provided both the mundane and exotic items which made up the museum's collections. The two-volume list of accessions, totaling some 192 closely written manuscript pages, is testimony to the general desire of the age to collect, classify, and observe the elements of the physical and man-made worlds. During the second decade of the nineteenth century, the museum contained (among other things) 269 paintings, 1,824 birds, 250 quadrupeds, 650 fishes, over 1,000 shells, and 313 books in the library; according to one authority, the total number of all objects exceeded 100,000.[8]

Further evidence of the museum's popularity may be found in figures for the museum's income and attendance. After some shaky years
in the 1790s when the museum brought in revenues fluctuating from
$1,172 to $3,330 a year, income traced a continuous upward path during
the first two decades of the nineteenth century: $2,910 was received in
1800; $4,213 in 1805; $8,380 in 1810; and $9,905 in 1815; the peak year,
1816, brought in $11,924. Lacking other evidence, we can derive rough
figures for annual attendance from the museum's receipts, since Peale
depended solely on visitors for income; he received no subsidies and
apparently did not accept (or was not offered) cash donations. A precise
figure for attendance cannot be derived from the receipts because Peale
offered special admission packages such as yearly tickets and charged
additional fees for special exhibits or events. However, given an admission fee of twenty-five cents, a rough count of the number of visitors
can be extrapolated from the figures for yearly revenue. This gives an
attendance of 11,620 people in 1800, 16,862 in 1805, 33,520 in 1810, and
39,620 in 1815; the peak year of 1816 may have seen 47,696 people enter
the museum—this in a city whose population was 69,403 in 1800 and
91,874 in 1810.[9]

Despite the museum's popular success, almost from the beginning
Peale realized that his vision for it was beyond the capacity of any one
person to realize and, moreover, that if he continued expanding his collections the museum would soon become an institution of general value
to the city, the state, and the republic as a whole. In 1792 he published
an address "To the Citizens of the United States of America" in *Dunlap's
American Daily Advertiser* expressing his gratitude to those who donated
specimens. He indicated his desire to expand his collections, and admitted that his "design" was "so vast" as to be "far beyond the slender abilities of an individual." His hope was that the importance and magnitude
"of the object" would attract more public support and "enable him to
raise this tender plant, until it shall grow into full maturity, and become
a *National Museum.*" Peale's conception of the utility of the museum meant
that state aid was not only desirable but indeed imperative, because
the museum contributed to the general welfare. Additionally, public support for the museum would be valuable in ensuring its growth and prosperity and in providing for its continuity once he and his family were
gone. State aid, in Peale's view, was the only means to provide funds
for the day-to-day operation of the museum as well as providing a solid
institutional foundation that would ensure its future.[10]

In seeking government support, Peale was influenced by European precedent and practice. Peale well knew of the European policy of state aid for institutions devoted to learning and science. Peale also had received the encouragement of European scientists and statesmen that he should and would receive state support. For example, after a private audience with Jefferson in 1805, the naturalist Alexander von Humboldt reported to Peale that he found it inconceivable that the United States government would not make the museum a national institution. Similarly, the French envoy Phillipe Rose Roume wrote to Peale, using the image of the enlightening sun to describe the effect of the museum on the American people and concluding with the assurance that Peale's efforts would entitle him to the "*droit incontestable*" of public support.[11]

At the time Peale founded his museum, he did not feel it necessary to delineate with precision its public and private nature because political and economic theory allowed a blurring of these categories with regard to activities and institutions viewed as promoting the general welfare. It was understood in postrevolutionary America that activities that could be shown as being eventually useful to the community, and that would not otherwise be undertaken, would be given encouragement by the state. Americans looked to the state governments as the guardians and promoters of the public interest; nor was the term *public interest* construed in a narrow sense. Projects in agriculture, manufacturing, commerce, the arts and sciences, and education were to be given careful consideration when seeking state aid. In his 1803 address to the Massachusetts legislature, Governor Caleb Strong noted that in the ideal commonwealth a wise government, its power resting in the people, would direct and aid diverse pursuits so that private advantage and the public good would "concur." In his address to the same legislature a few years later, Elbridge Gerry declared that state aid and patronage to varied pursuits "cannot be too much encouraged and supported." A political economist of the early nineteenth century argued that even special interests and monopolies were not to be denied aid if it could be shown that the "general interest of the community [was] still the object in view . . . [or that there would be as much reason] for the interest of the community to make the grant, as for . . . [the special interest or individual] to receive it." Local and state governments frequently intervened in such privately sponsored economic enterprises as turnpikes, canals, banks, and bridges that were regarded as essential public services requiring support or guarantees beyond the capacity of individuals; state legislatures aided private universities and colleges in the post-revolutionary era. The American Philosophical Society, America's first learned society, was perhaps Peale's model with regard to the question of state patronage of science and education. Before the Revolution, the society's greatest source of income was the Pennsylvania Assembly, and the legislature continued to aid the society, although to a lesser extent, after independence. In a similar example, which Peale probably knew about, the government of Massachusetts had founded and then aided the American Academy of Arts and Sciences.[12]

Given this practice and climate of opinion, it was reasonable that Peale should attempt to demonstrate that his museum was one of the institutions that contributed to the general welfare of society and to seek aid from the state and national governments. Peale conducted a campaign in the press to create a nationwide awareness of his museum and its beneficial consequences for American society. He published a series of appeals to the public like the one already mentioned, and he wrote or commissioned other articles for the press arguing in favor of such positions as the public benefits of natural history museums. In order to disseminate information about the museum and natural history to the public more efficiently, Peale acquired a printing press in 1804. As he wrote to a fellow naturalist, "[Having a press] will enable me to do many useful things to defuse Knowledge of Natural History and show the importance of such an Institution. This must be done, before I can exert to obtain government patronage." This educational campaign was intended to buttress Peale's more direct appeals for state aid, such as in 1792 when he submitted his first memorial to the Pennsylvania state legislature. This appeal requested that a committee be appointed to visit his museum and determine the "proper pecuniary aid" to be contributed by the state. The legislature tabled the memorial, perhaps, as Peale optimistically believed, because it was simply submitted too late in the session. Not discouraged, Peale made several more attempts during the 1790s to obtain aid from the Pennsylvania legislatures, and while he did receive favorable responses from legislative committees, he was not successful in getting the legislature to act in his favor.[13]

Having failed to obtain direct financial aid from the legislature, Peale's next campaign for state aid, beginning in the winter of 1800, was to obtain a larger building for his museum and its increasing number of specimens. There were two suitable buildings available: Independence Hall, which was vacant following the shift of Pennsylvania's capital to Lancaster; and Congress Hall, which would become vacant when the federal government left the city the following spring. Peale published an address in the newspapers to the "People of America and Citizens of Philadelphia." Philadelphians, he wrote, should be proud of the museum, but he warned them that if they did not "make exertions to foster an important school for their own and their children's use . . . some other city in the Union [would] rejoice in receiving [his] labours." And he reminded all Americans that "England, France, Italy, not only boast of their Museums, but cherish them from the public funds." Peale submitted a memorial to the state legislature "praying the loan of one of the unoccupied buildings in the city of Philadelphia." On February 24, 1800, the petition was read in the lower house of the legislature, tabled, and no further action was taken.[14]

Peale did not allow these setbacks to divert him from overseeing the expansion and improvement of the museum. Most important, in 1801 he learned of a significant find of fossil bones in New York State. With an interest-free loan from the American Philosophical Society, Peale organized an expedition that would succeed in exhuming and eventually reconstructing two almost complete skeletons of the American mastodon (fig. 66). The exhumation of the mastodon may be considered the first organized scientific expedition in the United States, and Peale's accurate recreation of the skeletons was of immense importance in the history of paleontology (fig. 81). It is worth noting that in constructing the skeletons Peale pioneered modern museum practice and techniques by using carved models to substitute for missing bones and carefully noting which sections of the skeleton were manmade. The mastodon enormously increased the reputation, prestige, and popularity of the museum; as a result, overcrowding became an even more severe problem. To solve the problem of the museum's lack of space, once again Peale sought government patronage.[15]

On January 12, 1802, Peale wrote to President Jefferson about his desire to make his museum a permanent public institution. Although he emphasized the utility of such an institution, Peale's description became lyrical as he "imagined" a great collection that "in one view" would "enlighten the minds of . . . [his] countrymen" by exhibiting the "wonderful and various beauties of Nature." Such an institution would prove to be "more powerful to humanize the mind, promote harmony, and aid virtue, than any other School yet imagined." And as a result, his arduous labor in collecting and preserving specimens would not end in their

dispersal after his death, but "would be crown'd in a National Establishment." He wanted to know Jefferson's "sentiments" about "whither the
United States would give an encouragement, and make provision for
the establishment of this Museum in the City of Washington."[16]

Jefferson, in his reply four days later, acknowledged the great value
of Peale's collection, and praised the museum keeper's "unwearied perseverance & skill" in collecting and preserving specimens. He wished
that the museum "could be made public property," but feared that Peale
would allow his [Jefferson's] "partiality" to the museum "to excite false
expectations . . . which might eventually be disappointed." Jefferson explained that the issue rested on "one of the great questions which has
divided political opinion in this country . . . Whether Congress are au-
thorised by the constitution to apply the public money to any but the
purposes specially enumerated in the Constitution?" Members of his
own party, Jeffersonian Republicans, who limited Congress to the exercise of only those powers enumerated in the Constitution — strict constructionists in modern parlance — "have always denied that Congress
have any power to establish a National academy." But some of these
Republicans, Jefferson added, "still wish Congress had power to favor
science, and that an amendment should be proposed to the constitution, giving them such power specifically." Jefferson further noted that
if a majority of the Congress believed that the national government had
the power to establish a national university, Peale's museum would be
purchased as the first step toward creating such an institution. But, as
an astute politician, Jefferson knew that a majority in Congress were
strict constructionists. Indeed, when Joel Barlow proposed a plan for
a national university in 1807, which Jefferson favored and viewed as a
"means" of satisfying his friend Peale and nationalizing the museum,
the measure went down to defeat in Congress.[17]

Bowing to political realities, Peale accepted Jefferson's judgment with
respect "to an Application to congress," and in February 1802 he reopened
his campaign for state support by presenting memorials to the House
and Senate of Pennsylvania seeking aid in obtaining a larger building
for his museum. The legislature this time responded positively and
granted Peale the use of the vacant Independence Hall (or Statehouse,
as it was also known). Peale welcomed the legislature's action, little sus-
pecting that it would be virtually the only support he would receive from
the state. Indeed, just in order to keep Independence Hall, Peale would
have to lobby the legislature regularly for their continued support, and

perform a variety of other tasks such as maintaining order in the state-house yard, a popular gathering place for drunks and prostitutes. In addition, starting in 1815 he had to pay a rental fee (he previously had only to maintain the building), a fee that would increase regularly and be the subject of much wrangling between the Peales and the state, and later the city of Philadelphia.[18]

Peale's dream that his museum would become a public institution was never attained. Its specimens were sold and dispersed, much of the collection going to P. T. Barnum and Moses Kimball, and some of the items were destroyed by fires in 1851 and 1865. Explanations for the museum's ultimate failure rely on the notion that the museum was ahead of its time and—there are two versions to this argument—that it was the forerunner of either P. T. Barnum or the twentieth-century Smithsonian Institution. Historians who see Peale as the forerunner of Barnum argue that, contrary to Peale's stated intentions, the museum was never a serious educational institution and that Peale was merely a "showman" who earned a good income by exploiting the public's fascination with unusual and exotic displays. One historian of science, who at least acknowledges Peale's goal of making the museum an institution of public education, nonetheless concludes that the "reality fell short of the ideal" and that the legislators, like most of the visitors, "regarded the museum as a kind of show . . . [and] were impressed by Peale's financial success but took it as proof that his museum did not need public support." The view that compares Peale's museum to the Smithsonian is far more complimentary: the reality did achieve the ideal, but the society was not ready to support that ideal. The two components of that ideal, which have been realized in the twentieth century, are Peale's democratic concept of a museum for all classes, directed to the research scientist as well as to the general public, and his method of displaying specimens in habitat groups, which satisfied the specialist and provided in Peale's terms, "rational amusement" for the populace. In this interpretation, Peale's museum failed because it was ahead of its time—a twentieth-century institution that could not obtain public support in the nineteenth century.[19]

Both these interpretations are ahistorical and fail to treat Peale in context. An incident in 1806 illustrates the point that Peale was very much a man of his time, but one who did not perceive that times were changing. The American Philosophical Society had permitted Peale to borrow its elephant skeleton to display alongside the mastodon but only on the understanding that he not advertise the elephant. The society knew full well that Peale depended on publicity and advertisements for attendance and income; its attitude indicates that the society's members resented the commercial aspect of the museum. Superficially, the incident would seem to confirm that Peale was a precursor of Barnum: Peale as nineteenth-century showman. However, for Peale the categories were not so clearly defined. The ideal in Peale's time — the eighteenth-century Enlightenment — was to unify separate realms of behavior and knowledge. Peale sought to close the gap between popular entertainment and scientific knowledge, and considered it proper and desirable to advertise an attraction if that would bring people into the museum for enlightenment.[20]

In Peale's mind, the commercial dimension was far less distinct from the public realm than it would be in the nineteenth and twentieth centuries. In 1800, he wrote to William Findley, a Pennsylvania state legislator, arguing that his museum should be made a state institution. Peale believed it was his duty to come to the legislature at a time when he was still able to aid in the further development of the museum and make it an important educational institution "by blending the amusing & the useful." As for his own individual gain or profit, he believed that he did "not ask for any advantage" for himself "which will not produce greater benefits for the State." He saw no inconsistency in the legislature making the museum a public institution and also "allowing profits" to him and his heirs. That the state legislators viewed the museum as a "show" that earned a profit did not mean that Peale conceived of himself as acting as a showman. Rather, Peale's conceptions of public versus private and education versus amusement had not evolved (as they were beginning to for the legislators) into their separate and distinct nineteenth-century realms; in the fluid situation of the early years of the century, the two parties were speaking across each other in different languages.[21]

Peale's very sense of an educational institution derived from the Enlightenment's sense of the unity and utility of knowledge. In many ways, the history of his museum mirrors the experiences of eighteenth-century learned societies in America. The most prominent of these societies — the American Philosophical Society — was established as a general body of learning in the expectation that the knowledge it generated would have application in such important areas of society as agriculture, manufacturing, and commerce. When Benjamin Franklin (fig. 73) issued a circular letter in 1743 proposing the creation of the Philosophical Society, he set forth a long list of activities which would be the legitimate concerns of the new society. The list included investigations of plants, cures for diseases, labor-saving mechanical inventions, husbandry, "Arts, Trades, Manufactures . . . Surveys, Maps and Charts," and "New Improvements in Planting." For Franklin, all of these miscellaneous investigations into "the Nature of Things" were a unity because they would "increase the Power of Man over Matter, and multiply the Conveniences or Pleasures of Life." Similarly, Peale's vision for his museum was that it become a repository in which "every art and every science should be taught. To this central magazine of knowledge, all the learned and ingenious would flock, as well to gain, as to communicate, information." Man would thus be able to achieve the same mastery and power as Franklin had envisioned: to know "from the combination of certain things the results," by comparing "the present with the past," to "calculate the revolution of the Planets," to "produce by the labor of the hands various and wonderful works of art, and with knowledge of the . . . lever, the screw, & the wedge . . . make machines to lessen labour, and multiply the conveniences & comforts of Life." All this man would be able to accomplish when he had at hand, as in a museum, the "subjects" of "nature" with which to "analize & know the component parts . . . by actual experiments." The inclusiveness of Peale's museum thus reflected the virtually pervasive Enlightenment belief that all knowledge had unity and utility. This belief was an Enlightenment axiom that reached its highest expression in Diderot's *Encyclopedia,* the goal of which was to collect, classify, and disseminate the universal body of knowledge. The eighteenth century's learned societies shared this objective, and Peale's museum — the world in miniature — was an even more explicit statement of this philosophy and one that came close to translating the ideal into reality.[22]

Toward the end of the eighteenth century, this vision of unity began to unravel; the pattern is clearly shown in the histories of the American Academy of Arts and Sciences and the American Philosophical Society. Their founders had expected that their organizations would make significant contributions to society. But by the late eighteenth century, these organizations were being criticized as too general, too "universal," in their programs and research. In the last decade of the century, organizations limited in scope to specific aspects of manufacturing or agriculture, such as the advancement of an industry or the improve-

ment of a breed of animals, were formed in nearly all the states in order
to address specific economic or scientific needs of American society. The
multiplication of these societies by 1800 is seen as an indication that the
broad, universal approach to knowledge formulated in the Enlightenment had broken down. To a great degree, Peale's argument for the
public support of his museum was predicated on its public utility, which
in turn looked back to the old Enlightenment faith that all knowledge
was unified and useful, and that all classes of people — "the unwise as
[well] as the learned" — would appreciate and value the "importance of
a well organized Museum." With a large segment of the public suspicious that scientists were more interested in abstract research than in
knowledge with practical application, it was not possible to build a great
deal of public support for science in general. On the other hand, it also
indicated the elitist attitudes of American scientists and their distrust
of popular science, when more and more professional scientists dismissed
as unworthy Peale's belief that the public's interest in the curious and
unusual, used with care, could contribute to the popularity of science.
Peale failed in his attempt to turn popular opinion in the United States
to the support of science, and also in his attempt to convince scientists
to seek popular support. The museum's failure was in part a consequence
of its being in an age of great scientific discovery but one in which science was not widely appreciated by the general public. The unpopu-
larity of science, and the scientists' distrust of popularity, were in part
consequences of the breakdown of the unified view of knowledge and
science that had prevailed during the Enlightenment. Government support at the state or local level would also not be possible once the Enlightenment's unified view no longer prevailed. The breakdown of this
unity undermined the support the museum would need in the nineteenth
century if it were to be made into a truly public institution.[23]

The importance of Peale's museum was long minimized by scholars
who saw Peale's activity as a museum "showman" as a declension from
his career as an artist. Subsequent work, most notably by Charles Coleman Sellers, has refuted this negative interpretation and established the
importance of the museum in the history of American culture. As well,
Sellers correctly saw that Peale's operation of the museum was the logical consequence of an integrated and coherent world view: the exhibition of the unities and harmonies of nature was a natural outgrowth
of ideas that went into his painting. But in arguing the case for the importance of the museum, Sellers and others have perhaps gone too far
in stressing the prototypical aspects of the institution. In a kind of Whig

interpretation of museums, the Peale museum is almost seen as a twentieth-century museum in eighteenth- and nineteenth-century Philadelphia because of its anticipation of modern museum techniques. What we have demonstrated is the extent to which Peale's conception of the museum straddled two worlds, an ultimately untenable situation. While the layout of the museum did anticipate modern practice, the philosophy that underlay its operation was rooted in an eighteenth-century Enlightenment conception of the unity and utility of all knowledge. In the nineteenth century, the "universalism" of Peale's "world in miniature" would be increasingly questioned by those who, skeptical of such all inclusive visions, would only support institutions and interests that could demonstrate an immediate practical utility to the state and society. Through unceasing effort Peale was able to keep the museum operating, but a culture that was increasingly unresponsive to his claim to serve the general good made it impossible for him to complete his life's task and to insure that his museum would be handed down to posterity.

NOTES

This chapter was originally published in the *Journal of the Early Republic* 8 (1988): 389–418. The authors would like to thank Dr. Lillian B. Miller, Editor, Peale Family Papers, National Portrait Gallery, Smithsonian Institution, for encouraging this study. We would also like to thank Milton M. Klein for his comments. An earlier version of this chapter was presented at the Joint National Meeting of the National Council on Public History and the Society for History in the Federal Government, Washington, D.C., April 24, 1987.

1. *Dunlap and Claypoole's American Daily Advertiser,* April 24, 1794. See also Sellers, *Mr. Peale's Museum; CWP; Selected Papers* 2:91.

2. *Dunlap and Claypoole's American Daily Advertiser,* April 24, 1794. For Peale's role in Philadelphia's cultural life, see *CWP;* for the cultural environment in Philadelphia, see Daniel Boorstin, *The Lost World of Thomas Jefferson* (1948; rpt. Boston, 1960), pp. 8–25, and Edgar P. Richardson, "The Athens of America, 1800–1825," in *Philadelphia. A 300-Year History,* ed. Russell F. Weigley (New York, 1982), pp. 208–57.

3. Peale's own account of the founding of the museum is in A(TS): 107–08, F:IIC. On Enlightenment thought in the late eighteenth century, see Henry F. May, *The Enlightenment in America* (New York, 1976), pp. 153–277, esp. 197–222. The world of the artisan in eighteenth-century Philadelphia has been detailed in Eric Foner, *Tom Paine and Revolutionary America* (New York, 1976), pp. 16–96. For the interconnection of Peale's artisan background and faith in the progress of enlightenment, see chap. 13.

4. For the phrase "world in miniature," see A(TS): 272. Peale's course of lectures on natural history which he delivered at the museum had as its central thesis the existence of a harmonious animal kingdom (Academy of Natural Science, Phila-

delphia, F:IID/3-26); see also Charles Willson Peale to Isaac Weaver, February 11, 1802, P-S, in *Selected Papers* 2:396-98.

5. The organization of the museum and Peale's interest in displaying embalmed corpses are detailed in an untitled broadside by Peale, dated 1792, P-S, F:IID/1B8-11. A graphic representation of the main exhibition area of the museum, with the portraits displayed above the cabinets, is Titian Ramsay Peale's painting "The Long Room" (fig. 72).

6. May, *American Enlightenment,* pp. 338-40; Charles Willson Peale, "Memorial to the Pennsylvania Legislature," December 26, 1795, P-S, in *Selected Papers* 2:136-38. For the phrase "Temple of Wisdom" and Peale's concern about religious opposition to the museum, see Charles Willson Peale to Andrew Ellicott, February 28, 1802, P-S, F:IIA/25C3-6; Charles Willson Peale to Isaac Weaver, February 11, 1802, P-S, in *Selected Papers* 2:396-98.

7. Peale discussed his admission policy and contrasted it with European practice in a letter to William Findley, February 18, 1800, P-S, in *Selected Papers* 2:276-81; also see A(TS): 318, F:IIC. For the European museum, see Richard D. Altick, *The Shows of London* (Cambridge, Mass., 1978), pp. 26-27; Edward Miller, *That Noble Cabinet. A History of the British Museum* (Athens, Ohio, 1974), pp. 62-63, 92; Toby Anita Appel, "The Cuvier-Geoffroy Debate and the Structure of Nineteenth Century French Zoology" (Ph.D. diss., Princeton University, 1975), pp. 38-41; Peale's Museum, *Guide to the Philadelphia Museum* (Philadelphia, 1804 and subsequent editions). For Peale's intention to compel the "unwise" as well as the "learned" to be active in cultural affairs, see Charles Willson Peale to Phillipe Rose Roume, December 25, 1803, P-S, in *Selected Papers* 2:628-31.

Peale's primary purpose in charging an admission fee was to obtain revenue for his family and for the museum's support. An additional reason cited by Peale for the fee was to control the crowds that would result if he allowed free admission. There may also have been a class component to Peale's admission fee, since the amount required was sufficiently high to exclude those at the bottom of Philadelphia's social structure. This may be evidence, then, of the attempt by the "respectable" classes in Philadelphia (including artisans and mechanics) to demarcate themselves from the culture and physical lives of the poorer classes. Peale to Findley, February 18, 1800; Susan G. Davis, *Parades and Power. Street Theatre in Nineteenth-Century Philadelphia* (Philadelphia, 1986).

8. Peale's Museum, 1803-1842, Records & Accessions, P-S, F:XIA/3-5. The totals of the museum's collection are in *CWP,* p. 346.

9. Museum attendance is calculated from the tables of museum income in "1808-1819 Peale's Museum, Current Expenditures," P-S, F:XIA/5. See Susan Edith Klepp, "Philadelphia in Transition: A Demographic History of the City and its Occupational Groups, 1720-1830" (Ph.D. diss., University of Pennsylvania, 1980), p. 342.

10. *Dunlap's American Daily Advertiser,* January 13, 1792, in *Selected Papers* 2:9-11.

11. Von Humboldt's conviction that the Jefferson administration would aid Peale is in Diary 20, P-S, *Selected Papers* 2:694; Phillipe Rose Roume to Charles Willson Peale, January 4, 1802, *Selected Papers* 2:381-86.

12. Oscar Handlin and Mary Flug Handlin, *Commonwealth. A Study of the Role of Government in the American Economy: Massachusetts, 1774-1861* (New York, 1947), pp. 53-56, 104; Governor Elbridge Gerry to the Massachusetts House and Senate, *Salem*

Gazette, June 12, 1810; George Rogers Taylor, *The Transportation Revolution, 1815–1860* (New York, 1951), pp. 378–83; Brooke Hindle, *The Pursuit of Science in Revolutionary America,* 1735–1789 (Chapel Hill, N.C., 1956), p. 140.

13. Charles Willson Peale to Dr. Edward Stevens, June 28, 1804, P-S, F:IIA/35A11–13; *Selected Papers* 2:19, 24, 83, 85, 136–38.

14. Charles Willson Peale, "Address to the Public," *Aurora General Advertiser,* January 27, 1800, in *Selected Papers* 2:274–75. See also Peale's letters soliciting state support for the museum to William Findley, February 18, 1800; to Thomas Mc-Kean, March 3, 1800, P-S, in *Selected Papers* 2:281–82; to Timothy Matlack, March 9, 1800, P-S, in *Selected Papers* 2:282–84.

15. The scientific background of the exhumation of the mastodon and an assessment of Peale's achievement is discussed in *Selected Papers* 2:308–13; John C. Greene, *The Death of Adam: Evolution and Its Impact on Western Thought* (Ames, Iowa, 1959), pp. 112–15; George Gaylord Simpson, "The Beginnings of Vertebrate Paleontology in North America," APS *Proceedings* 86 (1942): 130–88.

16. Charles Willson Peale to Thomas Jefferson, January 12, 1802, P-S, in *Selected Papers* 2:386–89.

17. Thomas Jefferson to Charles Willson Peale, January 16, 1802, Texas University: Hanley Collection, in *Selected Papers* 2:389–90; Charles Willson Peale to Thomas Jefferson, December 13, 1806, P-S, in *Selected Papers* 2:990–91; Dumas Malone, *Jefferson the President. Second Term, 1805–1809* (Boston, 1974), pp. 554–55.

18. Charles Willson Peale to Thomas Jefferson, January 21, 1802, P-S, F:IIA/25C1–2; *Selected Papers* 2:390–92, 393–96; Edward M. Riley, "The Independence Hall Group," in *Historic Philadelphia. From the Founding Until the Early Nineteenth Century,* American Philosophical Society, *Transactions,* n.s. 43 (1953): 30–33.

19. George H. Daniels, *Science in American Society. A Social History* (New York, 1971), pp. 130, 160; John C. Greene, *American Science in the Age of Jefferson* (Ames, Iowa, 1984), pp. 26–27. Greene does not cite evidence in support of his conclusion that the museum was regarded as merely a show. Neil Harris, *Humbug. The Art of P. T. Barnum* (Boston, 1973) covers the rise of sensational displays and exhibits in museums of the late nineteenth century.

20. American Philosophical Society, *Early Proceedings* (Philadelphia, 1884), p. 381.

21. Charles Willson Peale to William Findley, February 18, 1800. The development of distinct public and private spheres is surveyed in Richard Sennett, *The Fall of Public Man* (New York, 1976).

22. For the Enlightenment's ideal or "faith" in the "great unity of human knowledge" and the view of science as "a kind of cosmic education," see Charles C. Gillispie, "The Natural History of Industry," in *Science, Technology, and Economic Growth in the Eighteenth Century,* ed. E. Musson (London, 1972), pp. 131–32; and Franklin's circular letter, quoted in Boorstin, *The Lost World of Thomas Jefferson,* pp. 9–11; Charles Willson Peale, *Discourse Introductory to a Course of Lectures on the Science of Nature* (Philadelphia, 1800), p. 35; *Selected Papers* 2:706–07.

23. Peale to Philippe Rose Roume, December 25, 1803; John C. Greene, "Science and the Public in the Age of Jefferson," *Isis* 39 (1958): 13–26; Daniels, *Science in American Society,* pp. 152–56; Hindle, *Science in Revolutionary America,* pp. 357–59; Greene, *Science in the Age of Jefferson,* pp. 4–26.

13

"To encrease
the comforts of Life"

Charles Willson Peale and the Mechanical Arts

———❖———

SIDNEY HART

C HARLES Willson Peale, artisan, artist, and museum keeper, was
also an inventor and a reformer who fervently believed that
man's reason could be used as a tool to better his condition. He
was influenced by a broad movement, associated with the Enlightenment and the economic and social changes resulting from eighteenth-
century industrialism, that sought reform in the physical and material
conditions of life. Leading scientific, literary, and religious figures such
as Kant, Rousseau, Franklin, Rittenhouse, Rumford, Wesley, and Rush
were involved in this reform movement. They wrote on hygiene, infant
mortality, education, and poverty; they invented better stoves for health-
ier and more comfortable houses and experimented with new foods and
ways of cooking to improve the diet of the poor; they were involved
in temperance movements, sanitation, the founding of hospitals for the
poor, and child welfare; they wrote articles in the *Encyclopédie* on the
duration of life, hospitals, foundlings, and "political arithmetic" (national
statistics). Peale believed that his age was "a time of great discoveries,
more prolific than in 10 of the former centuries," and his enthusiasm
for technology and invention derived in large part from his faith that
these "discoveries" would improve the quality of life.[1]

Peale's inventions — his efforts at what in the eighteenth century were
called the mechanical and technical arts — have, however, been either

ignored or disparaged by historians. Peale himself expressed reservations concerning the time and energy he channeled into these efforts and away from his art and museum. He would become discouraged when an invention failed to win general acceptance and earn money; he would dismiss the invention as a "hobbyhorse" that he rode for a time and then discarded. Peale's inventions are not generally found in histories of technology because they were not in the paths in which future technology developed. For example, his design innovations in fireplaces and mechanical copying machines came just before the era of central heating and carbon paper. The scholarly consensus is that the energies Peale devoted to mechanical pursuits were wrong turns, misguided efforts, and, most unfortunately, distractions from his artistic and scientific pursuits.[2]

To judge Peale as a successful artist and naturalist and a failure as an inventor is to make a presentist evaluation that fails to consider his total interests and expertise and the role of technology in the eighteenth-century Enlightenment. If historians are to escape a "Whig" historiography of technology, they ought to study the "unsuccessful" inventions, not only those leading more or less directly to the technology of our own era. Peale's efforts may be viewed as "wrong turns" from our perspective, but in his own time they derived from the felt needs and ideals of his society.

Peale was involved in mechanics and invention throughout his life. As a young man in Annapolis in the 1760s, he worked as a saddlemaker, upholsterer, silversmith, and, most significantly in terms of preindustrial mechanics, a clock and watch repairer. Although he spent little time in this last trade, Peale was proud of the experience and detailed it with some fondness in his unpublished autobiography, commenting on the great amount of time he spent in learning to use the tools of this trade. As a young artist, Peale expressed this sense of pride and accomplishment by placing "a clock taken to pieces" in the background of his first self-portrait. Peale's enthusiasm for clocks reflected the very special status attached to these objects since the second half of the sixteenth century. Until the advent of the mature steam engine in the late eighteenth century, the mechanical clock was viewed as the apex of technology. By Peale's lifetime, the clock and its precision workmanship had become a popular metaphor for the world, the body, and the state. The clockmaker occupied, therefore, a very high position among artisans, and Peale, an artisan in mid-eighteenth-century Maryland, would still look to the clockmaker's workshop for the most advanced precision tools. These were the tools that he recalled learning how to use — tools he later in life adapted for his various mechanical pursuits. Throughout his busy life, Peale was able to devote time and energy to mechanical pursuits. Even while studying painting with Benjamin West in London — his stay there limited by finances and the need to return to his family in Maryland — he found the time to repair his teacher's "lock and bells."[3]

Peale lived in an age when it seemed that almost all great men — kings, statesmen, scientists, and literary figures — showed an interest in and displayed an aptitude for science and invention. Many of his friendships were based on that common interest. In 1776 he and David Rittenhouse experimented in the home manufacture of gunpowder and the development of better rifles with telescopic sights for Washington's soldiers. His friendship with Thomas Jefferson was strengthened in the late 1790s when they served on a committee of the American Philosophical Society to collect information on "American antiquities," with a special mission "to procure one or more entire skeletons of the Mammoth." When Peale later had the opportunity to exhume such a skeleton, Jefferson, as president of the United States, was quick to offer government aid. Peale corresponded with Robert Fulton and Joel Barlow on building a mechanical washing machine. He worked closely for many years with Benjamin Henry Latrobe and Jefferson to improve and promote the polygraph, a machine that duplicated writing. He and Thomas Paine discussed bridges more than politics. He was a signer of Oliver Evans's petition to Congress that sought to extend patent rights. He became acquainted with Patrick Lyon when he was requested by a friend in Annapolis to examine the inventor's new fire engine (he advised his friend to ignore Lyon's radical politics and purchase the engine). Peale and Alexander Wilson experimented with an old crossbow in an effort to determine "the true sustaining power of the bird in its flight." Even while painting Washington's portrait, Peale discussed mechanical matters with the president to make the time pass more quickly.[4]

When Peale moved to Philadelphia during the American Revolution, he located himself amidst a glittering array of scientific and technological resources. The American Philosophical Society, first established in 1743 and reorganized in 1769, had a great influence on Peale and his attitudes toward science and technology. Peale became a member in 1786, housed his museum in Philosophical Hall during the years 1794 to 1802, and was active in the society throughout the remainder of his life. Despite the range of their differences, the active members of the society shared a utilitarian view of science and technology. According to this view, the creator had designed nature for the use and benefit of man. The object of science was to understand this design, and the role of technology was to enable man to make use of that which was "furnished by the great and bountiful Author of Nature." Peale believed that all knowledge concerning the workings of nature would prove useful to man and could be used as a tool to better his condition.[5]

Philadelphia's other resources included the University of Pennsylvania, which with its medical school attracted scientists and other learned men to Philadelphia. Peale borrowed books from the Library Company of Philadelphia, the "father of American libraries." The federal capital was in the city from 1790 until 1800. The United Company of Philadelphia for Promoting Manufactures and the Society for the Promotion of Agriculture offered premiums or prizes for inventions or improvements. Philadelphia was also a center of commerce and manufacturing, boasting excellent brick kilns, an outstanding printing industry, breweries, nail and button makers, coppersmiths and hatters, and one of the most advanced shipbuilding industries in the nation. These manufacturers and Philadelphia's inventors and scientists benefited from a direct exchange of information.[6]

Inventions that "do good to our bodies"

The "Natural life of man," Peale believed, would be "200 Years," if he would "Reform in [his] Eating drinking & practice of Phisick." Peale studied and experimented with various eating and drinking regimens, and was a close observer and sometimes a practitioner of "Phisick." In 1803 he published a pamphlet containing his observations on health and longevity, and his letters and diaries reveal a continuing interest in the subject. Throughout his life he invented or designed various devices to improve health, extend life, and increase comfort. He manufactured artificial teeth, ground lenses for spectacles, and built an artificial hand for a member of the Pennsylvania state legislature. When Caspar Wistar, one of Philadelphia's leading physicians and a lecturer at the University of Pennsylvania's medical school, introduced models of human organs to teach students, he turned to Peale to construct a wax and papier-mâché model of the human throat and windpipe.

Peale's enthusiasm for mechanics often led him to view the human body as a complex machine—a view put forward by many prominent eighteenth-century medical authorities. George Wallis, for example, author of a popular medical work published in London and New York in the 1790s, defined the body as a "human machine." Physicians such as William Shippen lectured in Philadelphia on the anatomy of the human "machine." Peale wrote that an "*improper* mode of living," would derange the "machine" rather than allow it gradually and naturally to "wear out." The last phrase might be read as a loose comparison to a clock. Others in the seventeenth and eighteenth centuries were more specific in comparing the pulse to the ticking of a clock. Peale had artisan friends who treated back and spinal problems, broken limbs, and other "mechanical" dislocations and injuries. He believed that a good mechanic was preferable to a physician in treating dislocated and broken bones, and he once recommended a maker of carpentry tools as the best person to treat a broken leg.[7]

Regular bathing was a central idea in Peale's concept of good health and cleanliness. In the 1790s he used cold baths to treat himself and his family for yellow fever. Peale's outlook, however, was not typical in the eighteenth and the early nineteenth century. Standards of cleanliness varied, and for many the washbowl and pitcher were quite sufficient. The all-over bath was often considered a frivolous amusement or a sinful luxury, and in the winter months, a dangerous practice. Attitudes toward public bath houses had also undergone change. In sixteenth-century Europe, the fear of syphilis closed many public baths. The Reformation and religious climate of the seventeenth century associated bathing with sin, and one result was a general deemphasis on personal cleanliness and care of the body. As late as the 1760s proposals to establish public baths in Philadelphia were met with opposition from Quakers and other religious groups who considered such places as "unfriendly to morals." There was a gradual change of opinion regarding bathing and public bath houses in the eighteenth century. The Enlightenment engendered a renewed sense of the importance of the human body and cleanliness, and physicians also began to view the bath as a therapeutic measure. Epidemics, most physicians believed, were transmitted by airs, waters, and food, and thus personal hygiene was stressed as an effective way of saving lives.

The first home bathing devices in America began appearing in the latter part of the eighteenth century. In the 1790s Governor Thomas Johnson of Maryland may have had the first bathtub in the state in his home near Frederick. In 1780 Joseph Carson, a merchant and shipowner, paid four pounds and fifteen shillings for a shower bath, the first recorded in Philadelphia. The Drinker family of that city installed a shower bath in their backyard in 1798, although it was not until July 1799 that Mrs. Drinker overcame her fear, and for the first time in twenty-eight years experienced being "wett all over at once." By the end of the eighteenth century, a few more families owned shower baths and even tin-lined wooden bathtubs. In the first decade of the nineteenth century, bathing and the installation of private bathtubs were encouraged by the establishment of municipal water systems in many cities on the eastern seaboard. However, the large-scale use of bathtubs in private homes was not possible until the development of more adequate municipal water systems in the 1830s.[8]

Peale acknowledged the difficulty of "getting water to fill" the "plunging bath" and enthusiastically turned his attention to an easier way of bathing when, in the 1790s, he learned from Joseph Priestley that London hospitals were using vapor baths. In 1801 he patented a portable vapor bath for home use (fig. 82). The invention was noted with approval in a Pennsylvania medical school dissertation on bathing. The writer explained that the warm bath would act as a stimulus to remove "constriction induced on the blood vessels" in the initial stages of fevers when the patient was in a debilitated state. Peale's design was among the first of many portable baths to be developed in the nineteenth century. Although he did not profit from his invention, his donations of vapor baths to the City Hospital, the College of Physicians, the Pennsylvania Hospital, and to friends and relatives were much appreciated.[9]

Peale continued to design and invent devices to improve health until the end of his life. In 1826, when he was eighty-five, he placed advertisements in the Philadelphia newspapers notifying the public that he was engaged in the production of porcelain teeth. Not uncommonly for that era, Peale had begun losing his own teeth at an early age. Seeking a remedy when he was thirty-four, he borrowed a French text on dentistry and began making artificial teeth out of animal substances. Peale continued making teeth and experimenting with new substances throughout his life. He finally became convinced that he could manufacture superior teeth out of porcelain.[10]

Although Peale was not the first in America to manufacture porcelain teeth, his work was pioneering. In the first quarter of the nineteenth century, American dentistry was burgeoning. The Revolutionary War, which provided many young dentists with field experience, also brought to the United States French dentists who, having come with the French army, remained in America. These French dentists brought to America information and techniques from the most advanced nation in dentistry. Nonetheless, during this time there were few dentists even in the larger cities and no dental schools or professional associations. Training was by apprenticeship; there were no licenses or state regulations, and anybody could open a shop and call himself a dentist. Treatment often meant tooth extraction by methods characterized as "heroic."[11]

Until the late eighteenth century, the most commonly used materials for teeth were hippopotamus ivory, which was porous and stained easily; human teeth, which the poor extracted from their mouths and sold; and animal teeth, which broke easily. In 1789 Louis XVI granted the first patent for porcelain teeth. Glazed porcelain, durable and stain resistant, had obvious advantages. However, because the successful manufacture of porcelain teeth was dependent on the skill of the craftsman, porcelain teeth were utilized only to a limited extent in France and later in England.[12]

In 1813 Peale viewed Edward Hudson's small collection of French-made porcelain teeth which the Philadelphia dentist had purchased for $2,000. A few years later, Peale viewed a set made by Hudson, and judged them to be poorly manufactured. In January 1816 he wrote to Thomas Barnes and a Mr. Holmes, dentists in Boston who apparently had had some success with porcelain; he inquired the price of their teeth but did not purchase any. In 1817 porcelain teeth were being made by Anthony Plantou, a French dentist who had settled in Philadelphia. Plantou's teeth were later described by an American dentist as "very imperfect [and] brittle."[13]

In 1822 Peale purchased a set of teeth made by Plantou, but was dissatisfied with them. He felt that although Plantou had made some good teeth, "he was not a Mechanic." They do not please me," he wrote, "and I believe I can make a better sett after I can determine on the composition & proportion of methods." Peale experimented with different porcelain compositions and furnace improvements throughout the hot Philadelphia summer. At one point the furnace produced too much heat and discolored the enamel. In October he had an accident, destroying several teeth and damaging the furnace. Finally in December he arrived at a formula using "equal quanties of feltspar found near German-town & White Clay found at White Hill N. Jersey" which made a "fine Porcelain for teeth."[14]

In a letter to his son Rembrandt in February 1823, Peale described the laborious process of crafting porcelain teeth for his daughter, So-phonisba, who at thirty-eight, had only "2 teeth in her upper Jaw, and four front teeth in the lower." He first took impressions of the gums and jaw with beeswax and made plaster of paris casts from the wax. The teeth were carved separately out of the porcelain and glazed in the furnace. The beeswax cast of Sophonisba's jaw was taken to a brass founder who produced a cast from which a silver or platinum base was made. The teeth were then riveted or screwed to the base. The manu-facture and the fitting took two weeks. A few years later, Peale devel-oped a further refinement, making the teeth and base out of a solid porcelain block, an advanced technique earlier used by the French but abandoned because it was too difficult.[15]

In 1826 Peale decided to make his porcelain teeth production a "busi-ness of profit." He was determined to free himself of debt and had con-cluded that he could earn more money by making teeth than by paint-ing portraits. Peale charged $150 for a set of teeth, too much money for many who wanted his services, but, he asserted, "lower than other art-ists charge for such work"; in London, the price was $35 a tooth. He would try to reduce his price later, but would "not be confined to any such business" if he could not get "a handsome reward for . . . [his] labor." Peale met early opposition from the dentists in Philadelphia, but in July he received an important public endorsement from the Phila-delphia medical community. By late summer, after his newspaper ad-vertisement had appeared in other cities, he began receiving many in-quiries. Unfortunately, Peale did not live long enough to profit from his new profession, although he does receive recognition in histories of dentistry. His work on dentures came to an end just as dentists in Bos-ton and New York were beginning to experiment with porcelain teeth, and it was not until another decade had passed that the process became commercially successful.[16]

Peale's concern with health and comfort accounts in part for his in-terest in stoves and fireplaces. In the eighteenth century, the challenge to provide efficient heat for public buildings and private dwellings at-tracted many of the best scientific and technical minds. Prior to this time, Anglo-Americans preferred open fireplaces and radiant heating, which produced a feeling of warmth near the hearth, but did not heat the air, which was regarded as unhealthy. In 1744 Benjamin Franklin introduced his small open iron stove, an efficient mechanism designed to be placed inside the large American fireplace. The Franklin stove provided an open fire and radiant heat, but it also employed an air box that heated the air and circulated it into the room. Gradually the principle of warmer interior temperatures during the winter months was accepted as not only beneficial for health but also necessary for comfort. This change of attitude came about partly as a result of such technical developments as Franklin's invention, but it was also a product of the new interest and concern with human comfort. By the last quarter of the eighteenth century, stoves were in increasing demand in Philadelphia not only for private homes but also for schools, government buildings, and even churches, which had never been heated before. One historian has estimated that by the 1790s "probably every public building in Philadelphia that could afford it was heated by stoves."[17]

Peale's residence in Philosophical Hall placed him in a milieu where many fireplace and stove improvements were being examined and encouraged. Since the introduction of Franklin's stove there had been continuing interest and discussion, stimulated by Franklin and other members of the society, concerning new inventions and improvements in heating. One of these improvements was the work of David Rittenhouse, who in the 1780s developed a smaller, simplified version of the Franklin stove. In the 1780s and 1790s many Philadelphia homes, including the Peales', had a Rittenhouse stove.[18]

The need to heat the museum efficiently made fireplace and stove design of more than humanitarian or theoretical interest to Peale. In the mid-1790s, he became especially interested in finding efficient heating devices, because he had decided to keep his museum open during the evenings. He read an account of a successful new brick stove in France that he hoped to use in his museum. Peale built the French stove and tested it. Using a specified amount of wood, Peale kept an hourly record of the outside and inside temperatures on a cold January day. With an outside temperature just above freezing, he achieved a maximum temperature of 54 degrees, while using only a small amount of wood. Peale viewed the experiment as a success.[19]

In 1797 Peale and his son Raphaelle entered a contest sponsored by the American Philosophical Society with a prize of $60 for the best fireplace design affordable to the poor.[20] The society's contest might have originated in part out of the fears of Philadelphia's wealthy and powerful who were becoming concerned with the deteriorating condition of the city's lower classes during these years. The legacy of the city's radically democratic politics during the American Revolution convinced many wealthy Philadelphians that there would be social unrest if the situation of the poor worsened. The difficulties of the poor in heating their dwellings increased as the price of firewood climbed steeply in the mid-1790s, and city regulations were necessary to prohibit the purchase of firewood for resale in Philadelphia between September and March. Local wood was scarce and had to be shipped from New Jersey and the Delaware Valley; and there were recurrent demands to regulate shipping and carting rates. As firewood prices increased in the city, there were charity drives to provide fuel for the needy. By 1793, a privately financed fund was established to buy wood for the poor in the winter.[21]

Peale and Raphaelle experimented with several designs for chimney modifications and open fireplaces. One design contained the placement of a stove in a niche built into the front wall of the chimney; another had a "honey-combed" back wall that circulated warm air in much the same way as the Franklin stove.[22] The Peales' fireplace designs contained improvements developed in Europe in the last decades of the eighteenth century, the most significant of which were the designs of Count Rumford. In 1796 Rumford published "Chimney Fireplaces," which contained designs for smaller, more efficient fireplaces that would conserve heat. Peale and his son were aware of at least some of Rumford's designs and incorporated such components as slanted jambs, which reflected heat into the room. The Peales' design also included a sliding metal cover to be lowered from the mantel (to increase the draft or diminish the fire) and a damper (to open against the back of the chimney and prevent smoke from returning to the room). The Peales were the first to emphasize safety in a fireplace design, and they indicated that the fire could easily be extinguished by closing both the metal cover and the damper (fig. 83).[23]

In 1799 the Philosophical Society finally awarded its prize for new fireplace designs to the Peales. Peale and his son also received the first patent in America for fireplace improvements. The Philosophical Society did not consider the designs entirely original, but awarded the prize because of the skill with which the components "were combined and applied to domestic purposes." The society also took into account the fact that the Peales' entry had been submitted in 1797 and the society's award made two years later, when many of the improvements developed in Europe had become well known in America. The Peales' achievement in fireplace design should be viewed more in terms of application than innovative theory. Peale himself emphasized the "practicing hand," "utility," and "due management" of the invention. The patentee had a "duty," he wrote, "to make his invention as useful as possible to the public generally." The Peales charged $10 for the use of their design, defending the cost as payment for their time to supervise the construction of the fireplace.[24]

Peale continued to experiment with new designs for stoves and fireplaces. On March 8, 1801, he wrote to Thomas Jefferson four days after Jefferson had been inaugurated president of the United States. An ardent Republican, Peale offered his congratulations and expressed the hope that the new president would "still find leisure to devote some attention to the Minutiae of public good, in objects which promise the economy, convenience, and comforts of Life." The subject of his letter was the waste and inefficiency of the large American kitchen fireplace. He had studied Rumford's design for an elaborate brickwork structure, honeycombed with flues connected to small wood stoves, each designed for a particular-sized pot. The principle was to break down the large open fireplace into small, easily regulated stoves. Other refinements consisted of insulated double covers for pots; the use of pressure cookers, steam cooking, double boilers; an efficient roaster; and smoke conveyance through tubes to heat additional pots. Peale designed one of these stoves for his own use, built them for friends and relatives, and offered his design and assistance to such institutions as the Pennsylvania Hospital.[25]

For his museum of natural history, Peale designed the "smoke-eater" (fig. 84), a fascinating and complex mechanism that not only supplied sufficient heat but also became an exhibit itself. The basic principle, earlier employed by Franklin and the French, was to draw the smoke and soot particles down to the fire where they would undergo combustion a second time. A pipe drew the warm air under the floor to the outside of the building. Astonished visitors to the museum were able to look through a vent in the pipe and see a stream of smokeless hot air leaving the stove. The "smoke-eater," a marvel of efficiency, was (like the Franklin stove before it) too intricate a mechanism for the average person to build and maintain.[26]

A historian of technology has viewed all of the heating improvements sponsored by the Philosophical Society in this era, especially Peale's devices, as exercises in late eighteenth-century technological virtuosity, incapable of being produced for wide distribution. The delight in technological complexity that characterized some of these devices, such as

Peale's "smoke-eater," made them too costly as well as too complex for most people. But in any case, the undeveloped industrial and marketing base of the United States at this time would hardly have lent itself to the "wide distribution" of any invention. Peale realized that he would have had to sacrifice both his painting and his museum in order to travel around the country and promote his inventions, a sacrifice he was unwilling to make. Nevertheless, when his in-laws, the DePeysters, a prosperous New York mercantile family, arranged for him to demonstrate his fireplaces and stoves to the New York City government, he did sell and supervise the construction of many of them.[27] Moreover, although Peale was strongly in favor of inventors' obtaining a profit from their creativity and labor, his interest was primarily in the creation and design, and not in the economic development, of the invention.

"An easy means of preserving copies . . . two perfect originals"[28]

In 1803 John Isaac Hawkins was granted a patent for a pantograph mechanism that could trace profiles and copy drawings, music, and letters. Having emigrated from England at an early age and eventually settling in Philadelphia, Hawkins pursued his mechanical interests in the workshop of Peale's museum. Peale encouraged the young inventor and was especially enthusiastic about a device specifically designed to copy letters, which Hawkins called the polygraph (fig. 85). He offered "hints" to improve the invention, and when Hawkins returned to England in 1803, Peale agreed to refine and market the polygraph in the United States. During the almost five years he spent "perfecting" and marketing the machine, Peale was constantly advised by friends that the invention was "unprofitable" and that the extensive time he spent on it resulted in the "neglect of the Museum." Peale, however, viewed the polygraph as an invention that "deserve[d] attention," because it added to the "conveniences of life" and would "economise our time." It would, he believed, prevent quarrels and lawsuits, aid widows and orphans, and improve morals, "since none [could] be so lost to character as not to wish to be thought well of, by those who may view transactions so faithfully given by their corrispondence." He was convinced that once the polygraph was made reliable, his fellow citizens could not fail to recognize that such a "writing machine, which enables a person to make two three or more originals exactly alike . . . scarcely with more labor than in writing with a single Pen, is certainly belonging to this class of meritorious inventions." In 1804 he wrote to Hawkins, "[You have] reason to rejoice, for it is clear as sun shine to me, that the great utility of writing 2 or 3 pens with ease and at the same time correctly alike will finally secure a very extensive sale."[29]

Peale's enthusiasm for the polygraph derived in part from the demand in the eighteenth century for more accurate and efficient copying machines, primarily for technical or engineering drawings. Drawing machines had become important to designers during the late Renaissance, when the development of new ways of achieving perspective and depth made possible more realistic and accurate engineering drawings. In the eighteenth century, drawing techniques rapidly improved throughout Europe, and, particularly in France, objective drawings became an important means of expression to describe, catalogue, and quantify the natural and manmade world. This use of drawings, especially in depicting machines, found its highest expression in the hundreds of illustrations reproduced in the *Encyclopédie*. In England, British naval and architectural designers produced drawings that were not merely presentations of the product but were actually used in the construction phase. Perspective drawing in England was considered an important skill, and drawing machines were in demand. George III was tutored in perspective drawing when he was Prince of Wales and owned a drawing and perspective machine made for him by the king's instrument-maker, George Adams, an eighteenth-century London craftsman.[30]

In 1780 James Watt was granted a patent for a copying press, which he hoped to use for his engineering drawings as well as for his correspondence. Watt's device did not trace the original like the pantograph; it offset the original by pressing it against a dampened sheet of paper. In 1799, a patent was granted to English engineer Marc Isambard Brunel for the application of the pantograph to making "two or three similar writings or drawings at the same time and by the same person." The beauty and quality of the workmanship impressed many artisans, but the machine could not be made to operate efficiently. In 1804 Jefferson obtained one of Brunel's pantographs from Peale in order to "make a trial" of the device. Like others who saw the machine, Jefferson was charmed by its ingenuity, but he soon wrote Peale that although he understood the workings of all the parts and could find no fault, "he could not produce a copy of a single letter distinct," and gave up on it "as a beautiful bagatelle."[31]

In the United States, especially from the 1780s on, copying machines seemed to be most valued by statesmen. Jefferson, who owned a Watt copying press, in 1785 urged James Madison to buy one and wrote that he would have paid ten times the price if he could have had one from the date of the Stamp Act. Madison responded that he would buy a machine when he could afford it and added that government offices should have them. Benjamin Franklin ordered three machines from James Watt as soon as they were available, and Franklin sent one of them to Charles Thomson, the clerk of the Congress. In 1782 George Washington received a copying press as a gift and used it and another that he purchased at a later date for the remainder of his life.[32]

In creating a pantograph mechanism that could copy writing, the challenge confronting Hawkins and Peale was to design the parallel machinery of the pantograph so that both pens would move precisely with the same motions and with as little effort as writing with a pen. The writing surface had to be "a perfect plane," the rulers, "perfectly parallel," and the joints had to move "freely without any play." The pen holders had to be capable of fine adjustments, and pens had to be found or adapted to the requirements of the polygraph; even the ink had to have the right chemical composition. Peale considered the perpendicular support or the "vertical parallelograms" as the key to the successful operation of the polygraph. This part had to be designed so that the pens touched down simultaneously and moved with ease and precision over the length of the paper. Previous designs had failed because they could not solve this problem. Peale made a major contribution to solving the problem of equalizing pen pressure when he "hinted to Mr. Hawkins" that "vertical parallelograms" would help "equalize the touch of the Pens." During the years 1803–04, when Hawkins was in England, Peale occupied a great deal of his time with the polygraph — adding springs, bars, rollers, pulleys, and joints that would better enable the vertical parallels to move the pens in tandem.[33]

The polygraph prototypes experienced many mechanical problems, but Peale's belief in the value and utility of the machine determined him to perfect the model. On August 7, 1803, he wrote to Hawkins that he would produce a top quality product before any of the machines were sold. "Two or three persons," he wrote, "have been anxious to have them, but my answer is *that it is for their Interest that I keep them longer on hand, that they may receive them as perfect as possible.*" Peale sold two of the first models of the polygraph to Latrobe and Jefferson at a price far below the cost of producing the machine. Both men agreed to help Peale perfect it. This arrangement was ideal: the two men were mechanically inclined and friendly to new inventions, and they would help Peale transform a temperamental prototype into a marketable product that would work for those with little or no mechanical aptitude. "You will oblige me," he wrote Latrobe, "whether you think anything to be done, before we send the Polygraph into the world amongst fools and knaves."[34]

Peale's solution to most of the polygraph's mechanical problems was to design specialized tools that produced uniform parts for the machine. His work in this aspect of the invention reveals his considerable skill as an artisan. In early 1804 he had discovered faults in the alignment of the pen arms. Painstaking care with the workmanship and strict supervision of his workers failed to correct the problem. Finally, he traced the problem to his drill. Peale then designed an accurate bow drill in an iron frame. He had perhaps encountered this sophisticated tool when he had repaired watches, or perhaps he saw it used by sculptors, who needed such a tool to control the depth of holes. Peale encountered additional mechanical difficulties related to the angle and uniformity of the writing surface. For this, Peale designed a spirit level hinged to a "rack-quadrant" that enabled him at a glance to check the finished product. Special hardwoods, expensive brass for key parts, collets and other materials and techniques used by clock makers — all were employed for the parts requiring precise adjustments. By the fall of 1804, Peale had developed an entire workshop with specialized tools for each process in the manufacture of the polygraph, and he was optimistic that his quality control problems were solved. He wrote to Hawkins that "every piece has its Lock or place formed which it must be made to fit into to be drilled &c." so that they did "not depend on the accuracy of the sight of the workmen as formerly."[35]

Peale received public endorsements from both Jefferson and Latrobe, who throughout their lives praised the invention, and he sold several of the machines in 1804 and 1805. Hawkins did only slightly better in London. However, by the middle of 1806 Peale had to admit that the polygraph would not be a commercial success. He wrote to Jefferson that it had been "an expensive and unprofitable business," but that he had persisted in improving it because it had been a "favorite Machine." He had "persevered," he insisted, "in the hope of making them perfect and highly useful."[36]

The standard explanation for the polygraph's failure is that it was

too delicate a machine. It seems likely, however, that historians have
been given this impression as the result of the initial correspondence
between Peale, Latrobe, and Jefferson concerning the problems of the
prototype. The Latrobe and Jefferson endorsements only came, as Peale
had said, after the problems were solved. Jefferson continued to be a
satisfied user of the machine for the rest of his life, and when he became
president, he recommended its use to government officials and ordered
several polygraphs to give as gifts to friends and foreign dignitaries as
a model of American workmanship and ingenuity. Latrobe became completely dependent on the machine to maintain his business records and
used the polygraph until bankruptcy forced him to part with it in 1817.[37]

More than a decade later, Latrobe wrote to Jefferson about the polygraph:

> Notwithstanding the convenience, & great utility . . . which I find from
> the Polygraph, it is a fact, that Peale never could dispose of more than
> 60, 40 of which about, as his Son tells me . . . were sold by my recom-
> mendation. . . . I have often recommended them to Merchants, but they
> object that their *Clerks* "are always sufficient for the copying of their let-
> ters, & would otherwise be unemployed, & moreover never write a good
> hand for want of practice: & that they must copy their letters into books,
> for safekeeping, & for production in courts of justice."[38]

Latrobe acknowledged that these reasons accounted somewhat for the
commercial failure of the polygraph, but more fundamental in his opinion was the conservative nature of merchants, whom he characterized
as "generally a sort of Machines." Lawyers behaved in a similar manner, governing themselves by the "*practice* of their business." Thus, the
polygraph could not be introduced to "the most *writing* class of men,
& is used only by a few literary men."[39]

Perhaps the fundamental reason for the polygraph's commercial failure had as much to do with the nature of the American economy as
with the invention itself. At a time when there was no national advertising (newspaper printers in other cities were "requested" to insert advertisements), no network of distribution, and no techniques of large-scale
production, marketing the polygraph would have required an enormous
commitment of Peale's time and energy. When advised that traders
could sell the polygraph on commission, Peale replied that he did not
like "keeping accounts" and that he feared the "risk of losses by failures."
He was "determined . . . to avoid all such trouble."[40]

"Easy and safe passages over the waters of the United States"[41]

In his autobiography, Peale analyzed his mechanical interests as sudden moments of inspiration when his "fancy" would be "struck" by an "Idea" of an "improvement, which he conceived had a chance of becoming advantageous to the Public." At such times, he would "instantly" channel his energy and time "to accomplish such invention." Peale explained his interest in bridges as the result of a conversation with a friend on the importance of walkways to good health. When the friend regretted that the walkway in the statehouse garden was not longer, Peale was "struck" with an "Idea" to design a bridge that would connect the garden to a field across the street.[42]

During the summer of 1796 Peale built a model of the bridge and placed it in the "passage of the Philosophical Hall." The twenty-foot model received its most difficult test when "12 Indians and all stout men" stood on it at once. The bridge held, "although at the same time it looked so light that very frequently men have been fearful to cross it singly." The ends of the bridge rose when one person jumped on the middle of it, a movement described as "deformation" by a modern commentator. However, the model was freestanding and lacked abutments, which Peale rightfully considered crucial in an arched structure. By the fall of 1796, Peale was convinced that his design had great applicability for America's "numerous creeks and rivers" and could support an arch of 500 feet.[43]

Peale never indicated what influenced his bridge design, but its two most salient characteristics — the single arch and the wood planking — may be traced to incidents from a decade before he built his model. On a winter day in 1784, Thomas Paine, an old friend and political ally of Peale during the Revolution, went to view the great accumulation of ice on the Schuylkill River. Paine wondered whether the river's floating bridges would survive another winter, and he later wrote of a vision he had that day of a new "American" bridge — an iron, single-arch structure — designed to withstand American rivers. There is no evidence that the two men discussed bridges in the 1780s, but after Paine returned to America in 1802, Peale wrote to Paine and encouraged him to place his bridge models in the museum; he agreed with Paine that only single-arch bridges would be useful and an honor to the country.[44]

The other influence for Peale's design may initially be found in Thomas

Jefferson's letter of October 12, 1786, to Maria Cosway, containing Jefferson's famous dialogue between his "head" and "heart." Jefferson, in Paris, had gone to study the architecture of the Halle aux Blés, where he met Cosway. While his "heart" recalled his meeting with a charming woman, his "head" was engrossed with the architecture of the grain market. The structure had a remarkable roof, using an innovative method of construction originally conceived by the Renaissance architect Philibert Delormé (ca. 1510–70). The roof was not supported by heavy timber trusses but by arched ribs made of wooden planks. The design allowed the large amount of space between the ribs to be filled with windows, flooding the market with daylight, and providing a breathtaking sensation of graceful strength without massive bulk, much the same aesthetic feeling that Peale claimed for his bridge.

While in France, Jefferson acquired Delormé's 1561 study of timber framing. After he returned to America in 1789, Jefferson became a strong advocate of the architect's arch structure, proposing its use in American buildings and even mentioning its potential use in a bridge across the Schuylkill. Although there is no evidence that Jefferson and Peale ever discussed bridge design, Jefferson lived in Philadelphia during the early 1790s, became acquainted with Peale at the American Philosophical Society, and was associated with the museum. Given the relationship between the two men, with so much common ground in their interests in mechanics and inventions, it is likely that the subject was discussed.[45]

The direct influence accounting for Peale's interest in bridges was the widespread enthusiasm and public support in the 1790s for internal improvements. State legislatures were inundated with petitions and bills for the construction of turnpikes. The first successful long-span bridges in America were built as links in this new system of roads. In 1794 the Lancaster Turnpike was completed, linking Philadelphia to the rich farmlands of eastern Pennsylvania. A tremendous increase in settlements in western Pennsylvania and along the Ohio River made it evident that Philadelphia's continued prosperity and its ability to compete with such cities as Baltimore hinged on the construction of a reliable system of roads and bridges. It was also apparent that the vulnerable links in Pennsylvania's east-west routes were the floating bridges on the Schuylkill River and that a suitable design and sufficient funds were needed to construct a permanent bridge across the river.[46]

In the fall of 1796 Peale published articles in Philadelphia newspapers announcing his invention and requested that the Select Council view the model of his bridge. In January 1797 he was granted the first patent in the United States for a bridge design. Peale had come to the conclusion that his design could be used for the long-awaited permanent Schuylkill River bridge (fig. 86).[47]

In many respects Peale's approach to bridge design was similar to that of the major American bridge builders in this era—Timothy Palmer, Lewis Wernwag, and Theodore Burr. Like them, he used a scale model to test load capacity because there was in America no science of structural materials and no predictive and verifiable information of how materials would react when used in bridges. European architectural and carpentry manuals were the only reference works available to American bridge designers. Such works as William Pain's *The Practical Builder* (1774) instructed the builder in the basic principles of mensuration; Peale demonstrated his knowledge of these principles in his 1797 *Essay on Building Wooden Bridges.*[48]

Peale's choice of wood also placed him in the mainstream of American bridge design. The contrast with England is significant. In 1800 a committee of the House of Commons reporting on the planned construction of a new London Bridge considered only iron and stone as suitable building materials, because "a Work of such importance ought to be constructed of the most solid and durable Materials, and it is safer to depend on a Structure which, though more expensive in its Erection, is calculated to last for Ages without any considerable Decay." American communities were not concerned about the "Ages" but built the best bridge they could afford.[49]

Peale's use of the arch also reflected common usage, but his use of Delormé's construction departed significantly from the design of other bridges in the United States. The challenge to American bridge builders during this time was to span a broad expanse of water with a wooden structure using a minimum number of piers. Although only a few visionaries attempted single-span bridges, bridge designers agreed that American rivers, often filled with ice in the winter and destructive freshets in the spring, could not be spanned successfully by bridges with many piers.[50]

Palmer, Wernwag, and Burr designed their structures with massive timber arches combined with a truss. Wernwag, in his design of the "Colossus," which realized Paine's vision of a single-arch bridge over the Schuylkill, used three massive timber ribs, each "4 feet deep and one foot thick." His arch was also braced with a truss made of heavy timbers. The ribs of Peale's 390-foot arch would consist of only "six layers of plank, each two inches thick." Peale recognized that a truss was needed to provide rigidity; he believed that the curved boards of his rails would answer that purpose and save the expense of massive timber bracing.[51]

In 1800 Peale received an analysis of his design from the French Academy of Sciences. The authors of the analysis, Charles Augustin Coulomb and Gaspard-Francois-Clair-Maire Riche de Prony were two of France's prominent experts in engineering, applied mechanics, and large-scale public works. The authors were critical of Peale's effort, mainly because of Peale's lack of experience in bridge design and construction; but they were unwilling to pass final judgment and pointed to the necessity of several trials before any definitive evaluation could be made of such a novel design. They questioned if many of Peale's design features were sufficiently strong to support an extended arch. Significantly, the analysis compared Peale's design with Delormé's. The French engineers favored Delormé's technique of placing the planks on their sides, a distinction of which Peale seems to have been aware. Peale believed that part of the originality of his patent was turning the planks horizontally so that they could be combined in a laminated construction. Coulomb and Riche de Prony praised Peale's originality and characterized him as an "ingenious artist," "rich in resources." The analysis concluded that Peale's bridge had been studied with interest, and that the combination of Peale's "inventive mind" and further experience "will lead him to useful results."[52]

Peale's design, not considered for a bridge across the Schuylkill River, would have lacked the strength and rigidity necessary for such a distance. His design revealed his lack of experience in large-scale construction. The major American bridge designers, on the other hand, remained conservatively tied to the basic wooden arch and truss combination because the theoretical knowledge that could lead to new designs was largely unavailable in America at this time. The final selection of the design for the Schuylkill bridge is an illustration of this conservatism. In the initial construction of the bridge there were severe problems with the piers. Many proposals were submitted to discard the unfinished piers and span the river in a single arch. When a design ultimately was chosen that incorporated the piers, it was explained that while in "theory" an arch could be extended a great distance, "the point of practicability or discretion has never been precisely fixed," and "practical men shrink at the danger" of extending arches beyond 200 feet.[53] Peale's design might have been tried for small spans and probably would have worked. It seems likely that Raphaelle Peale, using his father's patent, built one or several bridges in South Carolina in 1805–06. Also, in February 1805 Peale noted in his Museum Accession Book, "Mr. Gallatin informs us that a Bridge something like C. W. Peales Patent was built 10 or 12 years since at the mouth of the Savage River emptying into the Potomac, on the road from Winchester, cheap and durable."[54]

There were other eighteenth-century men like Peale who dreamed of great bridges spanning rivers. In 1811 Thomas Pope proposed his fantastic "flying pendent lever bridge," which was to span the Hudson River in a single 3,000-foot arch. It, too, never was built.[55] Like Pope, Peale took evident delight in attempting a bold new design and aspiring to be more than a good artisan or craftsman. In America the men who did build the bridges of this period were practical, experienced master builders who accomplished all that was possible in a society that had hardly begun to move beyond the older crafts. The graceful bridges spanning American rivers would be built — albeit not in any design resembling Peale's — at a later time when the science and technology of the nineteenth century caught up with the aspirations of the eighteenth.

"To expand the mind and make men better; more virtuous and liberal"[56]

Peale's inventions derived from the reform impulse of the Enlightenment and the eighteenth-century aspirations for technological advancement, neither of which included visions of large factories and industrialized urban areas. Not until the second decade of the nineteenth century, when Peale viewed "large Manufactories," did he become aware of the industrial and urban direction of technology. In 1804, before his first view of nineteenth-century industrialism, Peale wrote to Jefferson that he had decided to use a part of his museum to "teach the mechanical arts" by exhibiting machines, models, and drawings "illustrative of various methods of workmanship." In this approach to technology, Peale would use his museum in the same way as Diderot and the *philosophes* used their encyclopedias: to demonstrate and classify the various branches of technology. The idea was to take the mystery out of technology so that, as Peale expressed it, "Many trades which are thought difficult to those unacquainted with them, will here be found easey." The purpose of this exhibit was not to aid in the establishment of large factories but to instruct farmers to employ their "vacant hours" in learning crafts so that they could supply themselves with "vast quantities of manufactured articles, without the neglect of agricultural pursuits." Learning these skills would not only protect the morals of farmers, who in "winter and in stormy weather" are "Idle" and may develop "vicious habits," but would give them profit and supply the country with "vast quantities of manufactured articles."[57]

Other Americans — such as Peale's friend Benjamin Latrobe, who had observed the course of industrialization in England — saw a different and far less bucolic future for technology. Since Latrobe had left that country (he wrote to Peale in 1803), the government and manufactures had become "interwoven." Latrobe used Adam Smith's classic description of the division of labor and told Peale of workshops where the people were either "employed in making pinpoints" or "pin's heads." He was appalled by this view of the future and hoped America would avoid such a society.[58]

But in 1803 Peale had not yet viewed such workshops, and he thought of machines only in terms of improving the moral and physical well-being of man and promoting "much good to the country." For Peale, technology and man's ability to invent and construct machines still remained a supreme indication of humanity's enormous potential, a divine mark of the creator's favor:

> The Supreme Creator in his goodness had indowed man with a reflecting mind . . . he can calculate the revolution of the Planets, he can produce by the labor of the hands various and wonderful works of art, and with the knowledge of the lever, the screw & the wedge, he can make machines to lessen labour, and multiply the conveniences of Life.[59]

In 1810 Peale gave the day-to-day running of the museum over to his son Rubens and "retired" to a farm in Germantown, Pennsylvania, to become a "gentleman farmer" like his friend Jefferson. Within a short time, he became involved in the construction of mill machinery for use on his farm and to power machines for a cotton manufactory for his sons Franklin and Titian. In order to learn as much as he could on this subject, Peale visited mills and factories in the area, and some of what he viewed in Germantown might have reminded him of Latrobe's description of English working conditions. In 1815 he wrote Jefferson that it would be "more beneficial to our Country to manufacture with small Machines in families, [than] by large establishments — where numbers of each Sex are huddled together to the great derangement of their morals & virtue." He had seen in Germantown "the Children of all poor families . . . employed in the large manufactories," who were paid fifty cents a week and received little schooling. And he had conversed with "an intelligent Gentleman of New England (near Boston)" who told him "that some very extensive Manufactories in that country have experienced the disadvantage of employing so many hands together, and that they are now dividing those large establishments into 2 or 3 smaller ones."[60]

Yet these foreboding visions of nineteenth-century industrialism do not appear fundamentally to have changed Peale's optimistic faith in man's ability to use the machine for his own improvement. He always returned to the theme of the "mechanical arts" and the "conveniences," or "comforts" of life. The unity of technology, utility, and reform — one of the Enlightenment's major contributions to western civilization — directed the expression of Peale's mechanical and spatial talents to inventions that aimed to improve the material conditions of life. Peale's inventions were, in the end, not exercises in technological virtuosity or peripheral expressions of his artistic talents but expenditures of energy directed to pursuits he thought would make life better. In all of this activity, he maintained the buoyant eighteenth-century belief that science and technology could be made the servants of man.

NOTES

The author expresses his appreciation to Lillian B. Miller, editor of the Charles Willson Peale Papers, for providing the opportunity and encouragement to write this chapter. I also wish to thank George A. Billias, Milton M. Klein, Gordon M. Marshall, and David C. Ward for their helpful comments on earlier drafts. An earlier version of this chapter was presented at a conference on Charles Willson Peale held at the National Portrait Gallery on October 23, 1981, and was originally published in the *Pennsylvania Magazine of History and Biography* 110 (1986): 323-57.

1. Historians of public health and medicine have long recognized the presence of this reform movement in eighteenth-century Europe and Anglo-America. See Richard H. Shryock, *Development of Modern Medicine* (New York, 1947), pp. 91-96; Richard H. Shryock, "The Origins and Significance of the Public Health Movement in the United States," *Annals of Medical History*, n.s., 1 (November 1929), pp. 645, 655n; George Rosen, *A History of Public Health* (New York, 1958), pp. 132-37. The bibliography of almost 1,900 entries in John Sinclair's *Rules of Health and Longevity*, 4 vols. (Edinburgh, 1808) indicates the interest in health and hygiene in the late

eighteenth and early nineteenth centuries. See also, Charles Willson Peale to John Isaac Hawkins, May 4, 1809, P-S, in *Selected Papers* 2:1198–1200. There were periods in Peale's life in which his interest in invention and reform was stronger than in art or science. See, for example, Charles Willson Peale to Thomas Jefferson, January 28, 1803, Library of Congress: Thomas Jefferson Papers, in *Selected Papers* 2:483–84.

2. Charles Willson Peale to Thomas Jefferson, May 2, 1815, P-S, F:IIA/55B10; Charles Willson Peale to Angelica Peale Robinson, May 5, 1816, P-S, F:IIA/57C9; A(TS): 237.

3. A(TS): 14, 16. For the status and popularity of clocks and clock metaphors in the eighteenth century, see Otto Mayr, "A Mechanical Symbol for an Authoritarian World," in *The Clock Work Universe, German Clocks and Automata 1550–1650,* ed. Klaus Maurice and Otto Mayr (New York, 1980), pp. 1–3; Rembrandt Peale, "Reminiscences," *The Crayon* 1, no. 6 (February 7, 1855), F:VIB/13B8. In *Emulation and Invention* (New York, 1981), pp. 49, 50–54, 135, 142, Brooke Hindle explores the relationship between art and invention at this time and emphasizes the role of the artist's "spatial intelligence" in the invention process.

4. For the respect accorded mechanics and invention in the eighteenth century, see, in general, Gary Wills, *Inventing America* (New York, 1978), pp. 97–100; Charles C. Gillispie, "The Natural History of Industry," in *Science, Technology, and Economic Growth in the Eighteenth Century,* ed. A. E. Musson (London, 1972), pp. 130–34; Peter Mathias, "Who Unbound Prometheus? Science and Technical Change, 1600–1800," ibid., p. 77; A. E. Musson, "Editor's Introduction," ibid., pp. 60–64; for Peale's friendships with David Rittenhouse, Benjamin Franklin, and Thomas Jefferson, see *Selected Papers* 1:98, 99, 160–61, 164, 165, 166, 338, 385, 419; *Selected Papers* 2:348; Gilbert Chinard, "Thomas Jefferson and the American Philosophical Society," American Philosophical Society, *Proceedings* 87 (1944): 267–70; *Early Proceedings of the American Philosophical Society . . . Manuscript Minutes of the Meetings From 1744 to 1838* (Philadelphia, 1884), pp. 269–70. For Robert Fulton, see *Selected Papers* 2:1049; for Thomas Paine, see *Selected Papers* 2:587 and Thomas Paine to Charles Willson Peale, July 29, 1803, P-S, F:IIA/28B11; for George Washington, see *CWP,* pp. 277–78; for polygraph discussions with Benjamin Henry Latrobe and Thomas Jefferson, see *Selected Papers* 2:614–16, 617, 618, 638, 639–40, 641; for Oliver Evans's petition, see *Selected Papers* 2:994–98; for Patrick Lyon's fire engine, see *Selected Papers* 2:631–32.

5. Meyer Reinhold, "The Quest for 'Useful Knowledge' in Eighteenth-Century America," American Philosophical Society, *Proceedings* 119 (April 1975): 120–21; Brooke Hindle, *The Pursuit of Science in Revolutionary America, 1735–1789* (Chapel Hill, N.C., 1956), pp. 190–215; Henry May, *The Enlightenment in America* (New York, 1976), p. 215.

6. John Thomas Scharf and Thompson Westcott, *History of Philadelphia* (Philadelphia, 1884), 2:1231, 3:2293; Thomas C. Cochran, "Philadelphia: The American Industrial Center, 1750–1850," *Pennsylvania Magazine of History and Biography* 106 (1982): 323–40; May, *The Enlightenment in America,* pp. 197–222.

7. Quotations are from Charles Willson Peale to Gabriel Furman, September 16, 1799, P-S, in *Selected Papers* 2:254–55; Peale, *An Epistle to A Friend, On The Means of Preserving Health, Promoting Happiness; And Prolonging The Life of Man To Its Natural Period* (Philadelphia, 1803), in *Selected Papers* 2:491–512; for Peale's work with teeth,

see *Selected Papers* 1:194, *Selected Papers* 2:1203; for Peale's eyeglasses, see *Selected Papers* 2:1006–07; for Peale's models of the human throat and windpipe, see *Selected Papers* 2:1185; for Peale's artificial hand, see Charles Willson Peale to Rubens and Rembrandt Peale, February 22, 1811, P-S, F:IIA/50A7–8; for his recommendation of an artisan to treat "mechanical dislocations," see Diary 20, in *Selected Papers* 2:703–04; Peale, *An Epistle to a Friend* 2:495; George Wallis, *The Art of Preventing Diseases and Restoring Health* (New York, 1794), p. 19; for the human body as a machine, see Richard H. Shryock, "Eighteenth Century Medicine in America," in American Philosophical Society, *Proceedings* 59, pt. 2 (1950): p. 289; Arturo Castiglioni, *A History of Medicine* (New York, 1941), p. 584; for the human body as a clock, see Otto Mayr, "A Mechanical Symbol," p. 4.

8. For Peale's treatment of yellow fever, see *An Epistle to a Friend* 2:502–03; and A(TS): 214–16; for typical outlooks on bathing and early bathing devices, see Harold Donaldson Eberlein, "When Society First Took a Bath," *Pennsylvania Magazine of History and Biography* 67 (1943): 30–49; Sigfried Giedion, *Mechanization Takes Command* (1948, rpt. New York, 1969), pp. 653–58; Shryock, *Modern Medicine*, p. 15; Cecil Kent Drinker, *Not So Long Ago* (New York, 1937), pp. 27–31; Lawrence Wright, *Clean and Decent, The Fascinating History of the Bathroom and the Water Closet* (New York, 1960), pp. 160–63; for bathing "unfriendly to morals," see Richard H. Shryock, *Medicine and Society in America, 1660–1860* (New York, 1960), pp. 40–41, 90–91; for cleanliness and benefits of bathing, see William Buchan, *Domestic Medicine; or the Family Physician* (Philadelphia, 1771), pp. 48–53; Samuel Tissot, *Advice to the People in General with Regard to their Health*, trans. J. Kirkpatrick (Philadelphia, 1771), p. 18; Henry Willson Lockette, *An Inaugural Dissertation on the Warm Bath . . . For the Degree of Doctor of Medicine* (Philadelphia, 1801), pp. 20–26; Sir Benjamin Thompson, Count Rumford, "Of the Salubrity of Warm Bathing" (1802), in *Collected Works of Count Rumford*, ed. Sanford C. Brown (Cambridge, Mass., 1969), 3:401–31.

9. Peale, *An Epistle to a Friend* 2:506–07; M. D. Leggett, ed., *Subject Matter Index of Patents for Invention, 1790–1873* (Washington, D.C., 1874), 3:1604; Lockette, *The Warm Bath*, pp. 13–18, plate, and description following p. 53; Wright, *Clean and Decent*, pp. 16–63; Charles Willson Peale to Philip DePeyster, April 23, 1801, P-S, F:IIA/24B4; Philip DePeyster to Charles Willson Peale, May 7, 1801, P-S, F:IIA/24B7; Charles Willson Peale to Dr. Dorsey, October 6, 1803, P-S, F:IIA/28F11; Charles Willson Peale to the College of Physicians, April 7, 1801, P-S, F:IIA/24B3; Charles Willson Peale to Managers of the Pennsylvania Hospital, November 30, 1808, P-S, in *Selected Papers* 2:1160.

10. *CWP*, p. 427; Charles Willson Peale, Diary 2, P-S, in *Selected Papers* 1:159; the French work was Claude Jacquier de Geraudly, *L'art de conserver les dents* (Paris, 1737); Charles Willson Peale to Rembrandt Peale, May 10, 1809, P-S, in *Selected Papers* 2:1203; Charles Willson Peale to Rembrandt Peale, July 9, 1826, P-S, F:IIA/72C8; Charles Willson Peale to Evan Thomas, January 12, 1827, P-S, F:IIA/72G3.

11. Walter Hoffmann-Axthelm, *History of Dentistry* (Chicago, 1981), p. 256; Vincenzo Guerini, *A History of Dentistry from the most Ancient Times Until the End of the Eighteenth Century* (1909, rpt., Amsterdam, 1967), p. 348; M.D.K. Bremner, *The Story of Dentistry* (New York, 1939), p. 69.

12. Bremner, *Dentistry*, pp. 60–61; James E. Dexter, *History of Dental and Oral*

Science in America (Philadelphia, 1876), pp. 20-21; Bernhard Wolf Weinberger, *An Introduction to the History of Dentistry* (St. Louis, 1948), 1:369-81; Guerini, *A History of Dentistry,* pp. 344-47.

13. Charles Willson Peale to Angelica Peale Robinson, November 12, 1813, P-S, F:IIA/52E7; Charles Willson Peale to Jefferson, May 2, 1815, P-S, F:IIA/55B10; Charles Willson Peale to Angelica Peale Robinson, May 5, 1816, P-S, F:IIA/57C9; Charles Willson Peale to Messrs. Holmes and Barnes, January 9, 1816, P-S, F:IIA/56F4.

14. Charles Willson Peale to Rubens Peale, June 14, July 9, October 4, 1822; January 19, 1823, P-S, F:IIA/67B10, 67C13, 67E6, 68A19; Charles Willson Peale to Angelica Peale Robinson, November 30, 1822, P-S, F:IIA/67G10; Charles Willson Peale, Diary 24, P-S, F:IIB/24.

15. Charles Willson Peale to Rembrandt Peale, February 9, 1823, P-S, F:IIA/68B11; Charles Willson Peale to John S. Miller, July 30, 1826, P-S, F:IIA/62D7; Charles Willson Peale to Rubens Peale, July 9, 1826, P-S, F:IIA/72C10; Bremner, *Dentistry,* p. 61; Weinberger, *History of Dentistry,* 2:283-88.

16. Charles Willson Peale, Diary 24; Charles Willson Peale to Rubens Peale, April 1, 1826, P-S, F:IIA/72B5; Charles Willson Peale to Rembrandt Peale, July 9, 1826, P-S, F:IIA/72C8; Charles Willson Peale to George Lauer, July 5, 1826, P-S, F:IIA/72C12; Charles Willson Peale to Rembrandt Peale, July 19, 1826, P-S, F:IIA/72D3; Dexter, *Dental and Oral Science,* pp. 24-26.

17. Eugene Ferguson, "An Historical Sketch of Central Heating: 1800-1860," in *Building Early America,* ed., Charles E. Patterson (Radnor, Pa., 1976), pp. 166-67; Samuel Y. Edgerton, "Heating Stoves in Eighteenth Century Philadelphia," *Bulletin of the Association for Preservation Technology* 3, nos. 2-3 (1971): 82; for the inefficiency of large fireplaces common in America, see Dolores Greenberg, "Energy Flow in a Changing Economy, 1815-1880," in *An Emerging Independent American Economy,* ed. Joseph R. Frese and Jacob Judd (Tarrytown, N.Y., 1980), pp. 41-42.

18. Edgerton, "Heating Stoves in Eighteenth Century Philadelphia," p. 85; "A Letter from Mr. C. W. Peale to the Editor of the *Weekly Magazine,*" *The Weekly Magazine* 1, no. 9 (March 1798): 265-69, in *Selected Papers* 2:209-15; Brooke Hindle, *David Rittenhouse* (Princeton, N.J., 1964), p. 247.

19. *Aurora General Advertiser* (Philadelphia), January 12, 26, 1796; see *Selected Papers* 2:140-41.

20. *Early Proceedings of the American Philosophical Society,* p. 231.

21. John K. Alexander, *Render Them Submissive, Responses to Poverty in Philadelphia, 1760-1800* (Amherst, Mass., 1980), pp. 9-48; Billy G. Smith, "The Material Lives of Laboring Philadelphians, 1750-1800," *William and Mary Quarterly,* 3d ser., 38, no. 2 (April 1981): 173-79; Morris Berman in *Social Change and Scientific Organization* (New York, 1978), writes of similar conditions in England. According to Berman, the Royal Institution and similar scientific organizations sponsored improvements in heating to help prevent social disorder (pp. 1-13).

22. "Chimneys," ca. 1798, P-S, F:IIA/22A10; Charles Willson Peale and Raphaelle Peale, "Description of Some Improvements in the Common Fire-place," *Transactions of the American Philosophical Society* o.s. 5 (1802): 320-24, in *Selected Papers* 2:192-97; Henry Kauffman, *The American Fireplace* (New York, 1972), pp. 197, 236, 238-43.

23. Brown, ed., *Collected Works of Count Rumford* 2:221-95, 516; Peale and Raphaelle Peale, "Improvements in the Common Fireplace," pp. 320-24.

24. *Early Proceedings of the American Philosophical Society*, pp. 280, 282; *P&M Suppl.*, p. 31; Edgerton, "Heating Stoves in Eighteenth Century Philadelphia," pp. 87–88; Charles Willson Peale, "A Letter to the . . . ," *Weekly Magazine;* on comprehensive design and invention, see Hindle, *Emulation and Invention*, pp. 50–54, 133, 135.

25. Library of Congress: Thomas Jefferson Papers, in *Selected Papers* 2:300–04; Brown, ed., *Collected Works of Count Rumford* 2:261–62, 322; 3:80–81, 84, 89, 105, 108–10, 113, 245, 322, 329; Lawrence Wright, *Home Fires Burning. The History of Domestic Heating and Cooking* (London, 1964), pp. 113–20; Charles Willson Peale to Managers of the Pennsylvania Hospital, April 2, 1801, P-S, F:IIA/24B1.

26. *The Weekly Magazine* 2, no. 25 (July 21, 1798): 353–54, in *Selected Papers* 2:218–21; Edgerton, "Heating Stoves in Eighteenth Century Philadelphia," pp. 85–86.

27. Edgerton, "Heating Stoves in Eighteenth Century Philadelphia," pp. 85–86; A(TS): 238–43.

28. Advertisement in *Poulson's American Daily Advertiser*, December 6, 1804.

29. Charles Willson Peale to Rembrandt and Rubens Peale, June 23, 1803, P-S, in *Selected Papers* 2:536–37; Charles Willson Peale to John I. Hawkins, April 22, 1804, October 7, 1804, P-S, in *Selected Papers* 2:656–60, 768–76; Charles Willson Peale, Diary 20, P-S, in *Selected Papers* 2:733–34; Charles Willson Peale to Benjamin Henry Latrobe, November 3, 1803, February 20, 1805, P-S, in *Selected Papers* 2:618, 811–12; Silvio Bedini, *Thomas Jefferson and His Copying Machines* (Charlottesville, Va., 1984), pp. 39–46. Ironically, Hawkins's adaptation of the pantograph—the physiognotrace—which copied profiles and became so successful, did not initially impress Peale.

30. Francis Pugh, *The Art of the Engineer* (New York, 1981), pp. 29–32.

31. H. W. Dickinson, *James Watt, Craftsman & Engineer* (1935; rpt. New York, 1967); Bennet Woodcroft, *Titles of Patents of Invention* (London, 1857), pp. 229, 424; for Brunel, see Thomas Jefferson to Charles Willson Peale, March 30, 1804, University of Texas: Hanley Collection, in *Selected Papers* 2:651.

32. See Bedini, *Jefferson and His Copying Machines*, pp. 15–19; Dumas Malone, *Thomas Jefferson the President: First Term, 1801-1805* (Boston, 1970), p. 419.

33. For the problem of pens moving with the same motion, see Charles Willson Peale, Diary 20, P-S, in *Selected Papers* 2:733–34; for comments on the writing surface, see Charles Willson Peale to Benjamin Henry Latrobe, October 30, 1803, P-S, in *Selected Papers* 2:617; Charles Willson Peale to Thomas Jefferson, April 29, 1804, P-S, in *Selected Papers* 2:663–66; for comments on joints, see Charles Willson Peale to John I. Hawkins, August 7, 1803, P-S, in *Selected Papers* 2:597–99; for pens, see Charles Willson Peale to Benjamin Henry Latrobe, November 3, 1803, P-S, in *Selected Papers* 2:618; Charles Willson Peale to Thomas Jefferson, February 26, 1804, P-S, in *Selected Papers* 2:639–40; for ink, see Charles Willson Peale to Thomas Jefferson, June 24, 1804, P-S, in *Selected Papers* 2:722–24; for "vertical parallelograms," see Charles Willson Peale to Thomas Jefferson, June 22, 1806, P-S, in *Selected Papers* 2:970–71.

34. Charles Willson Peale to John I. Hawkins, P-S, in *Selected Papers* 2:597–99; on selling below cost, see Charles Willson Peale to John I. Hawkins, P-S, in *Selected Papers* 2:768–76; for the assistance of Jefferson and Latrobe, see *Selected Papers* 2:614–16, 621–23, 651, 661–62; for "knaves and fools," see Charles Willson Peale to Benjamin Henry Latrobe, November 3, 1803, P-S, in *Selected Papers* 2:618.

35. W. L. Goodman, *The History of Woodworking Tools* (New York, 1964), p. 162;

Henry Chapman Mercer, *Ancient Carpenters' Tools* (Doylestown, Pa., 1929), pp. 214–15; Charles Willson Peale to Thomas Jefferson, April 29, 1804, P-S, in *Selected Papers* 2:663–66; Charles Willson Peale to John I. Hawkins, April 22, 1804, P-S, in *Selected Papers* 2:656–60; Charles Willson Peale to Benjamin Henry Latrobe, October 30, 1803, P-S, in *Selected Papers* 2:617; Charles Willson Peale to John I. Hawkins, October 7, 1804, P-S, in *Selected Papers* 2:768–76.

36. On Jefferson's and Latrobe's endorsements, see *Selected Papers* 2:746, 753–54, 847–49; on Peale's sale of polygraphs, see *Selected Papers* 2:738–39, 853, 868, 886–88; Charles Willson Peale to Thomas Jefferson, September 23, 1804, P-S, in *Selected Papers* 2:755–56.

37. Brooke Hindle, "Charles Willson Peale's Science and Technology," in *Charles Willson Peale and His World* (New York, 1982), p. 151; *CWP*, p. 308; on Jefferson's and Latrobe's endorsements, see *Selected Papers* 2:740–41, 811–12; Talbot Hamlin, *Benjamin Henry Latrobe* (New York, 1955), p. 484; for Jefferson's gifts of the polygraph, see *Selected Papers* 2:778–79, 849, 918; for Jefferson's recommendation of polygraph, see *Selected Papers* 2:828.

38. Benjamin Henry Latrobe to Thomas Jefferson, July 20, 1817, Library of Congress: Thomas Jefferson Papers.

39. Ibid.

40. Charles Willson Peale to Thomas Jefferson, June 22, 1806, P-S, *Selected Papers* 2:970–72.

41. *Aurora General Advertiser,* September, 27, 1796.

42. A(TS): 233–35.

43. Ibid.; Charles Willson Peale to Pardon Brown, October 26, 1796, P-S, F:IIA/20F13; Hindle, "Charles Willson Peale's Science and Technology," p. 151; Charles Willson Peale, *An Essay on Building Wooden Bridges* (1797), in *Selected Papers* 2:181–91.

44. David Freeman Hawke, *Thomas Paine* (New York, 1947), pp. 163–70; Charles Willson Peale to Thomas Paine, July 27, 1803, P-S, in *Selected Papers* 2:587; Thomas Paine to Charles Willson Peale, July 29, 1803, P-S, F:IIA/28B11.

45. Julian Boyd, Mina R. Bryan, Frederick Aandahl, eds., *Papers of Thomas Jefferson* (Princeton, N.J., 1954), 10:xxix, 444–45; Howard C. Rice, *Thomas Jefferson's Paris* (Princeton, N.J., 1976), pp. 18–19; Darwin H. Stapleton, ed., *The Engineering Drawings of Benjamin Henry Latrobe* (New Haven, Conn., 1980), p. 10; William Bainter O'Neal, *Jefferson's Fine Arts Library* (Charlottesville, Va., 1956), pp. 83–84. John Van Horne, an editor of the *Latrobe Papers* and librarian of the Library Company of Philadelphia, brought to my attention a letter from Jefferson to Latrobe of November 2, 1802, (Library of Congress: Thomas Jefferson Papers), discussing the Halle aux Blés, and demonstrating Jefferson's persistent enthusiasm for Delormé's architecture. Jefferson's role in promoting Delormé in America is also evident in the early nineteenth-century work of Robert Mills. Mills had made drawings for Jefferson in 1802 or 1803 while staying at Monticello, where he would have seen Jefferson's use of Delormé techniques; having been given use of Jefferson's library, he would have had access to Jefferson's copy of Delormé's work. See John M. Bryan, "Robert Mills: Education and Early Drawings," in *Robert Mills, Architect,* ed. John M. Bryan (Washington, D.C., 1989), pp. 15–16.

46. George Michael Danko, "The Evolution of the Simple Truss Bridge, 1790 to 1850: From Empiricism to Scientific Construction" (Ph.D. diss., University of Pennsylvania, 1979), pp. 3–5; Scharf and Westcott, *Philadelphia* 2:2141; Bayley Bartlett to Samuel Coates, December 21, 1794, Library Company of Philadelphia, Minutes, 4:16, 18.

47. *Aurora General Advertiser,* September 23, 27, 1796; *Philadelphia Gazette,* September 22, 1797; Select Council of Philadelphia, Minutes, City of Philadelphia, Department of Records; Charles Willson Peale to Timothy Pickering, September 27, 1796, P-S, F:IIA/21A5; Leggett, *Subject Matter Index of Patents for Invention* 1:149; *A Statistical Account of the Schuylkill Permanent Bridge* (Philadelphia, 1815). The city of Philadelphia was too financially strained to build the bridge, and in 1798 a company was incorporated by the Pennsylvania state legislature, which chose an English engineer to design and construct a stone bridge.

48. Danko, "The Evolution of the Simple Truss Bridge," pp. 13, 15, 47, 54; Llewellyn Nathaniel Edwards, *A Record of History and Evolution of Early American Bridges* (Orono, Me., 1959), pp. 34–35, 40; Carl W. Condit, *American Building Art* (New York, 1960), p. 6; Peale, *Building Wooden Bridges,* 2:184.

49. Edwards, *History of Early American Bridges,* p. 34; *Reports from Committees of the House of Commons, 1793–1802* (London, 1803), 14:12.

50. Danko, "The Evolution of the Simple Truss Bridge," p. 15; Edwards, *History and Evolution of Early American Bridges,* p. 33.

51. Danko, "The Evolution of the Simple Truss Bridge," pp. 20–23; Peale, *Building Wooden Bridges* 2:183–84.

52. Académie des Sciences, *Procès-verbaux des séances,* vol. 2 (Hendaye, 1800–04), p. 109; Charles Willson Peale to Timothy Pickering, December 27, 1796, P-S, F:IIA/21A5.

53. Danko, "The Evolution of the Simple Truss Bridge," pp. 9–11, 42; *Statistical Account of the Schuylkill Permanent Bridge,* p. 14.

54. Charles Willson Peale to Rubens Peale, October 14, 1805, P-S, in *Selected Papers* 2:896–98; Charles Willson Peale to Raphaelle Peale, P-S, October 14, 28, 1805, in *Selected Papers* 2:899, 902; Charles Willson Peale to Angelica Peale Robinson, October 29, 1805, February 18, 1806, P-S, in *Selected Papers* 2:903–04, 939; Museum Accession Book, F:XIA/3.

55. Condit, *American Building Art,* pp. 86–87. On the aspirations and achievements of American science and technology in the eighteenth century, see Hindle, *The Pursuit of Science in Revolutionary America,* pp. 378–79.

56. A(TS): 379. In this instance, Peale was referring to discoveries of "natural substances" and the advancement of natural history, but the words accurately reflected his belief that increased knowledge would make men better.

57. Charles Willson Peale to Thomas Jefferson, February 26, 1804, P-S, in *Selected Papers* 2:639–40; Gillispie, "The Natural History of Industry," pp. 130–34.

58. Benjamin Henry Latrobe to Charles Willson Peale, November 12, 1803, Maryland Historical Society: Benjamin H. Latrobe Coll., in *Selected Papers* 2:621–23

59. Peale, Diary 20, in *Selected Papers* 2:706–07.

60. Charles Willson Peale to Thomas Jefferson, June 18, 1815, P-S, F:IIA/55E1.

14

Charles Willson Peale's Belfield

Its Place in American Garden History

———◄◉►——

THERESE O'MALLEY

HARLES Willson Peale's country retreat, Belfield, was established at a time of significant developments in horticulture, agriculture, and landscape design in America. When Peale retired to his farm in 1810, Philadelphia still dominated the American intellectual and cultural world, and the Peale family was intricately involved in its success. Over the next decade, Belfield became the focus of Peale's attention as he attempted to integrate his scientific acumen and aesthetic sensibility in the creation of a garden. By manipulating the materials of nature according to the principles of art, Peale was able to combine the traditions of eighteenth-century picturesque gardening with nineteenth-century scientific achievements.[1]

This chapter is a preliminary study of a complex symbolic landscape; it can only begin to describe the major garden features of Belfield and to relate these to the mainstream of American and European garden history. Unlike many contemporary gardens of its day, Belfield is richly documented in paintings, drawings, letters, Peale's 1826 autobiography, as well as the remnants of the farm itself. One of the first descriptions of Belfield is found in a letter Peale wrote to his son Rembrandt in 1810, the year of its purchase. Interspersed with the text of the letter, Peale illustrated his "retreat"[2] in a series of pen and ink drawings (fig. 87). The letter described the 104-acre farm with several buildings including a "countryhouse,"[3] barns and stables, springhouse and mill. The property consisted of meadows, streams, orchards, and many mature specimens of weeping willows, tulip poplars, and lombardy poplars. The drawings suggest little progress at this early stage in the development of ornamental gardens, although Peale does mention the garden walks and lower garden as distinct from the farm gardens. Gradually, Peale added flowerbeds, shrub-lined walkways, garden buildings, a fountain, ponds, and sculpture.

The evidence suggests that Peale's garden shared many of the design characteristics of contemporary gardens in Philadelphia and its environs.[4] By the opening of the nineteenth century, Philadelphia had already enjoyed 100 years of landscape gardening. This area contained some of the most sophisticated estates in the nation, celebrated for their parks, gardens, and horticultural curiosities. The picturesque views and romantic scenery along the Schuylkill and Delaware rivers were ideal locations for the wealthy of the young republic to situate their country seats. Sweetbriar, the home of Samuel Breck, was one of the many great estates depicted by William Birch in his *Country Seats of the United States* of 1808. Overlooking a sweeping lawn, Sweetbriar had notable gardens and greenhouses. Another estate known as Lemon Hill, or Pratt's Garden (fig. 88), laid out in a somewhat formal, geometric style, was famous for its horticultural marvels. According to a record of 1795, it had a large and elegant greenhouse filled with citrus trees that figures prominently in many popular views of the estate. Lemon Hill was decorated by bowers, fountains, a grotto, and an artificial cascade. The summerhouses of bark and thatch were embellished with marble statues of Roman gods.[5] Belmont Mansion (fig. 89) had gardens with clipped evergreen hedges, topiary, a labyrinth, wilderness, and "a most perfect sample of the old taste of parterres." The owner, Judge Richard Peters, was known not only for his taste but also for his scientific acumen; he was the founder of the Philadelphia Society for the Promotion of Agriculture and author of a treatise on farming.[6] These are just a few of the contemporary country houses in the environs of Philadelphia with which Peale might have been familiar.

Peale shared with his neighbors a taste for landscape aesthetics that was shaped in part by landscape literature, the models of earlier American gardens in the area, and first-hand knowledge of European gardens. From the earliest days of the nation's founding, Americans had absorbed European landscape theory through imported books and from gardeners trained abroad. The Library Company, for example, ordered for their collection "Batty Langley's *New Principles of Gardening,* Humphry Repton's *Sketches and Hints on Landscape Gardening,* Switzer's Gardening and Parkinson's Flower Garden."[7] Peter Collinson, the British botanist and agent for John Bartram, presented to the library Philip Miller's *Gardener's Dictionary,* a compendium of known flora that was published in London and that contained New World specimens sent by Bartram.[8] These were some of the most influential texts for eighteenth-century European gardening. This imported knowledge, tempered by New World conditions and by native botanical experience, was employed within the first few decades of the country's existence to create distinctive American gardens and a body of literature. Bernard M'Mahon, a Philadelphia nurseryman from whom the Peales purchased trees and plants, wrote the *American Gardeners Calendar* (1806) which became a bible of gardening wisdom for native practitioners.[9]

Several landowners including Peale had visited the great gardens of Europe and brought back ideas to either emulate or accommodate to local conditions.[10] For example, Woodlands, the estate of Andrew Hamilton, may have been planned by the English designer George Parkyns after Hamilton returned from several years in London (fig. 90). It certainly was developed by Frederick Pursh, a German gardener who spent many years in Philadelphia. It was reported that at Woodlands there "was not a rare plant in Europe, Asia, Africa, from China and from the islands in the South Seas which he had not procured."[11] At Belfield, Peale, like many of his neighbors, appropriated elements of European gardens and garden ornamentation, translating them in such a way that they maintained their original pedigree yet expressed a peculiarly American character.

During the years 1810 to 1820, Peale transformed his property into a *ferme ornée,* an ornamented farm where the artful and utilitarian characteristics of Belfield were intermixed, and, as Jefferson said, "the attributes of a garden [were] interspersed among the articles of husbandry."[12] The *ferme ornée,* a garden type first described by Stephen Switzer in 1715–18 in his *Iconographia rustica,* continued to appeal to Americans well into the nineteenth century because it celebrated American agrarianism. The most influential gardens of the era, Monticello and Mount Vernon (figs. 91, 92), were both examples of the *ferme ornée.*[13] Although Peale's garden was created on a more modest scale than the Virginia plantations, it also combined ornamental and functional purposes for "healthy amusements."[14]

The effect of Peale's improvements at Belfield may be seen in his painting of 1815–16 (fig. 93) which he explained was a "view of the garden . . . as seen from what we call my seat in the walk to the Mill."[15] The view includes Peale's house in the center of the composition, set in the far ground on top of a hill. To the left is the six-pillared temple containing a bust of Washington that overlooked planted fields and the rest of the garden. In the center middle ground is a glass house that was built above an arched cave. A low hill falls down to the fountain and archway. The fountain basin is surrounded by terra-cotta pots, which Peale tells us were filled with Rubens Peale's flowers. The pots were probably similar to the pot shown in the 1801 portrait by his brother Rembrandt Peale, *Rubens Peale with a Geranium* (fig. 37).

Although there were a few gardens that retained the older style of clipped hedges, labyrinths, and parterres, such as Lemon Hill or Belmont, Peale tended toward a more "modern" taste, as described by Bernard M'Mahon in the *American Gardener's Calendar,* for serpentine walkways, rustic retreats, and a "natural assemblage."[16] At Belfield, it seems that boxwood hedges and flower beds were located close to the house, while the more irregular, naturalistic park was set further down the hill.

This so-called modern style was essentially Reptonian and prevailed in the United States at the turn of the nineteenth century. Humphry Repton's method of landscape produced varied effects by placing the house under management of art, while the park was in nature's province.[17] This meant that the gardens, while somewhat artificial near the house, became increasingly naturalistic as they moved farther out into the landscape. An example of Reptonian style can be seen at another Schuylkill estate, Solitude, where Birch said, "Formality was not wholly banished from the neighborhood of the house."[18]

Whether laid out in the "modern" fashion of Repton or the "ancient" style, the gardens around Philadelphia contained many of the same individual elements, such as grottoes, statuary, and temples. These classical elements became icons of the republican image that the early nationalists were struggling to define. The association of Roman virtue with agriculture resulted from the rediscovery in the eighteenth century of ancient texts by Virgil and the Younger Pliny on husbandry, villas, and plantations. As they set about establishing a new republic based on a classical model, early American landowners identified themselves as participants in a pastoral tradition. Peale embraced a classical republican imagery for his garden, reaffirming the agrarian ideal through ornament, inscription, and the productivity of his farm.

By 1813, Peale had built many garden features in and around the meadows and fields of Belfield, some of which he illustrated in paintings and letters to his children. In a letter dated November 12, 1813, Peale sketched an obelisk he built to "terminate a walk in the Garden" that extended straight out from the main entrance of his house. In his painting of 1815–20 (fig. 94), the obelisk is shown at the top of the hill visible from the main road to Germantown. Given its location and repeated mention in his correspondence, Peale obviously believed that the obelisk was an important addition to his garden. As he wrote to his daughter Angelica, he "read in [the] dictionary of art for [a] description" of the obelisk.[19] He was referring to the *Dictionary of Arts and Sciences* by George Gregory, published in 1807, which contained this section on obelisks:

> Obelisks appear to be of very great antiquity, and to be raised to transmit to posterity precepts of philosophy, which were cut in hieroglyphical characters; afterwards they were used to immortalize the great actions of heroes, and the memory of persons beloved.

Gregory's dictionary listed famous historic obelisks, including one that was erected to memorialize Ptolemy Philadelphus.[20] It is possible that Peale was linking himself with the ancient Egyptian who was associated with the library and lighthouse of Alexandria and had named the city of Philadelphia in the third century B.C. Peale followed Gregory's advice to finish the "truncated, quadrangular, and slender pyramid" with "inscriptions or hieroglyphics" which he placed on the pedestal.[21]

Like the pyramids of the past, Peale's obelisk was intended to mark "a place where [he] meant to have [his] body laid."[22] His choice of an obelisk was not surprising: Thomas Jefferson, with whom Peale corresponded regularly about Belfield, also designed one for his tomb at Monticello (fig. 95). Like Peale's, it too was inscribed with inspirational phrases.[23] The obelisk, used since Roman times and in Egyptian temple precincts from at least the twelfth dynasty, was frequently included in eighteenth-century English gardens such as Chiswick, Castle Howard, and Holkam Hall.[24] Jefferson had seen the obelisk in Alexander Pope's garden at Twickenham and, being much impressed by it, recorded Pope's inscription to his mother. As Peale was also quite enthralled with the poet's work, having read all of it,[25] he might well have known about the garden through either discussion with Jefferson or the many popular prints of the day. Both Peale and Jefferson were familiar with landscape literature such as the *City and Country Builder's Treasury* (1740) by Batty Langley, who recommended illustrated designs for obelisks.

The garden description that Peale wrote at the end of his life suggests that he ("the proprietor," as he called himself) wanted to create an ordered environment of cultivation—that is, a culture of the earth, the body, and the mind. The autobiography is a valuable document for understanding Peale and garden imagery of the period, as it serves essentially as another kind of self-portrait. In it Peale wrote, "The Proprietor made summer-houses (so-called) roofs to ward off the sunbeams with seats of rest—one made of the Chinese taste, dedicated to meditation."[26]

The Chinese summerhouse grew out of the current fashion for things oriental, a style called chinoiserie that was promulgated by pattern books by William and John Halfpenny, Thomas Chippendale, and Sir William Chambers, who designed the Royal Botanic Gardens at Kew.[27] The Chinese style was often seen in the zig-zag wooden latticework found in garden structures and furniture. For example, Thomas Jefferson sketched a design for a garden fence in the Chinese mode that showed a typical lattice gate used extensively at Monticello and the University of Virginia (fig. 96).[28] A garden seat from Chambers's book on Kew recalls Peale's description of the Chinese summerhouse's structure of thin posts with arched brackets holding up the roof as well as the "comfortable seats at back and sides." Recognizing that the Chinese were great philosophers, Peale dedicated this structure to meditation, inscribing it with a long verse that ended with these words: "Then let me ask myself, *why am I here?* am I blessed with more profound reason than other Animals, if so, *Lett me be thankful: let me meditate on the past, on the present and on the future.*"[29]

Another garden folly, a temple, was built by Peale's son Franklin on the top of the hill that provided a view of the rest of the garden. Peale described the structure in a letter to his daughter Angelica as having a hexagonal base with six well turned pillars supporting a circular top and dome on which was placed a bust of General Washington. Peale wrote that it "would have been appropriate to have had 13 pillars" for the temple, recalling the thirteen original colonies.[30] This structure was typical of picturesque gardens in the area and can be found in countless prints and drawings of gardens of the period. For example, Jefferson designed a similar pavilion as an icehouse for Montpelier, the home of James Madison.[31] In his temple, Peale transformed a traditional emblem, a classical portrait bust, into an American image. Peale appropriately selected George Washington because the first president was often called the American Cincinnatus, after the Roman general who had left his plough to take up the sword and then returned to his fields after the battle was won. Dr. David Ramsay, historian of the Revolution and a correspondent of Peale's, was inspired by this heroic image when, in 1779, he optimistically described the future American society which would be "formed out of heroes and statesmen, released from their present cares; some of which will teach mankind to plough, sow, plant, build, and improve the rough face of Nature; while others critically examine the various productions of the animal, vegetable and mineral kingdoms, and teach their countrymen to 'look through Nature up to Nature's God.'"[32] Peale believed that in this new society, where the leaders were educated and cultured, the priorities of the democratic government were clearly directed toward the pursuit of knowledge and education for the common man. Peale saw himself a teacher, a scientist as well as a cultivator of the land: his didactic garden allowed him to fulfill these roles.

Conscious of the historic moment in which he lived, Peale built a Pedestal of Memorable Events, another obelisk, on which were inscribed ninety historic dates in the New World, beginning with the first discoveries of North America and ending with the battle of New Orleans.[33] The decorative program of the pedestal recalled the ephemeral "Temple of Independence" that Peale built, inscribed with the names of all famous battles of the Revolution (fig. 97).[34]

Another echo of Peale's earlier celebratory architecture may be seen in the garden arch that is visible in the painting of 1815–16 (fig. 93) near the fountain on the left side of the scene. Peale transformed a toolshed into a small triumphal arch painted with a trompe l'oeil landscape and ornamented with several figures "representing statues in sculpture." In his autobiography, Peale explained in detail the emblematic meaning decorating the arch[35] so that the "design of those figures might be fully understood by visitors":

> He painted two pedestals ornamented with a [ball] to crown each, and the die of the pedestals, on one the explanation of the figures, viz. America with an even balance — as justifying her acts . . . .
>
> The fassie [fasces] emblematical of the several states, are bound together, inscribed by a rattle-snake, as innocent if not meddled with, but terrible if molested. This emblem of congress is placed upright as that body ought to be, with wisdom its base, designated by the owl; the beehive and children; industry and increase, the effects of good government

supported on one side, Truth and Temperance, on the other. Industry, with her distaff, resting on the cornucopia. . . .

Above the arch was inscribed: "A wise policy will do away wars, hence Mars is fallen," symbolizing Peale's abhorrence of war.[36] Peale continued to use some of the same emblems in his garden that he had used in his paintings, drawings, and ephemeral architecture. These images— cornucopia, fascia, rattlesnake, the beehive, classical gods and goddesses—had been used for centuries in the emblematic tradition that Peale inherited. Roger Stein has shown that Peale, throughout his career, imbued them with new meanings pertinent to American history in order to create an American national iconography.[37]

The last major monument in the garden was an artificial cave, a traditional garden element cited in classical sources and found in gardens since the Renaissance. Peale's arched cave, built in the hillside leading down to the fountain, was reminiscent of the grotto at Lemon Hill. That grotto was described by a visitor as "of a circular form, the side built up of rock and arched over head, and a number of shells."[38] This description recalls the famous shell-encrusted grotto on the banks of the Thames built by Alexander Pope. At Belfield, a greenhouse was built on top of the cave because of the constant humidity. This structure is seen in the center of the painting of 1815–16 (fig. 93), and it appears as a simple rectangular pavilion with espaliered trees hung on its facade. Terra-cotta pots filled with live plants sit on top like urns on a pedestal. The minute attention in this painting to details of trees and flowers (one can identify many of the species from the painting) is an extension of Peale's emphasis on the botanical component of the farm.

Along with a concern for ornamentation and agricultural success, Belfield shared with its contemporary gardens a deep commitment to botanical pursuits. Woodlands, Belmont, Lemon Hill, and Stenton were a few of the best-known estates whose collections of exotic and rare plants attracted the attention of botanists and horticulturalists internationally. In addition to collecting foreign specimens, the owners of these estates gathered native plant materials to document the abundance of New World flora and to experiment with new methods of scientific farming and horticulture.

That Philadelphia was preeminent in the field of botany is not surprising, considering that it was the center of early and continuous activity in the sciences. For example, one of the first botanic gardens in the country was begun by John Bartram in the 1730s on the banks of the Schuylkill. Bartram carried on an extensive exchange of plant material and botanical literature with the leading European botanists and collectors. Bartram contributed to the transformation of botanical sciences that took place during the eighteenth century as an increasingly ecological understanding of the natural world evolved. His garden was notable because he planted the specimens collected in the wilderness in the woods outside his house in conditions as near as possible to those in which the plant originated. This was a departure from traditional botanic gardens laid out since the Middle Ages in rectangular beds.

Like Bartram, Peale participated in the new wave of botanical sciences that promoted the study of plants in the natural landscape rather than simply in dried herbaria or gardens laid out with geometric rigidity. Long before Peale planned his garden, he attempted to demonstrate the interrelatedness of natural phenomena in his "world in miniature," the first natural history museum in the country. In it, he juxtaposed animals, bones, minerals, and ethnographic material. A contemporary description reveals this character of the museum:

> His natural curiosities were arranged in a most romantic manner. There was a mound of earth, considerably raised and covered with green turf, from which a number of trees ascended and branched out in different directions. On the declivity of this mound was a small thicket, and just below it an artificial pond; on the other side a number of large and small rocks of different kinds, collected from different parts of the world and represented in the rude state in which they are generally found. At the foot of the mound were holes dug and earth thrown up, to show the different kinds of clay, ochre, also various ores and minerals. Around the pond was a beach, on which was exhibited an assortment of shells of different kinds.[39]

Birds were arranged in cases with painted scenes that showed the foliage and terrain appropriate to their natural habitat. Peale's interest in the larger context of the animal world was expressed in his contrast of his museum with similar European institutions:

> It is not customary in Europe, it is said, to paint skies and landscapes in their cases of birds and other animals, and it may have a neat and clean appearance to line them only with white paper, but on the other hand it is not only pleasing to see a sketch of a landscape but by showing the nest, hollow, cave, or a particular view of the country from which they came, some instances of the habits may be given.[40]

Similar questions arising in natural history concerning the climate, soil, and growth patterns of living specimens also applied to plants. However, as Brooke Hindle has said, Peale was frustrated in his attempt to display botanic material in his museum, because plants did not retain a natural appearance once preserved.[41] Only a botanical garden where living plants were displayed could serve the needs of the new empirical sciences.[42] What Peale had achieved for ornithology, biology, geology, and paleontology in his museum could be done for botany only in a garden.[43]

Peale's advice to Jefferson, "Your garden must be a museum to you,"[44] confirms the idea that at Belfield Peale created a living museum of plants that would educate visitors about the natural world. He inscribed one of the garden follies with these instructions:

> Meditate on the creation of the worlds; which perform their evolutions in proscribed period! on the changes and revolutions of the Globe which we inhabit: — on the wonderful variety of animals inhabiting the earth, the air and the waters; their immense number and diversity: their beauty and delicacy of structure: some immensely large, and others gradually descending into a minuteness almost eluding our sight, even when aided by the microscope![45]

Although Belfield was not a botanic garden in the strictest sense, the history of botanic gardens during this period illustrates an attempt to reconcile aesthetic theory with changing scientific principles.[46] In the eighteenth century, as new and exotic plants were brought back to Europe by travelers, explorers, and naturalists, the old botanic gardens, which had hitherto been primarily medicinal in purpose, became museums of living plants and centers for research, experiment, display, and delight. The early nineteenth century witnessed the establishment of several botanic gardens in America designed for both scientific and aesthetic purposes. The gardens of Harvard, Yale, Princeton, the University of South Carolina, and the University of Pennsylvania were started within the first two decades of the new century. In addition to the obvious educational function, Peale recognized the naturalization and cultivation of useful plants taking place in these gardens as essential to the welfare of the national agrarian economy: "Natural history is not only interesting to the individual, it ought to become a NATIONAL CONCERN, since it is a NATIONAL GOOD, — of this, agriculture, as it is the most important occupation, affords the most striking proof."[47]

Even in nonscientific landscape gardening, the growing interest in exotics carried with it a recognition of their complex botanical properties. An enthusiasm among gardeners regarding the environmental determinants of plants led to a more scientific, ecological consideration of the material. For example, Repton, the leading landscape theorist of the period, had recommended that "beds of bog-earth should be prepared for the American plants; the aquatic plants . . . should grow on the surface near the edges of water. The numerous class of rock plants should have beds of rugged stone."[48] Therefore, the increasingly naturalistic, irregular design of picturesque gardening in the eighteenth century coincided with ecological trends in scientific gardening. For example, the Royal Gardens at Kew and Glasnevin, the botanic gardens at Dublin, and the Jardin des Plantes at Paris carried on the overriding botanical interest that characterized the period while integrating it with the aesthetic ideal of the picturesque landscape. Similarly, in America, early botanic gardens were arranged in systematic fashion for botanical study, but there were several that were notable because they displayed their scientific character with artistic designs of the highest quality. One such place was the Elgin Gardens of Manhattan (fig. 98), founded in 1801 by Dr. David Hosack, a faculty member of Columbia College and one of the first Americans to be elected to the Royal Horticultural Society of England.[49] When he announced its opening, Hosack attributed great social importance to his botanic garden: "We have every reason to expect that the establishment of a botanic garden . . . will . . . in a short time meet with the general design of protecting useful knowledge, and those arts which are most essentially connected with human happiness."[50]

Located on twenty acres at Fifth Avenue and Forty-seventh Street, the gardens were celebrated for their scientific endeavors as well as for their beautifully landscaped grounds. In a watercolor from 1811 (fig. 98), the main greenhouse and hothouses are shown surrounded by scattered trees and shrubs, the grounds traversed by a curving pathway, showing a typical treatment of a late picturesque garden. Dr. Hosack was in close communications with the most prominent figures of the day, including the Bartrams, Thomas Jefferson, André Michaux, and Charles Willson Peale.

Peale's belief in the importance of promoting botanical research and making this information available to the general public was shared by many of his intellectual and scientific contemporaries. Dr. Benjamin

Waterhouse, for example, a professor of medicine at Harvard, 1783–1812, encouraged the creation of botanical gardens in America's growing urban centers.[51] In his writings and lectures, Dr. Waterhouse exhorted the student of botany to "pass from the closet" to the gardens and fields in order to study the scriptures of nature, rather than books written by men:

> The utility of these institutions is self-evident. By public gardens, medicinal plants are at the command of the teacher in every lesson, the eye and the mind are perpetually gratified with the succession of curious, scarce and exotic luxuries, here the botanist can compare the doubtful species, and examine them through all the stages of growth, with those to which they are allied; and all these advantages are accumulated in a thousand objects at the same time.[52]

Waterhouse described the quintessential American garden for the turn of the nineteenth century as one in which the didactic, the scientific, and the aesthetic purposes of gardening were brought together. Peale was able to achieve this same union at Belfield, which embodied his own life's work in the arts, the sciences, and the education of the public.

The garden at Belfield should be seen as having incorporated a lifetime of meaning and significance both for aesthetic and scientific reasons for Peale and his family. Raphaelle Peale painted still lifes using the fruits and flowers of Belfield as models (fig. 99).[53] Rubens Peale was responsible for much of the botanical gardening: he planted exotic specimens collected from colleagues in both this country and abroad. His botanical interests, which developed early in his life, were addressed in his portrait by Rembrandt Peale in which Rubens holds a geranium, thought to be one of the earliest plants imported into the country (fig. 37). The seed is said to have come to John Bartram in Philadelphia from Peter Collinson in London.[54]

Belfield may be considered a self-conscious expression of Charles Willson Peale's individual character as much as any of his eighteen painted self-portraits. In justifying the detailed account of his garden in his autobiography, Peale wrote: "As the object of this work is to make the portrait of the man, it is proper to give all his friperies and follies, more properly, as all these things were made of wood and paint, which could last only a few years."[55]

Recognizing the ephemeral quality of his garden, Peale tried to record its details because he felt it was an important statement of his world view. In many ways, the statement that Peale made about his full-length self-portrait, *The Artist in his Museum,* is also appropriate to the creation of Belfield: "I think it important that I should not only make it a lasting monument of my art as a painter, but also that the Design should be expressive that I bring forth into public view, the beauties of Nature and Art, the rise and progress of the Museum."[56]

We can understand Peale's "improvement" of the property he purchased as an attempt to perfect the natural world, to order it as he did the natural history objects in his museum. In his retirement to Belfield, Peale brought together the emblems, forms, philosophy, and order that he had pursued in many media throughout his life. A fuller understanding of Peale cannot be achieved until a complete study of the garden, its sources, iconography, and botanical organization has been accomplished. The next volume of the Peale Papers containing the Belfield material should make this possible.[57]

NOTES

1. Kateryna A. Rudnytzky, "The Union of Landscape and Art: Peale's Garden at Belfield," National Endowment for the Humanities Funded Study, La Salle University, Honors Essay, 1986, pp. 8–10.

2. Charles Willson Peale to Rembrandt Peale, July 22, 1810, P-S, F:IIA/49D3–10. These pen and ink sketches, according to Jessie Poesch, were a copy of the original set that was sent to Peale's daughter Angelica on August 26, 1810. The sketches were first published and discussed as a set by Jessie J. Poesch in "Mr. Peale's 'Farm Persevere': Some Documentary Views," *Proceedings of the American Philosophical Society* 100 (1956): 545–56.

3. Rudnytzky, "Union of Landscape and Art," p. 38.

4. For a brief history of gardening in Philadelphia and environs, see Elizabeth McLean, "Town and Country Gardens in Eighteenth-Century Philadelphia," *Eighteenth-Century Life* 8 (January 1983): 142–44; and James D. Kornwolf, "The Picturesque in the American Garden," ibid.: 93–106

5. McLean, "Town and Country Gardens," p. 141.

6. Robert Wheelwright, "Gardens and Places of Colonial Philadelphia," *Colonial Gardens: The Landscape Architecture of George Washington's Time* (Washington, D.C., 1982), p. 27; W. Howard Adams, *The Eye of Jefferson* (Washington, D.C., 1976), p. 328.

7. Charles E. Peterson, "Library Hall," *Transactions of the American Philosophical Society* 43, pt. 1 (1953): 138n71.

8. Miller's *Gardeners Dictionary* (London, 1763, and subsequent editions) was very influential because it incorporated American material with Old World material and showed how to plant a "wilderness" with American specimens.

9. Charles Willson Peale, November 9, 1811, Daybook 2: quoted in Rudnytzky, "The Union of Landscape and Art," p. 25.

10. Many gardeners and designers trained abroad, such as Frederick Pursh,

George Parkyns, and George Bridport, were available in Philadelphia during this period and provided the latest information of European landscape fashion.

11. William Parker and Julia Cutler, eds. *Life, Journals, and Correspondence of Rev. Manasseh Cutler* (Cincinnati, 1888), quoted in McLean, "Town and Country Gardens," p. 144.

12. Quoted in William L. Beiswanger, "The Temple in the Garden: Thomas Jefferson's Vision of the Monticello Landscape," *Eighteenth-Century Life* 8 (January 1983): 131.

13. Monticello and Mount Vernon were influential because of their tremendous popularity among tourists as well as the close scientific, political, and social contacts between their owners, Jefferson and Washington, and many powerful landowners and garden builders of the time.

14. Edgar P. Richardson, Brooke Hindle, Lillian B. Miller, *Charles Willson Peale and His World* (New York, 1983), p. 96.

15. Charles Willson Peale to Angelica Peale Robinson, November 22, 1815, P-S, F:IIA/56C6–D6.

16. Bernard M'Mahon, *American Gardener's Calendar; adapted to the climates and seasons of the United States* (Philadelphia, 1806), p. 55.

17. Therese O'Malley, "Landscape Gardening in the Early National Period," *Views and Visions* (Washington, D.C., 1986), p. 137.

18. Alice B. Lockwood, *Gardens of Colony and State* (New York, 1931), 1:345–46.

19. Charles Willson Peale to Angelica Peale Robinson, November 12, 1813, P-S, F:IIA/52E7–13.

20. George Gregory, *A Dictionary of Arts and Sciences* (London, 1807), 1:281.

21. The design suggested by Gregory was as follows: "The proportion in the height and thickness are nearly the same in all obelisks; their height and thickness being nine or nine and one half, and sometimes ten times, their thickness; and their diameter at the top never less than half; and never greater than three-fourths of that at the bottom" (see Charles Willson Peale to Angelica Peale Robinson, November 12, 1813). The four inscriptions he included were: *"Never return an injury. It is a noble Triumph to overcome Evil by good; Labor while you are able. It will give health to the Body—peaceful content to the Mind; Neglect no duty; and Oy, voy, et se fais, si tu veux vivre en paix/He that will live in peace and rest, must hear and see and say the best."* The inscriptions were recorded by Peale in his autobiography [A(TS): 391]. For a discussion of Gregory's dictionary see Rudnytzky, "Union of Landscape and Art," p. 27f.

22. Charles Willson Peale to Eliza Peale, January 16, 1824, P-S, F:IIA/70A2–5.

23. Adams, *The Eye of Jefferson*, p. 209. For Jefferson's and Peale's correspondence, see Horace Wells Sellers, "Letters of Thomas Jefferson to Charles Willson Peale," *Pennsylvania Magazine of History and Biography* 28 (1904): 136–54, 295–319, 403–19; also see *Selected Papers* 2: passim.

24. Patrick Goode, and Jan Lancaster, *The Oxford Companion to Gardens* (London, 1986), p. 408.

25. *CWP*, p. 75.

26. A(TS): 390.

27. Sir William Chambers, *Designs of Chinese Buildings, Furniture, Dresses, Machines, and Utensils* (London, 1757). Thomas Jefferson owned a copy of this book as well as one of Chambers's, *Plans, Elevations, Sections, and Perspective Views of the Gardens*

and Buildings at Kew (London, 1763). See William B. O'Neal, *Jefferson's Fine Arts Library* (Charlottesville, Va., 1976), pp. 51–57.

28. Adams, *The Eye of Jefferson,* p. 334.

29. The entire verse read: "Meditate on the Creation of the *Worlds;* which perform their evolutions in proscribed periods! on the changes and revolutions of the *Globe* which we inhabit: — on the wonderful variety of animals inhabiting the earth, air and the waters: their immense number and diversity: their beauty and delicacy of structure: some immensely large, and others gradually descending into a minuteness almost eluding our sight, even when aided by the Microscope! *all* have ample support: — Then let me ask myself, *why am I here?* am I blessed with more profound reason than other Animals, if so, *Lett me be thankful: let me meditate on the past, on the present and on the future* (A[TS]: 390). For the interest in China, see Rudnytzky, *Union of Landscape and Art,* pp. 34–36.

30. Charles Willson Peale to Angelica Peale Robinson, August 2, 1813, P-S, F:IIA/52C11–13.

31. Thomas Jefferson, Icehouse and Garden Pavilion at Montpelier, Virginia, Home of James Madison, Photograph, Collection of Frederick D. Nichols and Ralph E. Griswold.

32. Gerald N. Grob and Robert N. Beck, *American Ideals* (New York, 1963), p. 225.

33. "A space was left to inscribe this memorable event, that the genius of America sent the first ship across the ocean by Steam" (A[TS]: 392).

34. Richardson, Hindle and Miller, *Peale and His World,* p. 183.

35. See chap. II for a discussion of the emblematic tradition in which Peale participated.

36. See Richardson, Hindle, and Miller, *Peale and His World,* pp. 177–79.

37. See chap. II. The relationship of Freemasonry, the building arts, and public decoration is a complex subject that warrants careful study. Further investigation must be made into Peale's relationship to the Masonic tradition, which employed the same imagery in its ritual and ornament. Many of Peale's colleagues were active in the Masonic fraternity and Peale himself was a member when he was much younger (*CWP,* p. 99).

38. Philadelphia Museum of Art, *Philadelphia: Three Centuries of American Art* (Philadelphia, 1976), p. 186.

39. Quoted in Sellers, *Mr. Peale's Museum,* p. 27.

40. Quoted in Rudnytzky, "The Union of Landscape and Art," p. 5.

41. Richardson, Hindle, and Miller, *Peale and His World,* p. 115.

42. Peale's model for this was the Jardin des Plantes in Paris with which he had close connections. It was a perfect example of the successful integration of a museum of natural history and a botanic garden. "Their museum is splendid," wrote Peale to his sons of the Paris museum (Sellers, *Mr. Peale's Museum,* p. 156). Peale's close friend and collaborator on the catalogue of his museum's collection was A.M.F.J. Beauvois, who later served as botanist at the Musée Nationale d'Histoire Naturelle.

43. Richardson, Hindle, and Miller, *Peale and His World,* p. 115. Recognizing this need, the American Philosophical Society tried to create a botanic garden in 1787, without success.

44. Peale to Jefferson, March 2, 1812, in *CWP,* p. 366.

45. A(TS): 390–91.

46. Botanic gardens, in this period, were typically associated with universities or medical schools that were engaged in botanical experimentation and the collection and display of plants, and that were generally opened to the public.

47. Charles Willson Peale, *Introduction to a Course of Lectures on Natural History, Delivered in the University of Pennsylvania, 16 November 1799* (Philadelphia, 1800), p. 12.

48. Humphry Repton, *Observations on the Theory and Practice of Landscape Gardening* (London, 1803), pp. 101–02.

49. Pennsylvania Horticultural Society, *From Seed to Flower: Philadelphia, 1681–1876* (Philadelphia, 1976), p. 110.

50. David Hosack, *Introduction to Medical Education* (New York, 1801), pp. 44–45.

51. Maurice E. Phillips, "Academy of Natural Sciences," *Transactions of the American Philosophical Society* 43, pt. 1 (1953): 269.

52. Dr. Benjamin Waterhouse, *The Botanist* (Boston, 1811).

53. Phoebe Lloyd, "Philadelphia Story," *Art in America* (November 1988): 154–71, 195–203.

54. Pennsylvania Horticultural Society, *From Seed to Flower*, p. 24.

55. A(TS): 392–93.

56. Charles Willson Peale to Rembrandt Peale, July 23, 1822, P-S, F:IIA/67D3.

57. Lillian B. Miller, Sidney Hart, and David C. Ward, eds., *Selected Papers of Charles Willson Peale and His Family. The Belfield Farm Years, 1810–1820* (New Haven, Conn., 1991).

15

Charles Willson Peale's Farm Belfield

Enlightened Agriculture in the Early Republic

◆

DAVID C. WARD

I N 1810, with a full life behind him as an artisan and inventor, artist, revolutionary soldier and political activist, and proprietor of
America's first great museum, Charles Willson Peale decided to
become a farmer. His reasons were personal, familial, and ultimately
philosophical in terms of the meaning of this decision for his view of
himself and the world. Peale wanted to move out of Philadelphia for
his and his wife's health. Retiring would also allow him to relinquish
the manifold tasks involved in the day-to-day operation of the Philadelphia Museum. In turn, this would clear the way for his son Rubens
to take charge and begin his career as a museum manager. And, although Peale never explicitly mentions this, it is hard not to resist the
conclusion that he was inspired by the example of his great friend Thomas
Jefferson, who had recently retired to Monticello and was eagerly looking forward to the life of the farmer. Peale, who shared much of Jefferson's outlook and world view (even down to their mutual love of gad-
gets), undoubtedly thought that farming would similarly provide him
with an interesting challenge to his curiosity, skill, and talent.

Today we might call Peale's decision a "career change" (or even a
"life crisis"), with all its implications of personal dislocation, shifting direction, moving to something different, changing course. For Peale, in
an era without specialization and with only the beginnings of the divi-

sion of labor, no such shift was required or implied. Peale's confidence in his ability to run a farm derived from an Enlightenment faith in the universality of knowledge and in the power of reason to surmount any intellectual or practical obstacle. Since he had been successful at everything else, it must have seemed logical to him that despite his urban background, he could be successful at farming.[1]

In 1810 Peale purchased a 104-acre farm for $9,500 in Germantown, a rural suburb of Philadelphia. The size of the farm was not out of line with similar holdings near Philadelphia. Farm size in the area had steadily decreased with urban growth in the eighteenth century. In 1765 the average size farm for Philadelphia, Bucks, and Chester County was 135 acres; given a continued diminution of acreage, Peale's farm was probably typical in size for its location. The price of $90 an acre was high (in the second decade of the nineteenth century, the average price per acre of a Pennsylvania farm was between $50 and $75), inflated by both the proximity to Philadelphia and existing improvements to the tract. The site had a farmhouse — a gambrel roofed structure built in the "German stile" — along with several outbuildings. It also had two streams and falls suitable for mill sites. Peale envisaged using a mill for powering labor-saving machinery, and he saw the eventual possibility of the development of rural industry.[2]

Peale first called his land Farm Persevere to express the determination which his life had required. He later changed the name to Belfield. This change, from a character trait to an aesthetic judgment, has led those interested in Peale as an artist to misjudge Peale's intentions and to concentrate on the aesthetic aspects of the estate. In particular, much of the attention of modern scholars has been devoted to Peale's construction of an ornamental garden which exemplified the principles of eighteenth-century English landscape gardening. In this emphasis, the fact that Belfield was a working farm, as its owner intended, has been minimized.[3]

This chapter concentrates on Belfield as farm. It examines Peale's philosophy of agriculture to see how this affected the practical aspects of the farm's operation — the hiring of labor, the growing of crops, the use of agricultural machinery. Focusing on the farming that was done at Belfield not only contributes additional insights into the life and character of Charles Willson Peale; it also provides a case study in the social history of agriculture in the early republic. An examination of the work force at Belfield may help us understand more about the problem of agricultural labor at the beginning of the nineteenth century. By tracing how Peale practiced farming at Belfield we can uncover the dimensions and limitations of the "Agricultural Enlightenment" in America.[4]

Belfield was distinguished from other mid-Atlantic farms in that the owner's family could not provide most of the labor. It is well to remember that although he was astonishingly active, Peale was sixty-nine in 1810. His wife, fifty-five, soon found the duties of a farm mistress onerous; in July 1813, she stopped doing the laundry for the workers because the job was too tiring. Peale's older children, of course, were pursuing their own careers, while the younger ones who were still at school or undergoing an apprenticeship could provide only intermittent labor. Belfield lacked the core group of family members who could be expected to shoulder most of the work on the typical farm.[5]

From 1810 to 1820 Peale hired fifty-five workers, thirty-one men and twenty-four women. Since two women were specified as black, it may be assumed that the remainder were white. These aggregate figures become more meaningful when they are broken down by year (see Table 1).[6]

TABLE I

Year	Total Workers	Men	Women
1810	3	3	0
1811	8	6	2
1812	14	8	6
1813	18	12	6
1814	17	10	7
1815	12	6	6
1816	12	7	5
1817	8	4	4
1818	7	4	3
1819	4	1	3
1820	5	3	2

The employment figures reveal Peale's fluctuating interest in his enterprise — rising to a peak in 1813–14 as he established the farm, and then declining as his interest in agriculture subsided. Hiring was usually done in the early fall (often October) at the conclusion of the previous year's harvest. Even though not all of the workers in a year would necessarily be at the farm at any given time, it does appear that Belfield was atypical in relying on large numbers of hired labor. Unfortunately, there are no case studies of other farms in the mid-Atlantic region that would provide a definitive answer to this question.

A further refinement in detailing work patterns at Belfield is to calculate the length of time workers remained at the farm (see Table 2).[7]

TABLE 2

Tenure (in months)	Total	Men	Women
0–6	28	18	10
7–12	14	2	12
13–18	3	3	0
19–24	3	3	0
over 24	6	4	2

This table indicates that there was a two-tiered system of employment at the farm. The majority of the workers were transitory, hired for a season or a similarly limited period of time, and moving on after the expiration of their term. Women, in particular, did not stay long at Belfield. Tenure at the farm was for a continuous and discrete block of time; that is, there were no workers who worked for a term in a given year and then reappeared later. Above this floating population was a cadre of more stable, long-term employees: those who served for more than a year and especially those who remained with the Peales for more than two years. The longest tenured man at the farm was Thomas Bowen, who worked there for three and a half years. His equivalent among the women was Katherine Keithler at three years, two months. Unfortunately, Peale rarely specified in his accounts what work was done by each worker. Such information would be useful in determining whether, for example, the long-term workers performed jobs of greater skill and value on the farm than the transitory workers. It also would permit an approach to the answer of whether Peale had the bad luck to hire incompetent farmers. He mentions that the first farmer he hired was unsatisfactory. Were the large numbers who worked for him under a year inadequate, convincing Peale not to renew their contracts?[8]

A partial answer to this question may be found in the wages paid by Peale. Peale's first farmer was hired to work on shares, that is, splitting expenses and profits with Peale. But this arrangement apparently was not continued after this man's brief tenure at Belfield. Instead, Peale's accounts indicate that workers were paid cash wages, usually on a monthly basis. Several of the workers' accounts indicate that they received food, board, and washing, thus in effect being paid more than a worker who received only cash. It must be assumed that in cases where subsistence was not indicated, workers had to find their own. Table 3 shows the wages for male workers.[9]

TABLE 3

Wage per Month	N
$8.00	1
$8.30 plus subsistence	1
$9.00	1
$10.00	9
$10.00 plus subsistence	4
$10.80 plus subsistence	1
$11.00	1
$12.00	4
$15.00 plus subsistence	1
$16.00	1
$24.00	1

Four workers' wages are not available. Two cases have been omitted; they concern workers who received wages that varied according to the season: one was paid $8 in the summer and $6 in the winter; the other $12 in the summer and $10 in the winter. There was no significant fluctuation in wages over the decade, although all the instances of men being paid $12 a month occurred after 1815. Although detailed figures for wages on Pennsylvania farms are lacking for this period, fragmentary evidence suggests that Peale's wages were probably higher than those at other farms at roughly this time. For example, a report from 1791 stated that farm workers received $60 and room and board per year. In 1828, Chester County farmers were paid between $80 to $100 and keep for a year's labor. The higher wages at Belfield may be accounted for by the farm's proximity to Philadelphia and the general scarcity of farm labor in the state. Of special interest are the three men who were paid the highest wages, since their salaries indicate that these were the most skilled workers employed at Belfield. The evidence from these cases indicates that Peale *did* hire unreliable workers. John Stump, who worked at Belfield from March 1814 to March 1816 at $15 a month, was the only one of the three who provided satisfactory service. Robert Davidson was hired in March 1814 at $24 per month but abruptly left on August 16.

Nicholas Spelman, who was paid $16 a month, lasted only from September 1813 to February 1814. In this time Peale noted that Spelman was absent from work on sixteen occasions — once to attend a horse race — and committed a number of other infractions. He quit on February 22.[10]

Peale experienced difficulties with some of his lesser paid workers as well. Barnet Haggerman, after working only two months in 1815, left without giving notice, much to Peale's chagrin: "I told him that I always gave a Months Notice & therefore I required the like notice from him."[11] Samuel Johnson, paid $10 a month, was repeatedly absent and missed work because of drunkenness. In August 1812 he missed several days in a row and Peale recorded this exchange on the twenty-fourth: "And this morning he came up and I asked him if he ment to work, he replied yes, do you want me to work, to be sure I do, I have work enough on hand that ought to be done." Johnson left Peale's employ the following month.[12] On March 5, 1813, Charles Pollock was "sick from drunkenness." He probably socialized with his fellow worker John Brown, who also missed that day, suffering the worse from drink.[13]

Workers whom Peale hired for specific jobs also occasionally turned out to be unreliable. On December 11, 1810, Peale wrote: "2 Carpenters came at 12 O'clock, one considerably drunk & the other not quite sober, they did & undid — talked & departed — I had great trouble to get any thing done — they made bad work."[14] On July 18, 1812, he paid off an unidentified worker with the comment that "by drinking he has so debilitated himself that he could not work today."[15]

While these instances were aggravating for Peale, it is doubtful that this type of behavior was exceptional for early nineteenth-century farm laborers. Nor would these occasional lapses contribute in any significant way to making Belfield unprofitable. In fact, given the relative infrequency with which Peale noted unsatisfactory behavior by his workers, he may well have experienced fewer disciplinary problems than average.

However, Peale's inability to hire and retain more highly skilled and experienced men does indicate a problem in the management and operation of the farm. As a neophyte farmer, Peale may not have been able to judge the talent of a prospective worker. Moreover, in an era when labor, especially skilled labor, was scarce, it is likely that the pool of competent farmers was small, and consequently Peale was forced to hire those who were not top quality; Nicholas Spelman clearly fell into this category. Conversely, when Peale was fortunate in hiring skillful workers, there was always the possibility that with their labor in such demand they could be lured away by prospects of higher wages or a better situation. For instance, in 1810, John Petterman told Peale that "his month was up, & he chuse to leave me because he had an offer of higher wages."[16]

In contrast to men, women workers were paid by the week. This may have contributed to their shorter terms than the men. Weekly payments may indicate that female labor was sufficiently available and undervalued so that long-term contracts were not necessary: they were hired for a brief period or a specific task and then dismissed. The possibility also exists, however, that women preferred the weekly payments because it allowed them flexibility in choosing when and for how long they would work. Unfortunately, we do not know enough about the labor market and hiring practices to resolve this question.

None of the accounts for women indicates that they received room and board. This probably means that they were either married or still living with their families. Women received substantially less than men, with only one woman even approaching the pay level of her male counterparts:[17]

Wage per Week	N
.75	2
$1.25	6
$1.50	15
$2.50	1

The two women who received the lowest wage were black. Apparently the women were more reliable than the men, since Peale noted that only one, named Lucy Briton, was frequently absent.

The examination of workers' wages provides details about the day-to-day operation of Belfield. Unfortunately, because of limited data, this does little to illuminate the lives of the workers themselves. Aside from the occasional comment about a worker's indiscipline, the data also does not reveal anything about the relationship between Peale and the people who lived and worked with him. As with most common or working people, their fate appears in history only in the shadowy and fragmentary traces left by the record of their employment.

Peale used his workers for the main task of raising and harvesting crops and for the ancillary work necessary to maintain and improve the farm. However, Belfield was not self-sufficient, and he had to rely on local (including Philadelphia) shopkeepers and artisans for goods and services. In the first year at Belfield he was especially reliant on hiring additional laborers to perform the tasks that were necessary to repair and improve the farm and its grounds. In 1810, there were twenty-six occasions on which Peale hired people for such tasks as building his springhouse, hanging doors and installing windows, repairing a hay barrack, quarrying, and hauling household items. On May 12 he paid Daniel Jones $5.20 for painting fifteen chairs. The smallest payment was $.66 to a girl for a day's washing. While Peale's use of part-time workers diminished as the farm became established, casual labor was still hired to supplement Belfield's complement of workers, especially during periods of heavy work such as harvests. On July 11, 1811, Peale noted that "A Reaper passing I engaged him for tomorrow at 1$ pr. Day & found." A year later, on July 14, Peale noted that he "went through part Germantown in search of Reapers—very difficult to be had this season."[18]

Other work had to be done off the farm. Lumber for Peale's buildings had to be purchased from local sawmills. Grain had to be ground at local gristmills, at least until Peale had his own mill running. Skilled work and specialized tasks had to be done by local artisans. For example, Peale settled the following—not atypical—account with Caleb Bickham, a blacksmith, on June 30, 1810:

Ironing 2 pr [illegible]	[$] 2.25
Bolt to Chaize	.25
Remooving 2 Shoes Cariage Horse	.25
To lessening the tire of my Waggon . . .	4.25
to Irons . . . for Waggon . . .	.75
To remooving Shoes	.25
The turning end Lightening Rods with ten hooks	2.00
2 Shoes to Carriage Horse	.50
12 Spikes	.37

On August 11 he gave Brickham $20 as partial payment for blacksmith's work, and on the fourteenth, he paid an additional $10. On September 27 he paid Brickham 62½ cents for making a "Weather Cock" for the hay barrack.[19]

Peale soon decided that local Germantown artisans did not meet his standards when it came to providing goods and services. A local shoemaker was found to be unreliable because he had developed a religious enthusiasm that led him to neglect his trade: "The building of Churches occupied his mind more than Bootmaking," Peale noted. More typically, the craftsmen and artisans did not have the requisite skills to do the work Peale wanted, and he had to turn to Philadelphia for equipment and supplies, undoubtedly increasing Belfield's operating costs.[20]

The remarkable feature of Peale's letters and his accounts during his time at Belfield is the absence of comment about what would have been the central concern of an ordinary farmer: the production and marketing of crops. For example, Peale apparently never recorded an overview of the layout of his fields and the amount of acreage he had under cultivation. The only map he made of Belfield, which is extremely difficult to decipher, shows a cluster of buildings — including the farmhouse, his tenants' house, barns, and sheds — surrounded by three rectangular fields. The map indicates that the field to the north of the farmhouse contains ten acres, but no other figures are given and the map is not drawn to scale. That Peale had three fields under cultivation is supported by his listing in 1815 of the "Eastern Meadow, Little Meadow [and] Field East of [the Road]." The land was watered by two streams, one running due south on the eastern edge of the property and the other angling southeast through the lower part of the western meadow.[21]

Peale's account book of his time at Belfield contains only scattered references to crop production and harvesting. Belfield's major crops were grains such as wheat, oats, rye, and corn, as well as hay for livestock, but Peale never provided a yearly account listing the amount of each crop he harvested. In his letters as well, he simply provided general statements of the progress of the crops. A letter to his son Rembrandt in August 1811 is typical and gives some sense of the activity on the farm:

> We have just began mowing our second Crop of Hay — The Clover field east of the House, is too good to be left to be trampled down by the Cattle, Therefore we shall take a pretty good Crop of Hay from it, next in turn is the Water Meadows, they will give a pretty heavy crop. . . . My Corn is very good. . . . The Petatoes very promising — Buck-wheat in Blosom — My Corn planted in March has given us an abundance of roasting — . . . My field where we had Oats, will be finished plowing in this forenoon, intended for wheat.[22]

In addition to the major crops, Belfield also produced dairy products, fruit, and poultry, which Peale attempted to market in Germantown and its surrounding area. Ironically, for a devout teetotaller, his most successful "crop" was currant wine, which was popular among Philadelphians. In general, however, Peale apparently met with indifferent success in his attempt at truck gardening. For example, in August 1811 he tried to dispose of his surplus potato crop by sending one of his farmers through Germantown with several bushels for sale. However, the potatoes, at roughly eighteen cents a bushel, were priced too high for the market and only one bushel was sold. Writing to Rembrandt, Peale mentioned that "We have an abundance of Chickens and some to spare, which brings us ½ a dollar a pr. in Germantown." Peale apparently did not find market gardening a profitable sideline to the farm, and in 1814, as he wrote to Jefferson, he discontinued the practice: "At one time I thought of sending Garden truck to market [but the] cost of Carriage with little dependance of getting an honest return, discourages the attempt."[23]

Although Peale remained at Belfield until 1820, he essentially stopped keeping detailed records of his daily activities by 1814. The random and incomplete nature of Peale's crop accounts makes it impossible to draw any conclusions about the relative efficiency and productivity of Belfield vis-à-vis other Pennsylvania or middle Atlantic farms. But their very incompleteness provides a clue as to how Peale approached farming and Belfield. Above all, Peale was concerned with the means of farming, not the ends. In his emphasis on technique Peale, not unlike Jefferson, represented the enlightened farmer who would apply his rational powers to make the natural processes of growing crops more productive and efficient. While not as extensive in its range of activities, Belfield was similar to Monticello in functioning as a sort of early American agricultural laboratory at which new theories and methods could be tried out. Peale was especially interested in using machinery to augment or replace manual labor on the farm as well as to control and harness the power of nature. Peale's use of machinery at Belfield contrasted with the usual experience in agriculture where machinery is used to replace human labor; at Belfield, machines supplemented the existing large complement of workers.[24]

Peale's interest in more efficient methods of farming focused on the preparation and seeding of the ground and improved methods of gathering and processing crops. Peale expressed his credo in farming as follows: "I have . . . learned that a small farm well worked and well manured, will produce as much profit, as one much larger, tended as is too commonly done, slovenly." To work a farm efficiently meant first to prepare the land properly. Peale's first concern was to establish the correct pattern of crop rotation so that fertility would not be lost through overuse. Following the advice of Jefferson, he used what was known among agricultural reformers as the "new three-field system" of crop rotation. The old three-field system had consisted of planting crops of corn and wheat, and then allowing a year for the land to lie fallow. The new system rotated corn, wheat, and clover, coupled with the extensive use of gypsum (or plaster) to reduce the soil's acidity and manures to maintain fertility. Clover, aside from its value as a food crop for live-stock, replaces nitrogen and other nutrients in the soil. Peale's concern to nurture his crops properly is reflected in his record keeping. In contrast to the fragmentary records he maintained of his farm's overall yields, he kept detailed records of his experiments in planting potatoes using different kinds of fertilizer. In June 1811, for example, he noted, "[potatoes were planted] on Rye Straw, without other Manure, as an experiment, having heard that Stable dung gives them a Strong taste — and all my other Potatoes had Stable Manure put into the ridges." Throughout the season, he continued to monitor the potato crop, and at the harvest in October, he recorded the yields which were obtained with the different methods of manuring, concluding that the crop planted with straw was not satisfactory: "Stable manure must bring a more certain crop."[25]

If the proper preparation and maintenance of the land was important, so also was the correct sowing and planting of the crop. Here Peale relied on machinery to ensure the efficiency of planting. First, he was concerned that his fields were plowed correctly, so he adopted Jefferson's famous mouldboard plow — one of the first attempts to design a plow following scientific and mathematical principles. Its advantage was that by calculating the optimum angle at which the mouldboard was curved, the farmer could get the plow to pass through the ground more easily, yet at a deeper level than previous plows. As Peale noted, the proper form of the mouldboard was

> perfect in form to turn the sod with the least possible resistance, an important qualification in this machine, as the work is also better done with least labour to man and Horses; the compleatly turning the sod without breaking it promotes the fermentation of vegetable covered into good manure — deeply plowed is also important.

Peale had dismissed one of his earliest tenant farmers because the man did not plow deeply enough, and he was determined not to continue

this wasteful practice. However, he had trouble finding workmen who
could fabricate a plow following his instructions. On August 19, 1811,
he finally did obtain a plow and found that it turned the sod over "handsomely." "She promises to be an excellent Plow," he wrote; but the plow
was poorly constructed. When it broke, Peale was stimulated to make
the plow himself. He used his steambath to bend a piece of white oak
to the desired curvature.[26]

Jefferson's new plow could also be used in innovative ways to increase
efficiency while conserving the land. Concerned with the erosion and
soil runoff that resulted when plowing was done in straight lines regard-
less of the topography of the land, Jefferson's son-in-law, Thomas Jefferson Randolph had invented the system of contour plowing. Jefferson
passed along to Peale Randolph's method of determining how the path
should be laid to travel perpendicular to the fall of the land, and Peale
reported to Jefferson that the method was successful: "I must say that
every one with whom I have conversed acknowledge the improvement
of making hilly ground equally advantagous as level field . . . though
none of my land is very hilly—even my Garden which is on the side
of a hill has received advantage by your lesson—." It is not known whether
any of Peale's neighbors followed his lead and adopted the new method
of plowing. In 1818, Jefferson sent Peale a new model plow especially
designed for contour plowing in hilly terrain, but it was found to be
unsatisfactory because it was too small and light.[27]

Peale experimented with other implements to prepare his land better
for planting. For example, following a pattern provided for him by the
noted agriculturalist Dr. William Logan, he constructed an early form
of harrow to dress the ground. The machine was horse drawn and consisted of a wooden framework with "5 hoes with colters [vertical blades]
united. 2 wheels before to regulate the debt [depth] the hows should
enter into the ground." Not only was this harrow more efficient but also
the use of five hoes simultaneously resulted in a corresponding saving
of labor, as the task of hoeing was consolidated.[28]

After preparing the ground, Peale used the latest in agricultural machinery to sow his seeds. The traditional method of sowing was by
"broadcasting," that is, scattering seeds by hand as the farmer walked
up and down a furrowed field. This resulted in wastage, as seeds thus
scattered failed to take root, and an irregular pattern of planting because of the haphazard dispersal of the seeds. The English agriculturalist, Jethro Tull, invented a grain drill by which seeds would be sys-

tematically inserted into the furrow at predetermined intervals and at the correct depth. Peale maintained that his drill was invented by his son-in-law Coleman Sellers, but the model he described is derivative and follows the general design perfected by Tull. Peale succinctly described its operation:

> A coulter oppened a shallow trench, a single wheel [of] the axle-tree of which turned round and pitts in it to hold 3 grains of Corn, which is taken from a hopper, and droped into a funnel which deposi[t]ed it into the ridge 22½ Inches apart — then a heavy Chain followed hooked to the machine . . . the chain dragging on the ground gathered the soil . . . [so] it was drawn over the Corn.

Not only did this drill regularize the sowing of seeds but it also simplified the tasks of planting. By consolidating several operations — the opening of the furrow, the dropping of the seed, and its covering — into one, the whole process was made quicker and more efficient, as Peale noted, "the opperation being the same as to labour, as the furrowing out of the ground." Peale was atypical in his adoption of a grain drill. The old method of broadcast seeding continued well into the nineteenth century. Peale ascribed the failure to use drills to the innate conservatism of people: "Men will not readily go out of an old track, for finding sometimes a trifiling difficulty, they become impatient, or too lazy to investigate causes, however simple — but chuse to do as their father and grand father had done."[29]

Peale could do relatively little to avoid the labor-intensive tasks (hoeing, weeding) involved in tending the crop while it was growing. And harvesting with the traditional technology of the cradle and scythe required large amounts of labor. However, in processing his grains and other crops, he again turned to machinery to simplify and speed the job. As in the case of the grain drill, the antecedents of Peale's machines were British, since British agriculturalists and agronomists pioneered in the development of improved machinery and techniques. Peale's threshing machine was derived from the pioneering work of the Scotsman Andrew Meikle. Meikle's machine relied on "a Drum with dashers to strike off the grain that is carried forward between fluted rollers, the sheaves carried to the Rollers in the manner of the carding machine i.e. a cloth mooving on two rollers — ." Peale also had an English machine for cutting straw. However, many of Peale's processing machines were made by American farmers or mechanics interested in agricultural reform. Peale used a clover mill made by Jonathan Roberts, a farmer from Montgomery County, Pennsylvania. Following the design of an unknown American inventor, Peale built a corn-shelling machine which used a system of knobbed rollers to strip kernels from the husk, thus superseding the time-consuming and wasteful practice of shelling corn by hand. He obtained Oliver Evans's patent machine for grinding coarse objects such as the plaster or gypsum he used to dress his fields. And some implements Peale devised himself to meet his needs as they arose: "I have attempted to make a Machine to take off the heads of Clover instead of mowing to get the seed—" Another of Peale's designs was for a milk cart which used a frame and gimbal to suspend the milk can so that it would not spill.[30]

To power his machinery, Peale exploited Belfield's mill sites, building a mill that used water power. Even with Belfield's water mill, Peale continued to experiment with other methods of obtaining power, and his major mechanical project at the farm was perfecting a windmill to pump water and power agricultural machinery. Peale adopted European technology and an innovation devised by Andrew Meikle to build a windmill with sails that could be regulated. By using springs to regulate the amount of the sail's surface that was exposed, the windmill's power output could be controlled, and the mill would not be blown down when caught by a heavy gust of wind. In part, Peale's experimentation with windmills was an exercise in mechanical virtuosity: technology for technology's sake. But Peale also conceived of windmills as providing a cheaper—yet still efficient—energy source than the emerging technology of steam. In addition to their cheapness of operation, Peale advocated windmills because he saw them as a more benign technology than steam or water power. Peale was concerned about the effects on the morals and welfare of Americans resulting from the concentration of industry. Such concentration, he observed, was encouraged because the technologies of steam and water power are most efficient when applied on a large scale. "I believe," he wrote to Jefferson, "it is more beneficial to our Country to manufacture with small Machines in families, than by large establishments." Windmills, inexpensive to erect and maintain, would encourage the decentralization of manufacturing and permit each individual family farm to be self-sufficient.[31]

Just as Peale's ornamental garden at Belfield exemplified the eighteenth-century aesthetic of managed nature, the farming that was carried on at the estate bespoke the owner's eighteenth-century faith in the powers of reason to improve life. In this, Peale ran counter to the usual conservatism of the agricultural world at the turn of the nineteenth century, a world that valued tradition over innovation, practice over theory. As Peale's comic failure at weeding suggests (he failed to pull the weeds out by the roots), his practical knowledge of farming was minimal. Rather, his approach was conditioned by his involvement with people concerned with agricultural improvement as well as by the manuals and treatises that laid out new methods of farming. "As I have every thing to learn about farming," Peale wrote, "I gain all the knowledge I can from my neighbors as well as from Books."[32]

Jefferson, as Peale's correspondence makes clear, was a key conduit of agricultural news and information. Their letters are a mine of information about agricultural machinery, crop rotation, fertilizers, and new methods of plowing and planting.[33] Peale also drew on the knowledge of local agricultural reformers such as Job Roberts and George Logan. More generally, in an age without rigid barriers between bodies of knowledge, the milieu of the Philadelphia intelligentsia, of which Peale was a part, was as concerned with agriculture as with science or mechanics. Although Peale apparently never joined the Philadelphia Society for Promoting Agriculture, its members were well known to him from other contexts. At the American Philosophical Society, for example, Peale associated with and doubtless learned from, among others, the silviculturalist William Hamilton and the botanist Benjamin Smith Barton. While Peale's contacts with individuals may be charted with some assurance, it is more difficult to know what he read about farming. He mentions the *Maison Rustique* and Bernard M'Mahon's *American Gardener*. He probably was also familiar with Job Roberts's *Pennsylvania Farmer* and John Beale Bordley's *Essays and Notes on Husbandry and Rural Affairs,* as well as those authors' minor writings. For instance, his use of plaster to restore the fertility of his fields probably derived from Roberts's advocacy of that method.[34]

What all these sources had in common was a concern for greater efficiency and conservation in making crops and tending the land. In this the agricultural reformers were strongly influenced by theories derived from European conditions and practice. The "Agricultural Enlightenment" in Europe concentrated on reforming agricultural practice by introducing new types of crops, making sowing, tilling, and reaping more efficient, and emphasizing practices such as manuring, fertilizing, and crop rotation to maintain the quality of the soil. Aside from a general preoccupation with applying science to agriculture, these reformers were concerned with breaking the grip of tradition on agriculture and ensuring that the land not be depleted through overwork and inefficient methods of cultivation.

Because agricultural reform was largely European in origin, its influence on American farming was limited. The American family farm could not afford Peale's commitment, either in time, labor, or money, to using advanced and innovative machinery. Added to this was the ingrained traditionalism of farmers which made them hesitant or recalcitrant in trying new machines and methods. Other uniquely American conditions further blunted the impact of the reformers' message. Above all, the ever increasing expansion of the amount of arable land did little to encourage American farmers to practice labor-intensive methods of cultivation and conservation. For example, while Jefferson and Peale agreed on the advantages of contour plowing, the method was not widely adopted by American farmers until much later in the century, when the extent of soil erosion made it imperative. Similarly, complicated cycles of crop rotation or elaborate methods of fertilization were not considered cost-effective by farmers inhabiting an apparently limitless expanse of virgin land. Finally, in addition to the factor of space, there was the inhibiting factor of time: there was simply not enough labor available on the American family farm to practice economically the intensive agriculture desired by the reformers. Peale himself noted that the failure of Belfield to turn a profit probably was caused by his hiring an excessive number of laborers as well as by the expense entailed in constructing and using advanced agricultural machinery.

Reflecting the ideology of its owner and embodying the creed of the agricultural enlightenment, Belfield lay outside the mainstream of American agriculture. To a degree, Belfield, like Monticello, represented a European variety, a hothouse flower that never took root in the (abundantly fertile) soil of America. It is significant that as Peale experienced the difficulty of practicing enlightened agriculture, he turned increasingly away from farming to an area of nature over which he could exercise his rational powers, namely, his ornamental garden. Yet if Peale's attempt to manage nature through agriculture was ultimately a failure, nonetheless the documents from Belfield provide a window into the world and activities of the enlightened farmer at the beginning of the nineteenth century. Peale's goal of a scientific and mechanized agriculture would not be realized until later in the century.

NOTES

The author thanks Lillian B. Miller, Sidney Hart, and Michael E. McGerr for their assistance in writing this chapter. In my research I relied heavily on two manuscript account books by Peale. For convenience, his Daybook 1806–1822, P-S, F:IIE/4–5, will be known as Daybook 1 and his Daybook 1810–1822, P-S, F:IIE/6, will be known as Daybook 2 in the notes that follow. Daybook 1 contains Peale's financial records and accounts, such as those with his workers. Daybook 2, while it also contains financial records, is more discursive and in many ways resembles a diary of Peale's time at Belfield.

1. For Peale's philosophy and his careers, respectively, as museum-keeper and inventor, see chaps. 12 and 13.

2. Daybook 2, p. 4; a convenient overview, including documents relating to the purchase of the property, of Peale's farm at Belfield is Jessie J. Poesch, "Mr. Peale's 'Farm Persevere': Some Documentary Views," *Proceedings of the American Philosophical Society* 100 (1956): 545–56; for farm prices and acreage, see Stevenson Whitcomb Fletcher, *Pennsylvania Agriculture and Country Life, 1640–1840* (Harrisburg, Pa., 1950), pp. 304–05; Charles Willson Peale to Angelica Peale Robinson, March 11, 1810, P-S, F:IIA/49A8–14.

3. Peale's only comment about changing the name of the farm was that his friends found the designation Belfield more convenient than Farm Persevere (Charles Willson Peale to Thomas Jefferson, August 19, 1812, P-S, F:IIA/51E3–10). For analyses of the aesthetic aspects of Belfield, see Kateryna A. Rudnytzky, "The Union of Landscape and Art: Peale's Garden at Belfield," National Endowment for the Humanities Funded Study, La Salle University, Honors Essay, 1986; chap. 14.

4. For the agricultural enlightenment in the Philadelphia region, see Simon Baatz, *"Venerate the Plough." A History of the Philadelphia Society for Promoting Agriculture, 1785–1985* (Philadelphia, 1985).

5. Daybook 2, p. 91; see Fletcher, *Pennsylvania Agriculture and Country Life,* pp. 107–10, for the dominance of family farms in Pennsylvania.

6. Source: Daybook 1.

7. Source: Daybook 1. It should be noted that only thirty men are included in the table because one individual's work time cannot be calculated.

8. Daybook 1, pp. 49 (for Bowen), 125 (for Keithler).

9. Source: Daybook 1.

10. Fletcher, *Pennsylvania Agriculture and Country Life,* pp. 306–08. The most recent study of wages in the Philadelphia region relies on the documents from Belfield so it cannot be used; see Donald R. Adams, Jr., "Wage Rates in the Early National Period," *Journal of Economic History* 28 (September 1968): 408–09, 420–21. For the accounts of the workers mentioned, see Daybook 1, pp. 85, 95, 81.

11. Daybook 1, p. 101.

12. Daybook 2, p. 85.

13. Daybook 1, pp. 81, 85.

14. Daybook 2, p. 33.

15. Daybook 2, p. 84.

16. Daybook 2, p. 9.

17. Daybook 1.

18. Daybook 2, pp. 9, 26, 51, 84.

19. Daybook 2, pp. 13, 19, 25.

20. Daybook 2, p. 57.

21. The map is in Charles Willson Peale to Rembrandt Peale, July 22, 1810, P-S, F:IIA/49D3-10; Daybook 2, p. 98.

22. For typical accounts that indicate Peale's sketchy record keeping when it came to Belfield's crops and yields, see Daybook 2, pp. 14, 25, 31, 39, 40, 42, 46, 48, 49, 51, 55, 60. Also see Charles Willson Peale to Rembrandt Peale, August 27, 1811, P-S, F:IIA/50D11-13.

23. For a description of the manifold activities at Belfield, including the attempt to sell chickens, see Charles Willson Peale to Rembrandt Peale, August 27, 1811. The fermenting of currant wine and the decision that truck gardening was too troubling may be found in Charles Willson Peale to Thomas Jefferson, November 14, 1814, P-S, F:IIA/54A13-B3.

24. For a superb introduction and documentary account of Jefferson's interest in practicing enlightened agriculture, see Edwin Morris Betts, ed., *Thomas Jefferson's Farm Book. With Commentary and Relevant Extracts from Other Writings* (Charlottesville, Va., 1976).

25. Charles Willson Peale to Thomas Jefferson, March 2, 1812, P-S, F:IIA/52B5-11. Peale's sentiments are remarkably similar to Nicholas Biddle's, who said in his 1822 address to the Pennsylvania Society for Promoting Agriculture: "We work badly too much ground, instead of cultivating well a little" (Baatz, *"Venerate the Plough,"* p. 34). See also Thomas Jefferson to Charles Willson Peale, August 20, 1811, Library of Congress: Thomas Jefferson Papers, F:IIA/50D7-8; Betts, ed., *Thomas Jefferson's Farm Book,* pp. 188-200; Daybook 2, pp. 47, 66-67.

26. Charles Willson Peale to Rembrandt Peale, August 27, 1811, P-S, F:IIA/50D11-13; Daybook 2, pp. 55-57; on Jeffersons' mouldboard plow, see Betts, ed., *Thomas Jefferson's Farm Book,* pp. 47-50.

27. Charles Willson Peale to Thomas Jefferson, December 28, 1813, P-S, F:IIA/52G1-6; Charles Willson Peale to Thomas Jefferson, April 10, 1820, P-S, F:IIA/64B9-10.

28. Daybook 2, p. 78.

29. Charles Willson Peale to Angelica Peale Robinson, August 1, 1813, P-S, F:IIA/51D12-14; A(TS): 394-95; Charles Willson Peale to Thomas Jefferson, December 23, 1815, P-S, F:IIA/56D13-E1.

30. Charles Willson Peale to Thomas Jefferson, December 28, 1813, P-S, F:IIA/52G1-6; Charles Willson Peale to Angelica Peale Robinson, August 2, 1813, P-S, F:IIA/52C11-13; Thomas Jefferson to Charles Willson Peale, June 13, 1815, University of Texas: Hanley Collection, F:IIA/55D11-13.

31. For Andrew Meikle's innovative windmill design and the history of windmills generally, see Stanley Freese, *Windmills and Millwrighting* (New York, 1957), pp. 1-16; Charles Willson Peale to Thomas Jefferson, June 18, 1815, P-S, F:IIA/55E7-12.

32. Charles Willson Peale to Thomas Jefferson, September 9, 1811, P-S, F:IIA/50E4-8.

33. For much of the Peale-Jefferson correspondence on agriculture, see Lillian B. Miller, Sidney Hart, and David C. Ward, eds., *Selected Papers of Charles Willson Peale and His Family,* vol. 3: *The Belfield Farm Years, 1810–1820* (New Haven, Conn., 1991). A useful selection may be found in Betts, ed., *Thomas Jefferson's Farm Book.*

34. For the milieu of scientific agriculture in Philadelphia, see Baatz, *"Venerate the Plough,"* chap. 2; Charles Estienne and Jean Liebault, *L'agriculture et maison rustique* (Paris, 1564), with an English edition in 1600 and many subsequent updated editions; Bernard M'Mahon, *American Gardener's Calendar* (Philadelphia, 1806); Job Roberts, *The Pennsylvania Farmer* (Philadelphia, 1804); John Beale Bordley, *Essays and Notes on Husbandry and Rural Affairs* (Philadelphia, 1799).

INDEX

NOTES ON CONTRIBUTORS

Sidney Hart is Associate Editor, The Peale Family Papers, National Portrait Gallery, Smithsonian Institution.

Carol Eaton Hevner is Research Consultant and Guest Curator, The Rembrandt Peale Catalogue Raisonne Project, National Portrait Gallery, Smithsonian Institution.

Robert J. H. Janson-LaPalme is Associate Professor in the Department of Art History, Washington College, Chestertown, Maryland.

Lillian B. Miller is Historian of American Culture and Editor, The Peale Family Papers, National Portrait Gallery, Smithsonian Institution.

Therese O'Malley is Assistant Dean, The Center for Advanced Study in the Visual Arts, National Gallery of Art, Washington, D.C.

Jules David Prown is Paul Mellon Professor of the History of Art, Yale University, New Haven, Connecticut.

Karol A. Schmiegel is Registrar at The Winterthur Museum and Gardens, Delaware.

The late Charles Coleman Sellers was Librarian of Dickinson College, Carlisle, Pennsylvania, and author of *Charles Willson Peale*.

Roger B. Stein is Professor of Art History, University of Virginia, Charlottesville.

David Steinberg, a doctoral candidate at the University of Pennsylvania, is a Fellow at the National Portrait Gallery, Smithsonian Institution (1990).

David C. Ward is Assistant Editor, The Peale Family Papers, National Portrait Gallery, Smithsonian Institution.

UNIVERSITY OF WINCHESTER
LIBRARY